How Our Departed Ones Live

THE EXPERIENCE OF THE ORTHODOX CHURCH

The Second English Edition

MONK MITROPHAN

Translated by
ARCHPRIEST JOHN R. SHAW

HOLY TRINITY PUBLICATIONS
THE PRINTSHOP OF ST JOB OF POCHAEV
Holy Trinity Monastery
Jordanville, New York

Printed with the blessing of His Eminence,
Metropolitan Hilarion First Hierarch
of the Russian Orthodox Church Outside of Russia

How Our Departed Ones Live
© 2015 Holy Trinity Monastery

PRINTSHOP OF
SAINT JOB OF POCHAEV

An imprint of

HOLY TRINITY PUBLICATIONS
Holy Trinity Monastery
Jordanville, New York 13361-0036
www.holytrinitypublications.com

First Printing 2005—ISBN 0-9771178-0-4

The original Russian language book titled:
"How Our Departed Ones Live, and How We Shall Live after Death"
was published in 1897 by Жизнь С.- Петербургъ.
Изданіе Книгопродавца И. Л. Тузова.

ISBN: 978-0-88465-401-8 (paperback)
ISBN: 978-0-88465-402-5 (ePub)
ISBN: 978-0-88465-403-2 (Mobipocket)

Library of Congress Control Number: 2015944163

Contents

The Story Behind the Rebirth of This Book

MY MOTHER, MARIA DMITREVNA PAVLENKO, née Schatiloff, who reposed a novice nun in 1987, was always close to bishops and high ranking clergy of the Russian Orthodox Church Abroad. Included among her clerical acquaintances, a close personal friend in her youth, was Saint John (Maximovich).

When my father, Vladimir Stepanovich Pavlenko, passed away in 1985, my mother asked me for some spiritual reading on the subject of death and dying. I had no such book in Russian and addressed Archimandrite Ambrose (Pogodin) (reposed October 31, 2004) from the nearby Menlo Park church (OCA). Father Ambrose is a well-known and respected author of theological works, a number of which were published by Holy Trinity Monastery, Jordanville, New York.

Father Ambrose said he had a certain rare book that my mother was sure to appreciate. My mother read the book and was very pleased. She highly recommended it, suggesting that if others had the same need in the future, to be sure to make it available to them. Years later, Mrs. Valentina Nikitechna Obermaier, née Saiapina, lost her mother with whom she was extremely close and shared a very strong spiritual bond. She suffered the loss of her beloved mother very deeply. Though Mrs. Obermaier is very well-read and is in possession of an extensive library of Orthodox spiritual books, she did not have among her books one that would specifically address her desire for more insight into the mystery of death. When she asked me for some additional reading, I suggested the book my mother had read on advice from Father Ambrose. We borrowed it again, and Mrs. Obermaier found it very comforting. This motivated her to have the book reprinted and made available in Russian. A suitable edition of the book was kindly made available by Mother Eugenia, the Abbess of the Convent of Our Lady of Vladimir in San Francisco, California. The main task was assigned to Mr. Alexander Miroshnichenko who took a loving and active part in seeing the publication come to light. It was a great joy to discover that this new printing was used to republish the book in spiritually re-emerging Russia, in not one, but many printings.

More time passed, and Mrs. Obermaier's beloved husband Hans became ill. A short time before his death, he, a German Catholic, became Orthodox and was given the name Ioann. After he peacefully departed, Mrs. Obermaier was inspired to have the book translated into English. Hans had not been fluent in Russian, and Mrs. Obermaier wanted her son and grandchildren to reap the abundant knowledge that is treasured in this important and rich publication.

Father John Shaw was asked to do the translation, which he accomplished in a very short time. After some delays and setbacks, the book is now ready for its first appearance in English. All those who have put an effort into its publication ask you to pray for them. We all thank God that He allowed us to participate in this, we trust, God-pleasing endeavor.

—Archpriest Stefan Pavlenko
2005

Translator's Preface

IT TOOK ME MOST OF THE YEAR OF OUR LORD 2001 to translate this book. The most time-consuming element in this was *not* translating the main text from Russian into English, but it translating the many proper names—names of people and places, which had been rendered in Russian characters when the book was published. These often required a bit of research to render correctly.

Thus, for example, the text might mention a certain "*докторъ Хвольфъ.*" This could be "Dr. Wolf," "Hvolf," "Wholf," or many other possibilities. To get the correct spelling, one must find out *who* [or *what place*] exactly is meant—and to find out what person or place is meant, one needs to know the correct spelling! In some cases, half a day might be spent in research, and there were some cases where doubts remain.

There was also a French edition of this book in the nineteenth century, and if that had been available to me, it might have solved some problems connected with the spelling of proper names. However, we had to make do with what was available.

These people and places were mostly known to the educated reader in nineteenth century Russia, and to bridge the resulting gap, I have added a number of explanatory footnotes to the text.

The original book was in two volumes, and only Volume I is currently available in the West. Perhaps in the future it may become possible to find Volume II.

—Archpriest John R. Shaw, Translator

Introduction to the English Edition

THERE IS A SAYING THAT "You can't judge a book by its cover." For this particular volume, that saying is more than true. From its title, *How Our Departed Ones Live, and How We Shall Live After Death*, it would seem to be another in a long list of books about what happens when you die. But this is not the case. In fact, this book goes far beyond just that small topic. I first encountered this book in its draft form when preparing for a talk about life after death. Archpriest Stefan Pavlenko offered to let me review files that he had which turned out to be the beginning of the translation of this book. The files were very helpful and enhanced my presentation. Over the next year, more files kept coming. I had agreed to read through the translation and provide some feedback about wording and so on. As I continued to read, I was astounded at the depth and breadth of this book. How much could one say about life after death, I had wondered, and yet there seemed no end to this stream of wisdom.

Certainly, the topic of the next life is indeed central to the book; however, in describing the heavenly afterlife, we are given also a description of this life: our creation, life before the fall and the effects of the fall, of life after the fall, of sin and its effect, of our salvation, of our destiny. We also learn about the communion of the saints and the heavenly host, as well as our own union and communion with those who have gone before and our prayers for the departed and the prayers of the saints for us. We learn about the nature of heaven and hell and of our destiny in the Kingdom of God.

More than just a book about death, this book is a catechism of the Orthodox Church. It provides a view of our faith, not from this world, but as if looking back from the next, revealing not how things are, but how things were meant to be, how they went wrong, how they are repaired, and the various results of all these events. This is a book for those who wish to know not only about the next life, but about this life and how to live in it. Truly this is a book that goes far, far beyond its title.

It has been my privilege to share this book in its Russian edition with a number of my Russian parishioners, and I eagerly await the opportunity to do the same with this new English language edition. It promises to be a major contribution to the ever-growing catalogue of Orthodox literature available in the English language.

—Archpriest David Moser

Death in Relation to Immortality
Concerning Death

1. The Origin of the Word and Concept of "Death"

THE WORD AND CONCEPT OF *death* first appeared on earth in the Garden of Eden, from the lips of God Himself, Who said to our first ancestors: "In whatsoever day ye shall eat of it, by death ye shall die."

2. The Appearance of Death on Earth

It is not known how long Adam and Eve lived in Paradise. The enemy's spite was not long in coming. All theologians are in agreement that the first man was a higher being, the likeness of the angels, and even the likeness of God; a being dedicated to divine Revelations and in all branches of knowledge moral and sinless. The present moral decline, progress for the worse or regress, is the result of ancestral sin.

Concerning the higher perfection of our ancestors one can judge from the fact that they were given no commandments, no moral laws such as we have been given, but only the easiest commandment. Probably all of the main laws of the spirit were already in the soul of man; it cannot have been otherwise. If man was set as king over all things visible, then he was the crown of God's creation.

The spirit was not weighed down by the flesh, and our forefather did not cry out as did St. Paul, "Who shall deliver me from this body of death?" But this moral downfall that St. Paul bewailed arose from the fall of Adam. With the fall of Adam, death of body and soul appeared on earth; "for by one man, sin entered the world, and through sin, *death*" (Romans 5:12), as the same St. Paul bears witness.

Thus death became the inheritance of our forefathers, and therefore of all mankind. Who does not know this concept and word: *death?* The savage and the educated man know it equally. All humanity knows two truths: first, that we shall die, and second, no one knows when.

3. The Definition of Death

As mysterious and incomprehensible as is the joining of the soul and body in the mother's womb, equally mysterious is the separation of the soul and body.

It is God's commandment that everyone be ready for death at all times. This is the common lot of humanity, as a punishment for sin; and, as a punishment, death is fearsome to the righteous and to the sinner. While commanding that we be ready for death, the Holy Spirit reveals the circumstances in which the righteous and the sinner pass into the life beyond the grave. The death of the former is beautiful and of the latter, dreadful.

The reality of these words was revealed to certain of the saints, who were pleasing unto God, for our edification.

According to the teaching of our Orthodox Church, "death is the separation of the soul from the body," after which the soul remains by itself while the body is committed to the earth and there disintegrates into its various components (elements). This is the lot of man on earth: death, of which the Holy Scriptures bear witness as follows: "And the dust shall return to the earth, as it had been, and the soul shall return to God, Who gave it" (Ecclesiastes 12:7).

4. The Universality of the Law of Death

The law of death is common to all humanity. Death is inescapable for each and every one. The law of God bears witness thus of the universality of the law of death: "Who is the man, who shall live and not see death?" (Psalm 88:49)[1] "It is appointed to man once to die" (Hebrews 9:27); "In Adam all die" (I Corinthians 15:22).

Death reaches a man when he has attained the limit of life determined for him by God's righteous judgment, so that he may complete the work assigned to him. Within this limit all that is beneficial to man has been provided, and therefore death is beneficial to him. It is also commanded that we should give thanks for all unto God's Providence. Therefore, Glory be to Thee, O God, Who hast arranged all things for our benefit. Blessed be Thy Name, O Lord, from henceforth and forevermore. St. Anthony the Great, looking into the depth of God's destinies, once turned to God with the following prayer: "O Lord, why

[1]The Psalms are numbered in this book according to the Septuagint text.

do some die in youth while others live to old age?" An answer came to him from God: "Anthony, watch thyself! For these are God's judgments, and it is not unto thy good to try them" (from the Lives of the Saints).

God has ordained for the soul to pass through three states, which comprise its eternal life: in the mother's womb, on earth, and beyond the grave. Why then should we be horrified, since all is the will of God, and we are the Lord's? We did not plan beforehand to be born on earth and recall nothing of our first state. Therefore let us prepare ourselves for our second birth unto eternal life beyond the grave. We have directions on how to prepare ourselves, and we already know what is to be after death.

Here is what St. John Chrysostom writes about death: "Death is terrible and frightening for those who do not know the higher philosophy, who do not know of life beyond the grave, who consider death to be the destruction of being. Understandably, death is horrible to such, and its very name is devastating. But we who, by the grace of God, have seen His unknown and secret wisdom and consider death to be a passing over, ought not to shudder but to rejoice and be of good spirit; for we leave this corruptible life and go on to another, which is unending and incomparably better" (Homily 83, commentary on St. John's Gospel).

5. The Reason for Death

The Word of God shows that God did not create death, but created man free of corruption (Wisdom of Solomon, 2:23); but "Through Satan's envy, death came into the world" (ibid., v. 24), along with sin.

Had Eve not gone into league with the devil, had she not been seduced by deceit, had she not fallen away from communion with God, then there would be no sin. "Righteousness is immortal, but unrighteousness is the cause of death" (Wisdom of Solomon 1:13–16); these words of Solomon which define the meaning and origin of death's appearance on earth, serve at the same time as evidence for the immortality of man. Solomon says that only the unwise see death as an end of existence (ibid., 3:2–4). Consequently, immortality was bestowed on man.

It was the breaking off of the soul's communion with God that constituted its death. Nine hundred thirty years after his soul's death, there finally followed the death of Adam's body.

6. The Unnaturalness and Necessity of Death

From the Holy Scriptures (Wisdom 1:13) it can be seen that death is contrary to man's nature, and therefore it is life that is natural to man. And so love for eternal life is natural for man. But with the fall, from the very time that man turned his love to that which was forbidden, love for eternity (which was natural) was replaced by love for the material, the temporary. The soul betrayed itself. It is entirely diseased and is attached to that which is not natural to it.

God did not create man for him to offend his Creator by breach of His holy will. God's desire was eternal bliss for man, as proven by man's nature which constantly desires and strives towards only that which is pleasant in life and hates and turns away from the unpleasant, from death. Thus, man is intended for a blessed eternal life, and sin is something unnatural; death is the consequence of sin and so is also unnatural to man; man was created immortal both in body and in soul.

The goal or intent of punishment is good: the cutting off of evil; and so death too is beneficial to man. After man's fall, as our Church teaches, death was needful as a means for holding back evil from spreading further. If Adam had remained physically immortal even after his fall, then evil would have been immortal, and there would be no hope of salvation for man. So as not to make evil immortal with man's immortality, it was forbidden to Adam to eat of the fruit of the tree of life (Genesis 3:22,23) immediately after his fall. By the same token, now that the power of death has been destroyed by the death of Christ the Saviour on the cross, and those who believe in Him are redeemed and justified from ancestral sin, death is also needful for the complete cleansing and extermination of evil from human nature, inasmuch as the root of evil is found in carnal conception itself.[2] It is in the conception, and therefore in the union, as it were, that joins soul and body, and therefore cannot otherwise be eliminated, than by the dissolution of that union. Therefore no matter how much a man might purify himself on earth, and no matter how perfected he might be in holiness, he still cannot altogether exterminate in himself the root of evil. He cannot free himself from the weight of the body, so as not to sigh together with St. Paul, "O wretched man that I am! Who shall deliver me from the body of this death?" (Romans 7:24; *Theology of Archbishop Anthony*, p. 242).

---

[2]The Holy Fathers of the Orthodox Church (St. Athanasius, St. Maxim the Confessor, and others) clearly state that no sin is committed at the time of conception, neither do we inherit a personal guilt at this moment; but every human being born into the world suffers the consequence of the fall, that is, he comes into the world with a corrupted nature.

7. The Beneficial Nature of Death

When things happen that are unpleasant for the soul and the body, which lies like a stone upon the soul, the soul is brought to sorrow, distress and often the risk of losing salvation, of losing the Kingdom of Heaven. Such circumstances are called temptations. Consequently, temptation is no joy for man, but a sorrow. Life has not been a joy for mankind since the minute that our ancestors fell, for then it was decreed that man should obtain the means of his existence by the sweat of his brow. Endless labor, diseases of the body, mental anguish, distress, temptations—these are what have filled our life on earth. Only the Saints have rejoiced in their sorrows; so there is no man who has been free of temptations. The holy, righteous, long-suffering Job asked: was not life itself a temptation?

There is not one human being that does not feel the weight of life towards its end. No matter how dear life is to a man at first, nevertheless, we often hear of the desire for death near the end.

While a man is on earth, distress and temptation never leave him, up to his death. Only death frees man from temptation. Is not death, which puts an end to sorrows, a benefit to man, one for which he should offer up thanks from his very heart?

All our life passes in temptations, which are needed for our salvation. What did St. David, the king, lack? And yet he expressed the truth of mankind, that old age is labor and illness. Was it not perhaps for this reason that he often cried out to God, "Woe is me, for my sojourn is prolonged," that is, death has not yet come. And our Lord Jesus Christ warned his followers, the Christians, that life on earth would be full of sorrows. Consequently, death for true Christians is an end of sorrows and should therefore be met with joy and humility. For death has already been destroyed by the death of our Redeemer and Intercessor, the Lord Jesus Christ, Who made death for Christians into a falling-asleep, a temporary sleep of repose. Death has been changed into a passage, that is, a moving from one place to another, from the visible world into the invisible, which is beyond the grave, spiritual, and, for Christians, incomparably and ineffably better. Therefore, Chrysostom cried out in exultation, seeing death as the beginning of bliss: "Where is thy sting, O death?"

The death of each and every believer is in the death of the Lord Jesus, Who gave us by His Resurrection a blessed eternal life. "I am the Resurrection and the Life" (John 11:25) teaches the God-Man; and we believe that the dead are alive in Him, if only they be not chaff, but members of the Church of Christ.

Death, viewed by itself, presents the action of Divine anger, softened by righteousness and love. Therefore death, seen in regard to the righteous, is a sign of Divine love, according to which their souls depart from this earthly, sad life, full of evil, into the kingdom of love, light, and bliss. This is the place to which their spirit was lifted up, and death for them, according to the word of God, is "beautiful"; as the attainment of a desired separation from the earthly, the temporary, the vain, so as to be with Christ: "having a desire to depart, and to be with Christ, which is far better" (Philippians 1:23); to be where the Creator decreed as the destination of man.

But viewed in relation to sinners, death is "bitter," as the action of Divine anger, mixed with justice; an eternal breach with what was dear upon earth and is no longer present beyond the grave. The bitter death of unrepentant sinners is of benefit to the state, the community, and the family, as the uprooting of a weed.

8. The Departure of the Soul

The soul, conjoined by the will of God with the body, is separated, again by the will of God, from the body with which it had previously formed a human being. Having separated, the soul passes over into the realm of beings like unto itself, into the spiritual, angelic realm; and depending on whether it has gained good or bad qualities, joins either the good angels in heaven or the evil angels in Hades. The Lord Himself revealed this truth in the parable of the rich man and Lazarus, teaching us that the soul, after leaving the body, that very day enters either Paradise or Hades. "Today thou shalt be with Me in Paradise" (Luke 23:43), said Jesus Christ to the wise thief.

This means that every soul after leaving its body will be either in Paradise or in Hades. When? "Today," said the Lord Jesus Christ. How are we to understand "today"? How does this agree with the teaching about toll-houses or with the Church's observance of the third, ninth, and fortieth day?

On earth there are days and nights and years, whereas, beyond the grave there is eternity—either bright or dark. For the soul to reach a bright or dark state beyond the grave, a certain space of time is needed which corresponds to the forty days on earth. The various states in which a soul is after its separation from the body correspond to specific days on earth. Since the state of the soul on the third day is known and revealed, as is its state in the next six days and in the following thirty days, the Church and those close to the departed person make use on these days of special means of seeking God's mercy.

And so, the word "today" signifies time beyond the grave, eternity. The third, ninth, and fortieth days are days on earth, but not beyond the grave where there is only "today" and none other.

The mystery of death is a door through which the soul, having parted with its body, enters eternity.

We see and know what then happens with the body, but as to what happens with the invisible soul, this we do not see. However, we have certain knowledge from the teaching of our Church, which is the pillar and ground of truth and which is infallible in its teaching, for the Holy Spirit teaches the Church.

The departure of the soul and the events which takes place at that time, the Holy Fathers explain as follows. The soul is met by angels good and evil. The sight of the latter is extremely distressing to the soul; it finds joy in the sight and the protection of the good angels. Then a man's good deeds and clear conscience are a great help and joy to him. Obedience, humility, good works, and patience help the soul, and, accompanied by angels, the soul goes in great joy to the Saviour. But a soul filled with passion and love for sin is taken away to Hades by evil spirits to suffer (St. Theodore the Studite).

Once two angels appeared to St. Macarius of Alexandria (a contemporary of St. Macarius the Great). "A soul," said one angel, "be it of a devout person or not, is frightened by the presence of fearful and terrible angels. The soul hears and understands the tears and wailing of those that surround it, but cannot utter a single word nor raise its voice. It is distressed by the long journey before it, the new way of life, and the separation from the body" (St. Macarius of Alexandria).

In the homily of St. Cyril of Alexandria on the departure of the soul, the sayings of St. Theodore the Studite and St. Macarius of Alexandria are filled out with the following information: "What fear and trembling the soul experiences until the final sentence is pronounced! The divine powers stand against the impure spirits and bring forth the good thoughts, words, and deeds that belong to the soul, which, amid the angels and demons doing battle over it, in fear and trembling, awaits either its justification and deliverance or condemnation and ruin" (St. Cyril of Alexandria).

The testimony of Taxiotes adds information on this subject to what was said above. He says that the good angels had with them a chest from which they took his good deeds at the toll booths and held them up against his evil deeds.

St. Gregory, the disciple of St. Basil, in a vision asked St. Theodora about the circumstances at her death and after it. "How can I tell you the physical pain, the fatigue, and the oppression that the dying are subjected to! The state of the soul at its separation from the body is as if one naked were to fall into a fire, burn, and be turned into ashes. When the hour of my death came, evil spirits surrounded me; some of them roared like beasts, others barked like dogs, yet others howled like wolves. Looking at me, they raged and threatened, and strove to attack me, gnashing their teeth. I was limp with fear, when all at once I saw two angels standing at the right side of my bed. Their presence calmed me. Then the demons drew back further from my bed. One of the angels angrily asked the demons, 'Why do you always come before us to those that are dying and frighten and distress every soul that is departing from the body? But do not rejoice too much here. The mercy of God is in this soul, and you have neither part nor share in her.' The demons were troubled and began to show my evil deeds that I had committed from my youth and cried out, 'And whose sins are these, did she not do this and this?' Finally Death appeared, very fearful in appearance, like a man, but without a body, consisting only of bare human bones. Death brought along various instruments of torture: axes, arrows, spears, scythes, pitchforks, scimitars, and others. My humble soul shook with fear. The holy Angels said to Death, 'Be not slow, but release this soul from mortal coils, swiftly and quietly set her free, she has no great burden of sin." Death came to me, took a small sword and first cut off my feet, then my hands; afterwards, with other instruments, he paralyzed all my members, separating them one from another at the joints. I lost my hands and feet; all my body became dead, and I could no longer move. Then he cut off my head, and I could not move even that, as it had become foreign to me. Then in a chalice he dissolved something and, holding it to my lips, forced me to drink it. The drink was so bitter that my soul could not bear it, shuddered and leaped out of my body, torn from it by force. The angels took it in their hands. Looking back, I saw my body lying inanimate, unconscious, and immobile. It was as if someone had cast off a garment and stood looking at it; thus I looked at my body in wonder. The angels held me, and the demons came towards us, showing my sins. The angels began to look for my good deeds and by the grace of God found them. The angels, with the help of God, gathered together all the good I had ever done and made ready to weigh it against my ill deeds. At that moment, there unexpectedly appeared our venerable Father Basil who said to the holy angels, 'This soul helped me greatly in my old age; I prayed to God for her, and God has given her to me.' With these words he took out a full, dark red bag and, giving it to the angels, he said: 'When you pass through the aerial toll booths and the wicked spirits begin to torture her soul, redeem her debts with this. I am wealthy in God's grace, gathered many riches by fasting and my labors, and I make a gift of this bag to the soul that served me.' Having said this, he departed. The wicked spirits were confounded, then raised up mournful wails and were gone. Then St. Basil returned again, bringing with him many vessels of pure oil and precious myrrh. He opened one after another and poured them over me; I was filled with a sweet spiritual fragrance and felt that I had changed and brightened. The Saint said to the angels, 'When you have done all that is proper, then bring her to the habitation prepared for me by the Lord.' After this the Saint became invisible. The angels took me, and we set off towards the East."

St. John of Damascus writes, "God, being good, will save the works of His hands, except for them that are among those cast off, who have trampled the true faith, so that the left side of the demons too much outweighs the right side. For men enlightened of God say that when at his last breath a man's works are weighed, if 1) the right side outweighs the left, then such a one shall give up the ghost among a throng of good angels. If 2) the right and left sides are equal in the balance, then without doubt God's love for mankind will prevail. If 3) the scales tip to the left, but only a little, then the mercy of God even then will make up what is lacking. These are three Divine judgments of the Master: righteous judgment, love for mankind, and great goodness. If 4) when the evil works have a very great preponderance,—here too is a righteous judgment—which rightfully determines condemnation." (from "Khristianskoye Chtenie," for the year 1827, part 26, "Homily on the Departed in Faith," p. 333).

These are all the circumstances that accompany the death of a man. Indeed, the Lord Himself, speaking of the death of the righteous man and the sinner, said in general terms the same thing: that the death of sinners is bitter, but that of the righteous, beautiful; for to the one was said, "This night thy soul shall be taken from thee" (Luke 12:20), and of the other, that the angels took his soul to the lap of Abraham (Luke 16:22). Consequently, the circumstances at the death of the one and the other must be similar to the descriptions by the Holy Fathers.

Thus, of course with the help of God's grace, it is up to us ourselves how our departure, our death, shall be; we can make it bitter or beautiful depending on how we carry out Christ's commandment to be ready for death at every hour and to repent, and believe in the Gospel. Therefore, constant repentance and an active, living faith in the Lord Jesus Christ will make our departing pleasant.

Not only the poor, such as Lazarus, will inherit life and be granted a blessed end, but the rich as well, if they are poor in spirit, wise in humility. Not only the wealthy, such as the rich man in the Gospel, will go to hell and have a bitter death, but the poor also, unless they bear their cross with magnanimous patience. And so, be ready, that is, prepare for death at every hour.

Fear and faintness before death are characteristic of man. All the Saints prepared themselves for this dread hour with tears, and their end was majestic.

"Lord!" quoth St. Basil the Great, "There is no death for Thy servants as they depart from the body and come to Thee, our God; but they pass over from that which is sad to that which is most beneficial and sweet, and to rest and joy" (Prayer at Pentecost Vespers).

And so, be reassured, brothers and sisters, death is not a destruction or the end of human existence. The soul lives in another world to which, perhaps, we too shall go presently. Our Lord Jesus Christ is the Conqueror of our death, and, consequently, of the death of our departed ones. Let us say to them in Him, not "Goodbye," but "Until we meet again, beloved spouse, good parents. Until we meet again, dear brother or sister. Until we meet again!" . . .

9. The Departure of a Righteous Soul

It can be seen from an angelic revelation to St. Macarius of Alexandria that the departure of a righteous soul presents a direct opposite to the departure of a sinful soul. A righteous soul, after separation from the body, is taken up by holy angels, protected by them, and moved to a land filled with light, joy, and bliss. The way in which such souls go is not surprising, since even on earth they were in the company of the Angels.

Here is what St. Ephrem the Syrian writes concerning the departure of a righteous soul: "The devout and the perfected ascetics rejoice in the hour of departure. Having before their eyes the great work of their asceticism (vigils, fasting, prostrations, prayers, tears, sackcloth) their souls rejoice to be called out of their bodies to a place of rest.

10. The Departure of a Sinful Soul

The death of a sinner is evil (Psalms 33:22),[3] as witnessed by the word of God itself. Why is it thus? Examine: What is a sinner? One who breaks the law of God, who tramples on His commandments. Just as virtue, reflected in the conscience, brings down upon the soul a joy not of this world, so likewise vice begets the fear of responsibility. Death, the passing over of the sinful soul, is evil, because the evil spirits whom the soul served without fear on earth, and with whom, like other sinners, it must be bound for eternity, meet the soul at the very moment of its departure. St. Macarius the Great reflects as follows

[3]Septuagint numbering and text.

on the departure of a sinful soul: "When a sinful soul departs from the body, a certain great mystery occurs. Hordes of demons, opposing angels, and dark powers come to it and carry the soul off to their realm. And one should not be surprised at this. If a man, still living in this world, subordinated himself to them, obeyed them, and became their slave, all the more does he become their captive and slave when he leaves the world."

"Separation from life," writes St. Ephrem the Syrian, "is extremely sad for the sinner, who sees before his eyes his carelessness and its bitter fruit. What regrets then seize the heart that has neglected its salvation while here!" (Psalms 136[4]).

From the writings of the Fathers we also know that sometimes the Lord, in His indiscernible plans, grants people who have not been devout to receive Holy Communion before their death, as the last gift of Grace in their lives; and on the other hand, He deprives even the righteous of this last Communion, for earlier sins, even though cleansed by penitence. As one of the spiritual means known only to Him, He uses sudden death as a punishment to cleanse the sins of youth, of ignorance, or forgetfulness (*Glukhaya Ispoved,*' by Polisadoff, p. 19).

11. The Third Day and the Tollhouses. The Significance of the Ninth Day, Fortieth Day, and Anniversary

Where is the soul immediately after it leaves the body? What is the significance of the third, ninth, and fortieth days? At what time or on what day does the soul undergo the aerial toll booths, and when, after its separation from the body, does the individual judgment take place?

St. Macarius of Alexandria conveys the following angelic revelation to us on the state of the departed during the first forty days after they are separated from their bodies.

When the mystery of death takes place and the soul is separated from the body, the soul remains on earth for the first two days and, accompanied by angels, visits those places where it had been wont to do what was right. It wanders about near the house in which it left its body and sometimes also remains near the coffin where the body reposes. But on the third day, in imitation of the Resurrection of Christ, which was on the third day, it is commanded to every Christian soul to ascend to heaven, to adore the God of all. This is the reason why the Holy Church has the custom of offering prayers for the soul of the deceased on the third day.

[4]See preceding note.

On the third day, thus designated, there is a commemoration of the deceased and prayers offered to God for him: a memorial service *(Pannikhida,* dirge) is celebrated. This day, both for the departed and for us who are still living, has a direct spiritual bond with the Resurrection of the Originator of our life, Who made a beginning of our blessed resurrection, and so of our dear departed one. On the third day, the deceased is buried. As we commit the body of one close to our heart to the earth, we turn our minds and hearts to the Conqueror of death, Who gave us the triumph of life over death. Our triumph, and the triumph of our dear departed, is in the Resurrection of Christ. The Church solemnly assures us, her children, that Christ is risen from the dead and to those in the tombs has bestowed life. And to your dear departed one—do you hear this?—life and resurrection are given only through Christ.

On the third day the body is committed to the earth, and the soul must ascend to heaven: "And the dust shall return to the earth, as it had been; and the spirit shall return to God, Who gave it" (Ecclesiastes 12:7).

The immeasurable space between heaven and earth, or between the Church Triumphant and the Church Militant, is a space in the usual conversational sense; and in the Holy Scriptures and writings of the Holy Fathers it is called "air." And so, what is called "air" here is not a thin material ether surrounding the earth, but space itself.

This space is filled with rejected, fallen angels whose whole activity consists in trying to turn man away from salvation and making him into a tool of unrighteousness. They act cunningly and maliciously on our inward and outward activity, so as to make us part of their downfall: "Seeking whom to swallow" (I Peter 5:8), as the Apostle Peter speaks of the devil. We have the witness of the chosen vessels of the Holy Ghost that the aerial space is the dwelling of evil spirits, and we believe this truth.

Thus, the seer of God's great secrets in the Apocalypse (Revelation) bears witness that the fallen angels were deprived of their heavenly abode (Revelation 12:8,9). Therefore, where is their station? In the Book of Job, the world is called their dwelling (Job 1:7), and the Teacher of the Gentiles openly calls them spirits of evil of this world, and their head, "the prince of the power of the air" (Ephesians 6:12; 2:2).

From the very moment that our first ancestors fell and were driven out of the Paradise of sweetness, a Cherub was assigned to the tree of life (Genesis 3:24); but besides that, another fallen angel also took his place on the path to paradise, so as to cut off man's entry. The gates of heaven were closed to man, and the prince of this world and age, from that time on, did not admit one human soul, departed from its body, into Paradise. Even the righteous, except for Elias and Enoch, along with the sinners, went down to Hades.

The first to go untroubled through this impassible road to Paradise was the Conqueror of death, the Destroyer of hell; and the doors of Paradise since that moment have been open. After the Lord, there followed the wise thief and all the righteous of the Old Testament, led by the Lord out of Hades. The Saints pass untroubled on this path, or, if they suffer at times the interference of demons, their good works nevertheless cover their failings.

If we, being already illumined by the light of Christ and having a free will to do either what is right or what is wrong, constantly are their captives, made workers of iniquity, carrying out their evil will, they will not leave the soul when it is separated from the body and must go to God through aerial space. They will not fail to lay claim to the soul, as having been a faithful servant to their suggestions (of thought, desire, and sense).

The demons present the soul's sinful activities in all their fullness, and the soul recognizes the rightfulness of this accusation.

Christians, living a life on earth that is not without sin, do not receive a blessed eternity directly. It is necessary for these shortcomings, fallings, and strayings to be weighed and evaluated.

If a soul has not come to know itself, has not completely recognized itself here on earth, then, as a spiritual and moral being, it must necessarily recognize itself beyond the grave. It must know what it has worked out for itself, what it has adjusted itself to, what sphere it has become accustomed to, what constituted its food and gratification. Heavenly justice wills it to recognize itself and, in this way, pass judgment on itself before the judgment of God. God did not and does not wish death to exist, but man himself willed it. Here on earth the soul, by the aid of Grace, may come to recognition and true repentance, and receive remission of its sins from God. But beyond the grave, in order to bring the soul to consciousness of its sinfulness, fallen spirits are used. Since they are the teachers of every evil on earth, they now present to the soul its sinful activity, reminding it of every circumstance when the evil was done. The soul recognizes its sins. Having come to know its own sinfulness, it anticipates the judgment of God upon itself; thus God's judgment defines what the soul has pronounced upon itself.

Repentance eliminates committed sins, and they are brought up no more, neither at the toll booths nor at the judgment.

The good angels, for their part, present the soul's good works at the toll booths.

The space from earth to heaven consists of twenty divisions or places of judgment, and the soul is reproached by the demons for its sins as it passes each. Each judgment seat, or as they are called in patristic writings, toll booth (and the evil spirits are called publicans), corresponds to a specific class of sins.

The publicans not only rebuke the soul for the sins it has committed, but also for those it has never been subject to, according to St. John Climacus (*The Ladder of Divine Ascent,* Step 7).

The order in which the toll booths follow one another we give according to the account of St. Theodora. On the way to heaven, towards the East, the soul encounters the first toll booth where the evil spirits stop it with its accompanying angels and set forth its sins of *word* (excessive, empty or idle speech, foul language, mockery, sacrilege, singing of unbecoming songs, disorderly outbursts, laughter, smirking, and so on).

The second toll booth is that of *lying* (every untruth, broken oath, vain use of the Lord's name, unkept promise to God, sins concealed from the spiritual father at confession).

The third toll booth is that of *slander* (slandering one's neighbor, passing judgment, denigration, abusive language, making fun of others while forgetting one's own shortcomings).

The fourth toll booth is that of *gluttony* (overeating, drunkenness, eating at inappropriate times and in secret from others, eating without prayer, breach of fasts, love of delicacies, stuffing oneself, feasting—in a word, all forms of serving one's belly).

The fifth toll booth is that of *sloth* (laziness and indifference in serving God, despondency, neglect of prayer in church and at home, parasitism, neglectful discharge of paid duties).

The sixth toll booth is for *theft* (every form of seizure and stealing, be it crude or dignified, overt or secret).

The seventh toll booth is *greed* and *miserliness.*

The eighth is for *usury* (money lending, covetousness, and taking the property of others).

The ninth toll booth is that of *deception* (wrongful judgment, unjust measures, and all other forms of untruth).

The tenth toll booth is *envy.*

The eleventh is *pride* (being proud, vain, thinking too highly of oneself, contempt, putting on airs, not giving due respect to parents, clergy, and civil authorities, insubordination, and disobedience).

The twelfth is that of *anger* and fury.

The thirteenth is the holding of *grudges*.

The fourteenth is *murder*.

The fifteenth is that of *sorcery* (magic, charms, the making of potions, incantations, spells, and witchcraft).

The sixteenth toll booth is that of *lust* (everything relating to this impurity: thoughts, desires, and acts; lust between persons not united in the sacrament of matrimony; fantasies of the sin of lust, dwelling on such fantasies; willingness to sin, delight in sin; voluptuous looks, impure feelings, and contacts).

The seventeenth is that of *adultery* (marital infidelity, the falling into lust by persons who have dedicated their lives to God).

The eighteenth is that of *perversion* (unnatural lust and incest).

The nineteenth toll booth is that of *heresy* (false sophistry about God, doubt about faith, apostasy from the Orthodox faith, blasphemy).

Finally, the last toll booth is *lack of mercy* (being unmerciful and cruel). Consequently, the passage of the toll booths is on the third day.

Bishop Makary writes: "The fact that the teaching about the toll booths has been in continuous, constant, and ubiquitous use in the Church since the fourth century clearly shows that it has been passed down to us by the teachers of the preceding ages and is based on Apostolic tradition (in his *Orthodox Dogmatic Theology*, Vol. 5, pp. 85–86.

Knowing the state of the soul beyond the grave, that is, the toll booths and appearance before God for adoration on the third day, the Church and relatives, in their love for the memory of the deceased, pray to the Lord that his soul may pass untroubled through the aerial toll booths and his sins be forgiven. The freeing of the soul from sins constitutes its resurrection unto a blessed, eternal life. And so, on the example of the Lord Jesus Christ, Who rose from the dead on the third day, a memorial service[5] is held for the departed, that he too may rise on the third day unto endless, glorious life with Christ.

After the soul adores God, it is commanded to be shown the various habitations of the Saints and the beauty of Paradise. The visitation and observance of the heavenly habitations continues for six days. The soul is amazed and glorifies God its Creator. And gazing upon all of this, it is changed and forgets its sorrow, such as it had whilst in the body. But, if guilty of sins, then seeing the enjoyment of the Saints, the soul begins to sorrow and to rebuke itself for leading a life of carelessness and failing to serve God as it should have done. After looking at Paradise, on the ninth day after its departure from the body, the soul is again

---

[5]Pannikhida.

brought before God to adore Him. And so, the Church does well in offering a prayer on the ninth day for the deceased.

Knowing the state of the departed soul beyond the grave, corresponding to the ninth day on earth, when the second adoration of God takes place, the Church and the relatives pray to God that the soul of the departed may be joined to the nine ranks of Angels.

After the second adoration, the Master commands that hell with all its torments be shown to the soul. As it is led, the soul sees everywhere the torments of sinners, hears weeping, moaning, and the gnashing of teeth. For thirty days, the soul is led through the divisions of hell, trembling, lest it too be judged to confinement there. Finally, on the fortieth day after separation from the body, the soul for the third time is taken up to adore God. And now, on the fortieth day after death, the righteous Judge determines a place for the soul appropriate to its deeds on earth. Thus the individual judgment of the soul takes place on the fortieth day after its departure from the body; consequently the Church does rightly in commemorating the departed on the fortieth day.

The fortieth day after the separation of soul and body is the day when the soul's fate beyond the grave is determined. This is the individual judgment of Christ, which defines the fate of the soul only until the great, universal Day of Judgment. This state of the soul beyond the grave, corresponding to its moral life while on earth, is not final and may change.

Our Lord Jesus Christ, on the fortieth day after His Resurrection, exalted the human nature He had taken into His Person to a place of glory, seated on the throne of His Divinity, "at the right hand of the Father" (Matthew 22:44); and so, on this model, the souls of the departed enter, on the fortieth day after death, into a specific place corresponding to their moral condition.

Just as the Lord, after completing the work of our salvation by His life and death, crowned it by His Ascension on the fortieth day, so also the souls of the departed, having completed their walk of life, receive their reward on the fortieth day after death: their place beyond the grave.

Just as the Lord, having ascended on the fortieth day, sits always "at the right hand of God the Father, until His enemies be laid as the footstool of His feet" (Hebrews 10:12,13), so also the souls of the departed, having received their place beyond the grave by the individual judgment of Christ, remain in that place—though not without the possibility of change—until the general Judgment of Christ *(Homily on the Commemoration of the Departed* by Archbishop Theodore, pp. 37–38).

This correspondence (parallel) between the states of Christ and the states of departed souls is recognized by the word of God (Hebrews 9:27,28).

And so, dear soul that mourns the death of one close to you, on the fortieth day lift up your mind and heart in faith to the Ruler of our life, who on the fortieth day ascended "to appear in the presence of God for us" (Hebrews 9:24), the living and the dead. Will the all-generous Father, having before Him His Beloved Son who bore the wounds of the cross for us, refuse Him in this intercession? Hold fast to faith in the love of the Lord, Who in His glory is occupied with our eternal fate, thine, and that of thy departed one. Pray to Him for the dead, that He heal the infirmities of the departed soul by His Grace, fill that which is lacking, forgive all his sins, and cleanse and establish him among those who have found mercy. Thy faith and prayer, with the help of the holy Church, will be of great help to the departed in determining his disposition until the Day of Judgment, at the individual judgment seat of Christ.

Since the Church knows the state of the reposed soul beyond the grave that corresponds to the fortieth day on earth on which its fate is decided but not yet finally—for bliss or torment—the Church and the relatives again hasten to help the departed. On this day a memorial service is held, so as to seek, so far as it is possible for us, the mercy of the all-good God for the dead.

And so, from all this we can see that the soul, after leaving the body, is on earth for two days and on the third goes up to God to worship Him. Then on the following six days it is in Paradise, and, finally, for the next thirty days is in Hades. On the fortieth day it is in its place, its state still not finally decided. The final fate of the soul is decided on the general Day of Judgment.

The anniversary, kept in the ensuing years, as well as the nameday and birthday of the deceased, are kept as special dates by good Christians. To show that death has not broken the spiritual bond and relationship between the living and the deceased, a memorial service is held and prayers offered to Him in Whom we have our salvation and life. We pray to Him Who said, "I am the life" (John 11:25).

Our prayer and our unfailing hope are in His promise to hearken to those that entreat Him: "Ask and it shall be given you" (Matthew 7:7), "For I desire not the death of a sinner" (Ezekiel 33:11), for whom I suffered, shed My Blood, and to whom I now grant life . . . "Only believe!" (compare Mark 5:36).

The Inner Connection and Mutual Relationship Between the Living and the Departed

1. The Spiritual-Moral Realm and Its Members

G OD'S SPIRITUAL AND MORAL KINGDOM, the kingdom of our Lord Jesus Christ, is made up of immortal, spiritual-moral beings (Luke 20:38; Romans 14:8,9), just as their Creator is Himself immortal. These beings are Angels and souls. The Angel and the soul are not impersonal spiritual powers, but truly personal spiritual beings (Rudakov's *Bogoslovie [Theology]*, p. 40). The soul, as long as it remains in the body, is on earth; after leaving the body, it passes on into the world of the Angels, the spiritual world beyond the grave. Man, by his dual nature of soul and body, stands on the border between the invisible and visible worlds, being a wonderful combination of the spiritual and the material, the heavenly and earthly, the eternal and the temporary. Man is a bond between this world and that beyond the grave. His immediate purpose is to be an earthly angel and a heavenly man.

St. Paul the Apostle teaches us that just as the living faithful belong to the Lord so do the faithful departed. The Lord recognizes only the faithful as His own, according to the words of the Lord Jesus Christ Who spoke of "The God of Abraham, and the God of Isaac, and the God of Jacob" (Luke 20:37), those who believed rightly in the One God. At the time of Abraham, Isaac, and Jacob, there was a great multitude of people on the earth, but since they did not believe in the true God, He does not recognize them as His own and is repulsed by them. They are not members of the great kingdom of God; and, in the words of Holy Writ, they are sons of the devil, lost to the kingdom of God and therefore not God's own. The faithful are called the sons of God; they are the Lord's and God is called their God. They are heirs of the kingdom of heaven.

The kingdom, or Church, of our Lord Jesus Christ is, was, and will be made up only of those who truly believe in Him. Consequently, all those who believed in Him in the Old and New Testaments, all those who believed in Him and have passed into the world beyond the grave, and all the good angels became

35

members of His Church, according to the words of St. Paul: "But ye are come unto mount Sion and unto the city of the living God, the heavenly Jerusalem, and to an innumerable company of angels" (Hebrews 12:22). These are the members of the spiritual-moral kingdom who make up the one spiritual Body of Christ, His Church (Ephesians 1:23; Colossians 1:18). The duties are the same for all members of the kingdom: to glorify God (Revelation 5:12; Philippians 1:10,11).

The members remaining on earth constitute Christ's Church vigilant, earthly, and visible; while those that have gone on to the life beyond the grave and been pleasing unto God, constitute, with the good angels, the Church triumphant, heavenly, and invisible.

But those that have not attained complete holiness while on earth and have also passed on into the world beyond the grave and remain there, as it were in a state of illness, have still not lost the right to be members of Christ's Church. All of these conditions of spiritual and moral beings have a bond and relationship among themselves. The members of the moral world, regardless of where they are, make up one indivisible whole. This means that each member, in a mere change of place, does not change his relationship to the other members.

The members of the spiritual-moral kingdom, as has already been said, are angels and souls; souls that are still on earth in the body and souls that have gone on to the world of angels. Their spiritual-moral nature corresponds to the spiritual and moral kingdom. This nature is the same for all and consists of reason and free will. For all spiritual-moral beings, there is one law of truth and holiness, one aim for being and action: moral perfection and bliss; and there are the same obligations for all. Here we have the unity that is between all the members of the kingdom of God, between the Church triumphant and the Church vigilant, or between the spiritual and the earthly worlds.

2. The Basis of the Union, Bond, Relationship, and Communion Between This World and the Next—of the Living with the Dead

The union, bond, relationship, and communion of this present world with that beyond the grave is not a flight of the imagination or some fantasy; but, according to the teaching of our Orthodox Church, the following four truths serve as the basis for this bond: 1) the same God for all spiritual and moral beings, both in this world and the next; 2) the spiritual-moral realm of angels and souls; 3) the spirit and its characteristics, and 4) the witness of Holy Scripture.

Our Lord Jesus Christ with His Grace is the first and main basis of the union, bond, relationship, and communion between this world and the next. God is one for all, the living and the dead. Before Him all are alive according to the teaching of the Lord Jesus Christ (Matthew 22:32). He is the common God of angels and souls, the Creator, King, Father, and Saviour of souls, both those that are still on earth in their bodies and those that have separated from them and are in the spiritual world beyond the grave.

The second basis of the union, bond, relationship, and communion of this world and the next is the spiritual-moral kingdom itself. It is impossible to picture a kingdom, a Church, or a society with members who are not in union and communion with their Master and with one another. It is impossible for the members of this Kingdom, the angels and souls, not to be in communication with one another, regardless of where they be: on earth in the body or in the world beyond the grave. Disjunction is not possible for them. The one nature of spiritual and moral beings, the one law, the one purpose of their being and activity, their common obligations all show that union and communication are inescapable.

The third basis for the union, relationship, and communion of this world and the next is the immortal spirit and its qualities: love, sympathy, and the like. Christian love, according to the teaching of St. Paul, is immortal (I Corinthians 13:8). Love abides in the heart on earth, and it abides beyond the grave also.

The fourth basis of the union, relationship, and communion of this world with the next is the witness of the word of God itself—of Holy Scripture. "Jerusalem which is above . . . is the mother of us all," as St. Paul taught (Galatians 4:26), and "Ye are no more strangers and foreigners, but fellow citizens of the Saints, and of the household of God; and built upon the foundation of the Apostles and Prophets, Jesus Christ Himself being the chief comer stone" (Ephesians 2:19,20).

These are the four bases on which our Holy Church affirms her teaching on the unbroken union and bond between those that live in this earthly world and those that have passed on into the life beyond the grave, into the spiritual world (*Dogmatic Theology of Archbishop Anthony*, pp. 2, 48).

3. The First Basis: The Lord Jesus Christ, His Grace, and Holy Faith

All people, not only the enlightened and educated, but even the most unlettered and primitive, the lowest levels of humanity, all believe that the dead live beyond the grave. But what is their conception of life after death? How do they picture it? What is their attitude toward the departed? What is their bond and communion with the dead? They picture all this in the crudest forms corresponding to their level of development. How many foolish ideas about the dead are there, not only among the primitives, but even among us Christians?

In his natural state after the fall, man lacks an organ for direct reception of the inspiration of the Holy Spirit; man is sharply cut off from the spiritual world by a strong barrier, the obtuseness of his senses. Faith in Christ alone has become our organ of communication with the world that is unseen, spiritual and beyond the grave.

Primitive peoples know that the dead live beyond the grave, but they do not know what relationship they have with them; they do not know how they are tied and in communion with them.

But the faith of Christ has revealed all of this to us. It has revealed the True God to us, it has revealed the mystery of our salvation; it has revealed our Saviour and Intercessor for us sinners; and it has revealed two states beyond the grave. It demands that we seek a blissful eternity for ourselves and others, for the living and the dead. The Faith has also shown the means that we are to use for our salvation and that of others, living and dead. Thus the basis of our bond and communion with the departed is Christ, His grace, and holy faith.

We have only to make our reason obedient to the faith in Christ, and we and our departed ones will be saved. Whosoever believeth, shall be saved (John 3:16), as Jesus Christ teaches. Only by faith can one see the future. Faith is an eye whose range of view extends beyond the limits of the visible, and the invisible is seen, and the future appears as the present. Faith demands love from us, the seeking of the kingdom of God, the bearing of our neighbor's burden, the readiness to depart at any time, the thought of the things above and not of the things of earth. All these demands of faith draw the mind and heart away from what is temporary and toward the eternal. They draw it to where our life and salvation is, to where our fathers, mothers, brothers, sisters, spouses, friends, and acquaintances that have gone before us live an immortal life. This is the place to which faith in Christ calls the mind and heart of the poor wanderer without breaking the bond and relationship between the living and the dead.

Immortal love will not cease. The heart senses that it will soon meet the object of its love. Faith joins the present with the future, the visible with the invisible. Faith joins man with the unseen God and with all spiritual-moral beings; it joins invisibly and spiritually.

The teacher of the Gentiles (the Holy Apostle Paul) teaches thus: "If we live, we live unto the Lord; and if we die, we die unto the Lord: therefore whether we live, or whether we die, we are the Lord's" (Romans 14:8). Consequently, both the living and the dead are the Lord's; both the former and the latter have one Lord Jesus Christ, the Saviour of those who believe in Him. It is natural to be concerned about one's salvation; but it will be made complete, if we keep in mind also the salvation of the departed whom the Lord loves. "Let this mind be in you, which was also in Christ Jesus" (Philippians 2:5), as St. Paul teaches. What is this that should be in us in imitation of Christ? He is the eternal Intercessor before God the Father for every sinner. And it is this intercession that should also be in us in Christ for each and every one, both the living and the dead. Christ demanded and demands this of us, saying: "Love one another, even as I have loved you" (John 12:34), and "seek first the kingdom of God (Matthew 6:33) for yourselves and for all people. Jesus Christ took the burden of our sins, and we, as the Apostle teaches, are obliged also to "bear one another's burdens and thus to fulfill the law of Christ" (Galatians 6:2). What can be more burdensome for a man than his sins? And so we can and, according to the commandment, we must take a vital, active part in the fate of the departed for whose salvation Christ was made man. By our true faith, we should put on Christ for the departed, just as a godparent at baptism puts on Christ and His grace for the one baptized.

Although the time of spiritual sowing is, for your beloved one who has reposed in God, already past, nevertheless, as a member of the body of Christ (the Church) he is still within reach of spiritual grace through the intercessions of the living members of the Church.

How then, by what means, shall the deceased be made Christ's, how shall the grace of salvation be his? In just the same way as a sponsor at baptism vouches for the faith of him who is baptized and thus opens for him full access to the grace of holy baptism, so those who are well pray for the health of the sick or adults for infants. In all these cases, grace is given for the faith of those who ask to those for whom intercession is made. And so, let our faith act for the deceased and bring him the grace of Christ.

Here are the conditions that are needed for the faith of the one that prays so as to bring the saving grace of Christ to the deceased:

I believe, O Lord, that Thou, Christ, the Son of the Living God, camest into the world not for the sake of the righteous, but to save sinners, and therefore to save my deceased one, the first of sinners.

I believe, O Lord, that Thou hast taken upon Thyself the sins of all that believe in Thee: therefore also the sins of my departed one.

I believe, O Lord, that Thy word is true and Thy promise immutable. Thou didst say, "Ask and it shall be given you" (Matthew 7:7); I ask Thy mercy for the one that has fallen asleep. For Thee this is possible, and my request is in accord with Thy desire to "save all," because Thou desirest not the destruction of a sinner.

It was Thy commandment to offer one's soul for the salvation of one's neighbor. Moses and St. Paul would rather have been excluded from the number of the chosen, if only their people could be saved. I too pray Thee, O Lord: rather let me alone perish, but my departed ones be saved for whom Thou hast shed Thy priceless blood. They are dear to Thee, and for their salvation I offer myself to Thee as a sacrifice.

All that I can do at Thy behest, with the help of Thy grace, without which I can do nothing, all this I am willing to carry out so that the departed may be saved. Didst Thou not say, O Lord, that we sinners and infirm ones should only desire good, and Thou shouldst fulfill it by Thy grace? I believe, O Lord, that hope in Thee shall not be confounded. The salvation of my beloved one is Thee and in Thee.

The Canaanite woman believed fully that Thou, O Lord, if only Thou wouldest, couldst heal her daughter from demonic possession. I, too, believe that if Thou willest, Thou canst have mercy, save, and deliver from eternal torment, making up what is lacking for salvation in the soul of the departed, by Thy grace, and healing the sinful ills of that soul. "The prayer of faith shall save the sick," as the Apostle St. James bears witness (James 5:15).

I believe, O Lord, that Thou didst die for all that believe in Thee. I believe that Thou in Thy death includedst the death of Thy servant, my dead one, and therefore hast given him life eternal, destroying eternal death for him by Thy death, and hast opened the way to resurrection, life, and rest for him.

Are these not Thy words, O Lord: "For God so loved the world" (John 3:16)—that is, people—and therefore I believe that my departed one is beloved of Thee. Having loved the world, God sent Thee, His Only-begotten Son, not to judge, but to save (John 3:17; 12:47). My mind and heart are entirely at peace in Thee, O most sweet Jesus, the Son of God, that Thou hast taken upon Thyself the sins of my departed one. For his sake Thou camest, for him Thou didst ascend the cross, suffer for him, die for him. Having risen, Thou didst ascend to heaven and sittest at the right hand of the Father in all Thy glory interceding for my deceased one by the wounds of the cross. He was the reason for Thy sufferings, O Lord, and therefore is saved by Thee.

The Lord Jesus Christ took upon Himself all the weight of the sins of believing humanity and gives us the grace to bear one another's burdens. Therefore, we can, with complete faith, take part in the life of the departed beyond the grave. Having sympathy for the state of those who have gone on before us into the other world, we are obliged to strive for their betterment in Christ Jesus, Who came to earth for our salvation. "Follow Me," (Luke 9:59) were the words spoken to one still living who had asked first to bury his father. This is the only way to help the dead. If the quick live without Christ, then a life not in the Spirit of Christ will not improve the state of the dead.

The Apostle Paul advises us to imitate him, as he did Christ, in praying for others, be they living or dead: "I could wish that I myself were accursed from Christ for my brethren's sake" (Romans 9:3), and he extends this prayer even to them that did not believe. This is the kind of self-sacrifice that our love for our neighbor, alive or dead, should attain. We should be ready to lay down our souls for the salvation of others, either living or departed. And so, let us pray that the Lord be merciful unto us, having mercy on the departed.

The departed will be at peace and pleased with us who remain still on earth when we express our love for them not only in word, but also in deed, by our true life. "My little children, let us not love in word, neither in tongue, but in deed and truth" (I John 3:18), as St. John, the Apostle of love, teaches us. Our love for the departed should correspond to the Lord's love for us: "Love one another, as I have loved you" (John 15:12); even unto the laying down of your life for your neighbor, as I too died for your salvation. Our love for the departed is commensurable with our love for the Lord. If we believe in the Lord, then we must believe that the dead live. If we love the Lord, then we should love them that live beyond the grave. This commandment of love does not separate the living from the dead, but conjoins them as St. Paul teaches: "Love dieth not" (I Corinthians 13:8).

4. The Second Basis: Life and the Order of Moral Development

Could one picture a kingdom, a society, a house, or family in which the members, spiritual-moral beings, were completely dissociated from one another, were completely independent of one another, did not know one another? Such a situation would be impossible for a kingdom, or a society, a house, or a family. If dissociation is impossible for the moral kingdom, then there must exist a bond, mutual ties, and communication among its members.

The Apostle Paul seeking to show this truth concretely, compares the spiritual-moral realm with our visible body and the bond of communion among the members of the spiritual-moral realm with the bond of communion among the members of our body. The condition of our body parts depends on their mutual relationship. The members of the body, depending on one another, help each other: "And whether one member suffer, all the members suffer with it; or one member be honored, all the members rejoice with it" (I Corinthians 12:26). When one member of a household is sick, the other members suffer with him. Disorder in societies or classes calls forth the participation of other societies; the bad condition of one state leads other states to think of helping.

Since those that pass over beyond the grave still remain living members of the body of Christ, we can conclude that there is still a close tie and a continuing, unseen relationship between this world and the next. An unbroken, inner spiritual bond remains between the living and the dead; it could not be otherwise.

Where there is life, there is activity, development. And where is there not life? Life is on earth and beyond the grave. The condition and the fate of departed souls are closely bound up with, and mutually related to, the life and activity of those living on earth. Activity and deeds tie the present to the past and the future. With the past, this is the consequence of what has gone before, and, with the future, it is the foundation for what is to follow. Deeds tie this world to the next, and they tie us, the living, with the departed. The past is reflected in our activities, as is the present and the future; there is glory and eternal memory for those who made a good beginning for the development of a given object! There is glory and eternal memory for those who have sown a good seed for continuing moral development. The departed have planted, and we enjoy the fruits of their mental activity. Clearly, present activities have their founders—our ancestors—who for that reason still live among us now in spirit and in their works.

Those remaining on earth develop the ideas of their predecessors, or they do battle with concepts they wish to eradicate. It is well if a good seed grows, and the present generation tastes good fruit; then there is good glory and eternal memory for those who went before. The Lord will reward them, and each, according to their works. Present activity in the Spirit of Jesus Christ is the fruit of the works of the departed, and their eternal peace is beyond doubt.

The soul is immortal and so are its works. Those who passed on have begun a work, and we continue it, and our descendants will go on to develop it further. Does not Moses live among us in his five books? Does he not still give us benefit through them? He will be the benefactor of all believing posterity until the

Second Advent of Christ to earth. Is it not one and the same to us, the living, to have a living teacher on earth or to have Moses from beyond the grave in his work? Is not the one as beneficial to us as the other? Should we not be as grateful to the one as to the other? Have they not both the same goal of teaching us? And so, the holy Apostles, Prophets, and Martyrs, and all the Saints are alive for us and among us in their deeds (as the Saints themselves put it: promising to remain with us in spirit). The great doctors of the Church live in their writings, and we should, and do, learn from them. Solomon, Socrates, and Plato still live with us, and we speak with them to this day about wisdom.

Does the present generation not taste fruits of the intellectual work of great persons? Do we not learn from them and develop their teaching? Frederick the Great, Napoleon I were disciples of Alexander of Macedon and Julius Cæsar. Archimedes laid the foundations for today's mechanics, and astronomy recognizes the calculations of Ptolemy. These are the benefactors of mankind. They offered benefit and still do and will till the end of the age. These are the benefactors of mankind, but there are enemies of mankind as well.

God Himself bears witness that the whole world lies in evil, and so there are people who fight with evil and win; but there are also those that are overcome by evil, who become its captives, slaves and, as zealots of evil, are lovers of moral disorder, opponents of truth, enemies of mankind. They sow hidden evil in societies and in individuals. In every evil event, the real workers are evident: those who develop the ideas of their depraved teachers of error, so that the leaders of this evil take part spiritually. Moral disorder causes both moral and material harm to individuals, to societies, states, and all humanity. Present activity consists of both the further development of their immoral ideas and the battle with evil. The present generation, both those that develop and those that resist, sees the dead malefactors as alive in their snares.

The enemies of family life, of society, and the state, of religion in general, wish to destroy the foundations of Christianity. They did evil by their teaching and life, continue to do so in their followers, and will go on doing evil in the world till its end. The villains did evil and perhaps did not suppose what dreadful fruit would grow from it in future generations. A bitter inheritance came down from such ancestors. The memory of such dead is not good, but a curse. Can they have peace in the Lord of peace and love? The ill as well as the good effect of the dead upon the living will end only with this world itself. Then all activity of good and evil will be limited to heaven and hell. Such is the law of moral development.

Having both good and evil people in our midst, we encounter both good and ill directions in life. It is for the present generation to perfect the good and trample down the evil. Thus we can understand that the zealots of good, which they developed and planted, tasted heavenly fruits while yet on earth; and after they passed on beyond the grave, they were rewarded with eternal peace. Heavenly joys should increase more and more, as the good they planted on earth gradually grows. Prosperity in Christ for the living calls down more and more the beneficent mercy of God on the dead. Good grows on earth, and, correspondingly, the glory of the departed grows in heaven. And, conversely, evil on earth cannot bring peace to its sowers beyond the grave. It grows on earth, brings about disorders, and the torment of them that founded it grows endlessly beyond the grave. It cannot be that evil would give its founder heavenly joy after death. The law of natural development is in full swing on earth: a new generation either develops the ideas of its forefathers or else does battle with the concepts of the past. Children follow and develop their parents' lead. The example of a departed friend is worthy of imitation, and so on. But the inner bond and mutual relationship between the condition and fate of the departed and the life of the quick, or between this world and the next, means that all the Saints and good souls beyond the grave sorrow for our sinful life on earth. They sorrow that their spirit did not find followers amongst us, that people do not follow the example of their life, that their teaching is rejected, that there are few who are in sympathy with them. While on earth, they suffered in spirit at the wrong they saw, resisted it with all the strength they had, and sacrificed their comfort and life for the truth. And now, seeing no end to moral evil, they cry out to God in heaven against those that despise truth thus: "How long, O Lord, holy and true, dost thou not judge and avenge our blood on them that dwell on earth?" (Revelation 6:10).

If our immoral, wrongful life on earth is a cause of sorrow to the Saints and good souls in the world beyond the grave, as being a life not in the spirit of Christ, then what shall we say of the state of souls in the other world who await help from the living?

Concerning useless prayer, the Lord teaches thus: "They honor me with their lips, but their heart is far from me" (Matthew 15:8, Mark 7:6). And so we pray, "Give rest, O Lord, to the souls of Thy departed servants!"

But can our departed fathers, mothers, spouses, brethren, sisters, friends, and acquaintances find rest in the Lord when we, their living children, spouses, brethren, sisters, and friends think and act contrary to the spirit of Christ?

What joy, what consolation do parents have in bad children? There is no more consolation than this to brethren, sisters, spouses, and friends from the living who do not know Christ and His holy will.

What can be more horrible than being in hell? And yet, according to the words of the Lord, even in that sorrowful state, the unfortunate rich man was troubled about the life of his brethren on earth. It was their way of life that caused his grief; he would not have grieved, had they been living righteously.

And so, we can live in such a way as to bring the dead either peace or sorrow. If we live in a way pleasing unto God, this is a development of the spirit of departed good fathers; we fulfill their measure (Matthew 23:32), and they are with us in spirit.

On the other hand, if we live sinfully, we develop the spirit of bad ancestors, and we fulfill their measure. Consequently, the spirit of our good forefathers is not with us, but it is confounded and distressed over the ruin of souls that trample their good beginnings.

So as not to break the tie and relationship with the good departed, we follow their example in everything. We try to develop their good ideas and to cut off and destroy all that is contrary to them. In this way we will be united with them; and at the same time, when we cut off evil, we thereby do a good deed unto the dead who have left these evil roots to posterity. By exterminating evil we silence the voice of a curse and thus help to cleanse and bring rest to the latter dead who were the cause, intentionally or not, of ill.

Only "Ask and it shall be given you; seek, and ye shall find" (Matthew 7:7; Luke 11:9), as the Source of Life taught us Himself. Not without reason was it said, "Ask, pray ...": for the grace of Christ—no matter how generous and powerful it is—does nothing by itself without our participation, for us or for the departed.

Only for him who is faithful and who asks are all things possible (Mark 9:23): "Be it unto thee as thou desirest" (Matthew 15:28). The righteous and all good spirits rejoice in our moral improvement. Just as the dead fathers were good and evil, so those who remain on earth fill the measure of their fathers; and the dead are still spiritually active in the living among whom the fruit and spirit of their fathers grow.

5. The Third Basis: The Immortal Soul of Man

Love unites us here on earth, often to the point of willingness to sacrifice one's life for a beloved person; but does it remain unchanged beyond the grave? If love reigns beyond the grave, then how is it expressed, and what sympathy has the other world for this one? What sympathy can there be between relatives separated by an inexorable death? What should the sympathy of the living be towards the dead?

The immortal spirit that abides in those on earth (the living) and in those that have passed on into the spiritual world beyond the grave, which penetrates the entire nature of man, both the soul and body, fills the soul with its immortal characteristics of which the most important are love and sympathy.

Love, sympathy, and the powers of the soul do not leave it in the new life beyond the grave, otherwise it would cease to be a soul. Consequently, the departed have love for the living and sympathize with them.

Sympathy is the fruit of love and is a vital taking to heart of a neighbor's situation. St. Paul bears witness that love is immortal, "never fails" (I Corinthians 13:8). Therefore, the state of the dead (their repose or unrest) is directly connected with the life of the living. In speaking of the members of our body, the Apostle speaks at the same time of the members of the body of Christ, His Church. Everyone is convinced from experience that his body parts serve, help, and sympathize with one another. In the very same way, people, wherever they might be, who make up one spirit and one body, must serve, help, and sympathize with one another. If only a soul has not lost divine love, then regardless of where it is, whether beyond the grave or still in the body on earth, it cannot fail to take a vital, active part in the state of souls close to it, no matter where they are. Under such conditions the dead have sympathy for the living, and the living are obliged to sympathize with the dead. The living and the dead, as members of the one spiritual body of Christ, according to the teaching of St. Paul, are in mutual sympathy, because they are bound by never failing immortal love. The dead sympathize with the living, and the living sympathize with the dead. If one member is in pain, then all the members suffer with it; and if one rejoices, then all the members are glad. This is the teaching of the Apostle Paul, that the dead love the living, and have sympathy for them.

Virtue, since it has a divine, unworldly origin, is reflected in the conscience of those who practice it and makes the soul glad with a heavenly joy. The departed are in sympathy with us and rejoice together with us, just as the holy angels rejoice in heaven over every repentant sinner as he does battle for virtue. This is the teaching of the Saviour Himself on the sympathy of the spiritual world for the state of people remaining on earth (Luke 15:10).

If the spiritual world beyond the grave rejoices together with those on earth who rejoice spiritually, then the opposite is also true: our harsh, sinful, and unrepentant life, our unrighteousness, causes sorrow for the spiritual world; the holy angels sorrow, the Saints sorrow, and our departed relatives sorrow, as can be seen from the concern of the rich man in Hades for his brethren remaining on earth (Luke 16:27,28). The Gospel bears witness that at the moment of death of the Lord Jesus Christ, the sun was darkened, the earth was shaken, and the veil of the temple was rent. At the moment of the death that trampled down the eternal death of those that believed in Him, many Saints who had died before rose up, came out of their tombs, and appeared to many of the living in Jerusalem. Such an event in the moral world—the death of the Lord Jesus Christ—evoked the participation of all His creation. The spiritual world, that beyond the grave, and the physical world were in sympathy with the mystery of the death of the God-Man.

On the resurrection of the dead at the moment of the death of the Lord Jesus Christ, Archimandrite Theodore (Bukharev) writes: "What drew these resurrected Saints to the holy city of Jerusalem and caused them to appear to many of the living? Was it not their profound concern for the poor people who had not recognized their Redeemer? Was it not the striving of the fathers who had entered into the joy of Christ's Resurrection to share that joy, so far as possible, with their living children as well?" (From his *Homily on the Departed,* p. 62.)

Did not the deceased wife of a priest feel sympathy for his ruinous situation when she appeared to him from the other world so as to bring him to his senses when he was rushing towards destruction? (See this account in Part II, "Appearances of Souls from Hades," p. 80–81.)

Before God all are alive; consequently the life beyond the grave, along with the present life, constitute a development of mental qualities and affections. The life beyond the grave is a continuation of the development of life on earth and should develop as a fruit does from the kernel of mental characteristics and inclinations on earth.

Where there is love there is sympathy. Beyond the grave, immortal love dwells in the kingdom of love and, along with love, sympathy toward love's object is inseparable: sympathy to lesser brethren, to us who are yet wandering on earth. Thus the condition of the world beyond the grave is in sympathy with the condition of this present life. The holy angels and all the Saints and all the still-imperfect departed *are* in sympathy with us and are vitally involved with us. We, for our part, can sympathize with their state beyond the grave and, by our life, either help or hinder the amelioration of the condition of those who are imperfect or those who are perfect. And so the spirit of man, with all its qualities (for example, love), serves as the basis for the inner, unbroken bond and close mutual relationship among the members of Christ's Church, between the living and the departed, between the other world and this.

If such is our bond and relationship with the world beyond the grave, then it remains for us to follow the spirit of Christ and let love for heavenly truth rule our hearts and let our philosophy be the same as that of the One responsible for our salvation.

6. The Definition of the Union, Bond, Relationship, and Communion Between This World and That Beyond the Grave

Having examined the basis for the union, bond, relationship, and communion of the world beyond the grave and that of this earth, it remains for us to say wherein such connections lie.

Faith brings about union, that is, oneness of mind. It unites man with God, and it unites all moral beings (angels and spirits) as St. Paul bears witness: "At the name of Jesus every knee shall bow, of things in heaven, and things in earth, and things under the earth" (Philippians 2:10). There is one flock of angels and men; the heavens rejoice with the angels, and the earth makes glad with people as our Orthodox Church teaches.

Faith binds people so closely together, internally and spiritually, that they seem to have one soul and one heart as did the first Christians. Such a bond between Christians, founded in the faith of Christ, is never broken by anything, if only the members of such a union remain and do not betray their active faith. The faith of Christians, living and dead, is one. We believe in the Lord Jesus Christ, we believe in life beyond the grave, be it blissful or tormented; and the dead, when they were on earth, believed in the same. We, the living, expect the resurrection of renewed bodies and their reunion with souls for eternal life; and the departed await the same. The object of our faith is one and the same, for the living and the dead. Consequently, faith leads to a union of the world beyond the grave (that of the departed) with this world (with the living).

Divine love, one of the characteristics of the immortal human soul, brings about a bond. That mankind should have such an indissoluble bond with God was commanded by God Himself: "Thou shalt love the Lord thy God with all thy heart, and with all thy soul" (Mark 12:30).

From the bond of moral beings with God, there proceeds a bond of love between moral beings (between angels and souls) as well. God demands true mutual love from us: "Love one another, even as I have loved you" (Matthew 6:33). He alone loves Me, who loves his neighbor. Consequently, the bond between man and God is closely tied with the bond between man and man. And so, all moral beings—angels, souls, and people, are inseparably bound. Even death is not able to break this bond, because the bond of love is the law of the Lord. Immortal love joins this world with that beyond the grave by an eternal bond. The bond of love is not only not weakened by death, but becomes even stronger. The image of a beloved person, one who has passed on into the world beyond the grave, lives in us; it lives in our mind and heart. As is the bond that we have with Christ by faith, such is the bond that we have through faith with our departed ones. A vital bond of love unites all members of the Church of Christ; the Church Militant on earth with the members of the Church in heaven (the saints) and with the members in the uttermost depths (Hades)—those who have not yet attained full holiness, but have not been deprived of the heavenly Kingdom.

Moral beings have obligations to God which also comprise their relationship with God. In regard to one another, they have both rights and obligations which make up their mutual relationships among themselves. While we are on earth we are in definite relationships with one another, of one society with another, one government with another. These relationships, especially for those united in the faith of Christ, do not cease even when one of the members of that union passes into the life beyond the grave. The relationships in this case do not end, but only take on another aspect, another character, corresponding to the way of life of the one who has passed on; and this is because those who have gone beyond the grave are also alive. And as the living and the dead retain a bond and union, the former have obligations to the latter. This means that the world beyond the grave is in a mutual relationship with this present world.

Fulfillment of obligations brings about a communion. In fulfilling their obligations to God, moral beings are in communion with God. In fulfilling their obligations to each other, they are in communion amongst themselves. Prayer to the Saints brings the living into communion with them. Fulfilling obligations to the dead brings the living into communion with the dead. When the living pray and do good for the sake of the departed a communion results. And so, the spiritual world beyond the grave is in communion with the present earthly world. Moral theology sets forth all the relationships and obligations of spiritual and moral beings to God and to one another.

The degree or strength of our bond and communion with the departed is determined by faith itself. The higher and more perfect the faith, the more vital the bond and communion between the present life and that beyond the grave. If there be no bond of love with our neighbors, there is no bond of love with God:

"If any man say, I love God, and hateth his brother, he is a liar" (I John 4:20), as St. John the Evangelist teaches; "In as much as ye have done it to the least of these my brethren, ye have done it unto Me" (Matthew 25:40), the Lord will say at the judgment. Consequently, the bond with God fully expresses the bond and communion of the living with the dead. If we do not love the departed, we do not love the Lord Who loves the dead as living members of His Church.

And so, although we are separated visibly for a time in the body, yet we remain invisibly in an unbroken bond and mutual communion if only we remain in union and communion with our Lord Jesus Christ.

The dead, remaining in a bond and communion with Jesus Christ—as St. Paul bears witness saying—"In the name of Jesus every knee shall bow, in heaven, in earth, or in the abyss" (Philippians 2:10) maintain a bond and communion with the living, especially with those close to their heart and with whom they were bound on earth by special ties of a love sanctified by the Lord. But if the departed are not in union and communion with the Lord, not of one faith with the living, and not Christians, then there can be no communion with the living or of the living with them. Then visible death forever breaks all communion of the living with the departed. The departed in the Lord, in union and communion with the living likewise cannot, on their own *part*, break the bond and communion with them; but the living can either weaken the strength of the bond and communion with the departed or else break it entirely. If faith is weak, love grows cold; with the cooling of love, they forget their obligations to the dead; and, as the obligations are forgotten, the communion of the living with the dead ceases.

Thus the union, bond, relationship, and communion that we have with the departed does not end with their death as long as we who remain on earth do not break it off of our own will. The dead always have a spiritual bond with us, and we, the living, by faith can always see our departed ones and hear their voice (funeral homily by Archbishop Platon of Riga, "Strannik" for February 1864, p. 139).

One can be far from the departed, or near. The greater our love for the departed and the stronger our prayer for him, the closer the departed is to us. The prayer of faith has such power to bring us close to the departed that we can feel his approach, the breathing of his soul near us. Tidings go from heart to heart above all at prayer. (Archpriest Ilia Putiatin, "Homily 263").

7. The Visible Expression of the Union, Bond, Relationship, and Communion of the Earthly World with That Beyond the Grave

If A relationship consists of rights and obligations and a communion in their performance, then this performance is understood to have its expression physically, visibly, palpably, in specific activities. And so, the union, the bond, the relationship between this world and that beyond the grave should be visible and palpable and be expressed physically.

Just as the invisible soul with its invisible activities (thoughts, desires, and feelings) is expressed visibly in its outward activity, so also its union, bond, relationship, and communion with the invisible world, here on earth, is expressed in certain physical actions which show its bond and communion with the world beyond the grave.

It is understood that the bond and relationship between spirits is expressed spiritually as fits its nature; but the connection and relationship of the spirit with the body must be expressed according to their nature, not only spiritually, but bodily as well. How do we express our love for one another, our confession of one faith? We express this *by deeds*.

Inner activities (thoughts, desires, and feelings) which are proper to the soul, once expressed by word or action, make up the outward activity of man or his deeds. Deeds are the visible expression of a connection and communication: the visible with the invisible, the earthly with the otherworldly, the spiritual with the bodily, the present with the past and the future, the human with the divine or the demonic, of man with God and His angels and with all the Saints, or of man with the devil and with his hosts of Hades and with the lost souls. Therefore our deeds bear the character of one or the other realm beyond the grave, be it of Paradise or of Hades.

Eternity is an unbroken and endless continuation of being. Man, having received life in the maternal womb, has entered into eternity. The Source of life is God. "I am Life" (John 6:35; 11:25; 14:6), as the Lord Jesus Christ taught. The life of the soul is its union with God. Therefore the reverse is also true: without God the soul is dead. The body is alive if the soul abides in it; and the soul is alive if God abides in it. The death of the body is its parting with the soul; but death for the soul is the removal of grace from it. And so, in a living body there can be either a living or a dead soul. The state beyond the grave is a continuation of existence on earth: either blissful (life) or sorrowful (death). On earth, a life in God and in His grace lays down a beginning of a future blessed eternity, while a life outside of God, without God and His grace, makes for a beginning of an eternity in Hades. And so, the present is closely tied and related to the future and serves as a trustworthy visible sign of the bond and communion of the living with the dead. The bond and communion of the living with the dead give special qualities to the present, qualities that are absent where there is no bond or communion. The life of all that are and have been pleasing to God bears upon it the mark of a bond and communion with the other world. Our future depends on the present. Faith which joins the present with the future, the earthly with the heavenly, makes angels on earth, heavenly people, while unbelief makes for living dead men. He that is resurrected on earth in the spirit has been resurrected for eternity; while he that has died in spirit on earth has died as concerns eternal life.

The quality or characteristic of every soul must without fail have its corresponding state (good or ill) in the life beyond the grave. This is an undisputed truth. As many as there are states in Paradise, so many must there be blissful states of the soul on earth as well corresponding to those in heaven. The mansions of Paradise, according to the words of the Lord, are many; so it is only proper to conclude that there are also many cells in Hades. As many enclosures as there are in hell, so many are there states of evil souls on earth. Regarding this correspondence of the life beyond the grave to this life, the Lord Himself taught: "The Kingdom of God is within you" (Luke 17:21). Therefore others also, if they have not the Kingdom of God within them, then they have hell within. There is a special mood to those who are inheriting the Kingdom of God and one particular to the captives of Hades. The character of the former is righteousness, peace, and joy in the Holy Spirit; that of the latter is bitterness and hatred. And so, those that dwell in Paradise and Hades have, on earth, corresponding like and equal characters of soul.

Of such states beyond the grave, both heavenly and hellish, there are seven, according to the Third Book of Esdras and St. Ambrose of Milan. This sevenfold number of states beyond the grave corresponds to the same number of judgments of God which take place in the world. Perhaps the sevenfold number of deadly sins (envy, pride, covetousness, luxury, gluttony, hatred, sloth) corresponds to states beyond the grave. There are seven states of Paradise and seven of Hades.

As the spirit of man unfolds and acts in him with its higher and lower aspects, just so do the spirits and souls that now make up the world beyond the grave, with their higher and lower aspects (Paradise and Hades), unfold and affect the earthly world.

Our activity, in which the world beyond the grave takes part, clearly expresses our union and communion with the spirits and souls of the unseen world.

All of paganism presents us with a bond and communion of men with evil spirits in a palpable manner; but Christianity presents a spiritual bond and communion (though invisible) with good spirits and souls through Jesus Christ. And the outstanding ascetics of Christianity were in a palpable communion with good and holy souls and spirits, and they visibly and palpably did battle with the spirits of evil (see, for example, the life of St. Anthony the Great).

The present is a reliable expression of the bond and communion of the living with those that have died. Look into the lives of individuals, families, societies, peoples, and you will doubtless recognize their bond and communion with the world beyond the grave. You will see whether or not the bond exists and even be able to note its degree.

Let us close our look at the truths about the bond and communion of the spiritual world and that of earth with the words of Archimandrite Theodore (Bukharin):

"As the grains of truth and good or the weeds of falsehood and evil gradually develop in the earthly world, so also the souls of the departed gradually mature in the world beyond the grave, as the fruit in a mother's womb, for the determination of eternal life. In this way, the harvest of the former cannot but relieve the womb of the world beyond the grave, and that of the latter, correspondingly, of the physical world (III Esdras 4:28–49).

"The world beyond the grave, the earthly world, and even the physical world walk in step, in a strictly uniform gait. Faith in Christ—living, active faith, inspired by His boundless love for mankind—makes us live members of His living body, the Church, through our sincere participation in the fate of the departed and striving to help them, such a faith is unto the salvation of the living and not to be brought to shame. 'Be it unto thee as thou wishest', as Christ taught. Such a faith saves both the living and the departed" (*Homily on the Dead*, pp. 69–70).

Faith saves both the living and the dead. The perfected dead intercede for us, the living, and we, the living, pray to God for the imperfect dead who are kept in Hades. Thus our salvation is well arranged in Christ our Lord Who took upon Himself the sins of all that believe in Him, whether they are in this life or the next. He is the God and Saviour of all that are faithful to Him.

8. The Union, Bond, Relationship, and Communion of This World with That Beyond the Grave

Man is spoken of as a little world in which there is such a wonderful harmony, an agreement among its parts. The soul is mystically united with the body; the spiritual nature united with the physical, has the closest of bonds and mutual ties. The word of God bears witness thus of the bond and relationship between the soul and body: "The token of a good heart, is a good countenance" (Ecclesiasticus 13:32). Anger is expressed visibly in the face and body; consequently, when the spirit is calm, the body flourishes, and when the body is infirm, the soul sorrows. The spirit of man embraces and penetrates all his nature, both the soul and body; therefore it has a bond and relationship with them. The soul is the concentration point of man's inner life. By means of the spirit and body, the soul enters into a relationship with two worlds: the higher and the lower—that is, the spiritual and the earthly.

The spirit of man knows its immortality, and this truth is deeply rooted in its consciousness; consequently, the awareness of immortality belongs to all mankind, beginning with our ancestors who were aware that they were immortal. As it had been determined for immortal beings, a breach of their obligation was to be punished by death. "The spirit of man," writes Archimandrite Theodore (Bukharev), "is inwardly bound with the body and has the most vital tie with it. It unfolds the higher and nobler organs of the body (the thoughts, in the head; the affections, in the heart), and its higher side acts through them; whereas, its lower side (subconscious and darker movements, and self-consciousness of life) acts in all the other organs. The spirit is quite foreign to any extension of feeling or material complication; it lives in spiritual order by the awareness of thought, moral movements, and inclinations. There is also an analogy to this microcosm (man) in the macrocosm of the universe. Thus, the world of thought and of the spirit, which is to unfold for us in the life beyond the grave, is in direct connection and relationship with the visible, earthly world; and unfolds its higher and brighter side to earth and those that dwell therein, as from the realm above. It was for this reason that the Lord Himself lifted up His eyes, ascending prayerfully to heaven (John 17:1). Its lower and darker side opens into the abyss (or "into the lower parts of the earth," in the words of the Apostle, cf. Ephesians 4:9). Yet in itself, this world in its heavenly or abysmal realms, exists and lives in an order that corresponds to man's inner world: an order of thought, love or hate, moral good or evil" (in his *Homily on the Repose of the Departed*, pp. 66–67).

St. Paul teaches that not only the soul, but the body also continues its life in the earth, in corruption itself; and he explains this mystery of God's wisdom as a seed sown in the ground. The matter of the seed is secretly bound up with the power of growing life, and in the decomposition of the seed's matter into its component elements there lies the flowering, the development of further life. Just so, the Apostle continues, an immortal spirit is natural to the body of one deceased (I Corinthians 15:51–54).

This apostolic teaching on the life of the body even after its separation from the soul is explained thus by St. Gregory of Nyssa: "As in a living man, the spirit, without complication, embraces and penetrates the whole complexity (composite nature) of the body, so also after its separation from the body, with the decomposition of the latter, our spirit, by its nature, finds it just as convenient and simple to have a relationship with the whole complexity (composite nature) of its body that has perished, while remaining in one or another realm of the spiritual world . . ."

All that takes place with the body in the time of its decomposition into its elements, as well as after that, all its flowering and development for a new life, does not take place without the involvement and sympathy of the spirit. The body ripens for its future spirituality; and the soul, at the same time as the body, gradually matures into a consciousness of its lot corresponding to its earthly life, a consciousness of bliss or ruin together with its inseparable earthly companion, the body, which is now new and spiritual.

And so, the soul has a relationship and sympathy with its body that is located on earth.

The spirit, not having a material extension and remaining with the soul in the body, is the basis for interaction and participation by the soul in its body which flowers for eternity. The body in the ground, the soul in the world beyond the grave, both ripen for the future; the first, in order to obtain appropriate spirituality, the second, in order to gain cognizance of its fate.

Everywhere there is life; everywhere there is growth; there is no idleness in nature. In the world beyond the grave, on earth and in the earth, there is flowering for eternity.

The order of things in the present, earthly, temporary life, as being subject to corruption and death, is completely opposite to the incorrupt and undying order of things in the future, spiritual, eternal life: "For this corruptible must put on incorruption, and this mortal must put on immortality" (I Corinthians 15:53).

The beings that dwell in the world beyond the grave are: good angels in Paradise, evil spirits in the aerial space surrounding the earth, the souls of Saints in heaven, the souls of the imperfect in Hades, and souls lost for the kingdom of heaven in Gehenna.

Here is the order of our exposition: first we shall look at the union, bond, relationship, and communion of the spiritual-angelic world with the present world; the union and communion of good angels with the earthly world and its inhabitants; then, the union and communion of the earthly, present world and its inhabitants with the evil spirits; further on, the union and communion of this world with that beyond the grave, that is, the living with the dead. And since in the world beyond the grave there are now three states of souls, therefore the relationship of the living to the dead is of three kinds: 1) to perfected Saints; 2) to the imperfect and 3) to those lost for the kingdom of heaven. And finally, we will show examples of actual appearances of the dwellers in the world beyond the grave to people on earth, both in their sleep and palpably.

9. The Bond and Communion of Those Living on Earth with the Angelic World in General

a) With the Holy Angels

Whoever does not believe in the existence of evil Spirits, it stands to reason, cannot believe in good angels either; nor does he believe the Scriptures and consequently doubts the existence of God. Such a one does not believe that he has an immortal soul subject to responsibility! Where would he assign the devout, the good, or the perverse after death?

The believer needs to make his reason subject and obedient to faith. Not only those things exist that are accessible to our senses, but those things also are real to which faith bears witness. For Christians perfected in the faith, the spiritual world sometimes, in certain cases, becomes accessible.

Revelation bears witness for us that, first of all, in the order of God's creation, angels were created. Their number is beyond count, and their place is the Third Heaven (*Theology*, Anthony, p. 96).

The activity of angels is the incessant praise of God, the vision of God's countenance, His service in the fulfillment of His will. The angels are bodiless beings with limitations, gifted with mind, will, and power.

The angelic, spiritual world (of angels and evil spirits) acts upon the soul and body of man both spiritually (mentally) and palpably (through feeling). The activity of men has already the character of one who lives in the spiritual world beyond the grave. Man's profound moral falling—"I do not that good which I will; but the evil which I hate, that I do" (Romans 7:15), as St. Paul wrote—the deadness of his soul and body, and therefore the extreme crudeness and dullness of his perceptions, make him unable to communicate through his senses with the spiritual, angelic world and with the good angels and evil spirits, except for certain cases which depend on the will of God.

Man cannot be in direct contact with the higher, spiritual world. The mystery of eternity and life beyond the grave remain a mystery to him so long as he is on earth. Only as much is revealed to him about this subject as he is able to receive and comprehend; those that have appeared to us from the spiritual world and those that have been lifted up for a time from earth to there were not able to convey what they saw and heard there, as to those who could not understand, accept, or conceive of such things. How could one convey to a child, only beginning to think, all the pleasures of life, and how could such a child envision and understand them? "Inexpressible words, which a man is not permitted to speak" (II Corinthians 12:4, NASV), as the Apostle Paul, who once was swept up to the third heaven, wrote.

"Eternity is so beyond expression," as Bishop John writes, "that it lays the seal of silence on every mind and tongue here. A small revelation of eternity in life here brings about a chaining, as if in death, of all man's senses and bodily organs" (his "The Mystery of Death," in "Domashnie Besedy" for 1869, Issue 48).

However, the higher man rises in his spiritual perfection, the more and the clearer communion with the unseen world is opened to him. Consequently, even now communion of man with the unseen world is possible and exists.

Since the nature, the goal of existence, and the activity and the laws for those who dwell in both worlds is the same, then it is possible, though not that easy, for there to be a communication between this earthly world and the spiritual world beyond the grave. What sort of a kingdom would it be, what sort of a home in which the members had no relationship to one another? If there were no communication between the moral beings, then how could the angels rejoice over a repentant soul on earth? With the fall of Adam the direct communication of this world with the spiritual world ended; there remained only indirect communication. The members of the moral realm are not dissociated in such a way that they would not know one another entirely.

As St. John the Divine bears witness, the number of good angels is two thirds, and they act on the soul and body of man; and, since the soul and body are in a mutual relationship, man, through his soul and body, can have a bond and relationship with the good angels. Sinners drive their angels away, while the righteous, those who fear God and who by their Christian battles cleanse their senses, have a bond and a constant relationship with the angels of light, and sometimes even a palpable communication. But with evil spirits they have nothing in common, save for the battle for truth, an invisible, spiritual, mental, and sometimes a physical battle.

The holy angels have appeared in dreams and also palpably to the Saints of God and to people of good life, proclaiming the will of God to them.

Concerning the bond and communion of the spiritual and angelic world with the earthly, with people, Jesus Christ Himself taught that the angels rejoice in heaven over people who correct themselves and turn to repentance, and that infants, and therefore all people, have their guardian angels in heaven (Matthew 18:10) whom God has commanded to keep man in all his ways, "lest his foot ever trip on a stone" (Psalms 90:11–12). Our guardian angels teach us faith and devoutness; they are the guardians of our souls and bodies who pray and intercede for us before God, and finally, they do not leave us when we pass into the world beyond the grave.

And so, since each of us has his guardian angel in heaven, what a close bond there is between the spiritual, angelic world and this present, earthly world! Thus there is a communication between the two worlds, only a spiritual, invisible communication. Yet sometimes, by the will of God, there can be a palpable communication between them. Our bond and relationship with our good guardian angels constitutes our obligation to honor and venerate them.

From the words of St. Paul, one should conclude that: 1) the holy angels dwell in the third heaven, and 2) they have the speech and words characteristic of their nature. The Apostle, swept up to the third heaven, heard there angelic speech and words (I Corinthians 13:1,2; II Corinthians 12:4). The words "let us attend," "Alleluia," "Holy God, Holy Mighty, Holy Immortal"—are they not uttered by the lips of angels in their heavenly homeland? Appearing on earth to people, the angels have spoken. Would it be pleasant for a moral being not to be able to share feelings with other beings like unto itself? Would the conversation between the dumb be of much pleasure if they had not first learned to write?

There is one nature for angels and souls (reason and will); the union, bond, and mutual relationship they share makes them into one spiritual and moral realm.

According to the teaching of St. Paul, the holy angels together with the souls of the righteous make up the heavenly Church Triumphant (Hebrews 12:22,23). Angels, like human souls, are indeed personal, limited beings.

Were there no union, bond, relationship, and communion between the angelic and earthly worlds, the Holy Church would not call both worlds to a common spiritual celebration and festivity on the feast of the Nativity of Christ. The dwellers in heaven, on earth, and in the abyss, as having one and the same nature (mind and will), the same laws, the same goal in being and activity, all together adore, glorify, and praise Him Who is the Cause of their salvation, Jesus Christ (Philippians 2:10). Perfected Christians are in a visible, palpable communion with the spiritual world, as this was especially in the early ages of Christianity. They saw, heard, spoke with beings not of earth; and the imperfect are in only an invisible, though real, spiritual communion with the angels.

b) With Evil Spirits

Since the time when Lucifer and his adherents fell, they were deprived of the right to be members of the kingdom of God. They are not of God. Pride, self-esteem, malice distinguish them from the good angels. Since the creation of man, their activity has consisted in the ruin of people. Laying out traps for people, they oppose every virtue, and man must force himself and his heart towards all that is good; "the kingdom of heaven suffereth violence, and the violent take it by force" (Matthew 11:12), as the word of God bears witness. The evil spirits act on the soul and body of man; and as the soul and body are in a mutual relationship and have a bond between them, so a man's soul and body can be in a bond and relationship with evil spirits. The unrighteous, the inattentive, and the careless sinner have a bond and communion with evil spirits: both an invisible, spiritual, mental communion and one that is sometimes palpable as well. But all the Saints have had a constant and fierce battle with them, and so now do all the followers of Christ, the true Christians.

The activity of the fallen angels is in opposition to the will of God; this activity, mixed with malice, envy, and hatred towards God and towards Christian man, seeking to make him too a sharer of their bitter fate, makes up the distinctive character of fallen angels.

If man indeed allows his activity to take on the character of the fallen angels, then of course he has a bond and communion with them, as one who carries out their will. Evil spirits act on his soul by means of suggestions, thoughts. A bond and communion with them is deadly for man, and therefore the Lord Himself calls the devil a murderer of men.

There are far fewer fallen angels than good ones, according to the testimony of the visionary St. John the Evangelist: they make up only one third. But nevertheless there are so many of them that, in the Saviour's words, they comprise a whole realm of darkness (Luke 11:18). Their evil activity towards God and man, as it develops more and more, makes them all the darker. The mind and will of evil spirits, due to their deliberate fall, took on a perverse direction; their mind turned to evil and their will to the fulfillment of evil intentions. Their strength, had it not been limited by God, would have destroyed everyone and everything, as can be seen in the case of the righteous Job. But without God's allowing it, they can do nothing, neither to man nor to beast, as demonstrated by their petition for the Lord to let them go from the demoniac into the herd of swine, something they were unable to do without God's permission (Matthew 8:31). Evil spirits are at all times, in every place building snares for man; they appear to us in the form of those departed this life, pretending to be deceased fathers, brethren, acquaintances, and friends; they appear in the image of Jesus Christ and His holy angels, so as to deceive the athletes of Christ.

Fallen spirits, having enticed us, cover themselves and their nets with virtues, so that people would not recognize them. They have appeared in dreams and in waking, not only to sinners so as to bring them to final ruin, but to the same end they have appeared unto the Saints of God. Appearing, they sometimes foretold the future which was already known in the spiritual world: for example, the temptations that were to befall St. Job the sufferer; the defeat of the Israelite king, Ahab; the temptation of St. John, the Archbishop of Novgorod, and others. As a whole, the future is not known to them; therefore, for the most part, as they themselves were misled, they also misled people and deceived them. They overcame the inexperienced, but were themselves overcome by the experienced; this is an obvious sign that they did not know the future.

Earth is the dwelling-place of man, while the air is the habitation of all spirits. But how closely is the air tied to the earth! Just as weeds grow among the good grass and tares among the wheat, so are the evil spirits and people mixed together. Just as evil is natural to the evil spirits, so too does evil belong to man from his youth as if naturally, only it too is mixed with good. A common abode and a striving towards evil, these are what join man and the evil spirits.

Thanks to God, as a result of our fall (the fall of our ancestors) there came about a dulling of all the senses, the loss of prior ability to act far beyond the limits of the visible world, to sense the unseen world, to see it, to hear and speak with its denizens. Were it not for this dulling of the senses, what would have become of man? He could not have withstood all the temptations of the devil, palpably acting upon him. He would have fallen irreversibly, as did the devil himself. Have many out of all Christendom attained such a purification of the senses? Only strict ascetics who helped by the grace of God could do battle with the enemies of truth. We are weak and feeble, shielded from our enemies by the dullness of all the organs of our bodies, so that our senses do not see, do not hear, do not feel all the cunning of the enemy. We do not see his activity with our eyes, but he still acts upon us invisibly: on the mind, by means of ungodly thoughts; on the will, by means of ungodly desires. Man's agreement or disagreement with such thoughts and desires constitutes his bond and communion, either with fallen spirits or with the good angels. For a Christian there is unceasing battle, constant falling and rising! With whom do we battle?—with thoughts and desires. The great ascetics also did battle with the evil spirits palpably.

Experience shows how varied the manifestations of evil spirits to people are even now, depending on the degree of the bond and communion people have with them.

10. In General About the Bond and Communion of the Earthly World with That Beyond the Grave, of the Living with the Dead

The members of the moral kingdom are not so cut apart as to keep them from knowing one another completely. The Apostle Paul came from the world beyond the grave and spoke mystically with St. John Chrysostom, invisibly for St. John, although St. Proclus saw them conversing. The Saints come to earth and work miracles: they heal the sick, speak with the living, and teach the latter. St. Anthony the Great saw the soul of St. Paul of Thebes ascending to heaven; St. Macarius of Egypt spoke with the dead, and they replied to him.

If, then, there is still a vital bond between the members of the Kingdom of God who have departed and those still on earth, then without doubt there must be a definite relationship between them. This relationship, because of the twofold state of the departed, also has two forms: the relationship of the living to the Saints who are in heaven, and the relationship to the imperfect who have not attained sanctity and therefore have not been found worthy of bliss, even though they are still not lost to the kingdom of God. Thus our Church teaches concerning the relationship of this earthly world to that beyond the grave (*Dogmatic Theology*, Archbishop Anthony, Section 347). In the world beyond the grave there is yet a third condition of souls: those lost unto the Kingdom of Heaven. Therefore, just as the living members of a body have no bond or communion with such members as are lifeless, paralyzed, or amputated from the body, so too there can be no bond and relationship between those members that are lost unto the Kingdom of Heaven and the remaining members of the spiritual-moral family, whose Father is God.

a) Of the Bond and Communion with the Saints

Among the departed there are those who, immediately after death, receive the Kingdom of Heaven, as did the beggar Lazarus in the Gospel: these are Saints. God acts through them on earth among the faithful by means of various supernatural works. Their glorified bodies, or relics, become the source of miracles. In their love for others, they intercede in prayer to the Lord for those living on earth; they intercede also for the departed who have not yet attained perfection. That the Saints intercede for the dead who are not in bliss, can be taken on the basis of the law of immortal love. If the Saints (for example, St. Mitrofan of Voronezh) while yet on earth prayed so earnestly for the dead, then how could one imagine that once in the invisible world they would not pray to God, before Whom they have boldness and in Whose presence they stand, for those people who are not in bliss? The Saints pray for all, wherever they might be, on earth or outside of it; and so they pray for the dead, and their prayers cannot be without effect, as St. James bears witness: "The effectual fervent prayer of a righteous man availeth much" (James 5:16).

And if the Saints have with us sinners a bond and communion, then it behooves us not to break but rather to support the bond and communion we have with our intercessors. For our part, we need to have faith, love, prayer to them, respect, honor, and the veneration of their relics as it is established by the Church. The faithful on earth call in their prayers upon the Saints of the heavenly Church and honor them as the friends who are pleasing to God, co-heirs of Christ, and elder brethren (John 15:14; Romans 8:17; Hebrews 12:23).

We, the living, see them as representatives of Christian spiritual perfection and, on the basis of our love and thankfulness for their intercession for us before God, we keep their memory: "Remember your teachers, who have spoken unto you the word of God" (Hebrews 13:7).

Veneration for the Saints is expressed through the feasts established in their honor, through veneration of their incorrupt relics, their icons, and all the objects left by them, such as garments, chains, and so on. Veneration of the Saints, as well as their relics and icons, is a teaching of our Orthodox Church.

This is the teaching of the Church on the bond and communion of the Saints in heaven with us who are still on earth: this bond and communion consists, for their part, of their prayers before God for us who are still on earth; and for our part, it consists of veneration and invocation of them in prayer for their help and cooperation towards our salvation.

That all the Saints take a vital part in the fate of those who live on earth can be seen from the words of the Saviour Himself Who said that the angels rejoice over a repentant sinner (Luke 15:7, 10); and since all the Saints dwell with the angels, therefore these too rejoice in the virtuous life of the living. And, on the other hand, the angels and all Saints sorrow over our sinful and inattentive life.

That the Saints pray indeed for those living on earth, St. John bears witness in his Apocalypse (Revelation 5:8) as he does concerning the prayer by the angels for those living on earth (ibid. 8:3–4).

The first Christians believed in these prayers and in the intercession of the angels and all Saints for us in heaven. This belief is expressed in the ancient liturgies (such as that of St. James), in the decision of the Seventh Ecumenical Council, and in the writings of the Fathers of the Church.

All the Saints, in leaving the earth and parting from us visibly in the body, at the same time promised to remain with us in spirit, if invisibly, yet in truth.

The first Christians believed that those who had passed on into the world beyond the grave did not break but continued their unseen spiritual bond and relationship with us who yet remain on earth. They expressed this belief in turning to the holy Martyrs and all who had been pleasing unto God, as to the living, calling them to communion in prayer and asking their intercessions before God.

b) The Bond and Communion with the Imperfect

The bond and communion of the living with the imperfect departed and the relationship of the living to them, as well as the visible means that express the bond and communion between the world beyond the grave and that of earth, is a subject calling for detailed examination. As its content is rather important, it will be set forth separately after the section "The Manifestation of Beings from the Spiritual World—Angels and Souls—to People in This World."

c) The Bond and Communion with Those Lost to the Kingdom of Heaven

Our holy Church prays thus for the departed: "Give rest, O Lord, to the souls of Thy servants, who have departed [this life] in the faith and hope of resurrection." This shows us whom the Church prays for and with whom She is in an unbroken bond and communion. Consequently, there is no bond and communion with deceased non-Christians and with the heterodox, as well as with those who are Christians in name only and those who have ended life in no way as

Christians: not in Christian faith and hope. The same applies to suicides, unless the suicide came about in unsound mind. For a true Christian, except a suicide, no form of death breaks the bond and communion with the living, with the Church. For a Christian, committed to the will of God, no violent death—for instance, drowning, burning in fire, strangulation, death in war or at the hands of brigands, being lost and perishing from exposure, heat, starvation, and so on—should be feared, because they do not break his bond and communion with all the members of the Church of Christ. The Saints pray for him and so do the living, as for a living member of the one living body.

11. The Manifestation of Beings from the Spiritual World—Angels and Souls—to People in This World

We said that the present, earthly world has a bond and mutual relationship with the spiritual world beyond the grave, and we showed wherein the bond and relationship consist. Now we will point out specific incidents from the past, and perhaps in the present, which are quite possible and to which in our carelessness or ignorance we have not referred: appearances to us of good angels, the perfected dead, the imperfect, and of evil spirits from the spiritual world.

As if it were a promise of this future union and communion, we have the evidence of both the revealed and naturalistic (pagan) religious teachings of manifestations to people, despite their sinfulness, of denizens of the spiritual world. Their appearances were in the Old Testament, in the New, among the pagans, and even take place at the present time. Our holy Church teaches that there is one flock of angels and mankind, and the powers of heaven invisibly celebrate with us. Angels and men have mixed and are in an invisible, mystical communion; and for more perfected Christians there can be, at times, also a palpable communication.

a) The Appearance of Good Angels on Earth

Anyone even slightly familiar with the Holy Scriptures knows that angels have appeared to people both in their sleep and while waking, by God's special providence, so as to be of service and lead them into the Kingdom of Heaven. These examples are found in both the Old Testament and the New.

The teaching of our Church and cases of angels appearing to humans on earth witness the close, unbroken tie and relationship of angels to us, as of elder brethren to younger members of one family whose Father is God.

Angels, willingly carrying out the will of God, as ministering spirits, take an active and vital part in the fate of mankind. Thus angels announce the will of God to people, watch over states (Deuteronomy 32:8), keep and have charge over human societies, regions, cities, monasteries, churches, and various parts of the earth (Revelation 7:1, 14:18), have influence over the private affairs of people (Genesis 32:1–2), strengthen and preserve (Daniel 6:22). Angels led the Apostles out of prison (Acts 5:19–20; 12:7–9), are present at the departure of the soul from the body, accompany it through the aerial toll booths, carry up our prayers to God, and intercede for us themselves (Revelation 8:3). Angels come to the service of men (Hebrews 1:14), instructing them in all truth, virtue, enlightening the mind, strengthening the will, and preserving them from ills in life (Genesis 16:7–12). Concerning the appearance of good angels, one can read in the Scriptures: Genesis 18:2–22; 28:12; Joshua 5:13–14; Luke 1:11, 26, 28; Matthew 2:13; Acts 5:19; 10:31; 12:7.

b) The Appearance on Earth of Evil Spirits

Just as tares grow among wheat, so does evil among the members of the spiritual-moral kingdom, that is, among angels and men. Among the sons of God, evil spirits roam about like lions: fallen angels, setting traps in every place and time for men, only to draw them away from the path of virtue. Among us are our enemies, as the holy Church teaches; their abode is the air which surrounds the earth.

Since man, through his spiritual side (mind and will), can naturally have a bond and relationship with beings like unto himself, therefore evil spirits also, like the good, act on our mind, will, and heart; and one either opposes and does battle with the evil spirits or else one enters into communion with them.

Acting invisibly on our soul by their cunning assaults, evil spirits have also appeared visibly and palpably. Whoever does not believe this must also doubt the temptations of our Lord Jesus Christ after baptism. Are there not many among the ascetics of Christ who have seen and spoken with them? When their onslaughts were overcome by the Saints, they were forced to take on various forms so as to ensnare a warrior of Christ. How many sorrows have they caused our soul and body? But, by the grace of God, they were unable to succeed. Someone will say: "But why do they not now appear visibly?" We answer: Who knows whether they do not, in fact, now appear palpably to the true servants of God? As for us sinners, what need is there for a visible appearance when we are already the zealous slaves of our passions, zealous in acting on their pressures and suggestions? Our foolish acts, words, and thoughts make us their cohorts and accessories. Understandably, such bonds and communion are harmful and ruinous for the world. Is not everything anti-Christian on earth the work of the devil? Do not his consorts and those united to him on earth bring about disorder, destruction, and ideas diverting man from his moral greatness?

c) Saints Appearing on Earth

The Lives of the Saints bear witness to us of the manifold appearances of God's Saints on earth. It is to be understood that their visits to people took place by the will of God. Leaving their heavenly homeland, they manifested themselves both in dreams and waking to those in need of their strong help. Are there many Saints to be found, who, out of their love-filled hearts, would not visit this sinful earth after their repose? Their visits to people were always accompanied by supernatural works, miracles, in which the name of God was glorified. Who can assert that now the Saints no longer appear? Has God's love towards humanity come to an end? Visiting the earth and its inhabitants, did they not bear witness in so doing of the existence of God and of life beyond the grave?

d) Appearances of Souls from Hades

Is this possible or impossible? It is possible! But why? Such as the soul was on earth, it remains the same in the new world beyond the grave. All is subject to the most good will of Him in Whose hands are the keys of Hades (Revelation 1:18) and Who is able to bring up from hell and to take down thither (I Kings [Samuel], 2:6).

In the Old Testament, Hades and death triumphed over the human race. All those who died, both the righteous, except for Elias and Enoch, and the sinners, went down to Hades, and Hades held fast its inmates. The Lord Himself, while still on earth, showed people the possibility of such manifestations, raising the dead. In the Old Testament, the chosen of God did the same: the Prophet Elias who raised up the son of the widow of Sarephtha; Elisseus (Elisha) who raised the son of the Sunnamitess (Shunammite woman), and others brought the souls of the dead back from the other world, from Hades (III Kings [I Kings] 17:22; IV Kings [II Kings] 4:33–37). But when the triumph of Hades and death was shattered, and we were redeemed by the God-man, then Hades was no longer able to hold its dead. The dead, it can be understood, by the will of God began to rise and to appear to the living as proof that Hades and death are no longer terrible to those who believe in the Redeemer Who is already come. Hades did not hold Moses who was to be with Christ on Mt. Tabor. The departed daughter of Jairus, the son of the widow of Nain, the four-day Lazarus freely left Hades and were resurrected. Hades could not hold them contrary to the will of Him in Whose hands are the keys to Hades. The prince of darkness sensed beforehand that he would be brought to nothing and trampled upon; and at the moment of our redemption, many deceased Saints rose and appeared to the living in Jerusalem (Matthew 27:52–53).

The disciples of Christ and many of the Saints raised the dead. If the dead could be raised, why should it be impossible for them to appear, by the will of God, for a definite good purpose? Not only the saintly departed appeared, but sinners as well who were still in an indeterminate state (Hades). Both appeared to the living, not only in sleep, but also palpably. The holy angels and Saints have appeared to people so as to announce the will of God. The appearance of the departed had the purpose of edifying the living, giving them faith in the real existence of the unseen world, even though it is beyond the reach of our physical senses in our fallen state.

Every Christian, even slightly familiar with Scriptural history, knows that angels and Saints, dwellers in the spiritual world beyond the grave, have come to earth; and there were cases when sinners, still imperfect and therefore in need of the Church's prayers, came to earth from Hades and appeared to relatives and acquaintances. As did angels and Saints, so too deceased sinners appeared to people on earth, either in dreams or palpably.

For man to have a visible, tangible communion now with the world beyond the grave is not possible. The whole world lies in evil, and our departed ones, having escaped from evil, would hardly be willing to visit us. One can picture what moral evil might result from the palpable communion of the two worlds. Our falling, and the devil's malice taking on all forms, would surely result in a dependable means of bringing all to ruin through a sensory communion with those who have gone on to the other world. Evil spirits would never cease to visit the living in the form of the departed who are close to the heart. The devil would pour out all his poison into mankind. Who can say how many would withstand such dreadful evil in communication with the dead?

The life beyond the grave, the lot of the righteous and sinners, our part in the improvement of the state of sinners asking God for the forgiveness of their sins, and the means by which we aid the departed, all this is witnessed by the appearances on earth of the dead to the living.

We know from history that the appearances to people living on earth of souls that have already passed on to the world beyond the grave took place in the Old Testament, among the pagans, in the New Testament, in the early ages of Christianity, and even in the modern, semi-Christian or anti-Christian world. And what of modem spiritism? Its adherents swear on their salvation to the truth of their beliefs, that they are visited by souls from the other world; and among them are hearts and minds enlightened by Christian light, even the highly educated! Now let us look at the historical evidence for the appearance of souls.

In the Old Testament, the Prophet Elias raised the son of the widow of Sarephtha, and a dead man was raised by contact with the bones of Elisseus (IV Kings 13:21). As a parallel to the summoning up of the soul of Samuel from Hades by Saul, one might bring forth the following examples from paganism. All humanity knows of the immortality of the soul and consequently also of its life beyond the grave; but as to where dead souls abide or where this world beyond the grave is located, this was pictured in various ways by the pagans. They recognized paradise, the place of the good in the other world, and hell, the place where evil souls went. The pagans recognized appearances of the souls of the dead to the living, and therefore the living were constantly in a union, bond, and communion with the denizens of the other world, that is, with their departed relatives and friends. In the view of crude, uneducated peoples, souls live in a dream-like state and appear to those living persons who fear even to remember them. As specters, the departed souls wander everywhere in the night and dwell in caves, pits, mountains, thickets, even on the sun and stars. They thirst for human blood and are overcome by sacrifices, prayers, and incantations.

The learned Greek philosopher and alchemist Democritus, who wrote a book called "Physics and Mystics," among other things, says in it that since his teacher died before having time to read him a full course of the sciences, he turned to incantations and, calling up from the netherworld the shade of his teacher, he conversed about science with him. His teacher said to him that all wisdom is to be found inside one of the columns of a temple, and there Democritus found the following three sayings:

> "Nature is born in nature,
> Nature conquers nature,
> Nature commands nature."[1]

Homer, in the eleventh canto of the Odyssey, draws a picture of Odysseus invoking souls of the departed from the world beyond the grave:

[1]Taken from the journal "Northern Star" [Severnaya Zvezdal], for 1878, No. 2, p. 29.

"I bared a sharp bronze sword, and having dug
A pit an ell wide and deep,
I made three libations to the dead, whom I called together:
The first, a honey mixture, the second, sweet-smelling wine,
The third, water and oat flour sprinkled over all . . .
Having made an invocation to the dead,
I myself slew a sheep and lamb over the deep pit;
Dark blood poured into it, and the souls of the dead
Came flying together, rising from the dark abyss of Erebus;
I then bared the sharpened sword, and with it
Sat before the pit, so as to impede
The approach of the lifeless shades of the dead
To the blood, until the blind seer Tiresias,
Whom I had asked, should give me answer.

Soon Tiresias' image appeared before him; Odysseus allowed him to drink his fill of the blood, and then Tiresias gave him the desired answer. Regarding the other shades, Tiresias said to Odysseus:

That one of the lifeless shades, whom thou[2] shalt let drink
Of the blood, will give thee a reasonable answer, but that
Whom thou lettest not drink will depart in silence.

The filial love of Odysseus to his dead mother called to earth:

Drawn by my heart, I wanted to embrace my departed mother's soul;
Three times I stretched out my arms to her in love,
Three times she slipped from me,
A shade or a dream . . .

The Babylonians, when they called up human souls from the world beyond the grave (according to the Arabic translation that has come down to us of the Babylonian writing "On Agriculture") would light a fire and cast into it various incense, pronouncing mysterious incantations as they did so. In the rising smoke, the soul materialized before them until it was quite solid. The Chaldeans believed that the souls of the dead abide in Sheol under the earth without blood and warmth of life, and that by incantations they could be compelled to reveal to the living their future fate.

---

[2]The earlier English forms, "thou," "thee," "thy/thine," have been used in this translation where the Russian had the corresponding forms.

In the New Testament, from beyond the grave first of all Elias appeared from paradise, and Moses from Hades with the Saviour as He was transfigured on Mt. Tabor with three witnesses: Peter, James, and John (Luke 9:28–32).

At the moment when Christ died, the risen dead preached the Resurrection of Christ. From the words of St. Matthew (27:52), one can see that the risen were Saints and that there were many of them. Certain of the ancient teachers of the Church felt that at that time those resurrected were the patriarchs and prophets, especially those related by blood to Jesus Christ, such as Abraham and David, or those who had served as His prototypes, for example Jonah, Melchisedek, and others. But others, reasoning that it would be hard for the long-departed to be recognized, thought that the risen Saints were of the number of those recently deceased, such as Simeon the Righteous, the Prophetess Anna, or Joseph the Betrothed. To this one might add that only those who were buried in the vicinity of Jerusalem arose, since the oldest tradition is that the crags where the tombs were located fell apart only near Jerusalem. The so-called Protevangelion of Nicodemus refers to the resurrection of the two sons of the righteous Simeon (in "Pascha, Gospodnya Pascha," Athonite publication, 1869, p. 31). The Apostle Peter, at the request of the widows in Joppa, raised up their deceased benefactress (Acts 9:40–41).

It fell to the Apostle Thomas' lot to preach the Gospel in India. He was appalled at having to preach in such wild lands. The Lord appeared to him, consoled him, promising to be with him. Thomas set out. On the way, he met up with a wealthy merchant named Abanes sent by the Indian king Gundafor to Palestine to search for an outstanding architect who might build a royal palace like those of the Roman Caesars. Abanes told the reason for his journey, and St. Thomas gave himself out for an architect. Abanes was happy, and the two set off for India. After they arrived, Abanes presented the desired architect to the king. Gundafor told the Apostle his desire to have a splendid palace like those of Rome, and Thomas undertook to build such a palace. The matter was decided. The Apostle received a large amount of gold and silver for the project. The king set off for other Indian states. The Apostle began to preach the Gospel and teach the people the Christian faith, generously distributing alms to all in need. Almost two years later, the king sent to learn how the building progressed. Thomas replied that it remained only to make the upper part of the palace, and for this he received again a considerable amount of money. Finally, the king was definitely informed that no palace was being built, and that the foreigner Thomas was only teaching the people a new faith and giving the royal treasures to the poor. The king, returning home, saw that indeed no palace had been, or was yet, under construction. At once he ordered Thomas and Abanes arrested and locked up in prison, intending to put them to a harsh death.

At this time the king's brother, who had heard of the king's unhappiness, became seriously ill and sent to tell the king that he was not up to bearing such royal sorrow and had weakened so greatly that it seemed as if he would die. Soon the sick man died. Then the king forgot about the displeasure that the Apostle Thomas had caused him and sorrowed and wept without consolation over the death of his beloved brother. An angel of God showed the soul of the departed all the heavenly mansions and, going about the higher habitations, showed him many bright and wondrous palaces of the righteous. Of all the palaces one especially was the best. Then the angel asked the soul, "In which palace wouldst thou wish to dwell?" The soul, looking at this wondrous palace, answered: "If it were only permitted me to live in some corner of this palace, I would ask for nothing more." "No," replied the angel who led him: "Thou canst not live in this palace; it belongs to thy brother! It was built for him by the foreign Thomas with the gold which he received from thy brother for building a royal palace." Then the soul said, "I pray thee, Lord, let me go to my brother and I will buy this palace from him for he does not know its beauty, and then I will return here again." The angel returned the soul of the departed to the body, and he that had been dead arose. Resurrected, as if waking from sleep, first of all he spoke to those about him of his brother and entreated them to let the king know and for him to come at once. The king, hearing that his brother was risen, rejoiced and lost no time coming. Seeing his brother indeed resurrected the king was beside himself with joy. He that was resurrected began to say, "O king! I know for a truth that thou lovest me, thy brother, and I know how bitterly thou hast wept over me. I know, good king and brother, that thou wouldest not regret giving me half thy kingdom to redeem me from death! Is it not true?" The king replied, "Thou knowest my love for thee and art not mistaken in thy hope." He that was resurrected continued, "If thou indeed lovest me so, then I ask from thee one gift. Refuse me not!" The king replied, "All that is in my power I will give thee, my beloved brother." Then the resurrected one added, "Give me thy palace, which thou hast in heaven and, in exchange for it, take my wealth." The king, hearing such a request, was plunged into thought, long remained silent, and finally asked: "What palace have I in heaven?" "Thou hast a palace prepared in heaven," said he that was raised from the dead, "such as thou canst not imagine nor hast seen nor canst thou see such in all the universe. This is the palace that Thomas built whom thou hast in prison. I have seen thy palace, wondered at its ineffable beauty, and wanted to dwell in at least some corner of it; but the angel that showed me all in heaven said, Thou canst not live in it for it belongs to thy brother; the foreigner Thomas built it for him.' I entreated the angel that he let me come to thee to obtain this palace. And so, if thou lovest me, give it to me, and take all my property." Then the king was doubly glad over his resurrected brother and the palace that Thomas had built for him in heaven, and he said to him that was risen: "Beloved brother, I swore not to spare thee anything on earth in my authority and power, but as for a palace in heaven, this I did not swear. But if thou wouldst have for thyself such a palace in heaven, then the builder is with me; he will build a like palace for thee also." After this it was ordered to bring the Apostle Thomas from prison. The king himself went forth to meet him and, falling down at his feet, asked forgiveness that he had sinned against him in ignorance. Then the Apostle Thomas gave thanks to God, baptized both the brothers, and taught them the Christian faith. And he that was resurrected, with much alms, also built an eternal habitation in heaven.

"In my land," recounted the blessed Cyrus, "a prince died and was buried fittingly. I was then a lad. Once, going past the cemetery I saw standing by one of the graves a man black as soot who called me to him. When I came up to him, terrified and dumb, he spoke to me thus: 'I wrote in my will that a certain sum of money was to be distributed to the poor for the deliverance of my soul. Why has this not yet been done? Go and tell them to do this by all means, for otherwise I shall forever stay Oin this condition in which I appear now'."

These manifestations of the risen dead bear witness to the strength of alms-giving, which cleanses sins and delivers from eternal death, as well as to the truth of the Christian faith.

For the sake of the glory of His name and might, to show His ineffable love to those true servants who strive for Him, and for the edification of the human race (Christians above all) God has fulfilled good wishes and prayers of living faith, as promised by the Lord Jesus Christ that even mountains should be moved and the dead raised to life, that is, by the power of faith and prayer He may call back departed souls from the other world, if only righteousness calls for this. Thus, Abba Milisius, passing by a certain place saw a monk whom someone seized as if he were a murderer. The elder drew near and questioned the brother. Learning that this was a slander against the brother, he asked those that held him: "Where is the murdered man?" They showed him. The elder, approaching the murdered man, ordered all to pray; and when he himself raised up his hands to heaven, the dead man arose. The Abba asked him in the presence of all, "Tell me, who murdered thee?" He answered, "I went to such-and-such a place and handed money to so-and-so, but he seized me and stabbed me, then carried me out, and cast me into the monastery of the Abba. But I ask you to take my money from him and give it to my children." Then the elder said to him, "Go and sleep till the Lord wake thee" (from the "Sayings of the Life of the Holy and Blessed Abba Milisius").

In the same way, the dead answered the questions of St. Macarius of Egypt which he addressed to them when the well-being, the faith, or happiness of those who suffered unjustly demanded it. Here is a similar case: in one community there was a murder which through false accusation was laid to the blame of a completely innocent man. The poor man, pursued, fled in fear to the cell of St. Macarius where he was seized. Neither tears nor oaths could convince the judges of his innocence, and the people who had gathered unanimously berated him as a murderer. At this uproar, St. Macarius came forth and learning what the case was asked, "Where was the victim buried?" They showed him the place where the grave was. Here, on bended knees and pouring forth an intense prayer to the Lord, the righteous man said to those standing round about, "Now the Lord will show if it was this man who committed the crime." He then called upon the murdered man by name, and the dead man responded from the grave. "By the faith of Jesus Christ, I command thee," said St. Macarius, "reveal to us: was it this man, accused by the people, who murdered thee?" "Not this was my murderer," replied the dead man loudly from beneath the earth, "not this one, whom they condemn."

St. Spyridon, the bishop of Trimythous in Cyprus, had a daughter, a virgin named Irene, as devout as her father. One of their relatives gave her some precious ornament for safekeeping. The girl, so as better to keep the thing committed to her care, buried it in the ground. After a certain time she died. When the owner of the ornament came back and did not find the girl alive, he began to demand his property from St. Spyridon. The elder, seeing in his relative's lost property his own misfortune, went to his daughter's grave and there asked God to show him before its time the promised resurrection. His hope was not in vain: the girl at once appeared to her father alive, showed him the place where the ornament was hidden, and again became invisible (from the "Miracles of St. Spyridon").

On October 22, our Church celebrates the Seven Holy Youths of Ephesus who rose after sleeping the sleep of death for 372 years to rebuke the unbelievers and those who doubted the resurrection of the dead unto life eternal and remuneration for earthly deeds. This wondrous, unimaginable event was as follows: Seven youths who lived in Ephesus at the time of the emperor Decius and were known to him, desirous of keeping the right faith in the Lord Jesus Christ, sold all their goods, distributed the money to the poor, and hid themselves from the emperor outside the city in a secret place, in a cave. Decius was forcing the Christians to offer sacrifice to the gods; this was the reason that the seven youths fled the city. Since they were known to the emperor, they too were supposed to worship the idols and offer sacrifice to them, but their absence forced the emperor to seek them out in hiding.

The youths, having hidden themselves in the cave and preferring to die rather than fall into the hands of the evil Decius, were heard by God, and shortly they all died in the cave.

After long searching, the emperor was told that the hidden youths had been found dead in a certain cave. Decius ordered that the mouth of the cave be filled in with stones. And so there passed 372 years, until the reign of Theodosius Junior when Christianity and many pastors of the Church were infected with the heresy of those who did not believe in the resurrection of the dead, retribution beyond the grave, and life eternal to come. The emperor Theodosius was contrite of heart and entreated God to show His mercy, revealing the truth. God fulfilled his petition.

The owner of the place where the cave with the dead youths was, desiring to enclose the site with a fence, as it was a pasture for his herd, took down the stones which had been used to close up the mouth of the cave. A few days after the opening of the cave, the youths were resurrected. Time had changed nothing: their bodies and clothes were incorrupt. They supposed that, having fallen asleep one day, they had awakened on the morrow, and again took counsel among themselves as to how they should act if Decius should find them and compel them to bring sacrifice to the idols.

One of the young men set off to the city of Ephesus to buy food. As he approached the city, he was amazed and unable to understand when he saw the sign of the Cross everywhere; and in the city itself he found nothing like what there had been when he and his companions left it. Everything had changed.

When he bought bread, the youth gave the merchant a coin. The coin from the time of the emperor Decius was a source of astonishment for the merchant. After several questions to the young man as to who he was and where he got the coin, the youth answered that he was a resident of Ephesus, named his parents, and told of how the previous day he and his friends had left the city to flee the persecution of Decius. As proof, he offered to show the way to the cave and his companions.

The expression "yesterday" used by the young man left everyone there taken aback. Bishop Marinus, with the city prefect Antipater and many of the people, went to the cave. Having entered it, they found on the right side a box with two silver seals. This box had been placed there by two Christians among those sent by Decius to fill in the mouth of the cave. In the box were two tin plates on which were written the names of these youths. The youths described all concerning themselves and the emperor Decius in detail to everyone. Everyone glorified God. They informed the emperor Theodosius of this miraculous event, and he hastened to the cave, saw, and spoke with the youths himself. From the depths of his heart he thanked God that his prayer had been heard and that the future resurrection of all and eternal life had been shown in this occurrence. In a short time, and in the presence of visitors, the youths again fell peacefully into the sleep of death.

Once St. Macarius of Egypt, passing through a desert, saw a human skull and asked it concerning the state of the departed beyond the grave. The venerable father often prayed for the dead and therefore desired to know the action of prayers. "Do you never feel any consolation?" asked the Saint. "No," replied the skull of a pagan priest. "When thou prayest for the dead, then we feel some consolation." This exchange assures us of the rightfulness and efficacy of prayers for the departed. So as to give His faithful servant a faith and consolation in the importance of praying for the dead, the Almighty Lord commanded the skull to bear witness to this truth. If, by the prayers of the Saint of God, even dead pagans receive consolation, then how can we doubt the value of prayers by the living for them that have reposed in Christian faith and hope? (From the life of St. Macarius of Egypt, January 19).

In the life of the blessed Andrew, fool for Christ (October 2), the following case of a resurrected dead person is described. In Constantinople, the daughter of a wealthy nobleman died. Preparing for death, she asked her father to bury her in a tomb in their vineyard located outside the city. Dressed in rich garments and ornaments, she was indeed buried in the place she had chosen. In the city, there had long dwelt a man who engaged in grave robbery, in robbing the newly buried dead. When this young girl was buried, the criminal noted her grave. On the day when he intended to carry out his crime, the thief encountered the blessed Andrew. The Saint, foreseeing his evil purpose and acting the fool, foretold him the punishment that awaited him: "At once after the act, thou shalt go blind," said the Saint, "as soon as thou hast stolen!" The malefactor mocked the Saint and gave no heed to his prediction, but only said, "We shall see how the words of one possessed are borne out, but I will go nevertheless!" As night fell, the thief went to the vineyard, cast aside the stone from the tomb, went inside, and took from the deceased all outer garments and decorations. But, seeing that the undergarments were also good, he took them as well and left the corpse naked. When the thief wanted to leave the tomb, the dead girl, by the will of God, rose, lifted her right hand, and struck him in the face, as a result of which he went blind at once. Having lost presence of mind, he stood immobile. The risen girl went out of the tomb, dressed herself, and began to say to her offender that he, not fearing God, had done thus to her not thinking what a sad state he had left her in to appear before the Judge in the day of resurrection. After this, she lay down in the coffin and slept the sleep of death. The thief remained blind forever after. If the dead, by the will of God and towards a definite end, hasten to share their joy with the living, their benefactors, and others known to them, then in this case the dead girl appeared so as to give expression to her displeasure. The righteous anger of the deceased was expressed not only in a rebuke, but also in striking the offender. This manifestation of the dead gives evidence how sorrowful for the dead are all of our wrongs and unloving attitude towards them.

St. Gregory the Dialogist tells of the appearance of a deceased sinner from Hades as follows: a priest was in the habit of bathing in a heated bath. One day, going as usual to wash himself, the priest met there a man he did not know who intended to help him undress. Indeed the unknown man removed the priest's boots and took his clothes. On the way out, the unknown one handed the priest a towel to dry his feet, gave him his clothes, and did all of this with surprising commitment. This attention went on over several visits. The priest, wanting to show gratitude to the unknown man, took with him two *prosphoras* (eucharistic loaves) and set off for the bath. The unknown man assisted him just as devotedly as before, and when the priest, already dressed, wanted to offer him the prosphora loaves in place of a blessing and as a gift for his love and assistance, the helper replied with bitter tears, "Father, why give me these? This is holy bread and I cannot eat it. I, whom thou seest, once was the master of this place, but for my sins here I am condemned. If thou wouldst do aught for me, then offer for me this bread to Almighty God and pray for my sins. And know that thou wast heard, if coming here thou findest me no more." With these words, he became invisible. The priest spent the entire week in tears and contrition of heart offering the sacrifice of salvation to God each day. Returning to the bath, he did not find the unknown man again.

Much is revealed to us, the living, in this appearance of a sinner from Hades: 1) how the deceased wish and expect our prayers and good done in their memory; 2) how much true benefit there is for them in these, and 3) the man who appeared from Hades said himself that he wanted nothing except prayers and the Unbloody Sacrifice.

The following is another case of a deceased sinner appearing from Hades attested to by St. Gregory the Dialogist, and also recounted to the deacon Peter to whom the Saint gave recognition as a friend. "In my monastery," thus begins the Saint, "there was a rule that none of the brethren should have any property. In the monastery, everything was in common. One of the brethren, by the name of Justus, took sick and, nearing death, he told his brother who was with him that he had three golden coins. This news soon reached me. Touched to the depths of my heart and at the same time seeking to help him that had sinned—and to keep others from breaking the rule of the monastery—I gave the following order: not to allow any of the brethren to visit the sick man as one excommunicated and deprived of contact with them, and, when he died, to bury him in a separate place, and to throw the three coins into the grave with him. Indeed, such an excommunication was a cause of grief to the sick man. He died and was buried as I had prescribed. Thirty days after the death of Justus, I felt sorry for him and ordered that for the next thirty days a daily Requiem Liturgy[3] should be held for the departed brother. Thirty days passed and at night, not in a dream but palpably, Justus appeared to his brother. The first question posed by the amazed brother to the apparition was, "How, brother, is it with thee?" The wraith answered, "Up to now it was ill, but now it is well, for now I have entered into communion." Capiosus, as the brother of Justus was named, told of this to the brethren. This was the thirtieth day that the prayers for the departed had been offered for the dead man and with them the Unbloody Sacrifice.

Thus, the dead man who appeared from Hades himself bore witness that he had been freed from captivity there.

In both cases the dead, by their appearance, expressed as it were their thanks and hastened to share their joy with their benefactors.

Deceased sinners have appeared on earth from Hades, witnessing their grievous state and asking the help of the living to whom they appeared manifestly. That this appearance of the dead was not a sensory illusion can be seen from the fact that when the living indeed turned to God with heartfelt prayer and did good works in memory of the departed, the latter again appeared to the same living people and bore witness to the betterment of their lot.

As for the beneficial consequences of alms for the departed, the following account has come down to us. The holy abbess Athanasia, before her departure

[3]"Requiem" is the first word of the Entrance Chant in the Latin Liturgy or Mass for the Dead, whose composition dates back either to St. Gregory Dialogue himself or to a time prior to his.

from this life, left orders to the sisters of her monastery to offer meals to the poor for forty days. But it happened that the sisters only carried out the instructions of their abbess for ten days. This negligence called back the Saint from the other world. Appearing in the company of two angels to certain of the sisters of the convent, she said to them, "Why have you broken my commandment? Be it known to all that alms and the feeding of the hungry for forty days for the soul of the departed bring the mercy of God. If the souls of the departed are sinful, then through this they receive remission of sins from the Lord; if they are righteous, then good works done for them serve for the salvation of those that do them" (*Lives of the Saints* for April 12).

The blessed Cyr-Lucas had a brother who after entering the monastic life was little concerned about his soul. It was in this state of carelessness that death found him. The blessed Lucas, sorrowing especially that his brother had not prepared for death as he ought, prayed God to reveal his lot. Once, the elder saw the soul of his brother in the thrall of evil spirits, and after the vision at once he sent someone to look at the cell of his brother. Those who were sent found money and belongings there from which the elder understood that his brother's soul suffered, among other things, for breaking the vow of poverty. The elder gave all that was found to the poor. After that, while he was praying, there was revealed to the elder a place of judgment where the angels of light argued with the evil spirits over the soul of his departed brother. The elder heard the cry of the evil spirits, "The soul is ours, it did our deeds!" But the angels said to them that the soul was delivered from their power by the alms distributed for it. To this the evil spirits objected: "Did the deceased ever give alms? Was it not this elder?" pointing to Cyr-Lucas. The blessed ascetic answered, "Yes, I gave the alms, but for his soul, not for myself." The crestfallen spirits, hearing the elder's reply, were scattered, and the elder, calmed by the vision, ceased to doubt and to sorrow over his brother's fate (*Prologue* for August 12).

"Once," related the holy martyr Perpetua, "in prison as we were all praying I unexpectedly pronounced the name of my deceased brother Dinocrates.[4] Brought to understanding by this unexpected occurrence, I began to pray for him with fervor and lamentation before God. On the following night I had a vision. I seemed to see Dinocrates coming forth from a dark place, suffering greatly from heat and thirst, dirty and pale, with the facial wound from which he had died. Between him and me there was a deep gulf, and we could not approach each other. Alongside the place where Dinocrates stood there was a reservoir whose edge was considerably higher than my brother was tall, and

---

[4]He had died at age seven of gangrene resulting from this wound.

Dinocrates was straining, trying to reach the water. I felt sorry that the height of the rim prevented my brother from drinking. I awoke at once after this and knew that my brother was in torment, but believing that prayer could help him in his sufferings, I prayed every day and night in the prison with lamentation and tears that he be given to me. On the day when we were in the stocks I had a new vision: the place that before I had seen as dark had become bright, and Dinocrates with a clean face and splendid garments was enjoying coolness. Where he had had a wound I saw only a trace of it; and the rim of the font was now no higher than the child's waist so that he could draw water from it without difficulty. On the edge there stood a golden cup full of water. Dinocrates, drawing near to it, began to drink, and the water in it did not diminish. His thirst slaked he went away rejoicing. With this the vision ended. Then I understood that he was freed from punishment."

The following appearance of a dead person from Hades bears witness to the power and efficacy of the prayers of the faithful, as well as to the state of sinners beyond the grave in Hades. An Athonite writes of a wondrous event involving two friends. Once in church they had occasion to hear a homily. The word of God had such a strong effect on the heart of one of them that he decided to change his way of life and become a monk, whereas the other continued his previous careless life and remained in the world. Soon death befell the layman and, touched by his decease, the monk, his friend, made heartfelt prayer to God to learn the fate of the dead man beyond the grave. God heard his prayer and sent him his friend from Hades so that he might give answer himself as to his condition. The monk had a dream vision of his dead friend. "How then goes it with thee, brother?" the monk asked his friend, rejoicing at the sight of him. "Wouldst thou know this?" moaned the dead man. "Woe is me! The unsleeping worm gnaws at me and gives me no rest in all eternity." "What manner of torment is this?" the monk continued to ask. "An unbearable torment," cried the dead man. "But there is nothing to be done, no way to evade the wrath of God. I was given freedom now for the sake of thy prayers, and if thou wilt I will show thee my torment. Only wilt thou see and feel it utterly, or in part? The whole torment canst thou not bear; know, therefore, and see only the part." With these words the dead man raised the lower part of his garment up to the knee, and horror, an unbearable stench so overcame all the senses of the sleeping monk that he awoke at once. All of the leg that his friend had bared to him was covered with dreadful worms, and from the wounds there arose such a foul stench that words cannot express it. This hellish stench so filled the cell of the monk that he could barely rush out of it, not managing even to close the door behind him so that the odor filled the whole monastery. All the cells were filled with it, and the distressed monks did not understand what it meant. For a long time this hellish smell did not disperse, and the brethren were forced to leave the monastery and seek shelter elsewhere; but the friend of the deceased could in no wise escape the foul stench once inhaled, nor wash it from his hands, nor cover it with any perfume. *(Letters of a Monk of the Holy Mountain,* Letter 6). By his visit and by displaying his wounds, the sufferer from Gehenna shared, as it were, his eternal, inescapable sorrow. Shared sorrow relieves the soul somewhat if others take part in it.

"In our time," wrote one hermit, "there was a certain brother by the name of John. Because of his book learning, he was made a reader with us. This brother died and some time afterward appeared, not in a dream, but openly to his spiritual father, Sabbas. He stood at the door of the cell, naked and burned like coal; with bitter moaning, he begged for mercy and pardon, confessing to his spiritual father the sin for which he bore such terrible torment. 'I always opposed and mocked the Law and the Scriptures,' said he. Soon this fearful vision disappeared from before the eyes of the spiritual father; frightened, he told no one of it, not even me who was ever with him, lest it prove to be a deception by demons. Some time afterward the vision was repeated again. With agonized wailing, the miserable sufferer asked his spiritual father, 'Tell, tell all the others of my sin. Otherwise, thou thyself shalt be tried!' Only then did Sabbas tell me all. Having learned in detail of the life of the departed brother, we were convinced that he was indeed such as he confessed himself to be, after death, to his spiritual father."

At the present time, by the will of God, and not without reason, there continue to be such appearances by the souls of the dead to the living. Thus in the life of priestmonk Anikita, among other things, there is the following account. Priestmonk Anikita (Prince Sergei Shakhmatoff in the world) having heard of the illness of his devout mother, set off to see her so as to take leave and to receive her blessing to enter the monastery. But finding her already lifeless, he wept bitterly that he had not been in time to receive her blessing. The devout mother heard his weeping and did not delay in consoling him by appearing. During a light sleep, she appeared to him with a bright countenance and said: "A blessing is much to give, but one can allow" (from *Life and Labors of Priestmonk Anikita*).

A certain clergyman lost his wise, well-bred, and devout spouse after sixteen years of married life. Their marriage had been made strong by true, sincere, mutual love; they had lived constantly in peace and concord, in steadfast faithfulness to each other and purity and formed, in the words of the Apostle, one body (Ephesians 5:31), one moral person. Profound sorrow and inexpressible grief overcame him. He fell into a depression and, shaken, was on the verge of a dangerous path leaning towards drink. "I do not know," the widowed priest goes on, "if I would have continued long on this ruinous path and where I would have gone on it had not my late wife stopped me. She appeared in a dream and, sincerely concerned for my situation, said to me: 'My friend, what befalls thee? Thou tookest a dangerous path, lowering thyself in the eyes of people and worst of all, canst lose God's blessing which till now laid upon our house. In thy calling even a small stain can seem great, and in thy place thou art seen far and wide. Thou hast six little ones for whom thou must now be father and mother. Hast thou indeed come not to treasure thy calling, achievements, and the respect thou hast till now enjoyed from all? Were thy life, good qualities, thy honor needed only by thy spouse? Think, my friend, about this. I ask and beg thee: reflect and consider rightly and make haste to leave this dangerous path which thou hast, to my inexpressible sorrow, so thoughtlessly and heedlessly taken. Thou grievest over separation from me; but, as thou seest, our bond is not broken. We can even now have a spiritual communion with each other. In the life beyond the grave, we can be united for ages in the lap of Abraham if we are found worthy. Thou complainest of an emptiness in thy heart; fill that emptiness with love for God, for thy children, and brethren; feed thy soul with the bread of angels as thou wast wont to call the word of God and wast fond of feeding thyself and thy family with it; strengthen thyself with thoughts of God and frequent divine service, pray to God for me and for thyself, for our children, and for the souls entrusted to thee.' This, the voice of my beloved spouse, reached deeply into my soul and had a beneficial effect on me. I accepted it as the voice of my guardian angel, as the voice of God Himself bringing me to my senses, and I decided to resist the temptation with all my powers. And thanks be to God and with His help I overcame the tempter and with firm step took my place on the right path (from the journal "Strannik," July 1865, "A Saving Voice from the Land Beyond the Grave," pp. 122–124).

A dweller of the Holy Mountain writes: A certain Archbishop A.V., who had suffered bitterly from attacks of melancholy, entreated God for help and once during evening prayers noted that in his front rooms a light was cast that grew gradually stronger and finally enveloped him. At this point he saw a woman, and as he looked carefully at her, he realized it was his deceased mother. "Why dost thou weep so, my child?" she asked, "and dost thou understand what thou seekest of God? For the Lord it is not hard to fulfill thy request, but dost thou know what thou deprivest thyself of by so doing? Knowest thou not what thou askest?" And giving him several counsels, she became invisible (*Letters of a Dweller on the Holy Mount, Collected After His Death*, p. 218).

In Orlov, in the province of Viatka, writes again an Athonite, there is a priest whom we shall call Fr. M. L., a close relative of mine; he passed the following account on to me. In his parish, about ten versts[5] from the city, there lived a peasant who was of an exceptionally meek and modest character. In 1848 or 1849, I do not remember exactly, this peasant suddenly took ill; at his request, Fr. M. gave him the last Holy Communion, and shortly after receiving the patient died. They washed him, laid him on a table, and prepared a coffin. Two hours after the sick man had given up the ghost, suddenly he opened his eyes, and sat up by himself on his bed which during his entire sickness he had been unable to do, being extremely weak. His first words, after he had opened his eyes and sat, were to send at once for the priest which was done without delay. "When I," says Fr. M., "arrived to see the revived man, he asked everyone else to leave the room as he wanted to speak with the priest alone." The members of the household went away, and the revived man sighed deeply and said, "Father, I was dying, I was taken by the angels, and presented before the Lord. When I appeared before Him and adored Him, He looked at me so mercifully, with such love that I cannot express it. His appearance—one cannot say how wonderful it was! At length the Lord said to the angels who had brought me, 'Why did you take him? He has a sin on his conscience which he never told in confession, having forgotten it out of length of time.' And at this, the Lord reminded me of my sin I had not confessed. I only then realized that indeed there had been such a thing with me, but I had forgotten it and never repented before a priest. 'Take him away,' said the Lord, 'and let him cleanse his soul before his confessor and then bring him again before Me.' "And after that," said the revived man, "I know not how I came to be alive again." Then he confessed his forgotten sin with some feeling, and Fr. M. read over him the prayer of absolution, asking to be remembered as his spiritual father when he should again be brought before the Lord. Fr. M. had barely read the prayer when the revived man, peacefully and untroubled, gave up his spirit to the Lord. Thus the Lord is merciful (from "Strannik," Volume I for 1860, p. 63).

Acting privy councilor Prince Vladimir Sergeevitch Dolgoruky, while he was ambassador to the Prussian court in the reign of Frederick the Great, was infected with the ideas of the Freethinkers. Having learned of this, his brother,

---

[5]A verst is an Old Russian measure of distance, about the same as a kilometer, roughly two-thirds of a mile.

Prince Peter Sergeevitch, wrote him letters more than once in which he assured him that he was in error, that without the true faith there is no happiness on earth, that faith is substantially necessary for the life to come, and so on. But all was in vain. Incessantly reading Voltaire, d'Alembert[6] and others, Prince Vladimir Sergeevitch laughed at the convictions of his pious brother. Once, returning from a visit to the king and feeling extreme fatigue, he undressed hastily, threw himself into bed, and soon fell asleep. Suddenly he heard some-one pull the bed curtains back and draw near to him, and a cold hand touched his, even squeezed it. He looked, saw his brother, and heard him say, "Believe." Pleased at the unexpected sight, the prince would have thrown himself into the embraces of his brother and friend, but all at once the vision disappeared. He asked the servants where his brother had gone, and hearing from them that no brother had come to see him, he tried to convince himself that this had been a dream. But the word "Believe" would not stop resounding in his ears and gave him no peace. He wrote down the date, hour, and minute of the vision and soon received notice that his brother, Prince Peter Sergeevitch, had passed away at that very date, hour, and minute. From that time on, he became a pious and faithful Christian and spoke often of this vision to others (*Consolation at the Death of Those Close to the Heart*, pp. 95–96).

The poet Zhukovsky presents two cases whose authenticity he vouches for. Here is one of these cases which is also certified by Prof. Pirogov. It happened in Moscow. A certain lady's favorite son was seriously ill, and she sat by his bed at night. All the mother's attention was concentrated on the suffering child, when all at once she saw her relative Moyer, who lived in Derpt, Livland,[7] standing in her chamber door. The apparition was so vivid that the troubled mother forgot her little one and turned with outstretched arms to the approaching Moyer. "Is it thee, M.?" But the visitor vanished at once. It turned out that, that very night, at that very hour, Mme. Moyer died in childbirth at Derpt. The other case, and many other examples of apparitions told by the author, we do not include here, but those interested can read them in the sixth book of the writings of Zhu-kovsky under the title *Something on Apparitions*.

In the *Dictionary of Russian Biography* (Словарь Достопамятныхъ Людей Русской Земли, published by Bantysh-Kamensky in 1836, Volume 5, pp. 94–95), we read the following. Once Ekaterina Ivanovna Stakelberg, when she was a maid of honor at the Palace in Tsarskoye-Selo (1767), was making her

---

[6]Jean LeRond d'Alembert or Dalembert (1717–1783), French mathematician and one of the two main collaborators (with Diderot) of the *Encyclopédie*.

[7]Today Derpt (Dorpat) is known as Tartu, Estonia.

toilette in the company of several other young ladies, among them the count-ess Elizaveta Kirilovna Razumovsky. In the midst of complete gaiety, Elizaveta Ivanovna, as it were involuntarily, gazed out the window and then looked again with greater amazement, then a third time at which jumping up from the chair she cried: "Father is here and came to the window!" She ran out into the garden to meet her father, but no one was there, and after long searching she finally was certain that her parent had not been there. When the Empress was told of this, she ordered a record made of the day and hour of the vision. A few days later, news came from Riga of the decease of Ekaterina Ivanovna's father which had occurred at the very day and hour when he appeared to his daughter.

There once were two friends who lived in great harmony. Once they were traveling somewhere and stopped for the night in a certain town: one stayed at the home of his friend, and the other who had no one, neither relatives nor friends, had to stay at an inn. The first who stayed with his acquaintance retired, went to sleep, and dreamed that his friend appeared to him and said, "Come at once, please, for the inn keeper is abusing me and even wants to kill me." This dream troubled him so much that he awoke and made ready to go to the inn and save his friend, but on the way changed his mind, thinking the dream must be nonsense, and returned home. But as soon as he went to sleep, again he had a dream in which his friend, dying in a pool of blood, rebuked him for not com-ing to help him and said: "I have already been murdered by the inn keeper, my body cut into pieces, and taken by my murderer outside the city and buried in fertilizer." This last dream was even more disturbing to the sleeper who awoke and at once went outside the city walls where he found his friend in just such a condition as was told him in the dream, and he brought the murderer to justice (from "Strannik," Volume IV, 1860, p. 105).

A young officer, Ivan Afanasyevitch Praschev, and his attendant soldier, the Little-Russian[8] Naum Sereda, are the figures in a mysterious event that took place on May 14, 1861.[9]

Here is what happened: Ivan Afanasyevitch Praschev and his attendant Naum Sereda were in a campaign in the Polish war of 1831. A short time before May 14, 1831, there were Gypsies in their camp, and so it was that a young Gypsy woman foretold for both of them, Praschev and Sereda, death on May 14. The simple-hearted Sereda took the prediction calmly and added, "Let God's will be done," but the heart of the young Praschev was troubled. When

---

[8]Older term for "Ukrainian."

[9]Dates given are according to the Julian calendar, which in the nineteenth century was twelve days behind the Gregorian.

the 14th of May came, Sereda was indeed mortally wounded, and as was dying he asked Praschev to send three gold coins that he had to his mother.

"By all means I will fulfill thy request with love and send not only these three gold coins, but also add of mine own for thy help," replied Praschev.

"In what way can I repay Your Honor's[10] kindness?" asked the dying man.

"Since the Gypsy woman foretold death on the fourteenth of May, and thou indeed diest, then come to me from the world beyond the grave on that day when I am to die."

"Yes, sir" replied Sereda, and soon after he died.

Praschev did not forget the Gypsy prediction, and every fourteenth of May was as if a day of passing on into the other world for him; and Sereda's promise to notify him of the day of his death prompted him to hold a Pannikhida each year on this day for the soul of the soldier Naum.

Exactly thirty years later, in the first hour of the night as it became the fourteenth of May, because of the splendid weather, Praschev, his wife, daughter, nephew, and daughter's fiancé were in the garden; the dog that always accompanied Ivan Afanasyevitch suddenly rushed into the garden walk, as usual when the dog spotted a stranger approaching. Praschev followed the dog and whom did he see but Sereda approaching him!

"Is it the fourteenth of May?" Praschev calmly asked the man from the other world.

"Just so, Your Honor. I am come to fulfill your order; the day of your death is come!" replied the unearthly guest and vanished.

Praschev at once, disregarding his family, began preparing himself in a Christian way for death: he went to confession, received Holy Communion, made all necessary *arrangements,* and awaited death. But death did not come. It was 11 p.m. on May 14. Praschev was in the garden with his family members. A woman's voice was heard, and the wife of the cook who was chasing her threw herself at the feet of Ivan Afanasyevitch seeking his defense, as he was the landowner. The cook was drunk, and in that condition he usually thought his wife was unfaithful to him and beat her. The cook ran up to Praschev and with a large kitchen knife wounded him fatally in the stomach. A few moments before midnight, therefore still on the fourteenth of May, Ivan Afanasyevitch died, having been notified of his death by Sereda who had dwelt thirty years in the world beyond the grave (from the journal "Niva," issues 15, 16 and 17 for 1880).

A similar occurrence of a dead soul appearing to the living took place in Italy in the sixteenth century. Here is how it was: "Two noted scholars of sixteenth

[10]Old Russian military form of addressing an officer of higher rank.

century Italy, Mercati and Marsigli, had differing concepts of the immortality of
the soul; one supposed that the soul departing from the body remains inactive
and dormant until Judgment Day, until the raising up of the dead; the other,
on the contrary, asserted that there is no inactivity in nature, and that the soul
therefore having reached the end of its life passes into other living bodies. So as
to ascertain who was right, Mercati and Marsigli, who had been close friends,
uttered a frightful oath and agreed that whoever of them should die first should
appear to the other and clarify for him the subject of their disagreement, if
only this should prove possible. Once, at night, when Mercati, in Rome, was
deep in study, he heard three strong knocks at his door. He got up and opening
the window saw a horseman at the entrance, wrapped in a white cape: "Thou
art right, my friend!" cried he to the amazed scholar and at the same moment
turned his horse and vanished like a storm into the fog. Two days later, Mercati
received notice that his friend, Marsigli, had died in Florence. (from the journal
"Severnaya Zvezda," No. 9, 1877, p. 180).

If one were to speak the language of modern nineteenth century unbelief,
then indeed, at times, there are strange things, mysterious by their nature. But if
the causes of strange incidents are sometimes assumed to be pure chance, then
examining an event closer and more carefully, one cannot fail to see in it little
known laws of psychic life. Thus far, there has not been an example of matter
and chance bringing forth life and consciousness. Here is a fact described in the
Moscow newspaper "Gattsuka," (No. 1, 1883, p. 7).

The persons involved in this mysterious case are two friends: the deceased,
Knyazev, and the living, Pobedinsky. Knyazev and Pobedinsky had to separate
after many years of sincere friendship for Pobedinsky was sent on a military
expedition during the Polish uprising. As they parted amicably, Pobedinsky
said, "If we should not see each other again *here*, then nevertheless we will see
each other *there!*" "No," objected Knyazev, "I will not die before taking leave of
thee." The friends parted. After several years of separation, Pobedinsky, on leave,
set out from Warsaw to see his friend Knyazev only to find him already dead
lying on a table. When evening fell, the visitor was given the deceased's study
as a room for the night. What Pobedinsky experienced that night is given in
his own words.

"I nodded, but it was not a pleasant doze after fatigue, but some deep forgetful
state. I heard silence prevailing all around and only the voice of the psalmodist[11]
broke the nocturnal stillness. About twelve o'clock, someone's steps awakened

---

[11] This was the chanter from the church, who read the Psalter over the dead all night according
to the old custom.

me ... I turned quickly ... began to listen carefully ... The steps came ever closer ... When suddenly in the doorway, between the door curtains, the tall figure of my friend appeared ...

"And, I swear to you, this was not a trick of the imagination. He stood, stretched out to full height, his dull eyes looking aimlessly somewhere at the wall. My hair stood on end. I could not cry out. My voice refused to obey. The dim light of the icon lamp fell directly on the face of the dead man and gave him some frightful expression. But then, the dead man moved, took several steps, cast his eyes about the room till they rested on me. To the end of my life I shall not forget that look. Deadly pale, the hitherto blank face of the deceased was transformed, as though warmth and light had been poured through it; the lights that had gone out in his eyes were lit again, and even on the pale lips there was a smile, and an all-too-familiar voice clearly pronounced, 'Pobedinsky, my friend! Is it thee I see?' And the dead man threw himself upon me, began embracing me ... In vain I tried with all my might to free myself from these fearful embraces: the lips of the dead man touched mine; the bony hands, like hooks, sank into my body. After useless attempts to get loose and moved by fear, of which one cannot give a clear conception, I lost consciousness.

"It was already morning when I came to my senses; around me people were fussing, and there was a gray-haired gentleman.

"Where am I? What happened to me?" I asked those nearby.

"Afterwards, afterwards you will learn everything," replied the gray haired gentleman who turned out to be a doctor. I waited impatiently for an explanation of my fearful nightmare. Was it really a dream I wondered, lost in guesses? Several languid hours passed. I felt so much stronger that I was able to get up from the bed and heckle the doctor with questions: what had happened to me?

"You had a bad faint," explained the doctor.

"And what of the dead man? Surely he did not really come to me?"

"It was not a dead man, but a live one that came to you."

"Then he is alive?"

"He was. A few hours ago, but now ... " And the doctor raised the door curtain to the hall. The dead man again lay on the table under brocade, and at his feet the mournful voice of the chanter was heard.

"Here is what I learned from the doctor: my deceased friend, before departing forever into eternity, had fallen into a lethargic coma. The psalmodist who had been reading the Psalter over him had gone out of the hall and gotten into a conversation. At this point, the seemingly dead man came to his senses, got off the table, and went into his study as he was accustomed to do. The cry of the chanter when he returned had awakened the whole house.

"Imagine our wonder," said the doctor, "and shock, when we saw the dead man lying on your breast!"

"And was he alive when you entered?"

"No. The spark of life flickered in the deceased for a few moments as if to fulfill the word he had given you: that he would not die before taking leave of you."

The Dogmatic Teaching of the Church Concerning Intercession by the Living for the Departed, and Requesting Forgiveness for the Sins of Certain Sinners

1. The Basis of the Church's Teaching Concerning the Possibility of Salvation for Certain Departed Sinners

WE KNOW THAT DEATH IS ONLY A PASSAGE from earthly life to that beyond the grave; that those who are joined by God on earth are not separated by death; that the inner, spiritual bond and mutual relationship continues between those who remain on earth and those that have passed into the world beyond the grave, as between members of the one spiritual and moral kingdom of Christ. The union, bond, relationship, and communion have a palpable expression for those on earth—visible signs—bearing witness to the unbroken spiritual bond and communion with those who have passed into the other world. Having shown wherein the bond and communion of the visible and invisible worlds consists (that is, between those on earth with the angels and fallen spirits and with the Saints) now we shall seek to show the visible, palpable expression of this world with the imperfect who have passed on, with those that have not yet attained full sanctity, and with sinners that are in Hades but are still not lost for the kingdom of God.

The manifest expression of the bond and communion of those on earth with unperfected sinners that have passed beyond the grave comprises the content of this section. The life and activity of those on earth, based on faith in the Lord Jesus Christ, is a faithful mirror of the bond and communion with those not yet perfected who have gone beyond the grave.

Life and activity are one and the same. Where there is life, there is activity, and where there is activity, there is life; consequently, the works of those still on earth will show, will bear witness to their bond and communion with those who have passed over. God, uniting people by an eternal bond of love, forbade through His Apostle Paul to mourn over the death of those close to the heart, and revealed means of retaining this bond and communion with the departed, in the case of a short separation, death. These means or actions by those remaining on earth are: 1) the very life of those still on earth, 2) their relationship to God and to the departed, 3) prayer for the dead, 4) giving of alms, and 5) the Divine Liturgy.

a) The Basis for Asking Forgiveness of Sins for the Dead: Love and Faith

Our holy Church bases her teaching on the possibility of lightening the state of certain sinners beyond the grave, and even freeing them from Hades, on: 1) the characteristics of the human soul: love and faith, 2) the Holy Scriptures of the Old Testament, 3) the teaching of the Gospel, 4) the Apostolic tradition, 5) the teaching of the Holy Fathers and Doctors of the Church, 6) the decisions of the Councils, and finally 7) we find actual facts on this matter in the lives of many Saints.

History bears us witness that there was and is no society, regardless of cultural level, that did not recognize and believe in the immortality of the soul, and therefore in life beyond the grave; and, judging by earthly life, in a happy or tormented state in the next world. The societies were conscious of this truth and believed in it, so that it is common to all humanity, and a common heritage of the human spirit. Besides this truth common to the spirit of man, another natural belonging characterized his divine origin: love.

Love and hate are natural to man: love of truth and hatred of evil. The Christian human being, from the time of his baptism, takes on not only the outward name of Christ, of being a Christian, but is also obliged to nourish within himself the spirit of Christ: heavenly, divine love towards God and neighbors on earth, as well as towards those who have passed on into the other world, as witnessed by St. Paul who says, "Let this mind be in you, which was also in Christ Jesus" (Philippians 2:5).

Immortal love is the basis for prayer as a whole and for prayers for the dead in particular. The boundaries of love determined by the Lord are to give one's soul for others and to have a vital compassion for the souls of those who have loved us and still do, but are separated from us by passing into the world beyond the grave. They naturally evoke in the soul, first of all, prayer which belongs to the nature of man. It is natural, a commandment, and repeated by the Saviour, on the basis of the law of love, to desire for oneself the same as one desires for others. Salvation—the kingdom of heaven—this is the object of man's desire for himself and for everyone.

This is the foundation of intercession and prayer for the departed hidden in the spirit of man, in love. God alone is sinless: we all sin, we are conceived in iniquities: in sins we are born, live and die (Romans 3:10–13; 7:18). All human activity presents a mixture of good with evil to a greater or lesser degree. Here is a moving reason for love, to intercede for the departed before the source of love, God.

The spirit of man, which is of divine origin, should include something divine within itself: "Be ye therefore perfect, as also your heavenly Father is perfect" (Matthew 5:48), as our Lord Jesus Christ taught; "Let this mind be in you, which was also in Christ Jesus" (Philippians 2:5), as the holy Apostle taught. The love of the Lord should be the example of our love towards our neighbor. The Lord came into the world for the salvation of all. All believing humanity is saved, naturally beginning its existence on earth and from hence passing on to its eternal destination. For this reason the Apostle taught that the Lord has power over the living and the dead, and therefore both are the Lord's. The Lord loved us while we were still on earth, as well as after passing over beyond the grave; He so loved us, that for our salvation He offered Himself as a propitiatory sacrifice to God the Father. Such love God demands of us also, that all might see that "ye are My disciples"; love not only for the living, but also for them that have passed on beyond the grave: "Love one another, as I have loved you" (John 13:34). The Lord Jesus Christ Himself and His holy disciples, the Apostles, taught undying love. They did not teach only to love the living, those still on earth. Speaking of the immortality of the soul, of eternal life beyond the grave, of the quality of true love, they taught that love does not die, that it goes beyond the grave along with its object, with the beloved person, that it is not in the nature of true Christian love to grow cold.

What became of the soul of the departed? It has only changed its position, condition, and place of location. It is not on earth, but its spirit and qualities have remained with it as before when it was on earth. Beloved objects have remained beloved beyond the grave, as before it loves its own and burns with love towards God. If it be so, then is it possible for the living not to love those who have passed into the world beyond the grave? Let someone prove that the commandment of love extends only to the living, is limited to earthly wanderings alone. If they can show that, then at the same time they will show that for them there is no God, no soul, no life beyond the grave! Without love, what can there be beyond the grave? The living, if only they have in them the spirit

of Christ, are obliged to love, indeed they cannot go against nature by not loving their departed. This is a sacred obligation, this is demanded by the faith of
Christ, this is a proof that we hold the Orthodox faith, that we believe without
doubt in the immortality of the soul and in life after death in which all humanity has believed and still does believe. How can one explain the indifference
of some to the dead, as if they no longer existed? Unbelief and cruelty are the
marks of such a soul! If the law of Christ, the law of the spirit, commands that
we love our enemies, then how can we become indifferent to our departed who
loved us and still love us?

All peoples have loved, and still love, those departed into the other world.
Loving them that have reposed, they have always shown them various honors,
and still do.

The Lord Jesus Christ taught: what thou wishest for thyself from God, do
the same to thy neighbor, even love thine enemy. All our relationships with
others, good and bad, the Lord takes upon Himself when He says: "As long as
ye did it to one of these my least brethren, ye did it to me" (Matthew 25:40).
We need mercy from God in this life and the next; therefore let us ourselves be
merciful to others here on earth and to those beyond the grave.

Before God all are alive, and we have the commandment of eternal, immortal love; it was commanded us to pray one for another, to bear our neighbor's
burden, to seek the kingdom of God; and all this not only for ourselves, but for
our neighbor, for without love for our neighbor, we cannot be saved: "Love ye
one another, as I have loved you." We must be ready to lay down our souls: this
is the perfect love demanded of us by the Lord. If mercy and kindness bring
the soul that receives them gladness, relief, joy, whether it be spiritual or physical mercy, and at the same time these things bring about pleasure in the soul of
the one who is merciful, who does good, then prayer for those who have passed
on into the new world beyond the grave is the first and main work of mercy.
"Ask and it shall be given you"—these words of the Originator of life do not
lie. Wrongly do certain philosophizers think that prayer for the dead is of no
help to them, that its benefit extends only to the living; we do not accept this lie,
but rather believe the words of Jesus Christ Who taught us that God is a God
not of the dead but of the living, and therefore we intercede through Him with
God not for dead who do not exist, but for the living who have passed on into
the world beyond the grave for life eternal. If on earth our soul has rejoiced and
attained a special state not of this earth; if circumstances surrounding it have
changed suddenly, mystically for the better; if fetters have fallen from hands and
feet; if unearthly visitors have appeared; if all this has taken place in a super-

natural way with the soul, only because of prayers for it that were offered up to God (for example, the Cypriote captives in Persia when their parents prayed for them, or the Apostle Peter by the prayers of the faithful), then what is to prevent the same soul in the life beyond the grave from tasting the fruits of those works of mercy performed in its memory on earth by the living?

The concept of life and the dim notion of the indissolubility of human souls in death hidden in the depths of the spirit remained something of which mankind was only vaguely aware. As indefinite as the mutual relationships between people were on earth, in a spiritual sense, so they remained equally indefinite between those remaining on earth and those who had passed into the world beyond the grave. Natural love, born into the spirit as a result of the fall of man, did not know the means of its true activity towards those who had gone beyond the grave. To sacrifice one's life, to bring oneself in sacrifice, to mortify oneself as visible signs of love for the departed, as well as similar unnatural acts, were taken for truth; and the mind, enriched and developed by scientific knowledge, adhered to this foolishness, erring in spiritual darkness. The ancient educated Romans had the custom whereby the bodies of the more noted dead were not buried in the ground but burned on a pyre, and by the pyre slaves were also put to death; in later times, gladiators hacked each other with swords and slew one another. All this was done out of love for the deceased with the purpose of obtaining mercy for him from the god of Hades (from *A Short Account of the Customs and Mores of the Ancient Romans,* Part 6, Section 5). Only the grace-filled light of Christianity, enlightening every Christian, scattered the darkness of spiritual ignorance. Jesus Christ revealed the secrets of life after death on earth and showed wherein the bond and relationship of the living with the dead consists. With all of their enlightenment (that is, scientific and not spiritual), the ancients did not know what they needed to do regarding their dead so as to bring them a significant benefit. The ancients did not know what even the Hebrews chosen by God did not fully know, though they had God's law and the Prophets. The ineffectiveness of certain rituals performed over the dead is shown in the words of the Lord Himself when He commanded one of His disciples (who had asked first to bury his father) to follow Him. Such burials belong, said the Lord, only to those that know Me not: "Let the dead bury the dead, but follow thou Me" (Matthew 8:22). Likewise the Hebrew law concerning the uncleanness of dead bodies was first broken by the Lord Jesus Christ when He showed its groundlessness in touching with His hand the bier of the deceased son of the widow of Nain (Luke 7:15); again when He touched the hand of the synagogue leader Jairus' daughter (Mark 10:40); and in Christianity dead bodies are not considered unclean. In another place, Jesus Christ openly rebuked the Hebrews for not knowing the state of the dead beyond the grave when He said, "Ye do err, not knowing that beyond the grave they do not marry, but live like angels" (Mark 12:24,25). He said that He is the Resurrection and the Life, therefore only the Christian life of the living who believe in Him is beneficial to the dead: "For I am the resurrection and the life" (John 11:25); of the dead, the dead and the living are Mine.

The Lord Himself opens the beginning of prayers for the dead in the word— "Love." "Ask." "Seek." Until now the mind and heart filled with love did not know what to do with regard to those that had taken their abode in the world beyond the grave; but now Jesus Christ, His grace, and the holy faith have revealed to the sorrowing heart how it should act as concerns the deceased.

The love that is inborn, natural to the human spirit, is the source of all virtues. One commandment of love was given by God through Moses; Jesus Christ, the founder of His Church, confirmed this very commandment in the New Testament. Jesus Christ taught us to love one another with a love not of earth but of heaven, divine, eternal. Love manifests itself first of all in prayer, in interceding before God for others. Consequently, prayer for the departed is the fruit of our love for them. Souls filled with true love for others, regardless of where they be—on earth or beyond the grave—cannot but take a vital interest in their state, cannot but sympathize with their sorrow or joy. They weep with them that weep and rejoice with them that rejoice, as is characteristic of love according to the commandment. Awareness by the living of the sinfulness of the dead brings them a feeling not altogether of joy. The sad heart finds consolation in faith where the possibility unfolds of saving the deceased, of delivering him from Hades, and of living together beyond the grave in the house of the heavenly Father.

Love without true faith does not know its real activity, and as if blind, it takes evil for good; at the graveside it murders a slave, so that the latter might carry a greeting to the deceased living in the other world, as did the ancient pagans, and as is still done in Africa, in Dahomey.[1] But love, given wings by Christian faith, does not shed blood, but obedient to the will of the Giver of Life, sees in Him alone the salvation of the dead, and therefore prays humbly to Him to grant repose to the departed and to have mercy on us who remain on earth. It prays because it is pleasing to God for us to help one another by our intercessions. The Holy Spirit Himself abiding in us teaches us to pray a true prayer, for

---

[1]West African state between Togo and Nigeria, annexed by France in the nineteenth century, independent in 1960, renamed Benin.

we ourselves "know not that for which it behooveth us to pray." Consequently the Holy Spirit teaches the living to pray for the repose of souls as a prayer for the salvation of the dead.

It has been shown that this bond and mutual relationship in the Church of Christ is expressed by outward, visible signs and actions. Wherever these visible signs are not to be seen, one can conclude with confidence that complete unbelief prevails. Only with faith is there a bond, union, relationship, and communion between the living and the dead. Without faith it is impossible to save oneself and help others to salvation. Faith, hope, and charity[2] serve as the first and main foundation for all the visible means that express our bond with those that have died. And so, our life, filled with living faith and good works, serves first of all as a visible sign of our unbroken bond with the departed. To help them that have passed on in their life beyond the grave, the living must lead a truly Christian life based on the Lord's commandment to one of His disciples who had asked first to bury his father: "Follow Me . . . Proclaim the kingdom of God . . . I am the Resurrection and the Life for all!" And so, the foundation on which is established the Christian's obligation to pray for the dead is love and faith. Our faith that the souls of the departed are alive, that the Lord's promise "Ask and it shall be given you" is not false, that the lot of the departed is in his power, this faith gives us the opportunity to intercede, to pray for the dead. This is the basis of our prayers for the dead on which we, the living, make bold to ask the all-generous God for mercy towards His beloved sinners.

The heart that burns with love for the departed, that is filled with faith in the Lord Jesus Christ, supported by the words of the Lord Himself that even in the world beyond the grave there is remission of certain sins, such a heart prays for the salvation of the dead in faith and hope.

"But why," writes St. John of Damascus, "should we consider it difficult or impossible to ask for the forgiveness of sins of the departed?" The path to freeing certain sinners from Hades, if they are believers in Jesus Christ and confess Him in Hades by their adoration, this path the Lord Jesus Christ Himself opened by the cross, having destroyed Hades and led out from it all who awaited His coming. As then, so now also He has the power and strength to lead sinners out of Hades if, it is to be understood, they are worthy of this. If there is only a reason, God desires to save sinners as He Himself bears witness: "I desire not the death of a sinner."

---

[2]This is a fixed expression in English; note however that "charity" and "love" are the same word in Russian.

If the intercession of the first martyr Thecla saved the pagan Falconilla after her death, if the intercession of St. Gregory Dialogus saved the pagan emperor Trajan with an order from God not to pray henceforth for the wicked, if the intercession of St. Macarius of Egypt brought consolation to pagans, if the empress Theodora obtained of God the pardon of sins of her dead husband Theophilus, the last iconoclast persecutor of Christians, then how can we as Christians doubt or simply not believe the words of the Lord Jesus Christ, Who gave His faithful a true promise to fulfill what was asked for in faith, if it be in agreement with His most holy will—to save mankind?

Tell us, what is impossible for God? The desires, the wishes of God are fulfilled at once; for God, all is possible. Who does not know that God desires the salvation of man? But without man's cooperation, his salvation is impossible. Salvation is given only to him that asks; all is possible, but only to the believer. As the members of our body, expressing the will of the soul, help one another, just so the members of the spiritual body of Christ, the Church, moved and warmed by the grace of God, bear one another's burden; and the living, moved by God Himself, intercede for the dead. God sent His Son, the Lord Jesus Christ, into the world so that those who believe in Him might be saved. This is the first and main basis of our hope in asking the pardon of sins of the departed through Jesus Christ Who took upon Himself the sins of our departed one also. Then many other means and methods have been given by God Himself for us to move God to mercy on the departed. If anyone, according to his ability tries to fulfill all that can bring salvation to the departed, is not such a one the instrument of God, working towards the salvation of the departed?

The endless grace of God is one of the foundations on which the Church bases its teaching that sinners can be helped in their state beyond the grave. "I seek not the death of a sinner": this is God's wish. Man must work towards this by his life by the means indicated by God to incline the All Merciful to kindness and to deflect the strictness of judgment. If the Church were not firmly convinced that certain sinners could, even after death, receive pardon of sins and be released from confinement in Hades, then she would not pray for them. She prays for them because she believes that the departed, if worthy of prayer, are saved by the prayers of the living. Thus the Old Testament Church believed, and so the New Testament Church believes according to the words of her Founder, the Lord Jesus Christ, that there is remission of sins for those that have passed into the world beyond the grave in faith and hope in Jesus Christ. This means that the living retain an undoubted hope in God, Who desires the salvation of all, including our departed. Consequently, after all that we can do for the departed in complete good will, accompanied by corresponding actions, our departed will be saved and will be communicants of heavenly joy. They will be communicants because the living prayed for them; and they prayed because this was the will of God: "Without Me ye can do nothing" (John 15:5). Has not God Himself promised to fulfill our petitions that are in agreement with His most holy will? The petitions of the living for the repose with the Saints of our departed, if only their sins do not constitute blasphemy against the Holy Spirit, will surely be fulfilled according to the word of the Lord Himself: "It shall be forgiven him, both in this world and in the world to come" (Matthew 12:32). This is so through his own confession and through works of repentance which witness his striving, as far as is possible, to wipe out his sins. These works of repentance which free the soul from Hades are: prayer, heartfelt contrition for sins committed, avoidance of sin, alms, and works of love towards God and our neighbor. Those who repent at the time of death, but are not in time to offer the fruits of repentance, obtain a lightening of their state beyond the grave; they are even fully freed from the torments of Hades by the intercession of the living who are commanded to pray for such sinners with repentance: "Let them (the living) ask, and life shall be given them (the dead)" ... "He that knoweth his brother to sin a sin which is not to death, let him ask, and life shall be given to him, who sinneth not to death. There is a sin unto death: for that I say not that any man ask" (I John 5:16). And so, regarding the dead who repented at the time of their death, we the living should pray for them with full faith and hope that their sins be remitted according to the promise of the Lord Himself. Other sinners, as the Lord Himself bears witness, will not be forgiven, neither on earth nor beyond the grave, as having rejected Christ and His grace and become hardened, unrepentant, impious sinners, outside of communion with the Church; concerning such it is useless to pray. Even St. John, having a heart overflowing with love towards others, in his First Epistle forbids prayer for such because their fate has been decided by the Lord: "it shall not be forgiven them here (on earth) nor in the life to come" (I John 5:16) (beyond the grave). This truth of the Saviour and the commandment of the Apostle, concerning for whom of the departed to pray and for whom not to pray the Holy Fathers of the First Ecumenical Council repeated in their Fifth Rule: "All who die with true repentance are free from deadly sin," it is said there, "because of the fact that they have repented; a deadly sin is when the sinner remains incorrigible, stubbornly resisting devotion and truth ... the Lord God is not in such, unless they are humbled and come to their senses from their fall into sin."

The words of the Lord Jesus Christ Himself: "ask and it shall be given you" and "sins shall be forgiven in the life to come" give us, the living, every hope, with the intercession of the Church herself and our own intercessions, to lighten the state of those sinners who have repented at death and consequently to release them from the torments of Hades.

The *Orthodox Confession*,[3] in the response to Question 65, bears witness: "Pious acts by the living are of benefit to those departed, even in grave sins; they turn Him to mercy Who has power to free the sinful soul from Gehenna." Likewise in the response to the Sixty-fourth Question: "Faith teaches us that many of the sinners, showing repentance at death, are freed from Hades by the prayers and offerings[4] of the living."

The faith of the holy Orthodox Church in the possibility of asking God for forgiveness of sins for those who died in repentance is expressed in the confession of this dogma by the Eastern Patriarchs in their "Confession of the Orthodox Faith"[5] (Article 18). The confession of this dogma is as follows: "We believe that the souls of those who have fallen into a mortal sin and at death did not despair, but still repented before departing this life, only did not have time to bring any fruits of repentance (heartfelt prayers with the shedding of tears and bended knees, contrition, consolation of the sick, and the expression of love for God and neighbor in actions), the souls of such people go down to Hades and suffer punishments for the sins they have committed, without, however, being deprived of the hope of relief from them. They obtain relief by [God's] extreme goodness, through the prayers of the priests and through good works done on behalf of the dead; and especially by the strength of the Unbloody Sacrifice which the priest offers frequently for every Christian of his flock and which the Catholic and Apostolic Church offers daily for all in general."

b) The Old Testament Scriptures

The most ancient literary text witnessing the efficacy and the use of prayers for the dead in the Old Testament is the Second Book of Maccabees (12:39–46): "After the battle, Judas came with his company to take away the bodies of them that were slain, as demanded by duty, and to bury them with their kinsmen in the sepulchers of their fathers. And they found under the coats of the slain

---

[3] *The Orthodox Confession of Faith*, or catechism, ascribed to Metropolitan Peter Moghila and adopted by the Greco-Russian Synod of Jassy in 1643.

[4] The Russian text here says "alms," but the Greek specifies the Eucharistic offering.

[5] Also called "The Confession of Dositheus," and approved by the Synod of Jerusalem in 1672.

things dedicated to the idols of Jamnia which the law forbiddeth the Jews: and all plainly saw that for this cause they had been slain. Then they all blessed the just judgment of the Lord who revealed the things that were hidden. And so betaking themselves to prayers, they besought Him, that the sin which had been committed might be forgotten. But the most valiant Judas exhorted the people to keep themselves from sin, forasmuch as they saw before their eyes what had happened because of the sins of those that were slain. And making a gathering, he sent twelve thousand drachmas of silver to Jerusalem for sacrifice to be offered for the sins of the dead, thinking well and religiously concerning the resurrection. For if he had not hoped that they that were slain should rise again, it would have seemed superfluous and vain to pray for the dead. But he considered that they who had fallen asleep with godliness had great grace laid up for them. It is therefore a holy and wholesome thought to pray for the dead that they may be loosed from sins."

There are certain further examples in the Old Testament of intercession by those on earth for them that have passed on into the world beyond the grave.

Jesus the son of Sirach, in his book called Ecclesiasticus,[6] since he was firmly convinced of life beyond the grave and of the need to help the departed, just as those remaining on earth, teaches to do good to both: "A gift hath grace in the sight of all the living, and restrain not grace from the dead" (7:36); "When the dead is at rest, let his remembrance rest, and comfort him in the departing of his spirit" (38:23).

The dying Tobit commands his son Tobias: "Lay out thy bread and thy wine upon the burial of a just man, and do not eat and drink thereof with the wicked" (Tobit 4:17). The Doctors of the Church attach the following meaning to this commandment: Tobit, realizing the importance and benefit of prayer for the dead, and so as to move the living to such prayer, left the commandment to offer shared meals. This devout and salutary custom of offering a "trapeza"[7] after burials or on other days significant for the departed (the ninth and fortieth days, anniversary, birthday, nameday, date of death, days of general commemoration of the dead) and inviting acquaintances, clergy, the poor, beggars, so that they would pray for the deceased—this was carried over into the early Christian Church and has continued to the present. Chrysostom, praising those who do thus, also teaches to offer such meals so that people will pray for the dead and by their prayers move God to mercy for the deceased (Homily 33 on Matthew). In the early Church, these meals for clergy and poor were held in the narthexes

---

[6]Called in Russian "The Wisdom of Jesus, Son of Sirach."

[7]From the Greek word for "table," used now of any church-related or religious meal.

of churches. Later, at the Council of Laodicea, it was forbidden to hold them in the narthex, and memorial dinners took place in houses (*The Rock of Faith*, Part I, Chapter 1).

The holy Prophet Jeremiah (Chapter 16) calls accursed and cast away from the face of God those who do not commemorate the dead or give alms at burials. If, in the words of the Prophet, those dead are accursed for whom prayers are not said, in whose name alms are not given, then on the contrary, prayer for the dead and alms given in their name make them blessed. Here are the words of the Prophet: "They shall not be mourned, said he, and not buried: for thus saith the Lord: enter not into their house mourning, and go not to weep nor console them, for I have taken peace away from this people, said the Lord, and mercy and compassion. And great and small shall die in this land; they shall not be buried nor mourned . . . And there shall be no breaking of bread, in their weeping unto consolation for the dead, and they shall not give cups of drink for consolation for their fathers and mothers. And do not thou go into the house of feasting to sit with them, and to eat and drink. For thus saith the Lord of hosts, the God of Israel."

The Patriarchs Jacob and Joseph left testaments at their death: the former, that they bury him not in Egypt, but in the land of Canaan: and the latter entreated that his body not be left in Egypt at the Exodus of the Hebrews thence. There was more reason to do this than a desire on the part of the Patriarchs to be buried with their own people; here one can see an inner, spiritual reason: the desire to be a communicant of the prayers and sacrifices that were offered for the dead. Here is the witness of the Book of Genesis: Jacob made Joseph swear that he would not bury him in Egypt, "But I will sleep with my fathers, and thou shalt take me away out of this land, and bury me in the burying place of my ancestors" (Genesis 47:30). And Joseph swore to it. Jacob died in the one hundred forty-seventh year of his age. The Hebrews considered themselves sojourners for a short time in Egypt, as shown by the words said by Joseph's brethren to the Pharaoh, after their arrival from Canaan and when they were presented by Joseph to Pharaoh (Genesis 47:4); and therefore, dying in Egypt, Jacob took it on oath from Joseph that he would not bury him in a foreign land, but would move his remains to the land that Israel would inherit. By designating the place of his burial the Patriarch Jacob foretold the future homeland of his people. When the time came for Joseph to die, he said to his brethren: "God will visit you after my death, and will make you go up out of this land, to the land which he swore to Abraham, Isaac, and Jacob" (Genesis 50:24). And Joseph swore to the children of Israel, saying: "God will visit you, Carry my bones with you out of this place." And Joseph died, being a hundred and ten years old (Genesis 50:25–26). And Moses took the bones of Joseph with him in the exodus from Egypt (Exodus 13:19). The body of Joseph, embalmed, lay not in a stone coffin, but in a wooden one, of a wood that did not rot. The coffin was hidden in one of the numerous caves in the hills around the Nile plain (Vlastov, "Exodus," Sacred Chronicle, p. 119). Joseph lived in the time of the Pharaoh Amenems III. After the exodus from Egypt, the body of Joseph was buried in Sichem, which had been given to him by Jacob at his blessing. Sichem was the capital of the Israelite kingdom, later of Samaria.

Here is the saying of Moses: "And Israel lived in the land of Egypt, in the land of Gessem and ruled it, and they bore children and were multiplied greatly. And Jacob lived in the land of Egypt seventeen years, and the days of Jacob, the years of his life, were one hundred and forty-seven years. And it came time for Israel to die, and he called to him his son Joseph and said to him: If I have found good will in thine eyes, put thy hand under my thigh, and swear that thou wilt show me mercy and righteousness, and not bury me in Egypt. So that I might lie with my fathers, thou shalt bear me out of Egypt and bury me in the tomb that is in the field of Machpelah, before Mamre, in the land of Canaan, which (cave) Abraham bought with the field from Ephron the Hettite as his property for burial (Genesis 47:27–30; 49:29–30). There, continued Jacob, they buried Abraham and Sarah, his wife; there they buried Isaac and Rebecca, his wife; and there they buried Liah" (49:31). And Jacob concluded his testament to his sons, and put his feet on the bed, and died, and was added unto his people" (49:33). This shows an awareness and confession of the immortality of the soul, of eternal life beyond the grave, and at that, of a life not isolated.

A living faith in the truth of God's promise to grant the land of Canaan to his posterity caused the Patriarch's mind and all his thoughts and his heart, with his desires to turn to the future of the chosen people of God. Compelled by extreme circumstances, the Patriarch lived in Egypt, but his mind and heart were where his posterity should dwell.

On the basis of the true bond and communion between the living and the dead, the life of the quick can be of great help to the condition of the departed. In the Old Testament, fasting on the part of the living was accounted to the benefit of the dead, as witnessed by the First Book of Kings (Samuel):[8] the inhabitants of Jabesh-Gilead learned that the bodies of the dead Saul (he had killed himself so as not to become a live sacrifice of the Philistines) and his three

---

[8] In the Septuagint Bible, there are four Books of Kings, of which the first two are those elsewhere called I and II Samuel.

sons Jonathan, Aminadab, and Malchishua were in Philistine control, and they set off thither and took the bodies. Returning home, they burned the bodies of Saul and his sons, buried the bones in Jabesh under an oak tree, and fasted seven days (I Kings 31:13). And David, when he learned of the death of Saul, rent his garments, wept, and fasted till evening with all those of his entourage (II Kings 1:11–12). David also wept disconsolately and fasted after the death of the glorious leader Abner (II Kings 3:35).

Naomi said unto her daughter in law, "Blessed be he of the LORD, who hath not left off his kindness to the living and to the dead" (Ruth 2:20).

Baruch prayed thus to the Lord for the dead: "O Lord Almighty, the God of Israel, hear now the prayer of the dead of Israel, and remember not the iniquities of our fathers" (Baruch 3:5).

The Book of Judges bears witness that the commemoration of the dead is prescribed by law in Israel. Four times a year, the daughters of Israel went forth to mourn the daughter of Jephtha the Gileadite (11:40).

The holy Prophet and King David bears witness that the state of the dead is improved by the solicitousness of the living, and that those who have already died can do nothing to help themselves. There is no repentance after death: "In Hades who shall confess Thee?" (Psalms 6:6),[9] or, "Not the dead shall praise Thee, O Lord, nor all they that go down into Hades" (Psalms 87:11). He that is dead can no longer help himself. In life, he had the means and methods for his salvation—the confession of sins and other virtues which he no longer has after death. Therefore David entreats the Lord to grant him healing in the present life: "Have mercy upon me, O God, according to Thy great mercy, and according to the multitude of Thy loving kindness, cleanse mine iniquity" (Psalms 50), before my departure from this life.

If in life there was no inclination to confess sins, then it should be understood that after passing into the life beyond the grave, in Hades, there cannot be this virtue repentance, as it is not proper to this state of the dead, a state corresponding to that of the evil spirits; and therefore David says, "In Hades, who shall confess Thee?" Repentance, be it complete or incomplete, as a virtue, is found only on earth, and those who act on it do not die, are not dead, but living; but those who do not know God and His law and do not do His will are not alive but dead, both on earth and beyond the grave. And therefore David wrote, "Not the dead shall praise Thee, O Lord, neither they that go down into Hades," because in their life the name of God was not hallowed in their actions, the more so it will not be hallowed beyond the grave—in Hades, in union with

---

[9] Psalms are given in Septuagint numbering.

the spirits of evil—with the enemies of God. David refers to those that know God and do His will as the living, but to the idolaters and unrepentant sinners, as dead. Only to the living, who worship the living God, does it belong to glorify Him here on earth, and beyond the grave, in paradise. But in Hades, death prevents one from praising and glorifying God.

Christ's teaching also began with the words, "Repent . . ." (Mark 1:15) said to people who were still on earth; consequently, repentance is appropriate only to a soul joined to a body; but after its separation from the body and passage into the world beyond the grave, it has neither the power nor the means for repentance: "Him that is not vested in a wedding garment, bound hand and foot, they cast into the outer darkness, where there will be weeping and gnashing of teeth." (Matthew 22:12–13) Therefore the departed can do nothing for themselves; only the living still remaining on earth can help them according to the Lord's commandment, "Love ye one another, ask and it shall be given you, seek the kingdom of God and His righteousness."

c) The Gospel Teaching

The witness of the New Testament on the efficacy of prayer for the dead is to be found in the teaching of the Saviour Himself about life beyond the grave, in the Apostolic traditions, in the rules of the Ecumenical and Local Councils, and in the teaching of the holy, God-bearing Fathers and Doctors of the Church.

The Lord Jesus Christ Himself bore witness to His disciples that beyond the grave, there is remission of sins for the dead, that is, through the aid of the living to whom was said: "Ask, and it shall be given you"; "Whosoever shall say a word against the Son of Man, it shall be forgiven him, but whosoever shall speak against the Holy Spirit, it shall not be forgiven him, neither in this age, nor the next." (Matthew 12:32). That means that sins not constituting blasphemy against the Holy Spirit will be remitted in the life beyond the grave (Mark 3:28–29). The main sins that are not forgiven either on earth or beyond the grave are: extreme unbelief, lack of remorse, hardening of the heart, stubborn resistance to divine truth, stubborn rejection of grace, combined with a turning away from everything that is holy and pleasing unto God (Hebrews 10:26,29). These sins are at the root of blasphemy against the Holy Spirit; but why are they not forgiven either in the life of this time or beyond the grave? Because the remission of all sins takes place (there is no sin that overcomes the mercy of God) only for him who repents of them. Jesus Christ said openly that the blasphemer shall not be forgiven, that is, the one who remains in his blasphemy; this means that he who has blasphemed but repented of it is forgiven.

Forgiveness takes place where there is an honest, heartfelt remorse with the desire of correction and with aversion to this confessed sin. Consequently there is no sin, regardless of what it might be, deadly or not, that would not be forgiven if only it be revealed in confession. A revealed sin is resolved, according to the words of Jesus Christ Himself: "Receive the Holy Spirit, and whosesoever sins ye remit, shall be remitted unto them; and whose ye retain, shall be retained" (John 20:23). A sin remitted on earth frees the one who reveals it from eternal torment; and the fruits of repentance, consisting of a penance fulfilled, correct the inner tendency to sin of the one who has repented. If, after repentance, a penance imposed by the priest either is not carried out or if there were no fruits of repentance due to death having followed, then such a deceased person can gain no small help from the intercession of the Church and from the prayers for him by those who remain among the living.

Sins constituting blasphemy against the Holy Spirit are not forgiven, because the moral state of the soul, as shown by these sins, is just such a state as that of remorseless demons (Archimandrite Michael, Gospel Commentary, Matthew 12:31–32, p. 221). This sin is not forgiven, because there is no awareness or remorse in the sinner.

That sins not constituting blasphemy against the Holy Spirit are remitted after the passage into the life beyond the grave, Jesus Christ showed in actual deed. While on the Cross He heard the heartfelt prayer of the repentant, wise thief: we are dying on crosses and soon will both be in the world beyond the grave. Thou art God, while I, by my deeds, am condemned. I know that even beyond the grave I must give Thee answer for all my wickedness; but I pray Thee, when thou goest thither, be mindful of me in Thy Kingdom . . . The thief did not ask the Lord to remember him here, but "when Thou comest into Thy Kingdom—be mindful of me," forgive me, and have mercy in the new life after death. The Lord accepted the prayer of the thief, not to remember his sinful life beyond the grave, and He said: "Today thou shalt be with me in paradise" (Luke 22:42–43). This means that, after death, in certain conditions, there can be remission of sins.

The holy Apostle and Evangelist Matthew writes that "The Lord gave His soul for the salvation of many" (10:45). For us, the living, there remains only to appropriate these Gospel words to the departed, that is, to understand that among the "many" our departed are included, and it shall be unto us (the living) and them (the departed) according to our faith, as the Evangelists bear witness:

"All things that ye ask in prayer *with faith,* ye shall receive" (Matthew 21:22); "All that ye ask for in prayer, believe, that ye shall obtain" (Mark 11:24).

Can the words of the Lord Jesus Christ be wrong, witnessing that He does not wish the death of a sinner, but desires his salvation? Is it not the Lord Himself, seeking the salvation of all, Who says to us, "All that ye ask in prayer with faith, ye shall receive"? Does not the Lord Himself demand undying love from us? And therefore, is not the true foundation of prayer for the dead love and the promise to fulfill that which is asked, so long as it be in agreement with the will of God? For this very reason the living entreat the Lord with full hope for those that have passed into the life beyond the grave: "Truly I say unto you, if ye have faith, and doubt not, all that ye ask in prayer with faith ye shall obtain." For the believer, all is possible (Mark 9:23); all is granted to the believer for his undoubting faith, whatever he asks in his prayers, if only it be in agreement with the will, the desire of God Himself. And since God does not want the death of a sinner, therefore the prayer of the living for the dead is in agreement with the will of God, and consequently is effective. Prayer, combined with faith, hope, and love brings the one who prays fulfillment of his petition from God, that is, mercy and repose for the departed.

In the parable of the ten virgins, which symbolizes the Last Judgment, the Lord says, "Those that were ready entered the marriage feast, and the doors were closed" (Matthew 25:10) This means that until Judgment Day the kingdom of heaven is open for the members of the Church; and the righteous enter with repentant sinners as well as sinners who have died but not in despair, with the aid of the living on earth and the Saints in heaven. But after the Judgment the gates of paradise will be closed and there will be no more entry there. If those who are drowning in water or burning in fire do not receive help in time, they perish; just so the imperfect soul beyond the grave will perish unless it receives help in time from those still on earth. If the living do not give a helping hand to the imperfect beyond the grave, then grace alone, strong and powerful though it be, will not save the sinful soul. Thus in order to draw the grace of Christ to the one that is perishing by God's incomprehensible love which wishes not the death of a sinner, living persons are selected and assigned who, not by themselves but by the grace given them, use various visible, outward means to save the departed soul which beyond the grave can of itself do nothing for its own salvation. The words "having power to cast into Gehenna" (Luke 12:5) or to commit the body and soul of the sinner to eternal death give us, the living, the consoling hope that He Who has power to destroy the sinful soul in Gehenna, can, by His power also save it from Gehenna as stated in the 65th Answer of the Orthodox Confession of the Catholic and Apostolic Church in these words: "Dying sinners are not necessarily cast into Gehenna, but rather this is in the power of God, as God can also forgive them for the good done for the benefit of the dead. They are of no small benefit to those who died in such sins." All this is the witness of Jesus Christ Himself who gave us the commandment to love, to ask, to seek the kingdom of God not for ourselves only, but for our neighbor, and that our intercession for the dead can be beneficial to them and can bring them eternal life.

d) The Tradition of the Apostles

The brother[10] of the Lord according to the flesh, St. James the Apostle, was taught by the Lord Himself to pray for the dead. We say by the Lord Himself because, according to the witness of the word of God—"for we know not what we should pray for as. we ought" (Romans 8:26)—consequently his prayer for the departed was inspired by the Holy Spirit under the direction of the Teacher and Lord Jesus Christ. Thus the departed are given, according to Christ's very words, an opportunity to receive the remission of sins, if only they had died as befits Christians. In turn, the holy Apostle taught Christians as follows: "pray one for another, that ye may be healed" (James 5:16). If the dead did not exist, then these words could relate only to the living, to those still on earth; but since those that have died are alive, living in another world, then this commandment lays the obligation on the living to pray for all members of Christ's Church regardless of where they might be—with us or apart, in absence, on earth or in the world beyond the grave. The word "healed," as one may rightly conclude, relates both to those still on earth and to those who have passed into the world beyond the grave, since the holy Apostle in his Liturgy[11] prays for those living on earth and for those departed into the world beyond the grave thus: "Lord, God of spirits and of all flesh, be mindful of those whom we have commemorated and those we have not commemorated, the Orthodox, from the righteous Abel down to this day; Thyself grant them rest in the habitations of the living, in Thy kingdom, in the sweetness of paradise, in the bosom of Abraham, Isaac and

---

[10]In Russian, as in the Semitic languages, the term "brother" also refers to a *cousin*. English "brother" would be *«родной брат»*, "first cousin" would be *«двоюродный брат»*, and so on. St. James was a blood relative, or *kinsman,* of the Lord.

[11]Although the oldest known manuscript of the Divine Liturgy, or Eucharistic rite, ascribed to St. James the Apostle date only from the twelfth century; recently a papyrus of the second century A.D. was found with a fragment of another early Liturgy, that of St. Mark, which has a comparable intercession for the departed.

Jacob, our holy Fathers, whence sickness, sorrow, and sighing have fled, where the light of Thy countenance visits and enlightens always."

The first Council was the Council of the Apostles in Jerusalem. Here unanimity in the preaching of the Gospel was confirmed: therefore the teaching of prayer for the dead was common to all the Apostles; so that wherever the Apostles planted Christianity, there was intercession for the dead, as is proven by all the ancient Liturgies of that time. The custom of praying for the dead came from the Old Testament Church into the primitive Christian Church. The first Christian Church, or Christian community, was the Church of Jerusalem, consisting of the Apostles and their disciples, whom the Holy Spirit guided to every truth (John 16:13). The same custom of praying for the dead was in all the Churches: in Alexandria, in Carthage, Caesarea, Constantinople, and Milan.

Of all the ancient Liturgies of the Orthodox Church, both those used in the East (such as those of St. James, the Brother of the Lord; St. Basil the Great, St. John Chrysostom, St. Gregory the Dialogist), and those of the Western Church (such as the Roman, Mozarabic [Paleo-Hispanic], Gallican and others), and finally the Liturgies of various ancient, separated Churches in the East (such as those of the Copts, Ethiopians, Syrians, Nestorians and others), however numerous and varied they may be, there is not one that lacks prayers for the dead. This is a sign that from the days of the very Apostles who gave the Church the order of the Divine Liturgy, there was never a time when the Christians did not pray for their departed brethren, even as part of their most important church service. (Archbishop Makary of Kharkov, *Orthodox Dogmatic Theology*, Volume 2, p. 597).

The Teacher of the Gentiles, the chosen vessel of the Holy Spirit, St. Paul the Apostle did not teach to sorrow for the dead, as do they who have no hope of the resurrection and the new, blessed eternal life beyond the grave. Knowing that all are guilty before God, and therefore the dead are not foreign to sin, he taught his friends Christian sorrow, the bearing of the burden of a departed neighbor, that is, sadness for the sins of the departed leading to heartfelt prayer for those that have passed into the world beyond the grave. Christians are given grace to bear the burden of others. Bearing the burden of others, we fulfill the law of Christ which is undying love. Jesus Christ did not cut off the dead utterly from the living, for He taught that before God all are alive; consequently the love He commanded extends to others who are beyond the boundary of the grave. The Apostles also, spreading the Gospel, joined the living and the dead, as shown by their teaching. The holy Apostle Paul taught that the dead and the living are

God's; therefore he does not divide but joins. The commandment of the Apostle James to pray one for another shows a direct command to pray for those who have gone on to the other world. To bear the burdens of others, not only those that live on earth but those also who have passed on beyond the grave, is what St. Paul orders us to do. Chrysostom explains wherein this bearing of burdens for the departed lies. Awareness by the living of the sins of the dead should give rise to weeping by the former, sorrow for the sins of the latter. This weeping is demanded of the living as being of benefit to the dead. Blessed, taught Jesus Christ, are those who weep for sins, by the law of love not only for their own but for the sins of others, living and deceased. Their consolation will be the fulfillment of their prayer, the remission of their own sins, and the remission of sins of those dead for whom they prayed. "This weeping of the living for the sins of the dead," says Chrysostom, "is good; this is high philosophy."

In another place St. Paul writes: "Remember your teachers" (Hebrews 13:7);[12] here by "remember" the Apostle commands us to remember, to commemorate the departed who have taught us the Christian life and to whom we are indebted for our present moral life, tasting the fruits of our fathers' labors and those of our brethren. In his Epistle to Timothy, the Apostle also commands us to pray both for the living and for the dead: "make supplications, prayers, intercessions, and thanksgivings for all men" (I Timothy 2:1–2). In the Second Epistle to Timothy, St. Paul desires that the members of the house of Onesiphorus might receive mercy from the Lord in the next world for the love they have shown him: "The Lord give mercy to the house of Onesiphorus: because he hath often refreshed me, and hath not been ashamed of my chains: . . . The Lord grant unto him to find mercy of the Lord in that day" (II Timothy 1:16,18).

St. John the Divine divides those who depart into the other world into those who repent of their sins at death and those who do not repent, the despairing. The former obtain remission of sins and life, but the latter inherit the punishment they merit for their life on earth: "If any man see his brother to sin a sin which is not to death, let him ask, and life shall be given to him, who sinneth not to death. There is a sin unto death: for that I say not that any man ask. All iniquity is sin. And there is a sin not unto death" (I John 5:16–17).

---

[12]The Authorized Version has taken the Greek in a different sense and translates this passage "Remember them which *have the rule* over you." Yet the original Greek [and the Slavonic] does not specify *living* teachers; it speaks of teachers in general without distinction of living or dead.

e) The Teaching of the Holy Fathers and Doctors of the Church

St. Dionysius the Areopagite, a contemporary of the Apostles and seer of divine things, a disciple of the holy Apostle Paul who attended at the passing of the Mother of God, in his mystagogical vision on the departed says: "The prayers of the Saints, both in this life and even more so after death, are effectual for those who are worthy of holy prayers, that is, for the faithful. The prayers of some for others have their value and strength before God."

St. John of Damascus writes, "St. Dionysius, divine hierarch and commentator on divine statutes, would hardly ask for that which was not well-pleasing unto God and the fulfillment of that which had not been promised by Him; for which reason he does not ask this on behalf of the unclean, that is, those dead who were not enlightened (that is, baptized)." And in another place St. John of Damascus writes: "Thus the holy hierarch asks that which is pleasing unto God and that which God will undoubtedly bestow." Here is the purpose of prayer for the dead: "Prayer is made that Divine grace will remit the sins of the deceased which were committed through human weakness, that they may take up their abode in the land of the living, in the bosom of Abraham, Isaac, and Jacob in a place whence all sorrow, sadness, and sighing have been removed; that Divine power in its goodness might overlook the impurities found in the departed by reason of human frailty for as Scripture says, no one is clean of stain" (St. John of Damascus, Homily on the Faithful Departed).

St. Athanasius the Great, in his *Homily on the Departed*, writes: "Although the faithful departed be laid out under the open sky, refuse not to invoke Christ our God in lighting oil [lamps] and candles: this is pleasing unto God and found worthy of a great reward. For oil and candles are a sacrifice, and the divine and Unbloody Sacrifice is a sacrifice of purification; good works toward the needy double every good return. By the grace of God, our efforts will not be in vain to achieve what we strive towards in faith. For the holy Apostles, sanctified teachers, and spiritual Fathers filled with the Holy Spirit and His indwelling power by His inspiration established Liturgies, prayers, and psalmody and annual days of commemoration of the dead. Such practices, by the grace of our God Who loves mankind, are to this day carried out and extend from the East to the West, from the North to the South, to the honor and glory of the Lord of lords and King of kings" (St. John of Damascus, *Epistle to Antiochus*. Question 34; and *Homily on the Departed*).

St. Gregory of Nyssa says that it is most pleasing to God and beneficial at the Divine Eucharist to commemorate the faithful departed. The same Saint, concerned for the salvation of souls, commands in mortal cases to communicate those forbidden or temporarily excommunicated.

St. Basil the Great prays thus for the departed: "Remember, O Lord, all those previously fallen asleep in the hope of resurrection and eternal life." Further on, he offers a prayer for those whose names the priest wishes to mention: "For the repose and remission of sins of the soul(s) of (Name) in a place of brightness, whence sadness and weeping have fled; give them rest, O God, where the light of Thy countenance shines" (Liturgy of St. Basil the Great).

St. Gregory the Theologian in his eulogy[13] for Caesarius, his brother, says of their mother: "The tidings were heard, worthy for all to hear, and the mother's sorrow was poured out in a good and holy promise to return to her son all his wealth, to offer it as a funeral gift." Further on he says, "Here is how I can honor thy memory, and I have already fulfilled it; but I will also fulfill another thing, by commemorating thee each year." This is the witness of a great worldwide teacher on prayer for the dead, and in general on all that is dedicated to God for the departed which he calls good and holy gifts.

The great ecumenical Doctor, St. John Chrysostom, taught by word and deed to pray for those who have passed over into the new world beyond the grave. In his Liturgy, three times there are prayers for them, and besides that he taught this virtue to his flock, showing the need, importance and benefit of such prayer both for those still on earth and for those departed this life. Here, for example, are several passages on this subject from his divinely inspired writings: "Those remaining on earth should not weep, not be distraught, but rather rejoice over the death of one close to their heart. One should not weep, but rejoice, whether the departed be righteous or a sinner. If the one fallen asleep was a virtuous individual, a good Christian, then do not weep for him but rejoice, for he has borne with love the whole burden of life on earth and passed on to true rest in Christ, because of Whom and for Whom he suffered more or less, defending and keeping the truth. But if the deceased was a sinner, then too one should rejoice, and not weep thoughtlessly, but rejoice that there will be no further growth of the evil to which the deceased was inclined. One should be troubled and weep, not at his death, but for the sins which he as a human being did. The contrition of the living for the dead, tears shed for their sins, should be mixed with undoubting faith by the living in Him Who took upon Himself the sins of all the world and therefore the sins also of our deceased sinner. Prayer, alms, the Unbloody Sacrifice help the departed much in the improvement of his state beyond the grave. If the prayers and sacrifices of Job for his children purified

[13]In 369 A.D.

them, then what hampers God from cleansing the departed of their sins for our prayers and offerings? Indeed God gives a return to some according to the prayers of others. To this end it was commanded that we should pray for one another so that some should be healed by the intercession of others. One hand washes the other, and both become clean.[14] Thus the prayers of the living for the dead save them both. To what end is distraught sorrow when the living can find mercy from God for the dead?" (Exposition of I Corinthians 15, Reading 41. Exposition of Acts 9, Reading 21). "If we begin to pray for those separated from us by place alone, our prayers will not be in vain or useless, because this is one of the means given by God for saving ourselves and others regardless of where they may be: on earth or in the other world. If it is said that our bodies are a temple of the Holy Spirit Who abides in us; then are not the prayers of the priest and deacon, as well as those in attendance, prayers for the dead by the whole Church and each of us Christians, a prayer of the Holy Spirit for the salvation of the departed?" In another place in his commentary on the Epistles to the Philippians and Galatians he says: "If the pagans burn those who die and their belongings with them, then how much more, O believer, shouldst thou send the believer's property with him, not as they do in order for it to become ashes, but so as to bring him greater glory thereby; and if the deceased was a sinner, so that God will forgive him his sins; but if he was righteous, so as to increase his rewards and recompense. Let us try," he taught his flock, "to show the departed a benefit and give him every possible help." Help and benefit for the departed are shown them by our prayers, alms, and the Unbloody Sacrifice[15]. Prayer for the departed cannot be in vain! The disciples of the Lord would not have raised it to a law for the priest to pray at these most awesome Mysteries for those departed in the faith, if they did not know how beneficial this prayer is for the state of dead sinners. St. John Chrysostom bases his teaching about the possibility of obtaining salvation for deceased sinners, of asking God for the forgiveness of their sins, on the means established by the Holy Spirit. These means are not in vain: prayer, alms, (Eucharistic) offerings. By means of them we obtain benefit for one another and consequently also salvation. In another place he affirms: "I vouch for the success of all these means." Therefore the improvement of the condition of sinners beyond the grave depends on us. Chrysostom, explaining the words of Jesus Christ to Martha, the sister of the dead Lazarus, "I am the resurrection and the life; he that believeth on Me, even though he die, shall live" (John 11:25), writes in his commentary on these words

---

[14]Russian proverb.

[15]The faithful departed are commemorated at every Eucharistic Liturgy.

(Discussion 62): "Since the Saviour is the Giver of life and of all good things, we must ask Him for improvement in the state of the departed. He, as God, gives life to whom He will."

Origen writes thus about the Book of Job: "We observe the memory of our parents, or we devoutly honor the memory of friends departed in the faith, both rejoicing in their [having found a place of] coolness and asking for ourselves also a devout end in faith."

The [former] pagan orator Arnobius, having been catechized by the Church, but not yet baptized, writes in his Fourth Book Against the Pagans: "What have our congregations done to deserve your destroying them? In them prayers are made to Almighty God, He is asked to bestow peace upon all, mercy on those in authority, the military, kings, friends, enemies, the living, and the dead."

St. John of Damascus, who collected the witness of all the preceding Fathers and Doctors of the Church, makes the following conclusion: "Initiates and eye witnesses of the Word who conquered the whole world, disciples and divine Apostles of the Saviour, not without reason and not without benefit established the commemoration of the faithful departed at the celebration of the awesome, most pure, and life-giving Mysteries which the holy, Catholic and Apostolic Church has kept since that time from one end of the world to another and will keep from now till the end of the world. For the Christian faith, foreign to errors, has accepted nothing that is useless and keeps unbroken all that is useful, pleasing unto God, and salutary" (*Homily on the Departed*).

"Now," writes this divinely inspired teacher of the Church in another place, "until the dread Judgment of the Lord is the time to help one another in all things and in attaining salvation. It is most pleasing to God Who loves His creation when we are concerned about our salvation and the salvation of others, when we do good works for the living and the dead." And so let us live for God and for others, not only those visibly with us, but also those that have passed on into the world beyond the grave yet not been cut off from us in spirit. Those joined by God Himself and who live in God are never separated. God does not join so as to disunite. The life of the living, pleasing unto God, will bring salvation also to the imperfect departed. The means indicated by the Holy Spirit and used by us in memory of the departed are not in vain, but will help them to free themselves from the torments of Hades. "As a sweet-smelling myrrh when a sick person is anointed with it involves both the one that anoints and the one anointed," writes St. John of Damascus, "just so do the good works of the living for the dead save both. Being good, God saves His creation, saves the work of

His hands, saves the rich and the poor, saves the learned and the unlettered, saves masters and servants, if only they do not reject faith in Jesus Christ."

Tertullian, in the book *On the Crown of the Warrior*, says: "We make the offering for the departed each year on the date when they reposed."

The hieromartyr St. Cyprian, Bishop of Carthage, who lived in the third century, repeats and reminds his flock of the rule of the Holy Fathers who lived before him. "No one dying should assign a priest as administrator of his goods, since the priest is a man who is obliged to serve God alone. Whoever breaks this rule is deprived of prayers and offerings after the departure of his soul from this life for distracting priests and servants of God from the altar." Consequently, if in this case there are no prayers for the departed, it means that they were and are offered for the dead who do not break this rule (*The Rock of Faith*, Part I, "Concerning a Good End," Chapter 3).

Eusebius writes: "All the people together with the clergy, not without tears and deep sighing, raised up to God prayers for the soul of the king and by this fulfilled the desire of him who was beloved of God" (*On the Life of the Blessed Emperor Constantine*, Book 4, Chapter 71). St. Cyril, Archbishop of Jerusalem, in his "Fifth Mystagogical Homily," writes: "We observe the memory of those departed before us: first of the Patriarchs, Prophets, Apostles, Martyrs, so that by their prayers and intercessions God might accept our prayers; then we pray for the deceased holy Fathers and Bishops; and finally for all who have departed this life among us firmly believing that this brings great benefit to the souls for which is offered the prayer of the Holy Sacrifice on the altar" (Part IV, Chapter 9).

Regarding prayer for the dead, St. Ambrose of Milan and the blessed Augustine bear witness. St. Ambrose prayed and asked forgiveness of sins for the deceased emperor Theodosius, while St. Augustine in his homily on devotion and love says, "Be attentive, brethren! We should not only show mercy to the poor during our lifetime, but also try to show it to the dead, bearing in mind what Judas Maccabaeus did: he said, 'It is a holy thought to pray for the dead that they be cleansed of sin.' For Judas knew that no one can claim a pure heart, reflecting that not even the stars were pure before God. Angels fell from heaven, the stars were not pure, and the infant whose life on earth continues one day is not free of sin. What then shall we say of ourselves? Surely we cannot boast of a pure heart? God forbid! Since we are sinners, conceived and born in sins, and leading a sinful life, and will die perhaps in sins that can be forgiven. And so all of us who shall pass through this life need mercy. Although we mortify our flesh by fasting and abstinence, although we bear all misfortunes with equanimity out of love for Christ: despite all of this the passions of this life are unequal to the glory that is to appear in us. Thus we need mercy since we cannot attain eternal life by our own merits. Wouldst thou have God be merciful to thee? Be thyself merciful to others. And so pray for the dead so that they, when they are in blessed life, may pray for thee."

Surely it cannot be that all these Saints drew false conclusions: they who walked in the air as they celebrated divine services, as did St. Basil the Great or who raised the dead, who healed all illnesses of the soul and body, who, in a word, wrought miracles? They prayed for the dead, and they, as they departed this life, left a testament to pray for them. Thus St. Ephrem the Syrian, having spent his whole left in penitence and weeping and having shown us an example of preparation for death, in his last will requested prayers and commemoration after the departure of his soul from the body, because he had no doubt that the priests of the Son of God could, with the holy offerings and the prayers they uttered, cleanse the sins of the dead. Dying, he asked his disciples to hold commemorations of him for forty days. His testament concluded with these words: "For the dead receive benefit when they are commemorated at the offerings by the living saints, and they are aware of the prayers offered in their memory. I exhort you tearfully, my dear brethren, and the whole throng of the church, as God takes me away from you, when ye stand in prayer, pray also for me. I ask you, my beloved, I exhort those who know me: pray for me with the same concern as I entreat you" (*Writings of the Holy Fathers*, "Homily at the Parting of a Priest with his Flock," Volume 18, pp. 23–24). In another place he writes: "There is no benefit to the departed in tears or in sorrow, nor in outward wailing: his works accompany him, his acts go with him, and only prayers and alms go along and keep him company."

Just so you should pray: pray early, pray late, and day and night, and none of your sighing shall be hidden from the Lord.

As St. Epiphanius assures us, there is nothing so beneficial to the dead as when they are remembered in prayer.

St. Dimitri of Rostov, confirming our hope of bringing salvation to deceased sinners, writes as follows: "As we offer our prayers for the repose of the souls of the departed servants of God of blessed memory, we have an undoubted hope that the sacrifice offered for their souls, the blood and water that poured forth from the ribs of Christ which takes place in the holy Chalice sprinkles and cleanses those for whom it is offered and for whom it is shed. And if the Blood of Christ—once poured forth of old on the Cross—has washed the sins of all the world, it and no other now also will cleanse our sins: if then the Blood of Christ has redeemed countless souls from enemy enslavement, now the same and no other will redeem the souls of those commemorated. If then the suffering of Christ justified so many, will not now the same suffering of Christ, recalled in the celebration of the divine Sacrifice, justify those for whom we pray? We believe without a doubt in the power of the Blood of Christ which flowed from His rib with water, that it cleanses, redeems, and justifies His servants" (*Homily on the Saturday of the Fourth Week in Lent,* Part 1). And in another place this Saint writes: "Prayerful commemoration of the deceased intercedes for the forgiveness of their sins, repose with the Saints, and the yearned-for vision of God" *(Homily at the Burial of T. Yushkov,* Part 5, p. 114). St. Dimitri of Rostov relates the Apostle's words "remember your teachers" directly to prayers for deceased teachers of the faith; and he himself writes that a man's first teachers are his departed parents, for whom he commands to pray without failing: "Remember your teachers, your father and mother, for from the beginning they are a man's teachers of his youth; likewise his teachers in the spirit, who have spoken to him the word of God . . ." (*Saturday of the Fourth Week in Lent,* Part 2).

We may conclude from all that has been said that all the Saints taught both in word and deed to pray for those that have passed on into eternal life. They taught, and, it can be understood, as chosen vessels of the Holy Spirit, they could not be wrong as to the lawfulness, the need, and the benefit of prayers for those departed this world. The Orthodox Church of Christ on earth, from her very beginning and to the end, has prayed and will pray for her members who are beyond the grave. She has taught not only to pray for them, but in their name, or in their stead, or simply to do good works for them unto those people whom the Lord recognizes as His lesser brethren and accepts our good works as done to Him: "Ye have done it unto Me!" Prayer, alms, the offering of the Unbloody Sacrifice, are means that change the condition of our fathers, brethren, and in general of all close to our heart.

All of the means enumerated, as being established by God Himself, as taught by all the Holy Fathers and Doctors of the Church, can change for the better the state of deceased Christians beyond the grave; and therefore blessed are those dead concerning whom there is a good memory on earth, a memory expressed in prayers and in general in all works of devotion by the living. And miserable are those dead, in the words of the Prophet, whose memory is not observed on earth and with whose death all remembrance of them ceases.

f) Decrees of the Holy Councils

The holy custom of praying for the dead, which existed in the Old Testament, was introduced by the holy Apostles into the Church of Christ also. St. James, in his Liturgy, prays for the dead. It is not possible that this truth was not shared by the other Apostles. The teaching on prayer for the dead existed in the first Church and in the early ages. In the fourth century, the composers of Liturgies, ecumenical teachers, and luminaries of the Church, Ss. Basil the Great and John Chrysostom, pray three times in the Liturgy for the departed. The prayer for the dead became an inseparable part of the Divine Liturgy, and the Sixth Ecumenical Council confirmed the afore-mentioned Liturgies, consequently it affirms prayer for the departed (Rule 32). The Council of Laodicea in its 28*th* Rule forbade celebrating or holding meals for the dead, that is, eating and drinking, in the churches. This restriction clearly shows that prior to this time there had been commemoration of the dead. This Council did not forbid prayers for them, but only setting forth meals according to the old custom in churches. Here is the decision of this Council: "That the so-called agape meals must not be held in houses of the Lord or in churches, and persons must not eat or recline at table in a house of God."

Timothy, Archbishop of Alexandria, who was at the Second Ecumenical Council as one of the one hundred eight Fathers, issues the decision, in agreement with the opinion of the Second Council, that the Holy Sacrifice not be offered for suicides. This prohibition reveals, as it were, the rule of offering the Holy Sacrifice, and consequently of praying, for the dead as a Christian custom and of using all means to bring repose to the souls of the deceased. Here is what this Saint writes in his Fourteenth Rule: "If anyone, being beside himself, shall raise his hands against himself or cast himself from a height, should there be the Holy Offering for him or no? Concerning such a one, the clergyman must determine whether or not he was genuinely out of his mind when he did this or not; for often those close to the one who suffered by his own hand, seeking to obtain the celebration of the Holy Mysteries and prayers for him, speak untruthfully and say that he was beside himself. Yet it may be that on account of human insult or from some other reason out of pusillanimity, he did this thing; and for such a one there should be no Holy Offering, as he is a suicide. Therefore the clergyman must investigate with care lest he fall under judgment."

The degree to which the early Christians were concerned for the salvation of souls that had passed into the other world is also shown by the fact that some, out of misdirected zeal, would put the Holy Gifts into the mouth of the dead person. The Sixth Ecumenical Council forbade such communions of dead bodies as not being in agreement with good sense. Those excommunicated for a time from Holy Communion for certain sins, in the case of dangerous illness, were resolved from excommunication and admitted to communion with the intent that the soul should not depart from this life without being resolved of its sins. This concern of the Church was expressed in one of the decisions of the First Ecumenical Council in the Thirteenth Rule. In the Apostolic Constitutions (Book 8, Chapters 41 and 42), not only is there mention of the commemoration of the departed as a lawful custom of praying that the Lord will remit every sin of the dead, voluntary or involuntary, but there are also rules prescribed as to how this custom is to be observed.

g) Actual Examples

We find evidence that dead can be forgiven their sins through the prayers of the living in the lives of the Saints and in grace-filled revelations. There were cases when deceased sinners themselves appeared to the living and bore witness of the change in their condition in the other world, as was said in the chapter, "Appearances of Souls from Hades" above. In the life of St. Gregory the Dialogist, Pope of Rome, we find a confirmation of this possibility. Once as he was going along a road, St. Gregory suddenly stopped and began to pray for the forgiveness of sins of the emperor Trajan who was already dead. Soon he heard the following words from God: "I have hearkened unto thy prayer and grant remission of sins to Trajan, but henceforth offer Me no prayers for the unrighteous." Both Western and Eastern sources bear witness to this. St. Gregory, called the Dialogist,[16] became Pope in 596 and died in 604, so that he lived in the sixth and early seventh centuries and was one of the greatest figures of the Roman Church. His prayers for the dead bear witness that at this time prayer for the departed was common to the East and West.

In the land where St. Benedict lived,[17] in their own convent, there were two young ladies of noble family. They had given a promise to God not to marry but to dedicate themselves fully to the Lord Jesus Christ. Indeed, in their self-control, they were great ascetics. Living in their own house, they did not notice how their great virtues of fasting and chastity were stolen from them by an awful evil: a loose tongue. In constant conversation they fell into judgment, slander, lies, and many other vices concealed in much speaking. Having learned of

[16]For his book called the *Dialogues* published in 593 and one of the most popular books of the time.

[17]Nursia in Italy.

this, St. Benedict threatened them with exclusion from Holy Communion. The fatherly measure of the Saint did not work, and they continued their iniquity as before. Soon both were overtaken by death, and they were buried in the church. After the burial of these young ladies, certain worthy persons noticed that each time the deacon said, "Catechumens depart!"[18] the young ladies who were buried in the church at once rose from their tombs and left the church. At length St. Benedict was told of this. The Saint of God, understanding the reason for the righteous anger of God, with a sad heart prayed for them to God and sent a prosphora[19] to the church where they were buried as an offering to God for their repose. After the Holy Offering, the young girls ceased to be seen leaving their tombs. This served as a clear proof for all that the prayers and offering of St. Benedict had obtained remission of sins and repose for these two girls.

In the life of this Saint, another case is given that shows how much it means for the departed when the living are concerned for the improvement of their condition beyond the grave. Thus, in the monastery where St. Benedict lived, there was one rather young monk who, out of excessive love for his parents, would secretly leave the monastery almost every day without the blessing of his superior. And in the end, God's punishment befell him. Coming to his parents' home as he was wont, he suddenly died. This was told at the monastery, and the brethren buried the deceased. But what happened? The next morning, the body of the deceased was found cast out of his coffin! Again they buried him, and again the next day the body was found outside the coffin. Then St. Benedict was told of all this, and he ordered the Unbloody Sacrifice to be offered for him and placed a particle of the Holy Gifts on the breast of the dead man to commit him to the ground. Indeed, after this the body was no longer cast out of the coffin, which clearly shows that the mercy of God was drawn to him beyond the grave (*Life of St Benedict*, March 14).

All the means established by God, since they are means towards the salvation of mankind, expressing visibly the bond between those still on earth and those who have gone on to the next world and not yet achieved perfection, serve at the same time as a reliable indication of the improvement in the state of the departed through the intercessions of the living moved by love for them and hope in God's mercy. They receive pardon and are freed from Hades. This is the doctrine of Orthodoxy; this is the teaching of our Church.

---

[18]In the Latin form then in use there was also the phrase "Let none who cannot pray with us remain."

[19]Eucharistic bread. In the sixth century leavened bread was still used in the West.

"Ask and it shall be given you; be it unto thee, as thou wishest": this is the promise of the Lord Jesus Christ Himself, and therefore it is true. Our wish, if it is in agreement with the will, the desire of Jesus Christ to save man, surely will be fulfilled, and the deceased will be saved. Otherwise the heart of the one who prays would not be warmed by grace to intercede for the dead. The living prays for the dead because this is pleasing to God. And if the intercession of the living for the dead is pleasing unto God, then the dead will be saved.

God is the same yesterday, today, and for all ages. God's providence for the salvation of the human race and His love towards mankind are the same as they were before. If the dead do not rise now to speak with the living about the salvation of both, the reason was stated by Abraham in the parable of the Rich Man and Lazarus: "the living will not believe" (Luke 16:31). However, the appearances of the dead to the living in sleep and in other visions palpably and providentially by the will of God have been, are, and will be. Here, for example, are two cases which cannot be doubted, two visions of the dead in dreams by the living that bear witness to the change for the better in their condition beyond the grave through the prayers of the Church and the intercession that was made known in the visions. Together with the vision of the freed dead person, the reason for his improvement was also given, a reason hitherto quite unknown. These two grace-filled revelations of the salvation of two departed persons took place not long before the time of writing this book. The first revelation gives witness to liberation from the torments of Hades in which the dead sinner had already been kept and tells how he was granted the kingdom of heaven together with all the Saints through the untiring intercession of his relatives; the second recounts the forgiveness of sins of a man through the intercession of his widow in whom the Apostolic words, "How knowest thou, O wife, whether thou shalt save thy husband?" (I Corinthians 7:16) were fulfilled.

Below we have written out the content of these revelations from their sources.

In the magazine "Strannik" ("The Wanderer," May 1862, page 263), there was published a revelation shown to Fr. Seraphim, one of the schema-monks of Mt. Athos. "The reason I entered the monastic life," as he began his account, "was a dream vision of the lot of sinners after death. After an illness of two months, I came to a state of extreme weakness. In this state I saw two youths who had come into my room; they took me by the hands and said, 'Follow us'. Not feeling my illness, I rose, looked at my bed, and saw my body lying peacefully on it; then I realized that I had left earthly life and must go into the world beyond the grave. I recognized the youths as angels and set off with them. I

was shown the fiery places of torment, and I heard the cries of those who suffered there. The angels, showing me which fiery place was for which sin, added:
'Unless thou cast aside thy sinful ways, this too shall by thy place of punishment!'
After this one of the angels seized a man out of the flame, and he was black as
coal, all burnt, and in chains from head to foot. Then both angels approached the
sufferer, removed his fetters, and at once all his blackness varnished; he became
clean and bright like an angel. Then the angels vested him in gleaming robes.
'What does this change in the man mean?' I ventured to ask the angels. 'This
is a sinful soul,' they replied, 'that was cut off from God because of his sins and
was to have burned eternally in this flame; but meanwhile his parents gave much
alms and commemorated him much at the Liturgies, held Pannikhidas;[20] and
so for the sake of parental love and the prayers of the Church, God has shown
mercy, and the sinful soul has been granted complete pardon. He is delivered
from eternal torment and now stands before the face of his Lord and will rejoice
with all His Saints.' When the vision ended, I came to myself, and what did I see
but people standing around me weeping and preparing my body for burial."

In *A Description of the Signs and Healings in 1863 from the Athonite Sanctuary
in Russia,* there was appended a lithographed letter addressed to the Athonite
priestmonk Arseny on December 21, 1863, of the following content:

"We sorrowed greatly," thus begins the nun Mother Dosithea of the Convent of the Saviour in Simbirsk, "over the death of our brother M. N. Chego-
daev which occurred in 1861 in Samara, and the more so because his death
was sudden, without a last confession and communion of the Holy Mysteries.
But then I had a dream, in which my late brother and I seemed to be walking together through some wonderful place. We came up to a new, seemingly
recently built village at the entrance to which there was a new, tall wooden cross,
and as one left the village there was a house of wonderful beauty, also new. As
we approached it, my brother said to me with a joyous look, 'See what a rich
village I recently bought, and for this purchase I am very, very much indebted
to my wife Tashenka;[21] she should be written to and thanked for the kindness
she did me.' 'And may I, brother, go inside your wonderful house and feast my
eyes on it?' He answered, 'Thou mayest; let us go and see how good everything
is in it'. Suddenly there turned up his wife, Princess Tatiana Nikiforovna, whom
my brother began to thank for everything she had done for him bowing to the
earth before her. The meaning of this dream soon became apparent. I received
a letter from Tatiana Nikiforovna in which she informed me that the Lord had

[20]Dirges, memorial services for the dead.
[21]Diminutive of the name "Tatiana."

helped her arrange for eternal commemoration of her husband, my brother, on the holy Mt. Athos when a venerated icon from the St. Panteleimon monastery on Athos was brought to Samara."

Can one not see in these two examples the exact fulfillment of the words of the Lord Jesus Christ: "If ye pray, then truly I say to you, all that ye ask in prayer, believe, that ye shall receive, and it shall be unto you."

In the magazine "Strannik," December 1864, page 125, there is an account of a dream that told of the improvement in the state of a dead person. In a certain village, an elderly chanter suddenly died. He had a son who was a civil servant. The unexpected death of his father shocked the son; the status of his father in the next world gave the good son no peace for almost a year. Having heard from acquaintances that at the Liturgy the most important time for the commemoration of the departed is during the singing of the chant "We hymn Thee, we bless Thee . . . ," when he was in church on the Monday of the Holy Spirit,[22] at this very point in the service, the mournful son prayed to God with particular devotion for the repose of his father. And what should happen? That night he saw his father in a dream, making three prostrations to him and at the third saying, "I thank thee, my son."

Like the Old Testament Church, so too the New Testament Church teaches and will continue to teach the possibility of certain sinners who believe in Christ the Saviour and offered repentance at death, but did not have time to show the fruits of repentance, being saved and delivered from eternal torment in Hades through the intercession of the Church and of the living who knew the deceased. Convinced of the truth of the aforementioned grounds, the Church firmly believes and therefore teaches her members to intercede before God for their departed fathers, mothers, brethren, sisters, spouses, children, friends, acquaintances and, by the law of love, in general for all Christians to whom the Lord Himself promised remission of sins beyond the grave to all those who die in faith and hope.

Thou, O Lord, having joined us by an eternal love, dost not cut us apart even in death; and setting a boundary of repentance at our departure from this passing life, demandest the prayers of the living for the dead, prayers for their sins. We believe, O Lord, that Thou givest unto them that ask of Thee; therefore through the prayers of those on earth for them that have passed into the world beyond the grave, Thou showest Thy mercy. Let us help one another, those on earth helping them that have passed into the next world, by means of acts pleasing unto God before that dread hour shall come when help availeth no more.

---

[22]The day after Pentecost, or "Whit-Monday," kept as a special feast day.

True, timely help surely brings a beneficial result: this is truth. Therefore St. John of Damascus writes, "Let us help one another and offer God, who loves brotherhood and is good and merciful unto souls, sacrifices of brotherly love. For He accepts them with great benevolence and applies the prayers of relatives as a good report unto those that have died suddenly and without preparation. For the merciful Lord desires us to pray to Him about this and is benevolent in fulfilling the prayers of His creatures concerning salvation; He is moved especially when someone prays not only for his own soul's salvation but for that of another. For in doing this, one rises to the imitation of God in asking gifts for others as it were mercy for himself; and fulfilling the measure of perfect love, obtains bliss, doing at the same time a great good for his own soul and that of another *(Homily on the Faithful Departed)*.

Further on, he also writes that the goodness and mercy of God will overcome the judgment of sin until Doomsday. Sin brings judgment, but repentance evokes the goodness of God. There is no sin that cannot be erased by penitence; but repentance has a time limit after which it no longer is possible. Blessed is he that strives for his own salvation, but more blessed is he that strives, not for his own, but for that of another. "For this is more pleasing and acceptable unto the merciful Lord that each should try to help his neighbor. God who is merciful desires that each of us do well unto others both in life and after death; for otherwise He would not have given us the occasion to pray for the departed at the Unbloody Sacrifice or to observe the third, ninth, fortieth, anniversary, and other days assigned by the Church for special prayers for the dead ..." (ibid.)

2. The Meaning of the Present Life of the Living inRelation to the Life of the Dead Beyond the Grave

This age (Matthew 12:32) of which the Saviour speaks is the entire expanse of time from His birth according to the flesh on earth until His second and glorious advent to judge the living and the dead. Thus the term "this age" means, for the entire Christian world as a whole and for each Christian in particular, the present earthly life. But "the age to come" (Matthew 12:32), in the words of the Saviour, signifies that endless expanse of time—or eternity—which each person enters after death. In general, the words "this age" signify all the time until the glorious second coming of Christ for judgment, and "the age to come" signifies the endless time after the general judgment of Christ. In the strict sense, eternity is time without beginning and without end (for example, God is eternal), but for the works of God's hands, eternity has its beginning. With their creation eternity opens up for them, and therefore properly speaking eternity begins for each person in the mother's womb from the moment of receiving life. Consequently, eternity for each person consists of three periods: being in the mother's womb, being in the world, and being beyond the grave. This age of which the Saviour speaks is the second period of eternity, and the age to come is the third period of eternity. In the first period the human being takes on a proper form and is prepared unconsciously for the second; in the second, however, he is consciously prepared, or develops himself, for the third period, that of existence beyond the grave. "Seek ye the kingdom of God and His righteousness" (Matthew 6:33): this is the commandment of the Lord Jesus Christ; but man is obliged to seek the kingdom of God and His righteousness not only for himself exclusively, but for all people as well, for all members of the kingdom of Christ, both on earth and beyond the grave. This is the fulfillment of the main commandment of love which serves as the foundation of the entire law.

The goal of the present life is heaven, union with God, eternal bliss; this is the destination of the Christian. "Love one another, be merciful one to another as your heavenly Father is merciful," teaches the God-man; and the Holy Spirit reveals visible methods, means, expressing love and mercy toward others, not only those on earth, but those also that have passed beyond the grave. A proper use of these means gives heaven to those of our departed who themselves did not manage, while on earth, to attain the goal of their life and to whom the words of Jesus Christ, "it shall not be forgiven in this world or the next" (Matthew 12:32) do not refer.

All the means for asking forgiveness of the sins of a dead sinner, means revealed by God Himself, serve as evidence of the possibility of lightening the state of the sinner beyond the grave, if only the deceased be worthy of them and if the living use them properly as the word of God bears witness: "They ask ill, therefore they do not receive" (James 4:3), or "Not everyone that saith to Me, 'Lord, Lord!' shall enter the kingdom of heaven" (Matthew 7:21), or "With their lips they honor, but their heart is far from Me, they honor Me in vain" (Matthew 15:8–9) and others. If God did not desire to save certain sinners, then He would not have given the means; and if He has given the means, then is this not obvious proof that He wishes to save them? And so, the first and main means of extending real help to our departed is this age, our own present life, founded on true faith in Jesus Christ.

If Jesus Christ Himself bore witness that sins are forgiven through one's own repentance of them here on earth, in this age, and if it is evident from His words that sins are forgiven in the age to come beyond the grave, sins that do not constitute blasphemy against the Holy Spirit, even though beyond the grave there is no more repentance for the dead, nor works of mercy, or of repentance, one can conclude that forgiveness of sins after death takes place only by the endless mercy of God. God's mercy has chosen the prayers of the Church, and the prayers and works of mercy done by the living, as the instrument of salvation of the departed. The living have the commandment to love, to pray, to bear the burdens of others, and to seek the kingdom of God both for themselves and for others regardless of where the others might be: on earth or in the other world. In other words, this age, or the present life of each of those still on earth, is a gift of God, a talent,[23] to be used for the benefit of oneself and one's neighbor, a means to change the condition of certain sinners in the other world. For this purpose the present age is given us. The meaning of this present age for the entire Christian world is set forth by the Saviour in the parable of the Rich Man and Lazarus (Luke 16) where the bond of love and the mutual relationship of this world and that beyond the grave are expressed by Abraham, Lazarus, the unfortunate rich man in Hades, and his brethren on earth. This age, which is to continue until the second coming of Christ, is a bond and mutual relationship between those on earth and those who have passed beyond the grave. At the judgment of the world only Christians will be judged, and the interval of time between the individual judgment and the universal has the purpose of showing in deed that we are Christians, that we live for God and neighbor, that we live for heaven.

Having passed beyond the grave, neither the righteous nor the sinner receives an immediate recompense which is to be given to the complete man, that is, after the reunion of the soul and body which will occur at the resurrection of the body. For this reason, according to the teaching of our Church, the righteous are in a state of preliminary bliss, and the sinners in a state of preliminary torment. Among the sinners in Hades there are those whose fate is not finally determined and who undergo some torment, as having offered only repentance on earth but not justified it by deeds. The secret of life beyond the grave for both the righteous and the sinner, but only till Judgment day, is revealed by the Saviour in this parable. The inner connection and mutual relationship of the next world and this will continue till the general Judgment of Christ. Jesus Christ Himself expressed all of this in the parable of the Rich Man and Lazarus. Let us cite a few passages from the commentary by Bishop Nikifor of Astrakahn and Stavropol on this parable (*Commentary on the Sunday Gospels,* Volume 2, Twenty-second Sunday [after Pentecost]): "The great and righteous Abraham carries on a short conversation, filled with love and compassion, with the rich

[23]In the Biblical sense—as in Matthew 25:15.

man who is a great sinner, addressing him as "my child." And so, the righteous are not wroth with sinners and do not hate them, but share their pain and sorrow at their state. Consequently the righteous in paradise see and recognize the condemned, just as those in torment see and recognize the righteous, known or unknown. That the sinners can see the bliss of paradise and its inhabitants has, in all likelihood, a definite reason, since it increases the suffering of the sinners: to the torments of Hades there are added the pangs of conscience, seeing the glory of the righteous. But the fact that the righteous can see Hades and its sufferers also has, in all likelihood, its reason: the righteous, seeing the condemned, sorrow and are filled with pity and mercy, and this sorrow decreases their joy and bliss. The purpose for this vision is so that the righteous might intercede and take concern for the salvation of the sinners. This vision will continue only till the universal resurrection when there will follow a complete recompense for both, perfect bliss or death, when the righteous will see the tormented no more nor the sinners the righteous."

Abraham says to the Rich Man, "they which would pass from hence to you cannot; neither can they pass to us, that would come from thence." Here it is evident that no one can of his own will pass from paradise to Hades nor from Hades to paradise; consequently, on the contrary, by the will of God, it is possible to go from Hades to paradise; God has the power to forgive an imperfect one his sins for any reason and to make him worthy of the kingdom of heaven. Here we have, as depicted by Jesus Christ, the state of the righteous and the imperfect beyond the grave in this intermediate period, and the significance of the present life of the living for the improvement of the state of certain sinners beyond the grave.

This age is an intermediate time between the two Advents of Christ, and the present life of every individual, consequently, is that time when Christ has come to save the world and not to judge it. The time for judgment is ahead: the age to come in which there follows the resurrection of the dead and the final resolution of the lot of every Christian beyond the grave. The fate of Christians in the life to come is not determined finally at their death, that is, at their passing into the world beyond the grave. The age to come has not yet dawned, and the Lamb of God Who takes away the sins of the world is daily sacrificed on Orthodox tables of oblation.[24] This sacrifice for the whole world while on the Cross reconciled man with God; the same, offered daily for the living and the dead, disposes the

---

[24]The reference is to the rite known as the *Proscomidé* held at the "table of oblation" where these words are pronounced at the cutting of the Eucharistic loaf, rather than on the altar table itself where the consecration will later take place.

Good One to mercy towards both, both being sinners. And so, on the basis of the nature of this intermediate time, the present age, the Orthodox Church teaches her members and herself prays at the offering of the Unbloody Sacrifice for all departed Orthodox Christians, pronouncing the names of some. Thus the purpose of this age is to obtain salvation in extending help for the salvation of others regardless of where they might be: on earth or in the next world. Our present life, despite all the sorrows it is filled with, should move the living to feel the greatest thanks to God for the possibility of asking forgiveness of sins for oneself and for the departed. How many joys and pleasures do we get merely from carrying out the desires of a beloved object despite all obstacles and failures! The desire to please someone we love also brings a feeling of joy. But what joy, not of this earth, should it bring the living to intercede for the dead who was once the object of love and respect! And now should not the striving to obtain the best possible for the departed, to console him—should this not bring the living, just as before, pleasure and spiritual joy? All of this is in the present life in which, despite its shortness, one can nevertheless do much. Chrysostom writes that this intermediate time expresses the boundless mercy of God towards the human race and gives those who have sinned or not believed the opportunity to wash away their shortcomings ("Homily 28" on the Gospel of St. John). For this reason the judgment has been postponed so as to give faithful humanity the opportunity of salvation. Jesus Christ Himself calls the present life "day" in which one should work, because, as He says, there will come the night (death), when no one can do good works. The Apostle Paul also calls our life an acceptable time, a day of salvation, because this time is designated for obtaining salvation for oneself and others, regardless of where they may be, on earth or beyond the grave. Having defined the meaning of the present life, the Apostle writes of its quality, appropriate to its meaning: "that we may lead a quiet and peaceable life in all godliness and honesty. For this is good and acceptable in the sight of God our Saviour, Who will have all men to be saved" (I Timothy 2:2–4).

Not all Christians pray to the same degree for their departed; some pray, others do not; some pray a true prayer joined to a life according to faith, while others pray only in words and show works opposite to their prayer: "with their lips they honor God, but their heart is far away." Thus not all who pray for the dead receive what they ask, just as not all the dead are found worthy of obtaining eternal salvation through the prayers of others.

Therefore those who pray and intercede truly and genuinely for the dead are instruments chosen by God to give help to certain dead who are worthy of the help of the living. Here is what St. John of Damascus says of God's choosing the living to intercede for the dead that are worthy of intercession: "After the death of such ones, the Lord will move their relatives, neighbors, and friends, will direct their thoughts and hearts and incline their souls to showing help" (*Homily on the Departed*). It is to be understood that for such true intercession, a true life is necessary. The purpose of our life is to extend the hand of help to others both here and in the next world. To love one's neighbor truly, with a pure heart, is natural for man, and this love should have its foundation in love for God. Without love for God, it is impossible to love one's neighbor. Truly loving God as the Apostle Paul teaches (Hebrews 10:35–39), we can have every hope that for our love to Him God will preserve those also who are dear to our heart, for He never wants to bring sorrow to those who love Him.

3. Intercession by Those Still on Earth for Those That Have Passed into the World Beyond the Grave—Prayer

Everything has its foundation, its reason: there is no action without cause. If we were certain that our offerings would not be accepted, that our petitions would be refused, would we so much as ask? Hardly. This is the truth. Hence the reverse is that since we are asking, we have some foundation that allows us to ask: "Ask"—and hope will receive what it asks in greater or lesser degree—"it shall be given you." The malefactor expects punishment for his crime; he knows that complete pardon is impossible, and therefore he does not ask it.

The spirit of man which is of divine origin and which makes him live knows its source and therefore turns to it. This turning of man to the Higher Being manifests itself in all stages of his development; this means that the spirit of man has in itself some basis for asking its Higher Being and for receiving that which it asks. The Hebrews had their basis for asking—the law of God Himself, while we Christians affirm our hope, our foundation on our Intercessor with God, the Lord Jesus Christ. On what did those who did not know the True God base their petitions? They, too, were not without basis in offering their sacrifices. Is there a single people on earth that did not have a divinity to which their mind and heart turned? There is no rule without exception, no family without its black sheep, and it is not surprising that among humanity there are those that do not know or have a God. Not all are healthy; there are the sick too.

Prayer for the dead is one of the works of mercy and includes as it were two virtues: prayer as a service to God, and the fruit of the prayer—the benefit afforded to the dead. Hence prayer for the dead is a work of devotion and a work of mercy. Jesus Christ Himself taught us that without Him we can perform no good work: "Without Me ye can do nothing" (John 15:5). To obtain God's mercy for oneself or others, either the living or the dead, is the natural striving of the human spirit expressing for the most part the will of God.

Prayer, according to the teaching of the Apostle and the Church universal, is the action of the Holy Spirit abiding in man. Hence if, as we said, turning to mercy is an expression of the will of God, then prayer for the dead, as a turning to mercy, expresses the will of God; and the Spirit of God Himself intercedes for us with ineffable yearning.

Our God is a God of the living and not of the dead; "if we live, or if we die, we are the Lord's," and "before God all are alive." The strength and effect of prayer spreads itself beneficially over the soul for whom it is raised up by the will of God regardless of where that soul might be located, on earth or beyond the grave. These souls are members of one great house, one spiritual body, having therefore one and the same nature, the same laws, the same purpose in existing, and therefore naturally they take active interest in one another's condition. The possibility and the form of benefit from our prayers for the dead was splendidly elucidated by St. Ephrem the Syrian in his testament in which he says that the dead have the same sympathy for the living when they pray for them as there is in nature between fruits. Thus, when the grape vine ceases its flowering in the field, at the same time the wine in houses undergoes fermentation. When certain garden vegetables planted in the ground are dormant, at that time the same vegetables kept in houses sprout.

To bear one another's burdens means to take a vital interest in the condition of another. As the Lord Himself took such a vital interest in us sinners that He took upon Himself all our sinfulness, as if guilty of all this before His Heavenly Father, and washed our sins in His blood and death; so we too, if the Lord took part in us, can we not take interest in our neighbors, asking salvation for them, can we not sacrifice for them all that we are able?

The power of prayer is beyond human comprehension. All is possible for one who prays. The history of the Old Testament and New Testament Church shows us the miracles of prayer. "Prayer," as St. Dimitri of Rostov writes, "is the key to heavenly treasures." "There is no such thing," writes one of the Holy Fathers, "as that which cannot be obtained by prayer to God, if only the thing asked for be good and asked for becomingly. Our sins are the main reason why our prayers do not reach their goal. Prayer should be raised up in contrition and repentance of sins. The Lord has been attentive to the heartfelt prayers of sinners also, but only when they prayed with penitence and heartfelt contrition for their sins.

Love, the first of all virtues, is love for God and neighbor; it includes fulfillment of the entire law. God is love and demands from His creation, man—who bears the image of God—sincere love towards others: "Love one another" ... "He that abides in love abides in God" (I John 4:8, 16).

Man was created for eternity, and the divine feeling of love cannot be temporary: love does not die.

He that abides in God abides in love. Love is expressed by visible signs. Prayer is an expression and at that, the true expression of pure Christian love. Prayer should be combined with love, faith, and hope which, according to St. Paul, will not bring to shame or mislead; and he that firmly places his hope in God will receive what he asks through the Lord Jesus Christ, our one sure Intercessor; Whatsoever we ask of God, He will do. (John 15:7; 1 John 5:14–15). For God to hear our prayer, according to the witness of the Prophet and Seer of God, Moses, we must abide in the fear of God. For our prayer to be effective we need 1) deep faith in God, 2) a devout life, and 3) piety, diligence, and humility in prayer. One of the elders was wont to say that for our prayer to fly unto God give it two wings: fasting and alms.

On God's part, all has been done for our salvation. Grace alone will do nothing for us without our participation, to the extent of our ability, in the work of our salvation. The Lord Jesus Christ said that God does not wish the death of a sinner, but wishes to save him, and for his salvation our cooperation is needed. He said, "Ask and it shall be given you; seek first the kingdom of God, and ye shall find it." There is no vanity for the disciples of Christ, His followers. To desire something for oneself is to desire it at the same time for all members of the body of Christ. Therefore "Seek the kingdom of God not for yourselves only, but for all members of My Church," which is made up of those still on earth, as well as those that have passed on into the world beyond the grave in faith and hope of resurrection. Whoever believes only prays; the unbeliever has no one to pray to and nothing to pray for. Prayer is the fruit of faith.

The Lord Jesus Christ taught us by showing in action that there are no dead in the proper sense of the word, that beyond the grave they live. At the foundation of the Christian life lies love which we are commanded to express not only in words but in deeds as well. The Apostles showed deeds expressing love, prayer for the members of the Church, and the bearing of one another's burden.

The Orthodox Church prays for the whole world, for all people, and only for the Orthodox[25] who in faith and hope have passed into the world beyond

---

[25]That is, in *public* prayer. *Privately* we pray for everyone: St. Gregory's prayers for the pagan emperor Trajan were answered.

the grave. It is enough only to believe in God, to be convinced of the truth of prayer for the repose of souls. If I forget he who has died, forget my relationship to him, then in what way shall I show that I loved him when he was on earth with me? If in truth I loved him when he was alive, then is it possible to stop loving him when he is dead? This does not make good sense.

To entreat the Divinity for mercy is the inheritance of all humanity of all times. The faith of Christ demands of Christians just such a seeking of mercy, of intercession before God through Christ, intercession both for oneself and for all the members of the Church. Only whilst abiding on earth man prepares himself for his future beyond the grave. The Church teaches that after death there is no repentance, there are no more means for the dead person to improve his state; only the living, in this case through the grace given by God, can help the dead by prayer. If it is a great achievement of virtue to sustain and save the present life of another, then how great is the accomplishment of obtaining for him life eternal, of seizing him from Hades, of saving one beloved unto the Lord Himself?

A friend is recognized in need. Can one imagine a greater need for the soul than the need of a sinful, imperfect soul beyond the grave?

See what a significance the one who prays for the dead takes on before God and the departed. To bury the bodies of the dead is a good work and belongs to all humanity. But in Christianity this good work calls for due honor as becomes a temple of the Holy Spirit. And so, burying the dead is common to all humanity, but prayer for the dead is the act of those who know the true God, the source of love and life. We do not know who is right or who is guilty before God, and we cannot know. God alone knows this. We know one thing: that all people are sinners. "There is no man who shall live and not sin," as the word of God testifies; "None is pure of stain, even if his life on earth is but one day" (Job 14:4). We know that all of us are conceived, born, and live in sins, and go into the next world incompletely cleansed of them. Only one thing remains for the living—carrying out that which was commanded: love towards all and prayer for all. The Giver of life and of remission of sins said Himself, "Ask and it shall be given you; I seek not the death of a sinner!" He Himself taught us to pray for this as follows: "And forgive us our trespasses!" This prayer was given us by the Lord Himself, and serves as the basis for all our prayers, including prayer for the repose of souls in which remission of sins is asked for the deceased. The coinciding of the words in the Lord's Prayer and in that for the repose of souls enables us to conclude that prayer for the departed is based on the Lord's Prayer. Further this forgiveness is asked for "us," that is, for the members of the Church of Christ. And where are these members? They are both on earth, and beyond the grave. "In the name of Jesus every knee shall bend, in heaven, and on earth, and in the abyss": if they bend the knee in adoration, then true worship of God involves full love to neighbors and even to enemies. If so, then those in heaven pray for those in the uttermost depths and on earth; those on earth pray to those in heaven and pray for those in the abyss. All those in heaven, on earth, and in the abyss as well pray to the God of all, calling out to Him through Jesus Christ: "Our Father!" As soon as He had committed this prayer to His disciples, Jesus Christ made this consoling conclusion: "Amen, Amen I say unto you: all that ye ask of God in prayer with faith in My name, ye shall receive."

4. The Church and Her Intercession

Prayer for the dead is a doctrine of the Orthodox faith. (Archbishop Anthony, *Dogmatic Theology*, Section 353, "Relationship to the Imperfect Departed, p. 255).

The teaching of our holy Orthodox Church concerning the life of the dead beyond the grave, the unbroken inner spiritual bond and mutual relationship between the living and the dead, and the visible expression of this bond and relationship that characterizes Christian involvement by the living in the state of the dead, all of this comprises one of the doctrines of Orthodoxy.

Loving one's departed, burying, and finally interceding for them before God are concepts common to all humanity in all times and places, concepts common to the human race; but their expression in the visible forms of love, burial, and intercession have not been the same among various people and at various times. The rules of the experienced holy men Tobit and Sirach, indicating the commemoration of the dead, were kept in the Old Testament Church and were known at the time when the Saviour came to earth for the salvation of the human race and the establishment of His Church. Although in the words and acts of the Saviour we do not find words directly affirming the obligation of commemorating the dead, yet at the same time we do not see acts contradicting this custom, as was the case, for example, with the concept of the Sabbath. The Saviour's teaching on the Sabbath seems to have gone against the ancient custom; thus also the ancient commemoration took on a new character. The Sabbath and the commemoration of the dead should be marked by works of mercy, works that bring man closer to God. If the commemoration of the dead were needless, then the Saviour would not have failed to find some occasion to say, "Ye err! Ye know not what ye ask!" But in such a case He only said to the living man who had asked first to bury his father and then to follow the Lord, "Follow

Me, and proclaim the kingdom of God; I am the life and the resurrection."The holy Apostles, the disciples closest to Christ, themselves prayed for the dead and by their example taught others to observe this duty towards the departed. Thus St. James, the kinsman of the Lord and first bishop of Jerusalem, St. Basil the Great, and St. John Chrysostom in their Liturgies prayed for the dead and have left us their prayer. St. Dionysius the Areopagite (*On the Church Hierarchy*, Chapter 6) bears witness that after the decease of the Apostles, prayerful commemoration of the dead was in use in church and in private.

If prayer is an expression of the will of God, then what would be the strength of this prayer by the whole Church, of all members of the house for one and the same object? Here is an example of the prayer of the Church with its beneficial effect on the soul. The holy Apostle Peter, through the prayers of the Church, during the night before he was to have been convicted, was led out of prison by an angel, unseen by anyone; the fetters fell away, and the guards near him heard nothing (Acts 12). Hence one can naturally conclude that prayer should have an equally beneficial effect on souls beyond the grave. The Church has always prayed for the departed and will do so till the Second Coming of the Lord to earth. At every church service, of which there are three, Matins, Liturgy, and Vespers,[26] the Church prays for both the living and the departed. The Church's aim is to sanctify man, to make him a participant in eternal, blessed life. Her concern for the lot of her members is alike for all: she is concerned for the salvation of both the living and the dead. St. Chrysostom calls this commemoration an apostolic ordinance and a command of the Holy Spirit. It is especially important that this dogma (the commemoration of the departed) is closely connected in the Orthodox Church with the Liturgies of St. Basil the Great and St. John Chrysostom in which the departed are commemorated three times: 1) at the Proscomidé,[27] 2) after the Gospel,[28] which proclaims unto all present the glad tidings of salvation of all who believe in Christ and of the remission of sins for all through Christ; immediately the deacon or priest intones the augmented litany, in which, in the tenth petition,[29] the Church sends up to God a prayer

[26]By this is meant three assemblies or gatherings for worship: early morning, later morning, and evening. In fact there are several other individual church services besides those named in the text.

[27]This is the preparation of the Eucharistic elements, the bread and wine that will be consecrated, at which the names of the living and dead are remembered in prayer by the priest. Because of the large number of names usually read, this part of the service came to be anticipated (held before the outward beginning of the Divine Liturgy). This commemoration is generally inaudible.

[28]Or after the Gospel and homily [sermon], if the local custom is for a homily to be given at this point.

[29]Today there are some variations in the text and the number of petitions.

for the departed thus: "We pray to the Lord for the Orthodox Patriarchs, for pious kings and devout queens . . . ,"[30] bearing witness to the unity and communion of the whole Church. This petition is said at the Liturgy, not only for all the departed who are close to us, but also those buried nearby, as well as all the departed no matter where they are buried—while at other services the petition mentions only the builders of the church whom the Church calls truly blissful and worthy of eternal memory—and for our fathers and brethren. After the augmented litany, at once there is pronounced[31] a special litany for the departed only. And, finally, 3) after the consecration of the Holy Gifts, the Church prays for the departed.[32] At evening church services the Church also prays for the dead, expressing in prayer the union, bond, relationship, and communion with them. Morning church services are also not without prayers for those that have passed into the world beyond the grave.

The Church also assigns her members days on which the remembrance of the departed is especially appropriate, that is: the third, ninth and fortieth days after the death of a member. St. Dimitri of Rostov writes, "The prayer of the Church and the offering of the Unbloody Sacrifice intercede and entreat the good God for the deceased" (*Homily at the Burial of Griboyedov*, part V, p. 110).

The Church prays for all her members, regardless of where they might be, on earth or beyond the grave, and the strongest means that she has for the salvation of her members is the Unbloody Sacrifice daily offered at the Liturgy. Divine services are divided into private (home worship) and public, or church services. Public or church services are those celebrated in church at the gathering or assembly of the faithful according to an established order or rite under the direction of a priest. The members of the Church are obliged to take part in public worship. Public services comprise Vespers, Matins, Night Vigil, the Hours, the Divine Liturgy, public or church Molebens,[33] and Pannikhidas on days of commemoration of the departed.

The Holy Church expresses her attitude to her members or children with concern, with solicitude for their wellbeing and salvation; the goal of all sacraments and church worship services is man's salvation.

---

[30]The text of the petition continues, "for the founders of this holy house, and for our fathers and brethren gone to their rest before us, and the Orthodox here and everywhere laid to rest."

[31]But not on Sundays or feasts—only on ordinary weekdays or at special Liturgies for the dead.

[32]This is the most ancient commemoration, found in all Liturgies, but it is usually inaudible.

[33]A *Moleben* is a general prayer service, popular in the Russian tradition, which can take many forms.

As soon as a person is born in the society of Christians, the Church in the person of the clergyman, hastens to him and his recuperating mother with a prayer to God that they may be kept and sanctified.

On the eighth day after childbirth, the Church gives the infant a name as a sign of his consecration to God and future obligations to Him and to the Church. On the fortieth day, the infant is brought into the church and over him is celebrated the rite of churching through which the newborn child is presented and led into the Church as her new member. At a time chosen by the parents, the sacrament of holy baptism is celebrated over the newborn. The Holy Church follows and hallows, as one might say, the whole life: the entire activity of man and all the more important moments of his life are sanctified by sacraments, celebrated under the aegis of the Mother Church. Concerned about her members on earth, the Church sees them off on their journey home, the Home of their heavenly Father; she does not forget them after they have passed into the life beyond the grave; her prayers for the dead are a clear sign of an unbroken spiritual bond of love.

The Holy Church, at each of her services, prays daily for those who abide on earth and does not forget them that have passed on to the world beyond the grave. Like the former, so too the latter are her members, her children; she is equally concerned for the salvation of both. Prayer in church is ecclesiastical prayer; prayer at home is private prayer. Prayer for the departed can therefore be either public or private, and one should pray for the departed everywhere and at all times. Departed sinners themselves, from Hades, having received pardon of their sins through the prayers of the Church and relatives still on earth, have appeared to the living on earth and borne witness of the change for the better in their otherworldly state, of their placement in the land of the living.

The aim of commemoration is to ask for pardon of sins for the departed and for the kingdom of God as promised by the Saviour Himself: "Seek the kingdom of God and His righteousness before all." There is only one means of our salvation for both the living and the dead: Jesus Christ and His sacrifice on the Cross which He offered for us. His blood cleanses our sins and consequently brings us life eternal. Without Christ there is no salvation; only "he that believeth in Him [whether alive or departed] shall live forever" (John 6:47).

a) The Liturgy

If the prayer of one man, Moses, asking mercy for an entire people, was so strong, then what should be said of the prayer of the whole Church, of all the faithful in Christ; and at that a prayer accompanied by the most powerful means of cleansing sins—the Unbloody Sacrifice—offered for the sins of all and consequently also for the departed, as they too are members of the Church of Christ. Those that abide on earth and those that have passed on into the world beyond the grave, as faithful in Christ, have Him as an intercessor before God as St. Paul bears witness: "For there is one God, and one mediator between God and men, the man Christ Jesus" (I Timothy 2:5). He is the mediator before God for all that are faithful to Him; He is both the sacrifice and the priest (Hebrews 7:17): His priceless blood shed for sinners cries out without ceasing to God the Father and Judge for clemency. Our every prayer to God, therefore also the prayer for our departed that are close to us and not found to be in mortal sins, can be strong and effective only when it is raised up in the name of Jesus Christ (John 14:14). He reconciled us with God and redeemed us from every sin when He offered Himself—His body and His own blood—to Him on the Cross as a sacrifice for mercy (Hebrews 9:14,26; 10:10). In the sacrament of the Eucharist to this day there is offered to God that same mercy sacrifice (John 6:51), the same precious Body of our Redeemer is broken for the life of the world, the same precious Blood is shed for the remission of sins (Matthew 26:26–28; Luke 22:19–20). Thus our prayer, both for the living and for the dead, is especially strong when it is joined to the offering of the Unbloody Sacrifice for all.

The strength of the Unbloody Sacrifice, which the priest can offer at the request of every Christian for his deceased ones, cleanses the sins of those who have died with repentance, in faith, and hope of the resurrection and eternal life.

According to the teaching of the Holy Fathers and Doctors of the Church, the most effective way of obtaining mercy from God and improving the lot of the departed beyond the grave, is the Unbloody Sacrifice offered for their repose.

For the cleansing of sins of the souls that are in Hades, and so for their release from thence, primarily it is the celebration of the Divine Liturgy that gives help. At the Liturgy, particles of bread are immersed in the Mystic Blood of Christ, symbolizing the washing of sins of the living and the dead; they are washed by this Blood which, according to the Apostle, "shall purge your conscience from dead works to serve the living God" (Hebrews 9:14). At the Liturgy, at this greatest of sacred services, Jesus Christ Himself is both the priest and the sacrifice (Hebrews 7:17,27), or in the expression of Saints Basil the Great and John Chrysostom, He is both "the Offerer and the Offered"; or, according to the teaching of St. John, He is "the advocate to the Father, and the propitiation for our sins" (I John 2:1–2). Chrysostom writes: "With such a great and powerful sacrifice, how can one not propitiate God for the dead, when it is Christ Himself, in the person of the celebrant, Who offers this sacrifice?"

Let us look at those passages in the Divine Liturgy in which the intercession of the Church for the dead is most evident. The celebrant bears the image of Jesus Christ, praying for the people and offering God a propitiatory sacrifice for their sins. During the Proscomidé, the first part of the Divine Liturgy, during the reading of the Hours, the celebrant makes remembrance of the entire Church (symbolized on the discos [paten] by particles cut from the third, fourth, and fifth prosphoras), commemorates the Saints who have been glorified (canonized), and prays for the living and the dead.

In the middle of the discos is placed the part taken from the first prosphora in memory of our Lord, God, and Saviour Jesus Christ, as the Lamb of God slain for the sins of the world. Around the Lamb (called the "Host" in Western parlance), as if gathered around their Redeemer, Head, and King, is all of His Church. Christ is our justification; His merits intercede for us before the Heavenly Father; He is the living, fruitful Vine, and we are the branches, through faith and holy Baptism grafted into this Vine by the grace of the Holy Spirit. From that day when, through the sacrament of holy Baptism, we were joined to Christ, all we believers in Christ became members of the one body of Christ; all as members of the one body have one Head, Christ; all have one life force, the Holy Spirit. This Spirit invisibly embraces and penetrates the whole Body of the Church and all Her members so long as they remain in union with Her; and acts in each member according to the degree of their acceptance, that is, to the extent that they are willing to follow the leadership of saving grace. At His right hand is placed the particle of the second prosphora which symbolizes the Queen and Birthgiver of God. At the left side of the Lamb, like the nine ranks of angels which stand before the Lord, nine particles from the third prosphora stand for the nine ranks of Saints. Below, in two rows, particles of the fourth, and fifth prosphoras symbolize those who have not yet attained full perfection and union with the Lord, the living and the departed in Orthodox faith. As they represent members of the Church, these particles are not cut out for communion, but to signify their communion with the Lord and among themselves. These particles do not constitute a cleansing sacrifice for the souls for whom they are offered. The cleansing sacrifice for souls is the Body and Blood of the God-man Jesus Christ offered on the Cross and now offered at the Altar under the forms of bread and wine unto the cleansing of the sins of the whole world. The particles represent those people whose names have been brought forward in prayer, and therefore they are not consecrated into the Body of the Lord and are not given in communion to the people. These particles are offered by the Church so that by means of them those persons for whom they were cut might receive grace, consecration, and the remission of sins through the Holy Sacrifice offered for the purification of the whole world on the Altar; for the particles lie beside the Body of Christ and are later placed in the Chalice where all is filled with sanctification, and spiritual gifts are sent down upon those whose names were commemorated. The particles are placed in the Chalice so that they will be moistened with the Blood of Christ; thus 1) the Saints are shown as closely united with God for the greater glory and rejoicing in heaven; and 2) the living and the dead, washed in this most pure Blood of the Son of God, have received the remission of sins and inherit life eternal as shown by the words pronounced at this moment: "Wash away, O Lord, the sins of those commemorated here, in Thy precious Blood" (Ivan Dimitrievsky, *Explanation of the Liturgy,* Section 135, 13 and 14).

After the second part of the Divine Liturgy called the Liturgy of the Catechumens when the Lord Jesus Christ is already present on the holy Altar in His Body and Blood, the Church presents all her children to Him who is mystically present on the Altar as if to a king who has arrived: "For to this end Christ both died, and rose, that he might be Lord both of the dead and living" (Romans 14:9).

The Church presents 1) the Saints, recalling them and thanking God for them as having achieved perfection and a blessed union with God and as constituting Her beauty and greatness. The Church gratefully remembers and glorifies in secret[34] and then exclaims thankfully for all to hear, "Especially for our most holy ..."

2) Next the Church prayerfully presents those who have died in the hope of resurrection. Inaudibly they are remembered, and the Church asks the Lord to be mindful of them, forgive their sins, and give them rest in a place of light, a place where there is no pain or sadness nor sighing; thus, for example, during the singing of "It is truly meet to bless Thee, the Birthgiver of God," the priest entreats God for the forgiveness of sins of all who have died in faith and hope on God's mercy. For the departed, the Holy Gifts constitute a propitiatory and intercessory sacrifice (Mikhailovsky, *Explanation of Orthodox Church Services,* p. 46).

3) The Church secretly presents those living on earth to the Lord Who is present on the Altar in the sacrament of His Body and Blood; but some are

---

[34]That is, in the prayer which is read inaudibly by the celebrant.

commemorated aloud, beginning with the Royal Family[35] in the prayer "Among the first, remember O Lord …" "And each and every one," that is, men and women (*Christian Reading* for 1848, Part II, pp. 80–81).

Since those presented to a king and those who stand in his presence are usually rewarded by the joy of associating with him, so the members of the Church, presented in prayer to Christ the King, receive a joyful and grace-filled communion at the prepared table of His Body and Blood (ibid., p. 82).

After communion, the particles cut from the eucharistic loaves in honor of the Saints and the living and the dead are placed in the Chalice containing the Body and Blood of Christ, and thus all members of the Church, communicants of the Body and Blood of Jesus Christ, are mystically united in Him as the Mediator of God and man (ibid., p. 85).

That the Divine Liturgy is the first and main means for cleansing the sins of departed sinners in Hades, on this we have the witness of all the Holy Fathers, Doctors, and Church writers.

From the words of St. Proclus it is evident that the Liturgy was not composed by these great men (Basil the Great and John Chrysostom in the fourth century), but essentially the same divine suppers, on the model of the Last Supper, were celebrated by the Apostles and their immediate successors. Basil the Great and John Chrysostom presented the Divine Liturgy in such a complete form that in later times the most inspired found nothing to change; a clear indication that in this they were guided not by human reason, but by that great mind whose seal leaves no place for the reason of man. Therefore the name "Divine Liturgy," besides the actual sacrament, belongs to it from the first to the last word. It is entirely divine in essence and in outward makeup (Belyustin, *Concerning Church Services,* p. 289).

The very first Christians were taught by apostolic example. Bringing their offerings (for the offertory)[36] in the name of the living, relatives and friends made various offerings in the name of the dead as well, and their names were proclaimed along with those of the living. From the very beginning of Christian societies, all members of the Church, living and dead, had a part in the presentation of offerings for the Holy Sacrifice. The living took part in body and spirit, the dead only in spirit (ibid., pp. 280–281).

[35] At this time (2005 A.D.) the Russian and other Orthodox thrones are vacant, and the exclamation mentions only the Church hierarchy. The civil authority is mentioned only in general terms.

[36] The Offertory, or Proscomide, at first was part of the Great Entrance procession, but later came to be anticipated before the service, as today.

The Unbloody Sacrifice, offered for the dead, intercedes and entreats the most Good God, as St. Dimitri of Rostov writes on this subject in his *Homily at the Burial of Griboyedov* (Part 5, p. 110). The Liturgy for the departed is the most powerful and effective means for asking the mercy of God for the dead. Can one not expect pardon and consolation for the criminal when on his behalf there is the intercession of the King's Son Himself? With undoubted hope one must expect that the Unbloody Sacrifice offered for all of our departed fathers, brethren, and sisters in the Lord will wipe away their sins, and that they will obtain the possibility of passing into a better state.

"We believe," write the Eastern Patriarchs in their *Confession of the Orthodox Faith* (Article 17), "that the Unbloody Sacrifice is the true propitiatory sacrifice offered for all who have lived and died in piety, and, as said in the prayers of this Mystery, it was given to the Church by the Apostles at the Lord's command for the salvation of all."

St. John the Merciful, Patriarch of Alexandria, himself often took concern for the sick, sat alongside the dying, helping with his prayers at the departure of the soul. He often celebrated the Divine Liturgy for the repose of souls saying, "The Divine Liturgy, celebrated for them that have died, is of great help to souls." In confirmation of this, he was wont to tell the event which took place in Cyprus.

The blessed Symeon, Metropolitan of Thessalonica, in his commentary on the Divine Liturgy, writes, "The particles bring to them for whom they were cut, manifold benefits; on this we have the tradition of the ancients. For the particles at the divine celebration represent those persons in whose name they are cut and for whom the sacrifice is offered. This is confirmed by the words of the priest at the proskomide: "Receive, O Lord, this offering at Thy heavenly altar.""

b) Days of Commemoration of the Dead, or Soul Saturdays

In the Church of Christ, every day the memory is kept of one or more Saints. Besides that, each day of the week is dedicated to a special remembrance; thus Saturday is dedicated to the memory of All Saints and the departed. Praying daily for the departed at every divine service, the Church demands that her members not forget their departed, that they pray as often and as intently as possible; but the Church demands especially prayers for the dead on Saturdays as days dedicated to the memory of All Saints and all the departed. Saturday was the Hebrew Sabbath, whose name means repose, rest. The Orthodox Christian Church dedicates this day to the memory of all those who have passed into the world beyond the grave, to the memory of the perfected (the Saints), and the imperfect whose lot has not yet been finally decided. The Church asks eternal rest for them from God, repose after an earthly life of many sorrows; and since Saturday, by God's own commandment, was set aside for God after six working days, thus may the life beyond the grave be an eternal Sabbath, a life in God, a day of rest and joy for those who have served the Lord on earth in fear. Besides the daily prayers and Saturday, there are also days in the year mainly dedicated to prayer for the departed. On all these days the Church, that is, all the faithful, have an especially vital involvement in the state of the departed.

These days are called Soul Saturdays and are divided into universal, general, and private Saturdays or local days of commemoration.

There are five universal Saturdays: Meatfare Saturday, the second, third, and fourth Saturdays in Lent, and Saturday, the eve of Pentecost. They go back to rules from apostolic times. The early Christians gathered at the cemeteries on these days, which is still done now, for the commemoration of the departed.

There are three local days of commemoration: 1) Monday or Tuesday after Thomas Sunday [Antipascha], that is, the first Sunday after Pascha; 2) August 29, the feast of the Beheading of St. John the Baptist, and 3) the Saturday of St. Dimitri or the Saturday before October 26, the date of the feast of St. Dimitri the Great Martyr. On the two last-mentioned, the Church for the most part prays for the repose of Orthodox soldiers and for all who have given their life for faith and fatherland.

1) SATURDAY IN MEATFARE WEEK

God did not deem that all should depart from earthly life in the same way. Various circumstances accompany the death of each individual. Not all are able to die at home, peacefully, amid family, friends, and with a priest to administer the Body and Blood of Christ to see them on their way. How many unforeseen, sudden deaths carry people off! How many have drowned in the sea, how many have burned in fires, how many have vanished without a trace when they lost their way in forests, in the mountains, the deserts; how many people have starved, frozen, been torn by beasts! Then epidemics, wars, evil people have swept so many from the face of the earth! Have all of these people someone left on earth to pray for them? And finally, do all those who remain on earth know the importance of prayers for the dead, and, at that, do all have the same opportunities to help the dead? These are the reasons that moved the Holy Fathers, on the basis of Apostolic tradition, to pray for the departed, besides each Saturday devoted to All Saints and the dead; also on certain other days of the year assigned entirely to common prayers for the dead who were not foreign to faith in Christ. The first such day of universal commemoration of the faithful departed is Meatfare Saturday. Why was this particular day chosen and not some other? We find the answer, first of all, in the character of Saturday as a day of rest and second, because the following day, Meatfare Sunday is the day when the Church commemorates the Second Coming of Christ and Doomsday; and as the living need God's mercy at the Judgment, so they precede this day with their own mercy towards the dead. At the same time, we also show that we have a close bond of love with all the members of the kingdom of Christ, with the Saints, the imperfect departed, and with those still abiding on earth; without this bond of love, salvation is impossible, and the battle of the living in keeping the fast is impossible. On this day, as on the last day of the world, the Church invites her members to common prayer for all that have died in faith, from Adam to this day; and each of those present prays not only for his own relatives and those close to his heart, but in general for all Christians who died in the true faith. This is the reason and the purpose for which this day was established, this Saturday of the last week before Cheesefare week when meat is not to be taken as food. The Saturdays before Meatfare Sunday and Pentecost are for the most part those spoken of as universal.

The establishment of this Soul Saturday dates to the early times of the Christian Church; this is stated in the Synaxarion[37] prescribed for this Saturday and confirmed in the order of church services laid out in the fifth century by St. Sabbas, on the basis of the most ancient tradition, and on the custom of early Christians to gather at the cemeteries on certain days to keep the memory of the dead, of which there is documentation from the fourth century (Chrysostom in "Homily 62" and "18." The service for Meatfare Saturday, and the Synaxarion for this Saturday).

11) SATURDAY BEFORE PENTECOST

As the concern of religion, the Church, and sacraments is the salvation of people, so the Church prays unceasingly for her members regardless of where they might be: on earth or beyond the grave. The Soul Saturday on Pentecost eve dates from the same period as does that on Meatfare Saturday. Just as before the commemoration of the last day of the world (on Meatfare Saturday) the Church intercedes for her imperfect members beyond the grave, so now before Pentecost, which symbolizes the first day of the kingdom of Christ revealed in power, the Church offers prayerful cleansing for the ignorances of the people

---

[37]That is, a reading at Matins on this day, explaining the observance.

and at the same time for the souls of the servants of God departed before us, asking for their repose in a place of coolness. "For the dead do not praise Thee, O Lord, neither do they who are in Hades dare to offer confession to Thee; but we, the living, bless Thee and pray and offer Thee sacrifices for their souls" (Prayer at Kneeling Vespers on Pentecost).

The beginning of the observance on this day is seen in the words of the Apostle Peter pronounced by him on the day of Pentecost where the Apostle speaks of the resurrected Saviour: "Whom God hath raised up, having loosed the pains of death" (Acts 2:24). In the *Apostolic Constitutions* it is said that the Apostles, filled with the Holy Spirit on the day of Pentecost, preached to the Jews and pagans about Jesus Christ, the Son of God, as the Judge of the living and the dead (Book V, Chapter 12).

III) THE SECOND, THIRD, AND FOURTH SATURDAYS IN GREAT LENT

The reason for the establishment of these Soul Saturdays is the spiritual effort in which Christians are then engaged. If, according to the teaching of the Apostle Paul, without love we are nothing then the very effort involved in the fast, if it is not accompanied by true mutual love, loses its meaning, and those who fast do not attain their goal: virtue loses its strength. Therefore, the Church is concerned that there be peace and love among all her members. Before taking up the Lenten effort, the Church had invited all her members on earth to show in deed that they abide in an unbroken bond of love and in communion with her members who are in the next world—with the Saints and with the imperfect departed. Continue the effort of the fast and to show that we in no wise depart from the commandment of the Founder of our Church, Jesus Christ: "Love one another," the Church calls her members to a universal commemoration of the faithful departed on the Saturdays of the second, third, and fourth weeks. And so, love is the basis for the establishment of these Saturdays. Another reason for their introduction is that on these days of Lent, except for Saturdays and Sundays, there is no Liturgy,[38] and the dead are, as it were, deprived of those boons they obtain from commemoration at the Liturgy. Thus the Church compensates for this by special prayers for the departed on the second, third, and fourth Saturdays in Lent. The remaining Saturdays in Lent, being dedicated to special commemorations, are not called Soul Saturdays, and prayers for the dead on them are according to the usual order.

[38]That is, no consecration of the Holy Gifts. The Liturgies that are celebrated on Lenten weekdays are called the *Presanctified*, because Holy Communion is given from the previous full Sunday Liturgy.

IV) TUESDAY AFTER THOMAS SUNDAY

The commemorations of the dead which the Church observes daily are discontinued during Holy Week and Bright (Easter) Week except at the Liturgy. At the Liturgy they continue as on other days;[39] but other commemorations, such as the reading of the Psalter over the deceased or the forty days memorial are not done during these two weeks.

It is not natural for the soul to be long dissociated from beings like unto itself, that is, from other souls. It shares its feelings, and this is a source of ease and joy. Conveying sorrow, it invites a being like unto itself to share its sorrow, and this gives a consolation beyond understanding. Likewise it hastens to share joy with others, again inviting to share in this. Since the soul exists not only for itself alone, but for the fullness of beings like itself, therefore according to the law that governs it, it cannot but rejoice with those that rejoice and sorrow with them that sorrow. And so, we have a joy in the Resurrection of our Lord Jesus Christ that nothing can exceed! The soul cannot hide this joy for itself alone. The Church has set apart Bright Week (the week following Easter Sunday, or *Pascha*) for the living to celebrate. But it is sad for a heart full of love, sad that there are beings close and dear, which nevertheless are not beside it; these are our departed ones. The Church, knowing our natural needs, has assigned to this end an encounter of the living with the dead for the sharing of the worldwide joy of salvation for all believers, a special day: the Tuesday after Thomas Sunday, the Sunday which by its very content corresponds to the spiritual communion of the living with the dead. "For what reason," asks St. John Chiysostom, "do our fathers now leave their houses of prayer in the cities and gather outside the city at the graves of their dead in the cemeteries? Because on this day Jesus Christ descended to the dead in Hades, to proclaim His victory over death" (Chrysostom's "Homily 62"). And therefore we too gather at the place where the dead are buried to celebrate together the common joy of our salvation.

These words of Chiysostom and the following teaching of St. Ambrose of Milan bear witness to the ancient origin of this commemoration of the dead after Easter, that is, Thomas Tuesday or Monday: "It is meet and right, brethren, after the feast of Pascha which we have celebrated to share our joy with the holy martyrs and to proclaim to them, as participants in the Lord's passion, the joy of the Resurrection of the Lord" ("Homily 77"). On Thomas Tuesday, or in some places on Monday, there are large gatherings, not in the usual houses but

---

[39]This means that the faithful departed are remembered at the Proscomidé and in the Eucharistic Canon, but not audibly for the congregation.

at the cemeteries. The living come and exchange the Paschal greeting with the dead, bringing with them decorated eggs which some, as they go home, leave on the graves.

Having shown the ancient origin of the custom of visiting graves and commemorating the departed after Easter, we should note that in the early Church all Christians were buried together, and among the martyrs other departed were buried as well ("Homily 77" of St. Ambrose of Milan). Chrysostom writes that the ancient Christians went to the graves or tombs of the holy martyrs and therefore to the graves of others also, just as today Christians visit cemeteries.

v) THE 29TH OF AUGUST

On this day the Church celebrates the Beheading of St. John the Forerunner and Baptist of the Lord. Sacred history bears witness to us that the Baptist suffered for the truth; and since Orthodox soldiers and in general all who have laid down their lives in battle for the faith, Tsar, and fatherland are like unto John the Baptist; therefore our Church celebrates a memorial for the most part only for those who have given their lives in battle. This day of commemoration was established in 1769, under the Empress Catherine II, during the war with the Turks and Poles.

In the order for the commemoration of Orthodox soldiers for August 29 it says, "This commemoration is to be celebrated by bishops, or in monasteries by the superior, and in other cathedrals by the senior priest in concelebration with the other clergy; in parish and village churches by the local clergy without fail."

vi) THE SATURDAY OF ST. DIMITRI

The Saturday before the feast of St. Dimitri the Great-Martyr (October 26) is added to the list of Soul Saturdays. Here is how and when this day of commemoration was introduced: the Grand Duke Dimitri Donskoy was born on October 26. During his rule, the prince of the Tartar Horde, Mamay, raised up the entire Horde against the land of Russia. Russia had a great Saint in the person of St. Sergius of Radonezh. The Grand Duke respected and honored the Saint and therefore came to him for advice: "Shall we go to battle against such a powerful enemy or not?" St. Sergius prayed, and then blessed the prince saying: "Thou, O Ruler, must take charge of the Christian flock entrusted thee, and with His help thou shalt obtain victory." At the same time he gave him two monks: Alexander and Andrew. At the battle of Kulikovo field, on September 8, 1380, the Grand Duke was the victor. This magnificent defeat of the Tartars came to mark the beginning of Russia's liberation from enslavement to them. Returning from the victory, the Grand Duke hastened to St. Sergius at the monastery of the Holy Trinity in Muscovy. Here, having held a commemoration of the soldiers that were killed, at the same time he proposed to the Church to hold an annual memorial for slain soldiers on the Saturday before the feast of his patron Saint, that is, October 26. From that time on, that Saturday has been added by the Russian Church to the Soul Saturdays, and Orthodox Christians on this day keep the memorial of their deceased relatives as on other days when the faithful departed are commemorated; they go to the cemeteries or they hold Pannikhidas in the churches.

VII) ROYAL DAYS OF COMMEMORATION

The established special days in the year for Royal Pannikhidas came about as follows. On June 21, 1584, the Grand Duke and Tsar Ioann Vasilievitch, with the blessing of Metropolitan Makary, established a common Pannikhida for deceased, devout princes, boyars, the Christ-loving military, the priestly and monastic order, and for all Orthodox Christians, "and commanded that this memorial be entered into the cathedral books" (*Acts of the Archeographic Expedition*, Volume I, 1836, Number 279) for which, in times of old in Russia, there was a special Pannikhida Ukase. For this reason, the list of deceased members of the Imperial Family commemorated on certain days begins with the Grand Duke and Tsar Ioann Vasilievitch (commonly called Ivan the Terrible) who reposed in 1584.

The Holy Synod prescribed how Royal Pannikhidas should be conducted on the days assigned to them in the register. The commemoration by bishops, monastery superiors, and other clergy was to be as follows: 1) Pannikhidas for the Emperors and Empresses and the Tsarevna Anna Petrovna should be celebrated by bishops and in monasteries by the head of the monastery on the days indicated in the register. Likewise, in the other cathedrals the superior priest should concelebrate with the other clergy and the clergy in parish churches; 2) celebration of Pannikhidas for rulers, Tsars and Tsarinas, and other high-ranking persons are left to the discretion of the bishops, only they must be celebrated, if not by a bishop, then by other clergy; in monasteries they should be celebrated by the superior and in other cathedrals and churches by the clergy for all members of the ruling family.

Only just reasons release bishops and pastors from the obligation of conducting memorials for the Royal Family. Such reasons are illness, absence due to urgent matters, and other like circumstances. The clergy of city cathedrals, external, and parish churches were to conduct such Pannikhidas monthly, that is, as many of such persons as names were indicated in a given month, but they must all be commemorated on the last days of each month, in one Pannikhida if desired.

If for some good reason this could not be carried out on those days, then by all means it was to be done on another day. When the commemoration of some member of the Royal Family occurred during Lent or on a Sunday or feast day then the memorial was to be conducted on the Saturday of that week.

But if the memorial of some member of the Royal Family fell in the days between Lazarus Saturday and Thomas Monday, that is, on Palm Sunday or during Holy Week or Easter week, then the memorial was to be done on Thomas Tuesday (Register of Memorials of the Royal Family).

5. Individual Intercession for the Departed by Relatives, Friends, and Acquaintances Remaining on Earth

Private worship services are what is performed by one individual or by one private society, at home or in church. Such services are the morning and evening prayers, among which there are prayers for the dead; the prayers before dinner and supper and after these meals, and the prayers at the beginning of any good work and after its conclusion. There are private services that are celebrated by a priest, such as the Pannikhida, the Moleben, or the Blessing of Waters.

If God desires the salvation of all men, then He desires to save the dead also, and therefore He commands the living only to follow Him. The living, following the Lord Jesus, have in Him the foundation for their hope that the dead, close to their heart, will be saved. The Lord Jesus Christ, faith in Him, and grace: these are the true and unashamed hope of the living for the salvation of the dead. The possibility of saving repented, deceased sinners who are, however, in Hades was given by the Destroyer of Hades Himself Who led out from thence those that believed in His advent to earth. If, after His resurrection, the Lord brought worthy souls out of Hades with Him, then why now, when there has not yet been a final judgment and when life and death are in His power and the keys to Hades are in His hands, should He not be able to save sinners who are worthy of this? As at the time of His resurrection, so also now He can, if only He is moved to mercy towards a sinner, unlock the gates of Hades and free captives from there who have not lost the desire and striving towards good and hatred and repugnance towards evil. Having once been indifferent while on earth to good and evil, here they cannot of themselves fulfill what is lacking for their salvation. This is the work of grace which fills what is lacking by the good providence of God, by the intercession of those still living on earth, and the intercession of the Saints who are already in the world beyond the grave. Finally, as the Apostle assures us, they have an all-powerful intercession before the face of God in our Redeemer Jesus Christ: "There is one Mediator of God and man, the man Jesus Christ, who gave himself as a ransom for all" (I Timothy 2:5–6).

Knowing the basis on which the Church teaches that the state of some sinners beyond the grave can be improved, let us look at wherein the private intercession of the living relatives of the deceased consists. The private intercession of the living for the dead should consist in a real use of the means indicated by God. Only then is the goal achieved of obtaining pardon of sins for the deceased worthy of such intercession. The visible signs—the means expressing an unbroken inner spiritual bond of the living with the dead or of those still on earth with the dwellers in the world beyond the grave showing the mutual relationship between them—these means, having been prescribed by God Himself, have the great and divine purpose of man's salvation. It is natural for people, who have the same nature and the same destiny to be actively concerned over the life beyond the grave of them that have passed on. God desires this, and therefore He has bestowed on man the means without which man's involvement would be useless to either the living or the dead. These means are the present life of those abiding on earth. There is a time for everything. This present life of the living and in general all the time till the Second Advent of the Lord Jesus Christ to earth is the time of prayer, intercession, seeking, sowing.

All is possible for the believer. The word "all" does not exclude that one may be saved for the faith of another. Prayer combined with faith, hope, and love penetrates the heavens. The Apostle Paul bears witness of this truth saying: "For He that spared not His own Son, but delivered Him up for the sake of us all [and consequently for our departed, so as to grant them salvation]: how shall he not with him also freely give us all things?" (Romans 8:32). Chrysostom explains these words of the Apostle thus: "If God gave over His Son for us and did not simply give Him over but delivered Him up to death, then how can we doubt the rest having received the Lord Himself? And this is the most convincing assurance, that every petition of the faithful, the more so if it is in agreement with the will of God, of course will be fulfilled by the heavenly Father." "Whatsoever ye shall ask the Father in my name, he will give it you" (John 16:23), taught our Lord Jesus Christ. Let us be obedient to the faith, if we wish salvation for ourselves and for those that have passed into the world beyond the grave. The present life, according to the teaching of the Lord, is intended for seeking the kingdom of God for self and for neighbor whether the neighbor be still on earth or have passed into the other world. According to the teaching of St. Paul, our life, the present, is the acceptable time, the day of salvation. Now the possibility is given, by methods indicated by God Himself, to propitiate the Lord for He is merciful and will cleanse our sins, that is, both of those still on earth and of those beyond the grave. These methods indicated by God are in force only till the end of the world and the Coming of Christ for judgment.

6. Almsgiving

After prayer for the departed, the second act of commemorating them is the giving of alms which we do either in their memory or in their name, that is, the giving of some earthly good to those in need: to the paupers, our brethren. This act of commemoration helps much to bring comfort to deceased sinners. The Lord Jesus Christ takes every help shown the poor as shown to Himself: "Ye have done it unto Me"; therefore He will not remain in debt to those in whose name He has accepted it. A glass of cold water, the widow's two mites: for all this a reward in due time has been promised.

The good works done by the living in memory of the departed have a significance as if the dead person himself did these good deeds. Charitable works in memory of the dead increase the number of those who pray for the salvation of the dead; for it is natural when one has received aid to pray for one's benefactors. Such prayers combined with faith do good unto the dead. We see many examples in history where, for the prayers of one, something was granted to another. For the intercession of the centurion, his servant was healed; for the intercession of the Canaanite woman, her daughter was healed. Therefore God, for the sincere intercession of such beneficiaries, can grant healing of the soul to the departed as well.

It is natural and understandable for anyone, that a man will sooner or later will certainly taste the fruit of his works, fruits of good or evil; the product of activity is inevitable: as ye sow, so shall ye reap! To each of us the Lord Himself will give a return for our works in due time. Our entire attitude towards our neighbor, all our activity, be it good or evil, turns upon Him that loved us even unto death. "He that is kind to a beggar lends to the Lord" (Proverbs 19:17). Naturally, anyone who may have seen good or respect shown to one beloved of us, knows how pleasant we find this; and if a beloved is ill treated, how sorrowful to us. If indeed man takes to heart all that is done to one who is beloved, then how much more so the Lord Whose love for us is beyond compare to any other love. And so, it is pleasing unto the Lord Jesus Christ that heavenly peace reign amongst us—divine love and joy not of this earth—so that we, children of one Father, might sympathize with one another's condition and take a vital concern in the sorrows and shortcomings of our neighbor. By compassionately helping our neighbor to the extent of our power we place Him that loves him in our debt, and we can be certain that He Who forgives our trespasses will not remain in debt to us. Spiritual and physical help to our neighbor is called assistance, alms, and, in general, charity. He that receives help gives thanks to him that bestows, to his benefactor, and the Lord will repay this benefactor. Charity, alms, given by the living in the name of the departed, have the same significance as if the departed himself had given help to his neighbor; and therefore it is natural that the fruits of alms belong to the dead; but the living, as the instrument of these alms, has a part in the heavenly reward.

Prayer and alms are among the works of mercy, the works of charity, and those that do them receive an appropriate reward in the place where truth, peace, and joy reign eternally. Prayer for the departed along with alms given in the name of the dead, put him in a favorable relationship with the Lord Jesus Christ, obliged by the acts of mercy done as if in the name of the deceased himself. The alms belong to the deceased. The true meaning of alms was known even in the Old Testament; the giving of alms to the poor at funerals goes back to ancient times, and the Hebrews had this custom. In discussing the basis for prayers for the dead, we have seen also the importance of alms as expressed by Tobit in his testament to his son Tobias and by the Wisdom of Sirach[40] and the holy Prophet Jeremias. The first mentioned teaches thus: "Almsgiving delivers from death, and it cleanses every sin and doth not let us walk in darkness . . . Share thy bread at the tomb of the righteous" (Tobit 4:10,17). The second mentioned teaches: "May the grace of giving be before all that live, and forbid not thy grace over the dead" (Ecclesiasticus 8:36). And finally, Jeremias speaks thus of alms: "Miserable and cast from the face of God are those dead, for whose salvation no alms are given" (Chapter 16).

This method of almsgiving which brings God's mercy to the departed, used in the Old Testament, was carried over into the Christian world, and, in accordance with the Christian law of laying down one's soul for friends and enemies, obtained a great significance and brought the one who did so a great reward in heaven: eternal bliss. "Blessed are the merciful, for they shall obtain mercy" (Matthew 5:7), and "Be merciful, as your Father in heaven is merciful" (Luke

---

[40]This Book is usually called Ecclesiasticus in English.

6:36). Behold the words of the Lord Jesus Christ Himself on the strength and might of alms and on the salvation they bring to the almsgiver, therefore, as being a sure means of obtaining the kingdom of heaven. "I say unto you, make to yourselves friends for yourselves by unrighteous mammon; that, when ye fail, they may receive you into everlasting habitations" (Luke 16:9), to which words of Christ the Doctors of the Church give the following meaning: when we die those beggars in Christ who have been the beneficiaries of our alms, and therefore heirs of the kingdom of heaven, will pray and intercede for their benefactors. These words relate to all true Christians. These words, however, were directed for the most part to the publicans and sinners who could also, even though through wrongful riches, receive the kingdom of heaven. But who can boast of the righteousness of his life, of his deeds? Whose works and life are utterly foreign to the love of glory, the love of pleasure, the love of silver, these fundamental sins? But if our life is not foreign to wrongdoing, and the life of the departed also was not foreign to wrongdoing, then let us make use of this saying for our salvation and that of our departed. Through the doing of good we obtain alms for ourselves and our departed through friends who, being beneficiaries through us, the living, will receive the departed and us into their mansions in the life beyond the grave. This is the teaching of the Saviour Himself concerning alms and their reward. Almsgiving is the fruit of love, its visible expression. The holy Apostles taught active love, good works, charity, and sympathy for the needs of others. The chosen vessel of the Holy Spirit, the Teacher of the Gentiles, says clearly that without true love all virtues are nothing. Our love should not be expressed in words only says the Apostle John, but in the works of love, consequently in works of mercy. The successors of the Apostles and after them all the pastors and teachers of the Church taught the people almsgiving both by word and deed.

It is a truth that for the faith of one, another receives: "Be it unto thee as thou askest ... Ask, and it shall be given you ... Every one that asketh shall receive." Prayer for another, alms for another or in the name of another, draw the grace and mercy of God to the one for whom we pray, or in whose name the alms are given. The loving heart naturally wishes for another, wherever he might be, here or beyond the grave, the same as it would for itself. It desires and seeks the kingdom of heaven, according to the commandment of Jesus Christ, both for itself and others. And here is the method, the means for obtaining eternal life beyond the grave, proposed to us by Jesus Christ Himself: alms for the needy, charity. Out of your riches help others, the poor, and they will prepare the kingdom of heaven for you, as the debtors of the lord prepared an eternal place with themselves for the overseer in the parable when he came to poverty. The glorious rich and the poor become beggars when the soul leaves the body; there is not the spiritual wealth needed for life beyond the grave; "there are no justifying works," as our holy Church teaches us. If all are guilty, all are deprived of the glory of God; then here is the means of salvation, offered by the Lord, the means that makes up what the soul lacks. Among the number of means that lighten the state of certain deceased sinners beyond the grave, Chrysostom notes alms also when he says, "If one is departed sinful, he should be helped as much as can be; only not by tears, but by prayers and intercessions and alms and offerings" (commentary on I Corinthians, Forty-seventh Discussion). He, again, writes on the Epistle to the Philippians (Chapter 1, Third Discussion): "Praying, ourselves, for the dead, let us move others to just such prayer. The means for this is almsgiving, giving for them often to the poor, the destitute." And in another place writing on Acts (Chapter 9, Discussion Twenty-one), he writes: "If we give alms, even if he be not worthy, nevertheless God will be moved. If for the sake of Paul He saved others, and for the sake of others yet again saved others, how shall He not do this for us?" And again he writes: "Let us not be concerned with magnificent funerals and rich caskets, but let us cause the widows, orphans, and all in need by means of alms to pray for the departed one." This means, even though not carried out by the deceased, nevertheless inclines God to mercy and to deliver the departed from eternal death (alms are not in vain).

How great the meaning of alms is can be seen from his teaching on this subject. "Nothing is so mighty, so strong in wiping away sins as almsgiving; virginity and fasting are the heritage only of the virgin and the faster, they do not save anyone except the ascetic; but almsgiving extends to all and embraces all members of the body of Christ." Chrysostom often conversed with the faithful about the beneficial results of alms and other works of mercy for the dead. Thus, in his *Commentary on the Gospel of St. John the Theologian,* he says: "Dost thou wish to honor the dead? Honor him with alms and good works, for alms serve for deliverance from eternal torment." Discussing immoderate weeping for the dead and rich burials as things of no use for either those who bury or for the departed he writes: "No small benefit is obtained for the departed in almsgiving in their memory. A luxurious burial is not love for the dead but vanity. For if thou wilt have compassion on the dead, I will show thee another way of burial and I will teach thee to lay down robes that shall rise with him and glorify him: these are the raiment of almsgiving. For this garment will always rise with him. Alms are a seal for him. From these, raiment shall glow forth at hearing 'ye have fed Me when I was an hungered' (Matthew 25:35). This makes men famous; it makes them bright; it places them in safety. Let us bury the dead in such a way as may be useful to us and to them unto the glory of God: let us give much alms for them; let us send them off with a glorious entourage."

"If the barbarians burn the property of the dead with them," says he in another place, "then so much the more shouldst thou, O Christian, send off with the deceased the property that was his, only not for it to become ashes as they do, but so that it vests the deceased in greater glory; so that, if he departed hence as a sinner, it might release him from sins; if he departed as one righteous, so that it might increase his reward and recompense." St. Athanasius assigns offerings made in the church for the departed to the same purpose, that is to say: candles, incense, and oil. "Whoever makes offerings for the dead," says he, "has the same purpose as a father whose child is young and completely without strength. If the child should suffer an illness, then his father in faith offers candles, incense, and oil in the divine house that they might be burned for the healing of the child from disease. It is not the child that holds and offers these things (a similar situation is met with at the renunciations at holy Baptism). Thus too we should think about one who has reposed in God: it is not he himself but others who hold and offer for him candles and oil and all that serves for his redemption; but the grace of God departs not from faith's intention." On the great significance of alms in regard to the dead, the blessed Augustine bears the same witness (On *Faith, Hope, and Charity,* Chapter 70).

7. Not All Intercessions of the Living are Beneficial to the Departed and Not All the Departed Benefit from the Intercession of the Living

Man must live for God and neighbor; in his life and activity the name of God must be hallowed. Activity should be founded, combined, and directed by heavenly, divine love. The piety of one is sometimes the cause of another's salvation. A wife saves her husband, and fathers obtain clemency through the prayers and piety of children, grandchildren, and great-grandchildren; dead are saved by the devotion of the living, that is, those dead who were themselves the first teachers of piety for their children who in turn fulfilled the measure of their fathers and by their devotion evoked the mercy of God to fulfill by grace the lack of their fathers and mothers.

When we, the living, with complete faith, hope, and love, insofar as it is given to man, make us of all that is within our power for the salvation of the deceased, then he is saved. God demands our participation, to the extent of our ability, in the salvation of others, be they living or dead. This is a dogma. If we wish to receive something from God, in agreement with His most holy will, we must do on our part all that is within our power, for Jesus Christ Himself taught us: "Only to him that asks is it given." The fulfillment of the petition depends on the degree and quality of the petition, for it was said, "Ye receive not, for ye ask ill" (James 4:3). Sacred history presents us with a multitude of examples relating to this dogma. Thus the Evangelist Mark writes, "When Jesus Christ entered into Capernaum and was in a certain house, straightway many were gathered together, insomuch that there was no room to receive anyone else. At the same time they brought unto him one sick of the palsy, and as they could not come nigh unto him for the press, they uncovered the roof where he was: and when they had broken it up, they let down the bed wherein the sick of the palsy lay, at the very feet of Jesus" (Mark 2:1–5). Only then the Knower of hearts said unto the sick of the palsy, "Son, thy sins be forgiven thee: rise, take up thy bed, and go to thy home" (Mark 2:11). See under what conditions the desire of the cripple and those who brought him was fulfilled. When everything had been done on their part, then the remission of sins followed. As the cripple, despite all his faith and hope in the Lord, could not help himself, that is, in this case he could not go himself to the Lord Jesus, and he needed the help of others, just so the sinner who dies in faith and hope cannot help himself. There is neither repentance for him nor works of mercy; only the living can help him by their interceding for him before God. And by the limitless kindness of God it is said to him, "Thy sins be forgiven thee, go to the house of thy heavenly Father."

This dogma is confirmed by many other examples as well. Thus, when the Apostle Paul was sent by ship from Caesarea to Rome in a ship of the emperor, there were up to 276 men with him on the ship. Over a period of several days there was a fearful storm at sea so that all those on the ship despaired of salvation. Then the Apostle said to them: "Be not troubled. Not one of you shall perish, but only the ship itself shall be lost, because this night an angel of God informed me, and I believe God that we shall not perish." But when the crew, sighting land, and desirous of saving themselves, would have left the ship in a boat, then the Apostle, despite his previous words that no one would perish, spoke the following words to the centurion: "If the crew leave the ship, then ye cannot be saved and will perish!" (Acts 27:22–31). And so the Apostle based the salvation of the sailors not only on the words of the Lord, but also on the service and help of the crew.

The same dogma is to be seen in the fulfillment of the petitions of the Canaanite woman, the man born blind, the ten lepers, in the resurrection of Lazarus, and in the fulfillment of the wise thief's request. "Without Me ye can do nothing good." To you belong only good desires, intentions, suggested by the Holy Spirit, while their fulfillment is Mine. Prayer for the dead, as a virtue, instilled by the Holy Spirit, is fulfilled by Me; to him that prays is given, according to his prayer, the salivation of the departed. This is the teaching of Orthodoxy. The endless mercy of God is joined to His endless righteousness. God desires the salvation of all people—this is mercy. But how can one save a sinner who has not attained salvation? Some reason must be found that could move the just God to mercy towards a dead sinner. The intercession of the living for the dead satisfies God's justice, and those worthy of salvation are freed from the torments of Hades. For our desire (the salvation of the dead) to be accepted and fulfilled by the Lord, there must be an active desire, that is, a life lived according to faith with the observance of all God's commandments. Such a desire is fulfilled by the Lord when the living have done all that they could for the benefit of the dead. God does not demand what is impossible for man, and His commandments, which are possible for man, are not burdensome, as St. John the Theologian bears witness. He fulfills the will, the desire of one who fears God, according to the Prophet David: "The Lord is close to all them that call upon Him, to all that call upon Him in truth; He will perform the will of them that fear Him, and hearken unto their prayer" (Psalms 144:18–19). Concerning those that have attained perfect love towards God, the Apostle Paul speaks in his Epistle to the Romans (8:35,39). There is no refusal of the prayers of the humble, there is no delay; coming from a contrite and humble heart, they go straight to the throne of the Highest: "The prayer of the humble has passed through the clouds" (Ecclesiasticus 35:17); "The Lord hath regarded the prayer of the humble, and not brought their entreaties to naught" (Psalms 101:18). Consequently, we may conclude that the reverse is true, that God does not fulfill the desires, petitions, prayers of people who do not fear Him. Those who fear God direct their life by His commandments. A life that embodies as far as is within one's power all the virtues—love, humility, meekness, righteousness, abstinence, chastity, truth, the keeping of all the commandments—such a life makes one's desires effective, worthy of fulfillment, and repose for their departed ones is possible.

But how is God to give peace to those departed sinners when those who pray for them are also sinners, thinking that prayer alone without a single virtue will help the departed—forgetting that God Himself says such intercessors "honor Me in vain; for they honor Me with their lips, but their heart is far from Me." With their lips they ask for the repose of the dead, but for God's love toward him they repay with hatred towards the Redeemer, that is, with their sinful life which is hateful to God. The word of God bears witness that God will not hear sinners and their prayers are not accepted: "If I have seen untruth in my heart, may God not hear me"... "When ye spread forth your hands, I will hide mine eyes from you; yea, when ye make many prayers, I will not hear; your hands are full of blood" (Isaiah 1:15). But we are all sinful, as witnessed by the word of God: "For who is pure of stain; none indeed, even if his life is but one day on earth" (Job 14:4). And the Saviour Himself expressed this truth as follows, seeing the condemned adulteress: "He that is without sin among you, let him first cast a stone at her" (John 8:7); and the Apostle writes: "For all have sinned, and come short of the glory of God" (Romans 3:23). For this reason, St. Tikhon of Zadonsk writes: "If we wish God to hear our prayer, then we must obey His commandments. Without this, our prayer is in vain, for God will not hear a sinner. If thou wilt have thy prayer heard, it must lead thee away from sin. Whosoever is a sinner and does not leave his sin, his prayers are not heard" (Volume I, Part IV, p. 88, Section 28). We are all sinners, all are guilty before God; however, these words apply not to all sinners, otherwise, to whom would the words of the Lord, "ask, seek" refer? The first sort of sinners are those who blaspheme against the Holy Spirit, who remain unrepentant, hardened, indifferent, in unbelief, concerning whom David writes, "I have hated all them that do iniquity; thou shalt destroy all that speak lies; the Lord turneth away from a man of blood and deceit" (Psalms 5:6,7). But the sinners of the second type are those who, as people wrapped in feeble flesh, fall and rise, and with tears of repentance take refuge with the healer of souls and bodies, the Lord Jesus, and with the Apostle Paul bewail their accursedness; their prayers, as the prayers of beloved children of God, are accepted and fulfilled: "If ye abide in Me, and My words abide in you, whatsoever ye desire, ask and it shall be unto you" (John 15:7). Was it not unto all Christians that Jesus Christ gave the one main and common prayer to God the Father, in which among other things we ask for pardon of sins: "forgive us our trespasses." Leading a life in true repentance, we receive pardon of our sins and fulfillment of our wishes that are in agreement with the will of God for example the repose of our sinful departed ones in the kingdom of heaven. "If any man be a worshipper of God, and doeth His will, him He heareth" (John 9:31). Further on, Jesus Christ, directing His words to His disciples, says: "Whatsoever things ye desire, when ye pray, believe that ye receive them, and ye shall have them" (Mark 11:24).

"Whatsoever"—this word includes all that is in agreement with the will of God, and the salvation of sinners is the desire of God. Therefore, prayer for departed sinners is according to the will of God and pleasing unto Him. Blessed indeed are such intercessors for the sinful dead who deliver their souls from eternal death and snatch them out of the prisons of Hades. Such benefactors receive an eternal reward in heaven together with those whom the Lord calls His faithful servants. St. Dimitri of Rostov in his homily "On Prayer" writes: "Prayer is the key to heavenly treasures. And there is nothing, as one of the Holy Fathers writes, that could not be obtained of God, so long as that which is asked for be good and requested as it should be. Our sins are the main reason that our prayers do not attain their goal. One should offer up prayers in a spirit of contrition and repentance for sins. The Lord has attended the heartfelt prayers of sinners also, but only when they prayed with repentance and sincere contrition for their sins" (*Collected Works,* Volume 2, p. 204). St. Tikhon of Zadonsk, in his instructions on the duties of the Christian, writes: "In order to be an intercessor for others before God, one should be pure and without vice oneself."

Having shown what is demanded of the living for his intercession to be of real benefit to the departed sinner in Hades, let us now look at whether or not all sinners in Hades can benefit from the intercession of the living, that is, can all those in Hades be liberated by our prayers? The Church prays only for all those who die in the true faith, and they will surely be freed from the torments of Hades. The soul that is still in the body must by all means take care for its future life, must be worthy that, after its passage into the life beyond the grave, the intercession of the living could bring it relief and salvation. "Each one," as the Apostle writes, "shall receive, according as he has done good or evil in the body." The intercession of the living is of benefit to those of the departed whose earthly life was a battle with the passions, who, although they died in faith and repentance, did not manage to lose their habits of vice to which they had been attached, did not manage to fulfill the conditions of true repentance in deed. St. Gregory the Dialogist says "the intercession of the living benefits only those of the dead who abstained in this life from acts of wickedness, benefits them to the point where they receive remission of the sins of weakness, ignorance, and forgetfulness, and the result of this is that they are led out of Hades to a place of light, refreshment, and peace."

St. John of Damascus writes concerning who among the dead is helped by the intercession of the living, "Everyone who has in himself the leaven of virtue (not all humanity, but only those who have this), yet who did not manage to turn it into bread, who wanted to do so but failed, either due to laziness, or to carelessness, or by human weakness, or through postponement from day to day, and was taken by sudden and unexpected death, such will not be forgotten by the righteous Judge and Master; but after death the Lord will stir up relatives, those close to the departed, and friends and will direct their thoughts, draw their hearts, and incline their souls to afford help and assistance to the deceased" ("Homily on the Departed").

Metropolitan Philaret of Moscow draws a concise, vivid, and striking picture of the state of those sinners beyond the grave for which the intercession of the living affords relief and salvation itself. "When the all-penetrating wisdom of God does not forbid prayer for the dead, does it not mean that it still permits one to cast a rope of help, even though not always one of absolute certainty, to those souls that have been separated from the shore of temporary life yet not reached the eternal haven, who between the death of the body and the last Judgment of Christ are teetering over the abyss; now rising in hope, now borne down by unbecoming deeds, now rising by grace, now pulled down by the remnants of damaged nature; now enthused by divine desires, now entangled in the crude, not fully shed garment of earthly thoughts" (Homily of September 25, 1852, at the consecration of the church of the Moscow Danilov Cemetery).

Sins that constitute blasphemy against the Holy Spirit—that is, unbelief, hardness of heart, apostasy, lack of remorse, and the like—cause one to perish forever, and for such dead the intercession of the Church and the living can do nothing to help since they lived and died outside of communion with the Church. And indeed, for such the Church does not even pray. The intercession of the living is of no avail to such of the dead as had no concern themselves for their life beyond the grave. And someone who led a life of vice, which was all sown with weeds filled with impurities and uncleanness, who never attended to the voice of conscience, but with indifference and blindness was submerged in the foulness of passions, who gratified all the desires of the flesh and gave no concern to the soul, whose every thought was occupied with carnal gratification, and in that condition met his end—to such a one none will stretch out a hand, but it will be with him so that neither spouse, nor children, nor brethren, nor relatives will give any help since God looks not upon him. St. Basil the Great says, "There is no clemency, and he belongs to the number of the condemned: the greedy, the rapacious, inexorable, merciless, those with hearts of stone." And further on: "During thine entire life, thou, drowning in pleasures and giving thyself up to luxury, wouldst not so much as glance at the beggars; what joy canst thou expect in thy death?" (St. John of Damascus, *Homily on the Faithful Departed*). In other words, the dead who are unworthy of the intercession of the living are not freed from Hades, because the intercession of the living extends only to those worthy of it or those worthy of being saved.

But who of the departed is worthy of the intercession of the living? He that more or less during his life is concerned for his salvation. Consequently, the lazy, the negligent, he that takes no care for his lot beyond the grave, will obtain no benefit from the intercession of the living, even if it were made.

God knows, that if the intercession you needed to give were insufficient for your departed, then God would not have permitted you to make this effort. But you were allowed, and this makes it easier to believe Him Who desires our salvation; and having permitted you, He says, "Fear not, only believe, and thou shalt be saved, thyself and those close to thee," rather than doubt as to whether the prayer is heard, will the dead be saved, and the like, which is clearly suggested by the enemy of our salvation. The enemy seeks to divert us from living faith to doubt, to disbelief in the Lord's promise to make them blessed who put their hope in Him: "Blessed are all they that hope on Him" (Psalms 2:12). The hope of Christians is Jesus Christ Who took upon Himself the sins also of thy deceased one. And so, whom is it better to believe: God Who desires our salvation, though it is not possible without faith, or the enemy who desires our condemnation, which is the lot of unbelief? Therefore being vitally involved in the salvation of thy departed, admit no doubts of his salvation. This is the craft of the enemy, for if the deceased were not worthy of salvation, then thou wouldst not be allowed to intercede for him; as witnessed by St. John of Damascus, God does not move anyone to pray for those unworthy of salvation, neither parents, nor wife, nor husband, nor relatives, nor friends: it is upon such dead that the words of the prophecy are fulfilled, that accursed are those dead for whom the living on earth do not pray. For those unworthy of salvation, there is no intercessor on earth; and there is no prayer, again because it is not pleasing to God; it is in vain because these dead are unworthy of clemency for their sins, constituting blasphemy against the Holy Spirit.

The blessed Augustine writes, "The dead that are unworthy of the intercession of the living obtain no relief in the next world from prayers, alms that are offered, and even from the Divine Liturgy itself celebrated for them by the living." But who are these that are unworthy? What sort of sinners are these?

There is a way of life that is not so honest as not to require the intercession of the living after death and not so bad as to make that intercession futile. This means that for the intercession by the living to bring benefit to the dead, there must be a certain merit on the part of the deceased through which, after death, it would be possible to gain relief through the intercession of the living. No one should expect to receive after death from God what he was indifferent to in life. For such a one in the next world, the intercession of the living is of no avail. The intercession of the Church and of all Christians in general for the dead does not relate to those who took no care for their salvation, who died in unrighteousness, without remorse, such as unbelievers, freethinkers, blasphemers, and haters of humanity, who have completely extinguished the light of Christ in themselves; for them, the intercession of the living affords no help, just as nothing can restore the growing power of seeds that have become rotten: the rays of the sun, good air, and nourishing moisture are lost on them. And on this basis the Church does not pray for deliberate suicides, unrepentant heretics, and sinners like unto them.

If there is no one to pray for dead persons, this is a bad sign. If there are no intercessors, this means there is no reason that would give rise to them. It is God's commandment that we should pray for one another, but true prayer is granted only by God Himself: "We know not what we should pray for as we ought: but the Spirit itself maketh intercession for us" (Romans 8:26). There is no good will of God towards such a soul, therefore its salvation is doubtful. Intercessors appear by the will of God, Who warms their hearts with the fire of divine grace, and they, taking a vital part in the life of the departed beyond the grave, intercede for him before God; they make up for the shortcomings of the deceased by leading a virtuous life, praying, almsgiving, and other means, insofar as is possible for them. St. John of Damascus says outright that they are chosen by God Himself to give the hand of help to the one that has passed on into the world beyond the grave, and therefore the salvation of such a deceased is undoubted, because the living have given him help as demanded by God Himself (*Homily on the Faithful Departed*). Those moved by God's grace to intercede before God on behalf of the departed have a sure hope for success in asking pardon of the dead person's sins, and in this we have the assurance of the great Saint of God, the universal teacher John Chrysostom.

No one knows how they will leave this world: will the soul be in full consciousness or not? Everyone has experienced to some extent a certain loss of consciousness when mentally or physically unwell. Thus, for example, when in a state of anger a person may act unnaturally, breaking divine and civil law. In a state of physical illness the soul forgets its obligations, because it suffers with its ill body. For this reason all the virtues by which the kingdom of heaven is obtained require full consciousness, and one definitely cannot hope to carry them out on the deathbed. If thou feel and realize that thou standest guilty before God and that thou fallest short, art unfinished in virtue, turn in the hour of death to those close to thee, so that they might fulfill thy shortcomings and smooth away thy sins by their intercession and by carrying out thy will. In making out a will and testament that expresses the last desire for salvation of the one departing, a desire that should also express the all-holy will of God for the salvation of the one who departs, Chrysostom advises the testator not to forget the Lord Jesus Christ and His lesser brethren, the poor. Forget not the Lord, as the One Who grants to the dying testator a new means of obtaining pardon of his remaining sins beyond the grave, sins not wiped out during the life of the testator; a means of moving those relatives and others still on earth to intercede before God for the repose with the Saints of their benefactor who has remembered them in his will. If the deceased testator is not evil, not a hardened sinner, not a heretic, but a Christian who has recognized that he is a prodigal son, and like the thief has confessed the Lord Jesus Christ, then like the repentant prodigal son and the wise thief he will inherit their lot: the forgiveness of sins and paradise. Repentance and faith are the means of salvation for a Christian; these two methods belong equally to the rich and the poor. Although a will is a means of obtaining salvation, nonetheless if the testator is foreign to repentance and faith, the testament he leaves will not save him. Likewise one with nothing to will to anyone after death, not having this means of gaining posthumous intercessors yet who is no stranger to repentance and faith, will still not lack his reward even for a glass of cold water, for rejoicing with them that rejoice, and weeping with those that weep. St. John of Damascus, regarding such dead as leave neither relatives after them who could pray for them nor means for the distribution of alms or the celebration of the Liturgy, writes: "The good God will save the creation of His hands, except only for those who clearly belong to the number of those cast away, who have trampled the right faith" (*Homily on the Faithful Departed*).

And so, God will accept the prayer of not all the living for the departed. By the same token, not all deceased sinners in Hades can benefit from the prayer of the living. Those who are lost to the kingdom of heaven do not gain from the intercession of the living, and indeed the Church herself does not intercede for them.

Among the number of those saved or rejected there will be both rich and poor, learned and unlettered, noted and unknown. Faith will save them or unbelief will bring them to eternal ruin. The sins of the faithful are forgiven on earth and beyond the grave through the intercession of the Church and neighbors, while the sins of the unbelievers, according to the words of Jesus Christ Himself, are not forgiven here or in the life to come. Here one should understand not the faith that the demons have, but faith justified by deeds of love towards God and neighbor.

8. Addenda

a) The Significance of the Third, Ninth, Fortieth, and Anniversary Days after Death. Kutya[41]

Speaking in general about what is demanded of the living to fulfill Christ's commandment—to seek the kingdom of God for oneself and one's neighbor, wherever he is, on earth or beyond the grave—we omitted mention of the significant days for the dead because they were spoken of in the first section, "Death in Relationship to Immortality." These days are: the third, the ninth, the fortieth, and the anniversary day after the death of a person. The Church demands that those remaining on earth honor these days especially in memory of the departed. As to the significance of these days, discussed in the above-mentioned first part of this book, here we will only add certain further information.

The third day after someone's death (called in Russian *trétiny*) is the usual day of burial and at the same time a day when the Church commemorates him or her in prayer. The commemoration of the departed on the third day goes back to the Apostles. This observance has its reasons. Some say that the Church observes the *trétiny* because on the third day the dead change their appearance. Neophyte of Russia finds the reason in the Resurrection of Christ on the third day. Others see the reason for this Church custom in the fact that the deceased was baptized and believed in the Holy Trinity: the Father, and the Son, and the Holy Spirit, bearing witness before God on the third day that the departed kept three great virtues to the end, namely faith, hope, and charity, upon which man's salvation depends and without which salvation is impossible. And finally, the basis of the *trétiny* is interpreted as lying in the triple nature of man: spirit, soul, and body which sin together and therefore, after the passage into the other world, require cleansing from sins, a cleansing that man himself cannot accomplish due to his infirmity. Therefore it is necessary—after the departure of the soul—when all the mental passions fall away of themselves—for us who remain among the living to ask and make entreaty for the soul before the all-merciful God.

The ninth day after death (called *devyátiny* in Russian), when one should commemorate the dead, is of Apostolic origin and, like the third day, has its reasons. Some say that the Church commemorates the dead on the ninth day because on that day the body becomes corrupt, except for the heart; Neophyte

---

[41]Often called "koliva", it is a food made from boiled wheat or rice, explained below.

of Russia finds the reason in the Church praying for the deceased to be joined to the nine ranks of angels. We ask the Lord that He, by the prayers and intercessions of the nine ranks of angels, cause the soul of the departed to dwell and repose in the choirs of the Saints and, after the Resurrection, to grant him a blissful habitation together with the angels.

The rule of the Church to pray for the departed over a period of forty days after death, and especially on the fortieth day itself, has too its reasons: some say that by the fortieth day even the heart falls into decay. But this explanation is not always in agreement with experience, as Benjamin, the Archbishop of Nizhny-Novgorod, writes in his book *Novaya Skrizhal*[42] (Part 4, p. 130). It should be noted that in the conception of an infant, the reverse order is the case: on the third day the heart is depicted, on the ninth day the body takes form, on the fortieth day the full appearance of a human being is manifested. Neophyte of Russia proposes a different explanation of the fortieth day (called *sorokúst* in Russian), the lamentation of the people of Israel which continued forty days after the death of Moses.

In general, the number forty is often used in the Sacred Scriptures: the lamentation for Moses lasted forty days; the Israelites wept forty days for the dead patriarch Jacob; the Hebrews in the desert were fed with manna forty years; Moses fasted forty days and forty nights, receiving the Law from God; Elias spent forty days and nights on his journey to Mount Horeb; the Lord Jesus Christ spent forty days and nights in the desert after His Baptism, and then after His Resurrection taught the Apostles the mysteries of the kingdom of God over a period of forty days. For this reason the Eastern Church[43] rightfully and devoutly made its rule from ancient times for forty days, and especially the fortieth day itself (in Russian, *soróchiny*). The holy Apostles established this custom in the Church of Christ, a custom that had existed among the Jews, of praying forty days for the dead. Just as Christ conquered the devil by spending forty days in fasting and prayer, so too the holy Church asks the Lord for grace for the dead, to conquer the enemy and obtain the kingdom of heaven. Simeon of Thessalonica writes: "The forty days are observed in memory of the Ascension of the Lord which took place on the fortieth day after His Resurrection, and with the goal that the deceased, having risen from the grave, might rise to meet the Lord, being swept up in the clouds, and thus be always with the Lord"

[42]Russian text reprinted by offset at Holy Trinity Monastery, Jordanville, NY.
[43]The Latin Church observed the third, seventh, and thirtieth days as opposed to the third, ninth, and fortieth.

(Archbishop Benjamin of Nizhny-Novgorod, *Novaya Skrizhal'*, Part 4, p. 129, Section 2).

On the anniversary day of the death of the deceased, and afterwards each year on this date as well as on the nameday of the departed, those relatives remaining on earth observe a memorial, showing by this that the bond of love is not broken by death, that the one who has fallen asleep lives in spirit with those abiding on earth, that he is immortal, that he will be renewed, that the spirit, soul, and body again will be united and constitute a new man.

Kutya or *kolyvo* is boiled wheat or other seeds[44] mixed with sugar or honey, giving it a sweet and pleasant taste. The meaning of *kutya* and its use at funerals, as well as at any memorial for the dead, is as follows: seeds bear life, and when they are sown into the earth they bring forth a new plant corresponding to the seed. So as to represent what awaits the body immediately after its separation from the soul and its future, Jesus Christ compares it to a grain of wheat and says, "Verily, verily, I say unto you, Except a corn of wheat fall into the ground and die, it abideth alone: but if it die, it bringeth forth much fruit" (John 12:24). From this, one can see that the spirit is inherent in the body even after the separation of the soul. Dwelling with the soul in the world beyond the grave, the spirit is present in the body. Just as the decomposition of the seed leads to its flowering, so too the decomposition of the body leads to its flowering for eternal life. In the words of the Saviour, where there is no decomposition, there is no flowering: but where there follows the decay of that which is planted, there is also a flowering: life, "it bringeth forth much fruit." St. Paul also compares the human body after the departure of the soul with a seed sown into the earth: "It is sown a natural body" (I Corinthians 15:44), to bring forth a new, spiritual body appropriate to the new, spiritual, eternal life. Seeds, seasoned with sugar or honey, signify the faith and hope of the living, and that the soul departed in faith will inherit a sweet, pleasant life beyond the grave. Sugar and honey used in kutya in general symbolize that for the Orthodox and the devout, after the universal resurrection, there will be a sweet and pleasing life.

And so, kutya is a visible expression of the confidence of the living in the immortality of the departed, in their resurrection and their blissful eternal life through the Lord Jesus Christ who gave His faithful servants resurrection and life everlasting. Simeon of Thessalonica (Chapter 374) writes: "We offer God seeds with various other fruits, by this expressing that man also, like a seed, like a fruit of the earth, put into the ground like a grain of wheat, will raise again by Divine power and, as if flowering, will be brought to Christ alive and perfect.

---

[44]Often rice mixed with raisins is used in the Russian tradition.

As the least seed, buried in the earth, afterwards brings forth an abundant, ripe, and perfect fruit, so too man, committed to the earth by death, shall rise again" (Archbishop Benjamin of Nizhny-Novgorod, *Novaya Skrizhal'*, Chapter 4, p. 133).

b) The Benefit to the Living in Praying for the Dead

The holiness of its origin and purpose and the importance of its actual benefit make prayer for the dead salutary for both the departed and the living.

The holiness of this prayer is revealed in its origin as a means given by God Himself to man for intercession for one another before Him and in its high purpose of saving the dead through the living. God wishes man to take part in the work of salvation. The kingdom of heaven is not simply bestowed, but is only for those who seek it for themselves and others. This is man's participation in the work of his salvation. By praying for the dead, the living take a holy part in the work of salvation of the dead, pray for them, and thus move the all-good God to mercy towards the departed: mercy is given to the dead by the intercession of the living.

Interceding for the dead, the living fulfill the commandments of love, and as they do this they become sharers of the heavenly rewards. Prayers for the dead bring salvation to the living, for they dispose the soul towards the heavenly and draw it away from what is passing and vain; they warm the heart with the purest love for God, fill it with the memory of death we are commanded to have, and thereby turn it away from evil; they give it the strength to refrain from willful sins and impart magnanimity and joyful bearing of sorrows mixed with hope for the future—a future not of this world. Prayer for the dead inclines the souls of the living to fulfill the commandments of Christ, to prepare themselves for departure at every hour. For to one who prepares himself constantly for departing this life, death ceases to be fearsome, but becomes joyous as a passage to the repose promised to those who serve the Lord. Departure combined with faith in Jesus Christ is joyous, as being filled with joy in meeting again those close to one's heart for whose salvation all has been done that depended on us. This is how great the benefit of these prayers is for the living.

c) The Contemporary Nature of Prayers for the Dead

A spirit that does not confess Jesus Christ as the Son of God come to earth in the flesh, born of the Holy Virgin Mary, such a spirit is of the devil. The dogma of the redemption of humanity by Jesus Christ is a Christian dogma.

There are concepts that belong to all humanity at all levels of development, at all times and everywhere, beginning with the first man, for example: the concept and striving towards a Higher Being, the thought of immortality, the hope of a better life beyond the grave, the need to propitiate an offended Deity. This need by a spiritual-moral being to propitiate God unfolded with the first man: Cain and Abel brought sacrifices to God. The whole human race feels the need for this and entreats God by various sacrifices, both for those on earth and for those that have gone on to the other world. The striving to propitiate a Higher Being, God, is part of man's spiritual and moral nature; it is natural for a fallen soul. Love comes naturally to the soul, consequently, it is natural to seek to propitiate God not only toward oneself, but toward all members of the spiritual-moral kingdom regardless of where they are, here, or there beyond the grave.

Only for the believer are all things possible, only the believer is saved—these are the Lord's words, justified by experience. Human knowledge cannot be without bounds. With its proud questions unanswered, the human mind, avoiding the indications of Divine Revelation, turns to denial, for example, of that which makes up the secret of the future beyond the grave. What reason moves some thinkers to reject prayer for the dead, to doubt its truth, benefit, and needfulness? Is this not the mark of a soul which the aforementioned lacks, and perhaps has even come to a complete loss of faith and love? If the word of God itself bears witness that all have sinned, that God alone is sinless, that God does not wish the death of a sinner, that inborn love, as commanded by Jesus Christ, strives with all its might to bring salvation to its neighbor and especially to those close and dear to our heart, then, after all that has been said, is there in the hearts of such proud and high minded thinkers love for others and faith in our Saviour?

There are false teachers who say that prayer for the dead is in vain because in the next world the soul already has what it prepared for itself while here. What awful hardness of heart, what darkening of the mind, and height of pride! What heart full of love, having been given the right of praying for other members of the Church, who make up one spiritual body, could be indifferent to the lot of its friend beyond the grave! What could hold it back from tears, from prayers for the state of the departed? It is ready for everything, for all self-sacrifices, if only its good will could be fulfilled. And there is nothing abnormal in this. Prayer and every good work can never be without fruit. If we are told that a sinner has died, then for this reason we pray for him for it is said: "Ask and it shall be given you." We ask for that which is pleasing to God Who desires the salvation of all. And if the object of our prayer is in agreement with the will of God, then our prayer, made in the simplicity of our heart, with full commitment to God, cannot be useless if only the deceased is a sinful Christian and not an apostate from Christ. I know that my deceased one is a sinner, because I believe the word of God which bears witness: "In thy sight [that is, of God] shall no man living be justified" (Psalms 142:2); and St. Paul, of the chief Apostles, the chosen vessel of the Holy Spirit, called himself accursed (Romans 7:24); and the divinely inspired King David called himself not a man, but a worm! What can be said after this, who among mortals can boast of his righteousness before God? Moreover, they will say to you that your departed one was not only a sinner, but left this world, perhaps, without proper repentance! We answer: who amongst us, be it the living or those departed this earthly life, has brought proper repentance? The strength, the degree of repentance, which is a gift of God, cannot be known to man. It is known only to the one Knower of Hearts, God. If God Himself bears witness that it is hard for a righteous man to be justified at the judgment, that means that there had not been full repentance. Only grace fulfills that which is lacking to those who repent, according to their desire for repentance: "For all have sinned, and are deprived of the glory of God" (Romans 3:23).

It is not the body, but the soul that is responsible for all man's activity, be it good or evil, visible as well as invisible. If the soul does not want something, then no compulsion of the body, however strong or continued, is carried out. The body in that case is only a visible instrument to perform the will of the soul, an instrument of the person's outward, visible activity. Of all the actions of the soul, one is the strongest and mightiest—prayer—by which man performs supernatural works. This truth is incomprehensible to those who have never and in no wise practiced it. Prayer is an invisible, spiritual act. Man cannot always understand how some manifestations take place, especially in the spiritual realm; for example, how can the action of prayer extend from the visible world into the other, invisible one? But explain how the prayerful activity of one soul abiding in the body has a beneficial effect on another soul also still in the body, bringing about that state that the first soul desired in prayer? Everyday experiences prove this truth. You pray for those close to your heart (an example that most have experienced) and see your desire fulfilled in them: the sick recover, one who is absent sends news by letter, and so on.

If your prayerful wishes were fulfilled for someone in another part of the world, then what is to prevent your lawful desires from coming true for a soul in the world beyond the grave which makes up only part of the common home of moral beings? The effects of prayer on the soul are the same regardless of where it may be; but how the action of prayer takes place is above our knowledge, this is the subject of faith—"Ask, and it shall be given you." The prayerful wish of the Cypriote parents saddened over their son's captivity and thinking him already dead in Persia, were fulfilled. Their desire was fulfilled though they did not see it palpably; yet they were convinced it was true later when they met him in person. Just so shall we one day be convinced that our prayers for the salvation of the departed were fulfilled when we encounter them in due time; we shall reap the fruit of our prayers when we hear from them of the gradual improvement of their state beyond the grave which took place through our love for them, through prayers to God for them, and generally from good deeds done in their memory. To doubt the efficacy of the prayers of the living for the dead is to doubt the value of prayers for those absent. With such doubts, prayer for another seems altogether in vain. This is the unnatural deduction to which carnal thinking brings one. Where then is the divine love born into the soul?

If it is true that there exists an enemy of good, then obviously he cannot bear to see good done by men. To destroy, to make the basis of virtue seem doubtful, this is the method of the devil who seeks to make man his accomplice. Remember the lie that he told to Eve in paradise: "Believe not . . . but eat!" Was it not from the Scriptures that the father of lies took the words he used to tempt God Himself, Jesus Christ, in the desert? To deceive is the devil's aim. Prayer for those who have passed into the world beyond the grave, which is one of the great virtues, has its enemies who, under the influence of that same enemy (the devil), misinterpret the words of Holy Scripture, such as, "God will repay each one according to his works." Taking these words of the Bible literally and not knowing their real meaning, they negate thereby the commandment of Jesus Christ on love. Is this not the same as what the devil once said in paradise: "Believe not!" Consequently, it would be in vain to pray for the departed. Not to pray is the same as not to have love; for if there is love, how can a loving heart be silent? This is what the devil wants: for us to cease loving those who have passed into the other world. But if the soul, at his suggestion (God forbid this to happen to anyone) should stifle divine love, is this not to become like the devil, to be together with him? Without love, all virtues lose their worth. Can we forget one beloved of us and of the Lord and not pray for him as desired by the enemy of truth and to forget him whom God loves? Not to pray for those beloved of the Lord Jesus Christ, who demands undying love, means not to carry out His all-holy will. There have been and are and will be enemies of truth, enemies of every virtue, and therefore prayer for those who have passed into the other world has enemies and will unto the end. St. John of Damascus, defending this truth, spoke with sorrow of its enemies—those in league with

the devil—for whom all deeds and thoughts that are good and pleasing unto
God constitute torture and agony, who are allergic to brotherly love and torn
apart by faith, mortified by hope, and stabbed by mercy. This unrighteous one
suggested to some the strange, foolish thought, quite contrary to divine law,
that all acts that are pleasing to God, done for the dead, bring them no benefit.
For, they say, it is written in the Scriptures, "Why is light given to a man whose
way is hid, and whom God hath hedged in?" (Job 3:23); "That every one may
receive the things done in his body, according to that he hath done, whether it
be good or bad" (II Corinthians 5:10); "In Hades, who shall give thee thanks?"
(Psalm 6:6); "God shall reward each according to his works; for whatsoever a
man soweth, that shall he also reap" (Galatians 6:7). And so, from the first days
of the Church of Christ, these and like passages came to be abused by certain
"sophists," as St. John of Damascus calls them. Thus, "For Thou shalt reward
each according to his works" and "every man shall reap what he soweth" and
similar expression refer, without doubt, to the Second Coming of the Lord to
judge the living and the dead; for then there will be no more help, and every
prayer will be ineffective. With the arrival of Doomsday, the time that has been
allotted for man to obtain his own and others' salivation will come to an end.
Time and means have varied. St. John of Damascus, relating these and similar
expressions to the end of the world, says, "These words shall indeed come true
for indifferent souls. Where can they then find the poor? Where the priest?
There is no place for prayer and alms. And so, till that hour comes, let us help
one another and offer sacrifices of brotherly love to God Who loves brotherhood and Who is merciful and kind to souls."

Life Beyond the Grave
The Inner Connection With the Preceding Sections

THE SOUL, AFTER IT SEPARATES FROM THE BODY, only now enters upon the true, genuine life of bliss meant for it, which was unattainable on earth and which is possible for the soul after leaving the body, after death. The soul begins to live in the world beyond the grave. The truth of immortality constitutes the subject of the first part: "Death in Relation to Immortality." In passing over to the other world, the soul, through the characteristic of undying divine love born into it, is not separated from those beloved to it and like unto it, but maintains an unbroken bond, an inner tie, a mutual relationship, and communion with souls that remain yet on earth. Or, one could say that the living have an inner bond and communion with the perfected dead, and this makes up the subject of the second part: "The Inner Connection and Mutual Relationship Between the Living and the Dead." Life beyond the grave in general, and that of the imperfect departed in particular is in a relationship with the life of those still on earth. The latter, on account of love, sympathize with the state of the imperfect departed in the other world and afford them beneficial influence by means of visible, palpable signs of the spiritual bond and communion with the imperfect. This is the subject of the third part, "The Dogmatic Teaching of the Church Concerning Intercession by the Living for the Departed." And, finally, the life itself of the dead beyond the grave is addressed—how souls live in the other world: as they did on earth or otherwise? Wherein does the life beyond the grave consist, and what sort of a life is it? This is the subject of the fourth part of the book: *How Our Departed Ones Live,* so important and necessary for our troubled time. This is especially true of the second half of the nineteenth century (and even more so in the whole of the twentieth and as we enter into the twenty-first century), which has been filled with a spirit of curiosity, doubt, little faith, and unbelief. And so, the subject of this part, "Life Beyond the Grave," comprising the doctrine of Orthodoxy, is closely bound internally with the truths of the first three parts, namely, with the truth of immortality (first part); the truth of the bond, union, and mutual relationship of spiritual-moral beings (second part); and, finally, with the truth of the genuine communion

169

of these beings, the interaction and mutual influence of this world with that beyond the grave, and likewise of the dead and the living, a truth known to the ancient world as well (third part). The contents of this present part of the book, *How Our Departed Ones Live*, is as follows:

i) Life beyond the grave in general.

ii) The first period of life beyond the grave.

iii) The Second Coming of Christ to earth. The resurrection of the dead. The final judgment of moral beings, and the end of the age.

iv) The second period of life beyond the grave.

Section I

1. Life Beyond the Grave in General

a) A Definition of Life Beyond the Grave

I believe that Thou, Christ, the son of the living God, didst come into the world to us sinners, in order to save those that believe in Thee from sin, accursedness, and death. I believe that Thou, Christ, the Son of God, didst take upon Thyself the sins of the whole world, obtaining thereby, for them that believe in Thee, forgiveness of sins and life everlasting beyond the grave. But what is life beyond the grave or what sort of life is it after death? Wishing to come to as much of an understanding as I can of this mysterious question, I remember Thy words, O Christ our God, "without Me ye can do nothing good, but ask and it shall be given you"; and therefore I pray Thee humbly and with contrition of heart, come to my help, O Thou that enlightenest every man in the world, that cometh unto Thee; Thyself bless and point out, with the cooperation of Thine all-holy Spirit, where we should seek the resolution of our question on life beyond the grave, a question so needful for our time, striving, as it is, to explain all that is seen and unseen to the glory of truth. For us the elucidation is needed in itself, but also to deflect two false directions of human thought that now are fighting for dominance: that is, materialism and spiritism, which are expressions of a diseased condition of the soul, an epidemic condition, contrary to Christian teaching.

There never was, is not, and cannot be anything more true than the prophecies of the word of God or the revealed and divine truths found in Holy Tradition and Holy Scripture. Here is one source for the resolution of our question, a source to which man was commanded to turn for answers in such cases. "Search the Scriptures" (John 5:39), or "Have ye not read, what was written for the ancients?" (Mark 12:10); or "The kingdom of God is in you" (Luke 17:21), or "Seek first the kingdom of God and His truth," and so on. From these words of the Holy Scriptures, we see two kinds of evidence concerning our question on life after death: outward evidence, outside of man (that is, Holy Tradition and Holy Scripture) and inward evidence, hidden inside of man (his spirit and the qualities of his soul).

And so, Divine Revelation and sensible teaching about the soul are the two main sources from which the undoubted truths flow concerning life beyond the grave. The Lord Jesus Christ Himself pointed to these two sources: Revelation and psychology. Tradition and Scripture represent life beyond the grave to us as a continuation of that on earth, in a new world under completely new conditions. Life beyond the grave is a continuation of earthly life, in the words of Jesus Christ, Who taught that the kingdom of God is within us, a kingdom of truth, peace, and joy in the Holy Spirit. If some—the good, the God-fearing—have paradise in their heart, then, on the contrary, others—the evil—have hell in their heart. And so, the state beyond the grave, that is, paradise and Hades, have their counterpart on earth in souls, a counterpart that constitutes, as it were, the beginning of eternal life beyond the grave. The character of life beyond the grave can already be seen in the life and activity of the soul on earth; and therefore, studying the moral state of souls on earth, we can see in advance their condition beyond the grave.

The mental state of Christian meekness and humility, joined with the repose granted by God's promise, fills the soul with heavenly peace. "Be meek and humble of heart, and ye shall find rest for your souls," as the Lord Jesus Christ taught. This is the beginning of a blissful, peaceful, untroubled life of paradise on earth.

An unsatisfied passionate state on earth, which is one unnatural to man, contrary to his nature, not in agreement with the will of God, is a reflection, in only a small degree, of the beginning of moral torment and the beginning of an eternal, unceasing development of passions in the soul: envy, pride, greed, carnality, gluttony, hatred, and sloth. These passions kill the soul even while on earth, unless the soul heals itself in time by repentance and resistance to passion.

Each of us, if attentive to himself, has experienced to some extent both of these inner spiritual states of the soul. We are free of passion when the soul is fully embraced by something unearthly, full of a spiritual joy we do not understand that makes one ready for any virtue, even complete self-denial and willingness to sacrifice oneself for heaven. Then there is the passionate state which makes us forgetful of ourselves and ready for any iniquity. It completely spoils all of human nature, both spiritual (the soul) and material (the body).

On earth some people are called alive, others dead. But who is dead? This is not a human being, but a part of a human being: the body. It is committed to the ground like a seed to flower, like a treasure[1] buried in the cemetery until a certain time. But the main part of man, the image and likeness of God his Creator, the soul is alive; it has gone over from the earth to the world beyond the grave, has taken up its abode and lives there. Jesus Christ bore witness to this truth, that there are no dead: "God is not a God of the dead" (Luke 20:38), and all are alive to God. Beyond the grave we all will be alive. Despite such a high technical development in our time, we see a spiritual and moral decline so profound that even the truth of the soul's existence beyond the grave is forgotten, the purpose of human life is forgotten. One may ask: Whom should we believe, the enemy of our salvation who suggests doubts that lead to disbelief in truths revealed by God or God in whom the believer is to be alive forever according to His promise? If there were not a new life beyond the grave, then what purpose would life on earth serve, what would be the use of virtue? God's wondrous providence clearly shows that man is created for immortality. Our life on earth is the beginning and preparation for life without end beyond the grave.

Faith in the life to come beyond the grave is a doctrine of Orthodoxy, and it is the twelfth article of the Creed. One may ask, What is life beyond the grave? We answer: It is the continuation of the present life, only in another sphere under completely different, new conditions. Life beyond the grave is a further continuation into eternity of the moral development of good and truth or else the development of evil, of untruth. Just as on earth life either brings one closer to God or distances him from God, so also beyond the grave some souls are with God and in God, while others are far from Him. The soul passes beyond the grave, taking away with it all that belongs to it: all its inclinations, its habits—be they good or bad—all its passions with which it has become linked, and for which it lived, will not leave it beyond the grave. Life beyond the grave is the manifestation of the soul's immortality bestowed upon it by God Himself in its purpose and substance. The image and likeness and the breath of life have made the soul a personal and an immortal being, just as its Creator is personal and immortal, eternal: "God created man for incorruption and created him in His Own image and likeness" (Wisdom of Solomon 2:23).

[1]Here there is a play on words in the Russian: *klad* means a treasure, that which is laid up, and *kládbische* is a cemetery, a place for burial.

With the concept of life beyond the grave, closely and inseparably bound are the concepts of eternity and immortality of the soul. Eternity is an expanse of time having neither beginning nor end and, consequently, consisting of the present only, without past or future. Eternity is a single continuous, present time, without change, always remaining. Such a concept of eternity applies only to God. From the moment an infant receives life in his mother's womb, eternity unfolds for a human being; he enters eternity, begins his unending existence, which makes him immortal. And so, according to the teaching of our Church, immortality is a state of the soul consisting both in the completeness of the soul's being, and in its maintaining of its personality and awareness (Archimandrite Anthony, *Dogmatic Theology*, Sections 337 and 33).

In the first period of eternity, when the infant is still in the mother's womb, the body, or outer man, is formed for eternity; in the second period of eternity, man's dwelling on earth, one might say that the soul or inner man is formed for eternity. In this manner, earthly life serves as a beginning for the third period of eternity, life beyond the grave, which in this case is an endless continuation of the moral development of the soul. In a general sense, eternity is a space of time with neither beginning nor end; though in regard to man, eternity has a beginning, but not an end. The concepts of eternity, immortality, and life beyond the grave are born into the soul of man; he knows them, and therefore they constitute a natural quality of all humanity in all times and places, beginning with our first ancestors,[2] no matter what the level of man's intellectual development. To be sure, until the light of Christianity shone upon mankind, the concepts of eternity, immortality, and life beyond the grave were pictured in false and crude forms. Ancient graves from prehistoric times contain evidence of these concepts existing in the awareness of prehistoric man. All beliefs which express a conscience promise man eternity, immortality of the soul, and either a happy or an unhappy existence beyond the grave. Consequently, the life to come, constituting a continuation of the present life, depends entirely on the character of that life. Whatever relationship the soul has here on earth to the Lord Jesus Christ, the Source of Life, such a relationship will be eternal as the Lord teaches: "The believer begins his eternal life on earth and will live forever; but he that believeth not is condemned even on earth for his unbelief and hath died on earth for life eternal." The good or bad state of the soul, begun on earth and developed more and more, will continue to unfold further and further beyond the grave for all eternity. However, the state beyond the grave of some souls, whose lot is not finally determined at the individual judgment, depends on the life of those

[2]That is, beginning with Adam and Eve.

living on earth. Properly speaking, life on earth and the life of those who remain on earth determine the life beyond the grave of certain imperfect dead.

Eternity, the immortality of the soul, and therefore its life beyond the grave are concepts of the human spirit, hence they are concepts belonging to all mankind, closely tied to the religious beliefs of all peoples, all times, and places regardless of man's moral and mental development. However, various peoples at various times have had differing pictures of life beyond the grave, and this did depend on their level of intellectual and moral development. Tribes at a lower level of development imagined life beyond the grave in the crudest forms as a complete continuation of earthly life with all its physical enjoyments and delights; while others conceived of a less pleasant life beyond the grave as if bereft of earthly joys. The world, in their view, consisted of an actual, living, present world, and another that was a realm of shadows. Such was the other world as seen by the ancient Greeks: a place where souls existed without purpose, as wandering shades (the view of Homer). Even now, the crudest peoples in the world, the Kamchadals,[3] the Greenlanders, the inhabitants of the Land of Fire, or of Nagasaki express a conviction of life after death in their beliefs and rites. Every wild man, dying, sets off for the realm of his fathers, the land of spirits. The living do not forget the dead, dedicating certain times to their memory. Let us take, for example, a short excerpt from a description of the holiday of the dead in Nagasaki ("Nature and People," March 1878). "As twilight falls, the inhabitants of Nagasaki set off in procession to various cemeteries. Lighted paper lanterns are set on the graves, and in a few moments such places of final rest are enlivened by a fantastic illumination. Relatives and friends of the departed bring various foods with them, especially fruit, intended for the dead; part of the food is consumed by the living and part is left on the graves. Various kinds of foods prepared for the dead only are put into special little boats and set afloat on the water, at the whim of the current, which will take them to the souls beyond the grave. There beyond the ocean is paradise, in their conception."

Savages, being firmly convinced of a life beyond the grave, seek to appease the dead by cruelty to prisoners of war, avenging blood with blood by blood vengeance. Death is not fearful to the savage; he goes to meet it with equanimity. Why? Because of a living faith in life beyond the grave.

All the burial customs and ceremonies that existed and still exist among ancient and modern peoples, in more or less clear features, express the beliefs and conceptions, divinations, and hopes of man for his future fate beyond the grave.

[3] A native tribe inhabiting the southern part of the Kamchatka peninsula in Eastern Siberia.

The truth of the immortality of the soul, its life beyond the grave, and, besides that, the truth of the inner bond and mutual relationship and communion of this world and that beyond the grave have been stated by representatives of national consciousness: by Socrates, Plato, Cicero, and the medieval writers. Savage tribes believe that the souls of the dead wander about their homes in the form of shades. Recognizing the truth of the soul's life beyond the grave, the savages hear in the very wind the languid moans of wandering shades. Souls borne by the wind, in the opinion of the poets of antiquity, were purified of earthly errors as, for example, Virgil wrote. Recognizing the truth of life beyond the grave, many savages pictured it physically and thought that the soul had need of gratifying bodily needs, for which reason they would put food, drink, weaponry, and objects of amusement into the grave with the dead. Lest the soul remain lonely in the next world without family, without servants, without horses and other appurtenances of life on earth, for this purpose they killed slaves, slew or burned the wives of the deceased at the grave. At the graves of nursing infants, the mothers would pour out milk, and the Greenlanders, if a baby dies, kill a dog and put it into the grave with the infant hoping that the clever shade of the dog will serve as a guide for the timid and inexperienced child in the next world. Despite all their lack of development, the ancient pagan peoples and the savages of today, coinciding in their lower level of development, have the idea of a moral principle in the retribution for earthly deeds after death. The work of Pritchard and Alger, who collected facts on this subject, serves as evidence of what we have said, that primitive peoples have a conviction of recompense beyond the grave. "Even among the undeveloped primitives," writes Mr. Caro (in "Christian Reading" for 1876, Part 1, "On the Origin of Belief in a Future Life"), "this conviction strikes us as to the subtlety of moral sense which cannot fail to amaze." The natives of Fiji, whom travelers describe to us as being the last of humanity in their development, are convinced that after death the soul stands before judgment. In all mythological sagas, though more or less crude in form, almost every people has the concept of a preliminary examination of souls before the judgment over them. "In the view of the Hurons," writes Parkman, "the souls of the departed must first undergo a journey filled with all manner of obstacles and dangers. They must cross rapids by a flimsy plank which shakes under their feet; a fierce dog on the opposite bank will not let them cross over and tries to throw them into an abyss. Further on, they must go along a path that winds between shaking crags that fall on them, crushing the travelers who do not know how to avoid danger. In the opinion of animist Negroes, the souls of good people on the way to the Divinity must undergo persecution by evil spirits, *dinis,* whence came their custom of offering sacrifices to these *dinis* for the dead. In classical mythology, at the gates of Hades we meet up with the three-headed Cerberus who must be placated with sacrifices. The Guinean Negroes are convinced that two spirits, one good and the other evil, accompany the soul after its departure from the body. On the way an obstacle is met with: a wall closes off the way. A good soul with the help of the good *jinni,* easily flies over the wall; an evil soul, on the contrary, is broken against the wall. This concept is quite reminiscent of the bridge "al-sirat" among the Moslems. In the world beyond the grave, in all pagan beliefs, there are places of reward and punishment.

Before the true light of the Christian faith shone upon humanity, life beyond the grave was conceived of in a highly confused and unclear way. The full and vivid form of individual immortality always remained something foreign to a non-Christian conception. Therefore, as soon as the question of life beyond the grave passed from the realm of religion into the realm of philosophy, the latter found no better way out for the soul than being merged with the divinity itself, or with the world spirit, in which case there could of course be no question of the soul's continued existence after man's death. All peoples believed that after death the soul continued its existence beyond the grave; and that continuing to exist it did not cease its bond with the living, with those still on earth. And as life beyond the grave was seen vaguely by the ancient mind as something unclear and mysterious, therefore the souls that had passed over aroused a kind of fear, a mistrust, among the living. Believing in an unbroken bond of the dead with the living and in such an influence as the dead can exert on the living, the latter sought means to dispose the denizens of the other world to love for the living. These means used in deep antiquity were: respect for ancestors, sacrifices, special religious rites, and incantations; also necromancy, the false art of calling up the shades of the dead—an ancient pagan spiritism in which the one who invoked shades was called a necromancer, an ancient pagan medium.

Mankind bases its faith on life beyond the grave 1) on Divine Revelation found in Holy Tradition and the Holy Scriptures of the Old and New Testaments, 2) on Jesus Christ and His glorious resurrection, 3) on the teaching of the Church, 4) on the teaching of the Holy Fathers and doctors of the Church, 5) on the concepts of God, the soul, and its qualities, 6) on the conclusions of sane reason, and 7) on the evidence of secular writers. This is whereon humanity, from its appearance on earth until the present day, has based its faith in immortality and unshaken conviction that there is life after death. We said that mankind bases its faith in life beyond the grave first and foremost on revealed truths found in Holy Tradition and Holy Scripture. We know that after the first man, the forefather of the human race, for a long time the art of writing was unknown; and therefore there was nothing written, there were no books, but the truths and rules of life and, in general, all that was significant in those times was passed on orally. In this way all religious truths that were passed on from generation to generation came to Noah who conveyed them to his sons and they in turn to their new, post-diluvian posterity. The nations that descended from the sons of Noah knew the truth of life beyond the grave as part of their tradition until the time when each people codified this in their written beliefs. Consequently, the truth of the immortality of the soul and of its everlasting life beyond the grave were kept in tradition until Moses was the first to make repeated mention of them in his divinely inspired Scripture, in various parts of his Pentateuch.

And so, if the truth of life beyond the grave was kept in tradition until Moses, if it was passed on from ancestors to descendants, much helped by longevity, then the question arises: Did our first forefathers know of their immortality and did they have any conception of life beyond the grave? Hearing the word "death" from God, Adam and Eve knew at once that they had been created immortal. Condemned to death, they soon heard also of their Redeemer from sin, condemnation, and death. Consequently, the concepts of immortality and life beyond the grave were known to Adam. This revealed truth was passed on from Adam and from generation to generation, so that all nations of antiquity definitely knew the idea of life beyond the grave from tradition, but their concepts of it varied.

That awareness of life after death was common to all mankind as Chrysostom bears witness saying, "The Hellenes[4] and the barbarians, the poets and philosophers, and in general the whole human race are in agreement with our belief that each is recompensed in the next life for his deeds" ("Homily 1.X. on the Second Epistle to the Corinthians"). This witness of a Christian writer on the existence of an awareness of the afterlife in tradition is supported by another witness, the pagan philosopher Socrates who said: "I am convinced that a man's fate is assigned him after death and that, according to the eternal faith of all mankind, for the good this fate will be better than for the evil."

Divine Revelation, both in the Old Testament Scriptures and in the New, has revealed the truth to man concerning his personal existence beyond the grave. The word of God, as truth, is and should be the source of all our knowledge (science); all our discoveries should be confirmed by it and in agreement with it. All knowledge must derive from the one basic truth of Christ, Who Himself bore witness of this: "I am the Light of the world, and everyone that

---

[4]That is, the ancient Greeks.

comes to me shall not remain in darkness" (John 8:12), that is, he shall be enlightened spiritually. All sciences enlighten the spiritual side of man (the soul) but not the physical side, the body. Thus, the first writer of Divine Revelation, Moses, several times in his writings states this truth, though not as clearly as it is expressed in the New Testament. Here are the words used by Moses to express this doctrine of life beyond the grave: "God said to Abraham: Thou shalt depart to thy fathers in peace" (Genesis 15:15). It is known that Abraham was buried in Canaan, while the body of his father Tharra[5] was buried in Harran, and the bodies of his ancestors in Ur. The bodies lie buried in various places, but God says to Abraham, "Thou shalt depart unto thy fathers," that is, thy soul shall be united beyond the grave with the souls of all thine ancestors who are in Sheol (Hades). And further on Moses writes, "And Abraham died ... and was gathered to his people" (Genesis 25:8). In just the same fashion Moses describes the death of Isaac also saying that he "was gathered to his people" (35:29). The patriarch Jacob, overcome by grief over the death of his beloved son, said, "In sadness I shall go down to my son into the nethermost parts" (37:35). Here again is expressed the same dogma of the immortality of the soul and the continuation of personal existence beyond the grave and the meeting with a beloved son. The word "nethermost," used by Jacob, signifies a mysterious habitation beyond the grave. Jacob, feeling the approach of death, said: "I am gathered to my people ..." (49:29,33) and died, and was gathered to his people. God commanded Moses to prepare for Aaron's departure from earthly life with these words: "Let Aaron be gathered to his people ... and let Aaron depart and die" (Numbers 20:24,26). Then the Lord said also to Moses: "And thou, when thou shalt see the land of Canaan, shalt be gathered to thy people" (27:13). And the Lord said to Moses, "Avenge the children of Israel of the Midianites: afterward shalt thou be gathered unto thy people" (31:1,2). All the men of Korah, according to the word of Moses, were swallowed up by the earth, and they went down alive into the uttermost depths (16:30). And the Lord said to Moses: "And die in the mount whither thou goest up, and be gathered unto thy people; as Aaron thy brother died in mount Hor, and was gathered unto his people" (Deuteronomy 32:50); "And when all that generation was gathered to their fathers ..." (Judges 2:10). The Lord said to King Josiah: "I will gather thee unto thy fathers" (IV Kings 22:20). "Why died I not from the womb?" cried Job in the midst of his temptations "Why did I not give up the ghost when I came out of the belly? Why did the knees prevent me? or why the breasts that I should suck? For now should I have lain still and been quiet,

[5] Also written Terah (Genesis 11:26).

I should have slept: then had I been at rest, With kings and counsellors of the earth, which build desolate places for themselves; Or with princes that had gold, who filled their houses with silver: Or as an hidden untimely birth I had not been; as infants which never saw light. There the wicked cease from troubling; and there the weary be at rest. There the prisoners rest together; they hear not the voice of the oppressor. The small and great are there; and the servant is free from his master" (Job 3:11–19). "I know," says Job, "that my redeemer liveth, and that he shall at the latter day raise up this my crumbling body from the dust, and in my flesh shall I see God: Whom I shall see for myself, and mine eyes shall behold Him, and not the eyes of another" (Job 19:25–27). Further on, is not the awareness of a future, everlasting life beyond the grave unfolded in the Psalter, the book of the King and Prophet David? In all things a preference of heavenly things to those of earth is expressed and the desire for eternal communion with the One God Who is all things for man; here also belong his prophetic images of the redemption of mankind by the Divine Man (Psalms 15:11; 16:15; 48:16; 72:23).[6] The holy David bears witness that the state of the departed is improved through the solicitousness of the living, and that the dead can no longer do anything to help themselves (Psalms 6:6); "Then shall the dust return to the earth as it was: and the spirit shall return unto God who gave it" (Ecclesiastes 12:7); all these and similar expressions contain the idea of eternity. Further, the Prophet Job says: "Before I go whence I shall not return, even to the land of darkness and the shadow of death; a land of darkness, as darkness itself; and of the shadow of death, without any order, and where the light is as darkness" (Job 10:21–22). The passages here quoted from the Old Testament serve as a direct refutation of the false view of certain critics, who suppose that in the Old Testament, nothing whatever is said about the immortality of the soul and about its personal life beyond the grave. Such a false opinion was completely refuted by Henri Martene and by Professor Wholfson, who in this regard afforded an important service by discovering in the Crimea the graves and tombstones of Hebrews who had lived before the birth of Christ. In the inscriptions, one can see the vital faith of the Jews in the immortality of the soul and in its life beyond the grave. This important discovery also fully refutes another absurd view of Renan's who supposed that the Hebrews had borrowed the idea of the immortality of the soul from the Greeks.

All the above-cited passages of the Old Testament on personal, conscious, and effective life beyond the grave show the complete falseness of the opinion that nowhere in the Old Testament is there mention of life after death. Those

[6]Septuagint numbering.

that slander the Old Testament, claiming that it is silent on life after death, call the passages quoted above neither more nor less than "poetic imagery." The Founder of the New Testament, the same Lord Jesus Christ who founded the Old Testament as well, draws humanity similar pictures of life beyond the grave, for example, in the parables of the King's Banquet (Matthew 22), a depiction of a society celebrating the arrival of the King at the banquet and the casting out of the unbecomingly clothed guest, that of the ten Virgins, of the Rich Man and Lazarus. Did not all the teaching of the Lord breathe, not an earthly, but a heavenly life? His Sermon on the Mount and conversation with the Sadducees present a teaching on life beyond the grave and such a life as is like that of the angels. Having given revealed truths to the Old Testament Church which served as a preparation for the New, He opened the veil that had hitherto been closed and which separates this life from that beyond the grave. Referring often to the Old Testament and passages in it relating to man's life after death, Jesus Christ showed the resurrection of the dead in actual fact: the son of the widow of Nain, the daughter of Jairus, the four-days' dead Lazarus, all called forth from the life beyond the grave. Was it not an actual fact, one that witnesses the life beyond the grave, that Elias and Moses appeared at the Lord's glorious Transfiguration on Mt. Tabor? Having revealed the secrets of life beyond the grave to man, the lot of the righteous and of the sinners (Matthew 8:11–12), the Lord showed the resurrection and therefore life beyond the grave by means of His teaching, life, passion, redemption of man from eternal death, and finally by His Resurrection. Jesus Christ Himself and His resurrection from the dead gave evidence and incontrovertible proof of the immortality of the soul and of its life beyond the grave. He was the first, as the new Adam, the founder of a new humanity, to rise from the dead and by so doing demonstrated for all to see and feel, beyond all attempts to disprove it, that there is eternal life beyond the grave. Every attempt made against life beyond the grave by a haughty mind could still have some place, had it not been for the resurrection of Christ. Then only materialists, atheists, nihilists, and others like unto them could wander in the darkness, thinking carnally. The main, dominant thought of the New Testament is the restoration of the lost union of man with God for eternal life, for genuine, true life which begins for man, according to the bliss intended for him, only beyond the grave. The Christian ideal is life beyond the grave, and death does not exist for those that believe in Christ. Death's triumph is destroyed, and life beyond the grave is visibly expressed over the burial place of every Christian. What, for example, does a cross over a grave signify? It is a visible sign, a full conviction, that the one who reposes beneath this cross has not died, but is alive, because for him eternal death has been mortified, and through this cross life everlasting has been bestowed. Can life be taken from one who is immortal? And here, the Saviour Himself, pointing out to us our higher calling on earth, teaches us the immortality of our souls thus: "Fear not them that kill the body, but cannot kill the soul" (Matthew 10:28); consequently, the soul is immortal. He shows us this very immortality of the soul in the parable of the Rich Man and Lazarus, where the souls of both, after departing the body, exist; and also: "God is not a God of the dead, but of the living" (Luke 20:38). Here is the clear teaching of God Himself on the immortality of the soul. "Whether we live, or whether we die, we are the Lord's," testifies St. Paul. But if we are the Lord's, and our Lord is not a God of the dead but of the living, therefore before God all are alive, both those still on earth and those who have taken up their abode in the world beyond the grave. They are alive for the Lord, alive for His Church, as Her members, for it was said to them: "He that believeth in Me shall live forever, and if he die, he shall live" (John 6:44; 11:25). If the dead are alive for the Church, then they are alive for us, for our mind and heart. The soul, together with the inclinations it has made its own on earth—be they good or evil—passes over into the world beyond the grave. Filled with love, and in the kingdom of love, it loves its own who remain yet on earth, and cannot forget them.

Did not the holy Apostles, their successors, and many Saints show, together with their teaching of immortality and life beyond the grave, this truth in actual practice? They raised the dead, spoke with the dead, as if with the living, directing various questions to them, for example the Apostle Thomas asked the slain youth, the son of the pagan priest who had killed him and received an answer. To be sure, while proving the divinity of the Lord Jesus Christ, these miracles bore witness at the same time to immortality and the life of the soul beyond the grave. All the doctors of the Church had as the main subject of their teaching the life beyond the grave and keeping man from eternal ruin. The Church's use of means to improve the lot of the dead shows unshaken faith in the life beyond the grave. Faith in the life beyond the grave has always corresponded to thought of and faith in a Divine Higher Being. With a lessening of faith in God, faith in life beyond the grave and a reward after death was also lost. And so, whoever does not believe in life beyond the grave, does not have faith in God either.

Here are the passages in the New Testament[7] that witness man's life beyond the grave, and which have been examined in detail where the subject was

---

[7]Note that the verse numbers, and in some cases even chapter numbers (in the Old Testament, for example, in the Prophecy of Isaiah), may differ somewhat from one version of the Bible to another.

discussed: the teaching on life beyond the grave (I Corinthians 15; Hebrews 9:27; Luke 20:38; and others); the teaching on the existence of the unseen world and its influence on the visible world. The activity of the visible world is activity of the invisible world, or, the character of man's activity bears the marks of the invisible world, of beings good or evil (Matthew 4:1–11; 12:24; 13:39; 16:27; 17:14–21; 25:41; Revelation 12:7–9; Jude 6; II Corinthians 11:14–15; Hebrews 1:14); the teaching that life beyond the grave begins on earth (Matthew 16:27); the teaching that the dead are alive; on life in society after death; on encounters, union, a bond and communion in paradise (Matthew 8:11; John 17:21–25; I Thessalonians 4:17); the teaching on the bond and relationship of those in the world beyond the grave with those still on earth (Matthew 22:32; Luke 20:38; Ephesians 2:19–20); the teaching on heaven and hell and on various degrees of bliss and punishment (Luke 12:47–48; 16:24; John 3:3; 14:2; Romans 2:6; I Corinthians 2:9; 15:39–42; I Peter 1:8; Mark 9:43–49; Matthew 5:22, 29–30; 13:42–43; 9:28; Revelation 14:10; Jude 7); the teaching on the resurrection and on eternal dwelling together in company (I Thessalonians 4:13, 16–17; John 5:28–29; 10:27–28; Matthew 8:11; 13:30; 24:31; Luke 13:28–29; Romans 8:11; Philippians 3:20–21); the teaching on an incomplete reward in the first period of life after death, and on a full reward only at the Day of Judgment (Revelation 6:11; 11:18; II Corinthians 5:10; II Timothy 4:8; Colossians 3:4; and others); the teaching on the time of our death, the coming of Christ to judge the world, and the end of the world. At Doomsday, all secrets will be made known (Matthew 24:42, 44; 25:13; Mark 13:34–37; I Corinthians 4:5; Revelation 3:3; and others); the teaching on the life of the Saints in paradise (Philippians 1:23; Revelation 7:9–17; I John 3:2; Matthew 22:30; Luke 23:43; John 14:2–3; 17:24; II Corinthians 5:1–8; I Thessalonians 4:14; and others); the teaching on Doomsday and on everlasting torment and eternal bliss, in which the body shall take part (Matthew 22:11–14,30; the entire twenty-fifth chapter; Mark 16:16; Luke 16:23–26; John 3:36; Revelation 14:11; II Thessalonians 5:11; I Corinthians 15:42–44; Philippians 3:21); the teaching on the end of the world, on meeting and remaining in common activity beyond the grave (I John 2:18; Revelation 1:3; 3:4; 6:9; 7:9–10; Matthew 24; John 14:2–4); the teaching that man's soul goes at once after the individual judgment to its place assigned in the world beyond the grave which constitutes the further continuation of its moral development in good (paradise) or evil (Hades), the development of the moral state in which it crosses the threshold of new life (Luke 16:19–31; 23:43).

b) Nomenclature of the States of Souls Beyond the Grave or of the Places Where They Abide

All the great minds of antiquity, for example Plato, Socrates, and others, realizing and sensing their own immortality and the life to come, nevertheless, despite all mental efforts, could not elucidate the life beyond the grave. It is self-evident that at the lower and more ancient levels of development, man still did not know where to assign the souls of the dead; and in his conception, of which we can get some idea from the primitives of today, these souls wandered in a vague, air-like form around their abandoned homes.

Little by little, thought and imagination created more or less definite places of habitation for the departed souls, with such names as countries or fields of souls, islands of the blessed, and so on. Next, out of awareness of good and evil and rightful reward for the one or the other, these places usually were divided into two realms, the typical character of which has a more or less distant similarity to the concepts of heaven and hell.

God is omnipresent; however, there is a special place of His presence where He appears in all His glory and remains eternally with His chosen ones, according to the words of Jesus Christ: "Where I am, there shall My servant be" (John 12:26); "where" signifies a special place in the universe where the righteous forever abide with God. Consequently, on the other side, whoever was not a servant of the true God, will not be with God after death, and therefore a special place is required for such in the universe. Here is the beginning of a teaching on the two states beyond the grave: one of reward, the other of punishment.

In the mystery of death, the soul, separated from the body, lives and feels. It passes over into the land of beings like unto itself, into a land of spiritual beings, into the realm of angels. And, according to the character of its life on earth, it is joined either to the good angels in the kingdom of heaven, or to the evil angels in Hades. The Lord Jesus Christ Himself bore witness to this truth. The wise thief and the beggar Lazarus were placed in paradise at once after their death; but the rich man was at once taken down to hell (Luke 23:43; 16:19–31). "We believe," as the Eastern Patriarchs affirm in their Orthodox Confession of Faith (Article 18), "that the souls of the dead enjoy bliss or undergo torment according to their works. Having parted from the body, they at once pass over to joy or to sadness and trouble: however, they experience neither perfect bliss nor complete suffering, for each will obtain either complete bliss or complete torment after the common resurrection when the soul will be reunited with the body in which it lived either virtuously or depravedly."

A careful examination of the word of God reveals to us that there are various conditions of the departed beyond the grave. The Book of the Wisdom of Solomon, in Chapter 3, sets forth the teaching on the twofold status beyond the grave: 1) bliss, the state of the righteous, and 2) punishment, the state of the wicked and of sinners: the third to fifth chapters inclusive are devoted to life after death: the repose of the righteous and the self-reproach of the wicked, of sinners. These two states, of the righteous and of sinners, or the places where, according to their character, they are, also bear various names. The first state, or the place of the saved, is called by different names in the Scriptures: the kingdom of heaven (Matthew 8:11), the kingdom of God (Luke 13:20, 29; I Corinthians 15:50), paradise (Luke 23:43), the house of the heavenly Father, the heavenly mansion or bridal chamber, as the Church sings,[8] "I see Thy bridal chamber, O Saviour, decorated," and other names as well (John 14:2; Matthew 19:21; Luke 12:33; Hebrews 4:9–10; 10:34; 13:14). But the state of the outcasts, or their place, is called Gehenna, where the worm dies not and the fire is never extinguished (Matthew 5:22, 29–30; 10:28; 18:8,9; 25:41,46; Mark 9:43,48), the fiery furnace, where there is wailing and gnashing of teeth (Matthew 13:50), the lake of fire and brimstone (Revelation 14:10; 19:20; 20:10,14,15; 21:8), the outer darkness (Matthew 22:13; 25:30), the abyss, fearsome even for the evil spirits (Luke 8:21), Tartarus, the darkness of Hades (II Peter 2:4), the land of eternal darkness where there is no light (Job 10:22; II Peter 2:17), Hades, hell (Isaiah 14:15; Hosea 13:14; Matthew 11:23; Revelation 20:13–14), the prison of spirits (I Peter 3:19), the nethermost parts of the earth (Ephesians 4:9), the uttermost depths (Philippians 2:10; Job 11:8; Revelation 5:3) and the well [or key] of the abyss (Revelation 9:2). The Lord Jesus Christ calls this state of condemned souls, for the most part, simply "death"; and the souls found in this state, the condemned sinners, He calls "dead men," for "in death there is no remembrance of Thee, in the grave who shall praise Thee?" (Psalms 6:6), "But we, Thy people and the sheep of Thy pasture, will confess Thee, from generation to generation, will proclaim Thy praise" (Psalms 78:13). Therefore the concepts "death" and "dead man" refer to the life beyond the grave, and for the most part to the state of the condemned, that of Gehenna; for death is a drawing away from God, from the kingdom of heaven, or in short, the deprivation of true life, of bliss.

[8]This is a chant sung at Matins during the first part of Holy Week.

c) The Periods of Life Beyond the Grave. Age. Personal, Conscious, and Active Life

Man's life beyond the grave comprises two periods: 1) life beyond the grave before the resurrection of the dead and the general Judgment, or the life of the soul, and 2) life after this Judgment, the life of the whole man. In the second period of life beyond the grave, all have the same age, according to the teaching of the word of God.

The Lord Jesus Christ Himself expressed His teaching about life beyond the grave as follows to the Sadducees: "God is not a God of the dead, but of the living; for all are alive unto Him" (Luke 20:38). This is evidence of the personal continuation of being (life) of the soul beyond the grave in general. All, both the people on earth and those beyond the grave, the righteous as well as the unrighteous, are alive, live an unending life, since they were meant to be witnesses of the eternal glory and power of God and of His justice. The Lord Jesus Christ taught that God is not of the dead, but of the living, that there they do not marry, as was the case on earth, but they live as angels of God. The Saviour said outright that beyond the grave souls live as angels (Luke 20:34–36); therefore the state of souls beyond the grave is a conscious one, and if the souls are alive like angels, then their state is also an active one, as our Orthodox Church teaches, and not an unconscious or dormant state as some suppose. The false teaching on a sleeping, unconscious, and therefore inactive state of souls in the first period of its life beyond the grave, which is not in agreement with the Revelation of the Old and New Testaments, nor with healthy reason, appeared as early as the third century in Christian society as a result of an incorrect understanding of certain expressions in the word of God. Thus, the Arab scholars known as psychopannichites, taught that man's soul, as if in sleep, remains in a sleeping, unconscious, and inactive state, like its organ the body, in the first period of life beyond the grave until it is reunited with its body. In the Middle Ages this false teaching appeared, and even Luther sometimes ascribed an unconscious state to souls beyond the grave. During the Reformation, the main proponents of this teaching were the Anabaptists,[9] or 're-baptizers', whose sect originated in Friesland[10] in 1496. Subsequently this teaching was developed by the Socinian[11] heretics, who denied the Holy Trinity and the divinity of Jesus Christ, and by the Arminians, those who followed the teaching of Arminius of Amsterdam, in the seventeenth century. The false teaching does not cease to develop even

[9]From Greek *ana-*, meaning "again," and *baptizein*, to baptize.

[10]An area in northern Germany and in the adjacent Netherlands.

[11]These were the followers of the Italian Protestant, Faustus Socinus [Fausto Sozzini, 1539–1604], and his uncle Laelius [Lelio Sozzini, 1525–1562].

in our time; the writing of Fries in 1856 is proof of this. The Revelation of the Old as well as the New Testament presents us with the doctrine on life beyond the grave, and at the same time tells us that the state of souls beyond the grave is personal, individual, conscious, and active. If it were not so, then the word of God would not show those who are asleep acting consciously. In the Old Testament, for example, the entire fifth chapter of the Book of the Wisdom of Solomon shows the conscious existence of souls in Hades. Then the Prophet Isaiah (in Chapter 14) draws a prophetic picture of the king of Babylon entering Hades and how he was met there. The picture is filled with poetry, but at the same time it expresses the full awareness of those on earth of the personal life beyond the grave of souls separated from their bodies, and shows this life beyond the grave as being conscious and active as well. "Hell from beneath is moved for thee to meet thee at thy coming: it stirreth up the dead for thee, even all the chief ones of the earth; it hath raised up from their thrones all the kings of the nations. All they shall speak and say unto thee, Art thou also become weak as we? Art thou become like unto us? . . . They that see thee shall narrowly look upon thee, and consider thee, saying, Is this the man that made the earth to tremble, that did shake kingdoms?" (Isaiah 14:9–10,16). A similar poetic picture of life in Hades, and the arrival of the Pharaoh there, and his meeting with other kings who had died and gone down to hell before him, is vividly depicted by the Prophet Ezekiel: "Whom dost thou pass in beauty? Go down, and be thou laid with the uncircumcised. They shall fall in the midst of them that are slain by the sword; she is delivered to the sword; draw her and all her multitudes. The strong among the mighty shall speak to him out of the midst of hell with them that help him; they are gone down, they lie uncircumcised, slain by the sword. Asshur is there and all her company; his graves are about him; all of them slain, fallen by the sword; Whose graves are set in the sides of the pit, and her company is round about her grave; all of them slain, fallen by the sword, which caused terror in the land of the living. There is Elam and all her multitude round about her grave, all of them slain, fallen by the sword, which are gone down uncircumcised into the nether parts of the earth, which caused their terror in the land of the living; yet have they borne their shame with them that go down to the pit. They have set her a bed in the midst of the slain with all her multitude; her graves are round about him; all of them uncircumcised, slain by the sword; though their terror was caused in the land of the living, yet have they borne their shame with them that go down to the pit; he is put in the midst of them that be slain. There is Meshech, Tubal, and all her multitude; her graves are round about him; all of them uncircumcised, slain by the sword, though they caused their terror in the land of the living. And they shall not lie with the mighty that are fallen of the uncircumcised, which are gone down to hell with their weapons of war; and they have laid their swords under their heads, but their iniquities shall be upon their bones, though they were the terror of the mighty in the land of the living. Yea, thou shalt be broken in the midst of the uncircumcised and shalt lie with them that are slain with the sword. There is Edom, her kings, and all her princes which with their might are laid by them that were slain by the sword; they shall lie with the uncircumcised, and with them that go down to the pit. There be the princes of the north, all of them, and all the Zidonians, which are gone down with the slain; with their terror they are ashamed of their might; and they lie uncircumcised with them that be slain by the sword, and bear their shame with them that go down to the pit. Pharaoh shall see them, and shall be comforted over all his multitude, even Pharaoh and all his army slain by the sword, saith the Lord GOD. For I have caused my terror in the land of the living; and he shall be laid in the midst of the uncircumcised with them that are slain with the sword, even Pharaoh and all his multitude, saith the Lord GOD" (Ezekiel 32:19–32).

The awareness of immortality, of the personal life of the soul after death, after its departure from the body—and at that, a life that is aware and active, rather than insensate and dormant—this awareness is proper to the human soul, the common awareness of mankind in all times and places, regardless of man's stage of development. Every human being, good or evil, continues beyond the grave his personal, endless existence, as our holy Church teaches. The soul, passing on into the world beyond the grave, takes all its passions, all its inclinations, habits, virtues, and vices with it. All its gifts, by which it showed itself on earth, remain with it.

Section II

1. The First Period of Life Beyond the Grave

a) A Definition of This Period

After the soul has parted from the body on earth, it continues its existence by itself in the world beyond the grave during this first period. The spirit and the soul continue their existence beyond the grave, enter into a state either of bliss or of torment from which they can be delivered by the prayers of the holy Church. In this way, the first period of life beyond the grave still includes the possibility for some souls to be delivered from the torments of Hades until the time of the Last Judgment. But the second period of life beyond the grave has only a blessed or else a tormented state. The life beyond the grave of the first period is a development leading to a new, final period of existence, corresponding to the qualities that the soul has acquired on earth. The first period of the soul's life beyond the grave is its condition immediately after leaving its body on earth and its stay in the world beyond the grave, until it is reunited with its resurrected body to receive its reward for its life on earth. The state of the soul from its separation from the body until the individual judgment was examined in the first part of this book, "Death in Relation to Immortality"; the state of the soul, or its lot, after the individual judgment until the universal judgment comprises the subject or content of the present section.

2. In General Concerning the Life and Activity of the Soul and of Its Distinct Powers Beyond the Grave

a) The Soul and Its Organ of Activity, the Body — Immortality of the Soul and Body — The Activity of the Soul on Earth and Beyond the Grave — Internal and External Activity

If man were a product of nature alone, as the materialists think and teach, seeing in him only a material nature, and denying his main or spiritual part, then one might ask: Why is it that in man's striking activity, besides what is common to animals, one sees also works that are possible only for the spirit? Thus, for example in such things as nutrition, rest, sexual activity, and so on, man, like animals, is a product of the earth; but in such matters as love (not carnal, but spiritual), in striving towards that which is true, beautiful and good, another nature (a spiritual nature) is shown in him. As a creation of the hands of God, meant to be a witness to the glory and power of his Creator, man could not be a finite being in both soul and body. God did not create, only to have His creation destroyed. The soul and body are works of God; consequently, both soul and body are immortal, are not destroyed. After the soul departs from the body, the soul lives in a spiritual world appropriate to its nature, while the body returns to the earth; man, placed between the visible and invisible worlds, those of nature and of the spirit, lives and acts in both worlds, both on earth and outside of the earth; in the body on earth, but in mind and heart outside of the earth, either in heaven or in hell. So strong and mysterious is the bond of the soul with the body, and so strong their mutual influence on each other, that the activity of

the soul on earth, directed towards what is true, exalted and beautiful, is much
held back and weakened by the body, as Jesus Christ Himself bears witness:
"The spirit is willing, but the flesh is infirm" (Matthew 26:41), which was not
the case immediately after the creation of the world; for then all was perfect,
and there was no discord in anything: the body was supposed to be, as in fact
it is, an instrument for the manifestation of the invisible, God-like soul, with
its mighty powers and amazing activity. Because the spirit is wakeful and the
flesh is weak, the battle is incessant, a battle for truth, a battle in which the soul
weakens; and often, together with the body, it falls morally, as if unwillingly
despite its desire, turning away from truth, from the goal it was intended to
reach, from the aim of its life, of its natural activity. "For that which I do I do
not understand," as the chosen vessel of the Holy Spirit, St. Paul, cries out in
sorrow, "for what I will to do, that do I not; but what I hate, that I do. Who shall
deliver me from this body of death?" (Romans 7:15,24). The activity of the soul
on earth, to a greater or lesser degree, presents a mix of good and evil, righteousness with unrighteousness. On earth the body works as a hindrance to the soul's
activity, but there in the other world, in the first period, these obstacles will be
removed by the absence of the body, and the soul will function only according
to its mood acquired on earth, either good or evil; while in the second period
of its life beyond the grave, even though under the influence of the body with
which it will again be united, this influence of the body, already changed into
one that is fine, spiritual, and incorrupt, will even aid the soul in its activity, having been freed from its present, crude needs, and having obtained new spiritual
qualities. Besides that, the Spirit of God Himself "searcheth all things, yea, the
deep things of God" (I Corinthians 2:10), and abiding on earth in the souls
and bodies of them that love God, will remain all the more with such lovers of
God in the further unfolding of truth. Under this beneficial action of the Holy
Spirit, all the mental powers, attaining unto what their nature seeks, can only
be filled with joy from the gratification of that which it desired, and the soul
will reach its bliss, its natural purpose. On earth, all the activity of the soul, as it
strives toward truth, is constantly complicated by all manner of difficulties and
sorrows: "In the world ye shall have tribulation" (John 16:33). This is the lot of
man on earth after his fall in paradise, the lot determined once and for all by
God Himself for Adam (Genesis 3:17), and in his person for all humanity, and
repeated by the Lord Jesus Christ for the new, spiritual man as well. Only the
forcing of oneself, that is, overcoming obstacles, brings gratification of desire
and hence joy. All virtues, regardless of any obstacle to their fulfillment, bring
an unearthly, spiritual joy to those who practice them, a joy in which the infirm

body takes part more or less, and the man, as it is said, is in bliss. But beyond the grave the infirm body will be transformed in its time, and will further the activity of the soul in its purpose: and that evil, in which the whole world lies, will not be there beyond the grave, and man will be eternally blissful, that is, all the activity of his soul will attain its eternal purpose. If on earth the true bliss of the soul was achieved by striving towards complete freedom from the triple lust of love for glory, love of pleasure, and love of money, then beyond the grave, the soul being completely free from this ill, will enjoy eternal bliss, in being foreign to all servitude, to all captivity of sin; if on earth it freed itself as much as possible from this enslavement to passion, unto the freedom of the sons of God, or constantly, hating sin, bewailed its captivity, awaiting humbly, patiently, and in complete commitment to the will of God, it will be released from the body of sin.

The invisible, inward, spiritual activity of the soul serves as the basis for all of man's visible, earthly activity, so that man's present visible life fully represents the invisible soul and all its characteristics. If the soul, by the determination of the Creator Himself, is immortal, that is, continues to live beyond the grave, and life is usually expressed by activity, then it is right that where there is life there is activity, and where there is activity, there is life. Consequently, the activity of the soul continues beyond the grave also. Wherein does the activity of the soul beyond the grave consist? In the same things as it did on earth. The sum total of all that its individual faculties do constitutes the activity of the soul. As its powers functioned on earth, so will they continue to function beyond the grave.

The life of the soul consists of its self-awareness, and the activity of the soul consists in carrying out spiritual-moral obligations. The activity of self-awareness is put together out of the activities of the individual mental powers, out of the activity of thinking, the activity of desiring, and the activity of the senses. The life of the soul in the first period of life beyond the grave is a purely spiritual life, an inner life, consisting of a profound delving into self, thoughts of self, and therefore self-knowledge. Removed from the body and from the material world, it is not distracted, and its powers now act without hindrance, striving towards truth. In this form the Lord Jesus Christ depicted life beyond the grave and the activity of souls in the first period after death in His parable of the Rich Man and Lazarus. The souls of the righteous man and the sinner are represented as alive and consciously acting, inwardly and outwardly, that is, their internal and external activity is depicted. Their souls think, wish, and feel. If the life beyond the grave is a continuation, a further development of earthly life, then the soul, passing over into the world beyond the grave with its earthly tendencies, habits, passions, with all the content of its character, continues its development beyond the grave also: activity that is good or evil, depending on the character of its earthly life. The earthly activity of the soul is only the beginning of its future life in the next world. True, on earth the soul can change its activity, from good to evil, and the reverse, evil to good, but that activity with which it passed into the grave is the one that will continue to develop into eternity. The object of the soul's action both on earth beyond the grave is the same: striving towards truth which must be naturally born into its inward and outward activity.

The body and all its organs do what the soul wishes, they carry out its will. This is their normal function, the object of their activity. The invisible soul acts visibly only by means of its organs. The organs by themselves are lifeless instruments. Consequently, if these organs are taken away from the soul, surely it does not cease to be a soul? It was not the body that brought life to the soul, but the soul to the body; consequently, even without the body, without all of its external organs, it retains all its powers and abilities, and their action, just as on earth, continues beyond the grave; the only difference being that their activity will be incomparably more perfect, as witnessed by the words of Jesus Christ, in which despite the immeasurable chasm that separates paradise from Hades, the deceased rich man, being in hell, saw and recognized both Abraham and Lazarus, who were in heaven; not only that, he spoke with Abraham. And so, the activity of the soul and all its powers in the world beyond the grave will be much more perfect. Here, on earth, we see distant objects with the aid of telescopes; nevertheless our vision cannot be perfect, since there is a limit beyond which sight, even helped by a telescope, cannot extend itself. But beyond the grave even a chasm does not prevent the righteous from seeing the sinners and the condemned from seeing the saved. While yet on earth the righteous, by living a Christian life, purified their senses and attained a natural state such as that of the first people before the fall, and the activity of these righteous souls went far beyond the bounds of the visible world. They understood, saw, heard, and felt the object of the spiritual world. They were in communion with spirits and souls. After this, how can one doubt or be better consoled than by that life to come when we shall live together forever, know one another, and always see one another. Because the soul, while in the body on earth, saw a person and other objects, it was the soul that saw and not the eye; it was the soul that heard and not the ear; smell, taste, touch were all felt by the soul and not by the members of the body. For this reason, these powers and abilities of the soul will be with it beyond the grave also; for it is either rewarded or punished, as one alive, feeling either reward or punishment.

The activity of the soul (man) should be based on love, which is the essence of a pure, healthy mind; activity mixed and directed by a Christian love that seeks not its own; the goal and aim of activity is the kingdom of heaven according to the commandment of the Lord Jesus Christ: "Before all else, seek the kingdom of God, and His righteousness." In all activity the name of God should be hallowed, as the activity of man should be an expression of the will of God. This is the natural activity of the soul which constitutes its purpose, as opposed to unnatural activity contrary to its nature and proceeding not from the will of God but from man's evil whim. In general, the normal, natural purpose of the soul's activity is to strive towards truth while on earth. But since our desires and strivings are endless, beyond the grave this striving towards what is true, good, and beautiful continues forever. Even the pagans, for example Plato, wrote of this purpose of the life and activity of the soul: "The goal worthy of human life, and the only goal, is to attain truth." In other words, this thought belongs to the spirit of man; therefore it is common to humanity, natural, inborn in the spirit.

If the life of the soul beyond the grave is personal, independent, and active, then this activity of the soul beyond the grave comprises the soul's activity: 1) towards God, 2) towards others, and 3) towards self.

All the powers or abilities of the soul, acting together, make up the activity of the soul; so that, without the soul, the powers by themselves do not exist, and their action is absent. The powers of the soul, acting on earth, act also in the other world when the soul passes there. Thus, the rich man mentioned by the Saviour in the Gospel (Luke 16:22–25) went down to hell in the soul after death. Here Jesus Christ represents all the activity of the soul in Hades, in its full extent. All the soul's powers are in action; conscience shows the reasons for the already unavoidable misfortune of the present; the action of the inward and outward senses bring about a cheerless torment, and, finally, the activity of the will strives without success to lighten the state of the soul, and the action of the memory of his brethren on earth and concern for their lot after death is a sign of the inner feelings and activity of the mind which have as their object the fate of his brethren who still remain on earth.

If it is natural for the soul to live in the society of beings like itself, if these beings (souls) are united while still on earth by God Himself in a bond of undying love, the souls are not separated by the grave, but, as the holy Church teaches, they also live in a society of spirits and souls. This is the unbounded family of the one heavenly Father whose members are the children of God; this is the immeasurable kingdom of the one heavenly King whose members the

Church not infrequently calls the citizens of heaven. But children in a family, citizens in a state, live in a society in various mutual relationships.

The soul, living in society, lives first for God, second for itself, and third for others, for beings like itself. These relationships of the soul to God, to itself, and to others bring about activity in it of two sorts: inward and outward. The inward activity of the soul consists of the relationships to God and to its own self, while its outward activity is made up of its various relationships to other beings and to all that surrounds it, both in this life on earth and in the world beyond the grave. Such is the dual activity of the soul on earth and beyond the grave. Self-awareness, thought, knowledge, feeling, and desire make up the inner, personal life of the soul. But the outer, communal life consists of varied activities towards all that surrounds it: toward beings and toward inanimate objects.

3. Inner Life — Inner Activity

a) Feeling — Mind — Memory — Will — Conscience — Their Activity Beyond the Grave

The very first and lowest step or, so to say, the foundation of the soul's activity consists of its internal and external feelings. A feeling is a power, an ability of the soul which receives impressions of objects by means of its external organs, the instruments of its activity. There are six such external organs and as many corresponding feelings and three internal feelings that correspond to them.

SENSES

External:	*Internal:*
Feeling	Attention
Smell	
Touch	Memory
Taste	Imagination
Sight	
Hearing	

The soul, as a spiritual-moral being, is obliged to carry on a spiritual-moral life; and therefore all its activity, as well as the activity of each of its separate powers or abilities, must be moral. Consequently feeling also, as an ability or power of the soul, must base its moral activity on its natural, inborn moral obligations. The fulfillment of the moral obligations that are natural to the soul comprises its activity on earth and therefore also beyond the grave. Thus, the performance of a natural moral obligation, or simply of the law, is something good for man, for his soul, and for its separate power or ability, since the purpose of man is to achieve bliss. Therefore the lawful activity of all the senses, both inward and outward, consists in bliss, for them individually and acting in harmony in the soul's entire concerted activity. Both the senses and the soul are in bliss. And so, bliss is attained only by the fulfillment of the moral law, through the performance of one's moral obligation. Whatever state you wish for your soul in the next world, place it in that state on earth, even though by forcing it; and so teach all your soul's powers the activity that you can encounter beyond the grave. In this way the senses have a moral law for their actions with which they must bring their activity into agreement: what to do and what not to do.

The unique and natural function of the senses is the striving toward truth: toward that which is true, good, and beautiful. Our senses should find and see in all of God's creation only the glory of God; but all that can bring the senses that which is contrary to their purpose (drawing sensuality to that which is unlawful, sinful) should be rejected as abnormal, contrary to the soul's nature. The senses, when they have been taught their natural function, delight in that which belongs to the glory of God; in all that exists, to see, hear, feel God as the Creator of all things visible and invisible and to find pleasure in the natural purpose of the senses. With such a character, the function of the senses will continue even beyond the grave in the kingdom of God's glory where the natural function of the senses will be fully gratified. The activity of the senses reaches its goal, and in the reaching of a goal there is bliss. Only physical, material objects which are . visible and spiritual, non-material objects, which are invisible, are the cause of pleasant and unpleasant mental states. By means of the senses which belong to the soul, it receives impressions of objects which bring about one or the other state of the soul. A pleasant impression brings about desire and an unpleasant impression, unwillingness. As long as the object brings about a desire in the soul through the senses, this is bliss on earth, and it will be the more so beyond the grave where, in the words of the Apostle, the senses will meet with objects that the eye has not seen nor the ear heard, and which the soul has not thought of with its mind. Here the joyous action of the senses will unfold and consequently there will be endless desire. Thus, the action of the senses is the first basis for the soul's activity, an activity that serves as the foundation for another: the will (of desiring or not desiring). These two activities of the senses and the will lay the foundation or form the main activity of the soul, that of the mind (thought and knowledge). The activity of the mind, including all the activity of the soul, will comprise the soul's entire activity, that of self-awareness. And so, for the state of the soul beyond the grave, blissful or tormented, the activity of the soul is needed, without which its life is unthinkable, manifested as it is in actions (feeling, desiring, thought, and self-awareness) of the soul.

The first and foremost of the external senses is vision. Its lawful and unlawful use, which causes it—along with the soul in general—good or evil, was taught by the Lord Jesus Christ Himself when He said, "Whosoever looketh on a woman to lust after her hath committed adultery with her already in his heart" (Matthew 5:28). Such use of vision is contrary to the law, not natural, separates a man from God, and deprives him of a blissful life beyond the grave. Bishop Non, glancing at the outward beauty of Pelagia, wept because he was less concerned for his own soul than she was for her appearance. Here is the lawful, moral use of vision, completely opposed to that use of vision that was made by the wife of Pentephres[12] towards the comeliness of Joseph. Striving towards truth, towards the light, scatters the darkness of impurity. There is one law for mental activity in general: the striving towards truth, from which is inseparable the spiritual, unearthly joy that is the fruit of lawful moral activity; this law of activity, in particular, belongs to every mental power. Consequently, it serves as the basis for the activity of all the senses, including vision, which should have for its object on earth all that reflects the glory of God, in which the Name of God might be hallowed. There are enough of such objects beyond the grave to last for all eternity, both for outward and inward vision in a life of bliss (in paradise), to see God there eternally in society, to see the holy angels, and to see the participants in bliss: all of the Saints and those close to one, who on earth were dear to our heart and with whom we were united by God Himself in an eternal bond of love; and, finally, to see all the splendors of paradise! What an inexhaustible source of blessedness for the sense of vision and for its activity!

But since evil has been mixed with good since the time our first ancestors fell into sin, one should in no wise admit as objects of the sense of vision those things, or qualities, or actions in which the poison that can destroy the soul is to be seen; one should distance one's glances from such sources of temptation (Matthew 18). Wherein the sense of vision finds pleasure on earth, that is, what it will seek beyond the grave. The activity of seeing on earth, developing in what is true, beautiful and good, will find its further development beyond the grave

---

[12]The captain of the Pharaoh's guard was named, in Egyptian, Pet-ef-Re, or "Belonging to the Sun." In the Septuagint this name appears as Petephre or Pent-ephres, in the Hebrew as Potiphar, Phutiphar (Genesis 39:1).

also for all eternity, in the kingdom of truth, beauty, and goodness, in the kingdom of Him Who said of Himself, "I am Truth" (John 14:6).

But if one has accustomed his sense of vision to an unnatural situation on earth, to an activity that is contrary to his nature and purpose, and has found pleasure on earth for his vision in the breach of truth, what further development of this pleasure can he hope for beyond the grave? All that is abnormal, contrary to nature, is evil; consequently, actions contrary to the law, destroying good, will produce an absence beyond the grave of that to which the sense of vision was accustomed on earth. If even on earth it is no small loss to a man to be deprived of the sense of vision, and life beyond the grave is a life of deprivation as punishment for sinners, then one should understand that among the first deprivations, according to the word of God, will be the lack of vision. In Hades the sufferers will not see one another in the dark fire, as the Church teaches; sinners in hell are deprived of the pleasure of seeing one another. Therefore, the bliss of the righteous demands the sense of vision, or else without it bliss would not be possible. From this sense we pass on to the reliable conclusion that only with the senses is bliss or punishment possible. The Old and New Testaments, bearing witness to the life beyond the grave, represent the souls as having a sense of vision. The rich man and Lazarus are depicted by the Lord as seeing each other. Therefore, in paradise the saved will all see one another. The Old Testament Scriptures bear witness to the life of the soul beyond the grave and do not deprive it of senses. In Hades, in the unresolved state, although the prisoners there do not see one another for they are deprived of this joy, nevertheless for the increase of their sorrow they do see the saved in paradise. This is in the first period while there is still an undetermined state. The soul's vision, according to the teaching of the Scriptures, is in particular the higher sense of the soul, a sense that embraces the entire psychic life and penetrates it from its most hidden foundations to its most outward manifestation in communion with the visible or material world and the invisible, spiritual world; a sense that penetrates everything connected with the perception and mastery of external impressions.

The natural purpose of the sense of hearing, like that of vision, is the striving for truth. If Eve's hearing had been open to the commandment of God and had been turned away from the seductive words of the devil, this would have been the natural, lawful, proper action of hearing, and its bliss, along with that of the entire soul, would not have ceased. And so, hearing should be directed on earth towards what is natural, good, and beautiful and should bring the soul impressions that are unto salvation, lawful. If one develops on earth the power of hearing in its natural purpose, unto salvation, then beyond the grave this power will find an inexhaustible source of bliss for itself and its activity. Where there is always heard the voice of exultation and of those who celebrate, where the activity of hearing will always be a source of joy, what the ear did not hear on earth, there it will hear. Nothing will disrupt the bliss of hearing which depends on and is conditioned by the blissful state of the soul. Beatitude of soul demands constant beatitude in the soul's various powers, therefore it demands a blessed activity in the power of hearing. The Old and New Testaments, speaking of life beyond the grave, everywhere represent the soul as not being deprived of this sense of hearing. The rich man in the Gospel and Abraham are depicted by the Lord as not being without a sense of hearing in the world beyond the grave.

The purpose of the mind's activity is to strive towards truth, that is, to know its Creator, God, the origin of all origins, the cause of being for all that is seen and unseen. The mind of all humanity seeks and strives towards truth. Consciousness of divinity is something innate, born into the human spirit, therefore the concept of the divinity is common to all mankind, belongs to all humanity of all times and places. The object of the mind's activity is knowledge of visible and invisible nature, and finally, the main activity of the mind is self-knowledge, a full, true knowledge of one's own spirit, as an individual being, personal and independent. And so, the content of the mind's activity, or of the activity of knowing oneself, is made up of the activity of the individual spiritual powers: thought, knowledge, feelings, and desires. The activity of the mind on earth, the knowledge of both good and evil, will always remain limited, as St. Paul teaches, to "knowledge in part," that is, despite all efforts of the human mind, its development on earth does not end, and, according to the law of eternal life, mental activity is its further purpose which will continue beyond the grave; then knowledge will, according to the Apostle Paul's teaching, be much more perfect, "knowledge no longer in part, but as it is" (I Corinthians 13:10,12): "In Thy light, O Lord, we shall see light" . . . in our mind and our conscience.

The activity of consciousness, composed of the activity of the individual mental powers on earth, when darkened by passions, habits, inclinations is not natural, and then consciousness does not function rightly. As a poison that a man has taken, even in the smallest dose, acts more or less destructively, harmfully, on the entire system, so too a moral untruth, no matter how small, once taken by the mind infects the entire intellectual system, and all the activity of the soul and its individual powers will be struck by moral infirmity. But beyond the grave, the self-awareness of each person will present the soul the most detailed and vivid picture of all its earthly activity, good as well as evil, in full clarity with the help of all the different mental powers, for example, the memory and others.

All deeds, words, thoughts, desires, and feelings will stand before the soul at judgment in front of the entire moral world.

The main action of the mind which sharp-sightedly and strictly watches over the state of the soul, over all the activity of the various powers of the human spirit, is self-awareness, a true conviction of one's own infirmity, weakness, lowliness. Only such humility in seeking and striving towards truth, aided by that basic truth spoken by the eternal law for man—"without Me ye can do nothing"—can lead man to his eternal purpose, to everlasting blessed life in God, with God, and on earth. Jesus Christ Himself taught us that the kingdom of God is within us, both on earth in a foretaste of bliss and beyond the grave in a true abiding in paradise. There, too, this activity of self-awareness continues, as demonstrated by the words of the righteous who are to answer at the Judgment: "When did we see Thee hungry or thirsty?" (Matthew 25:44); or the rich man's awareness of his present, sorrowful situation, when he sought to free his brethren who were still on earth from the cause of perdition: "Send them Lazarus, so that he can bear witness of the reward beyond the grave, lest they too come to this place of torment, so that they might change their sinful life to one of virtue." Here is the awareness of the unfortunate rich man in Hades, awareness beyond the grave, which includes the activity of the individual intellectual powers: memory, will, and feelings.

The soul's self-awareness constitutes its life, consequently self-awareness, making the soul a personal being, belongs to it even beyond the grave; for the soul continues its personal being beyond the grave also. Life, or the activity of self-awareness, as has been said, makes up the actions of the individual powers or abilities of the soul which, however, have no existence apart from the soul and therefore have no activity. They belong to the soul, and the soul acts by means of them. The soul with its powers passes beyond the grave and there continues to act, that is, even beyond the grave the individual powers of the soul continue their activity. Let us look at the activity of the individual powers that make up a common whole beyond the grave: 1) thought, 2) knowledge, 3) feeling, and 4) desire.

The object of thought both on earth and beyond the grave is truth. The natural purpose of this power is the attainment of the soul's destination: eternal life. All that is pleasant to God, all that is in agreement with His all-holy will is an object of thought on earth and beyond the grave. The way a man thinks on earth is already an indication of the society he will belong to beyond the grave, because there, the soul will not depart from the shape of thought it has acquired while on earth: the striving towards good, or towards evil.

The object of the power of knowledge is also truth. All that is true, beautiful, and good is the natural assignment of knowledge, and the soul strives to know it. Since the extent of what can be known is so limitless that all man's efforts on earth can reveal only the smallest fraction of it to him, the power of knowledge belonging to the immortal soul continues its activity beyond the grave, for all eternity. It will find objects for knowledge, and knowledge cannot come to an end, for if it did it must needs cease its activity which would be incompatible with the immortal soul, eternally active.

Wherever life beyond the grave is presented, in both the Old and New Testaments, everywhere the soul is shown retaining a full memory of its own earthly life and of those with whom it was in various relationships on earth. Thus our holy Church teaches (*Orthodox Theology* of Makary, Volume II, p. 656)—and her doctrine is true and fully in agreement with the conclusion of a healthy mind, the soul not changed in its state beyond the grave through deprivation of any of its powers including memory. The rich man in the Gospel remembers his brethren on earth and is concerned about their life in the next world. Since the soul's activity is comprised of the various actions of its individual powers, one cannot have full awareness of self (the action of the mind) or complete self-condemnation (the action of the conscience) without the action of the memory which reproduces all that is past and all that is present in the consciousness.

In the first period of life beyond the grave, those in paradise and in Hades are united by a bond and communion with those still on earth; they vividly remember and love those still on earth who were dear to their heart. Those, however, who were filled with hate in earthly life, if they were not cured of this malady, hate also in the life beyond the grave, by which we understand Gehenna where there is no love.

The will is a power, that is, an ability of the soul that orients the whole activity of the soul and its individual powers according to its desire. The natural purpose of its activity is to dispose the activity of the soul and its individual powers in a manner demanded by God's law and the conscience. The will should so direct all the activity of the soul that it will carry out its natural, inborn purpose: the will of God. The characteristics of the will's action are agreement or disagreement with the law of God and with the conscience. Agreement or disagreement with the will of God begun on earth, turns in the next world into either a complete flowing together with the will of God or else a union with the enemy of truth, into embitterment against God.

The activity of the senses and desires is the basis for thought and knowledge. And as self-knowledge cannot be taken away from the soul by the grave, therefore the activity of the senses and desires, which make up the basis for knowledge, must be admitted also in the next world. Where there is no activity of the senses, there is no desire, no knowledge, no life; consequently the immortal soul has the action of the senses beyond the grave, without which a reward is impossible, as confirmed by the word of God and by healthy reason.

The essential, natural quality or action that belongs to a given object or objects and characterizes them, is what distinguishes them from other objects. This quality or action is such that without it the object loses its true, essential, natural purpose, loses its reason for being. The manifestation of these qualities constitutes a law for the object, and it must function according to that law, so as to fulfill its purpose and reach the goal of its being. But since the purpose, the goal of creation in general, is not a burden of existence but bliss, in which alone the glorification of one's Creator is possible, therefore all that is essential or natural to the object cannot weigh it down, but on the contrary constitutes a benefit for it; therefore, the law in this case is not a burden, as St. John the Apostle bears witness of this: "God's commandments are not heavy" (I John 5:3). The law is not a constraint, a use of force, but a natural demand, its fulfillment necessary and easy, and, as a demand of nature, therefore carrying it out should be good and positive for the subject that acts. For example, love is a quality born into the soul of man and belongs to him alone in the highest degree. Love is an essential, natural quality of man, without which man ceases to be man and fails to reach his goal, distorts his nature; for man, love is a law, and fulfilling it brings him a benefit and a joy both on earth and beyond the grave. In fulfilling the law of his nature, man fulfills the demands of his conscience, which is also an inner law, the voice of God Himself, bringing unearthly joy to the heart of His servant while yet on earth. With the law fulfilled the purpose is reached, and man's purpose is peace, joy, and bliss, as the Lord Jesus Christ bears witness of this truth: "Be meek and humble of heart, and ye shall find peace for your souls"; this peace is on earth. Then the effect of conscience is that the heart is at peace, since otherwise, if there is an evasion of the natural purpose, of what is demanded by the spiritual-moral nature, the conscience's effect is the opposite: the heart is troubled. On earth, there are means to heal what is ailing and thereby ease the conscience but in the next world, what can calm it, what can bring it peace? The action of the conscience on earth, as well as that of the other mental powers, is only the beginning of its action beyond the grave. Simplicity of soul and purity of heart are states of the soul appropriate to blissful life in paradise. And so, the activity of the mind, the will, and the conscience consists in the demands of fulfilling their lawful, natural function.

The activity of the conscience in the world beyond the grave consists first of all in the inner life or activity of the soul. The activity of the conscience both on earth and beyond the grave is the action of its judgment, its denunciation, and then either peace or gnawing, being troubled as a consequence of self-condemnation. Self-knowledge is the action of the mind, and self-condemnation is the action of the conscience, it is the inner spiritual life and activity of the soul beyond the grave. Who has not experienced the activity of the conscience while still abiding on earth? After doing anything virtuous, any good deed reflected in the conscience; the heart is filled with a special joy not of this earth. And on the contrary, after doing evil, breaking the law, when this is reflected in the conscience, the heart is in a state foreign to peace, a state filled with fear, which is sometimes followed by hardness of heart and embittered despair, unless in due time the soul is healed of the evil it has done by the means given to man by God, the Physician of souls and bodies. Here are two completely opposite states of souls, resulting from the action of conscience. These two states will bring about their own further development beyond the grave through the operation of the same judging conscience which rewards or punishes for the moral state there had been on earth.

Conscience is the voice of law, the voice of God in man who was created in the image and likeness of God, and as a natural and inborn power of the soul, it will never leave it, regardless of where the soul may be. Its action is judgment and condemnation, its sentences everlasting, never falling silent throughout eternity. Its action in the state of the saved in heaven and in the state of the condemned in hell never ceases. The judgment of conscience, the judgment of God, is unbearable; and this is why souls on earth that are pressed by their conscience and do not know how to heal or pacify it by the repentance of the Prodigal Son or the Publican, of the Apostle Peter or the harlot, seek to avoid its condemnation and the languishing of the soul by attempting suicide, thinking to find in this an end to the pangs of conscience. But the immortal soul passes only into its immortal state beyond the grave corresponding to the state of the soul before death; and a soul tormented by conscience on earth passes beyond the grave in the same state of self-condemnation and eternal rebuke.

Once freed from the body, the soul enters into a natural life no longer diverted by anything. Self-awareness, the full awareness of one's life on earth with the action of memory, the vivid picture of an entire life's activity, as the basis for the present life beyond the grave, blissful or outcast, will make up the life of the soul, its self-awareness beyond the grave, and the action of conscience, of self-accusation; it will bring this life either eternal repose or eternal rebuke in which there can be no shadow of peace, for peace is found where there is neither reproach, nor rebuke, nor the prosecution of the law.

4. Outward Life — Outward Activity

a) The Union, Bond, Mutual Relationship, and Communion of This World with That Beyond the Grave, and the Union, Bond, Relationship, and Communion Between Souls Beyond the Grave

If the soul's inward life unfolds in its immortality and expresses its internal activity, and if the fullness of this inner life, that is, its purpose demands that it not be alone but in company with beings like unto itself, as the Lord Jesus Christ teaches, then for there to be community life, the soul must have outward activity beyond the grave, so as to express mutual relationships between spiritual-moral beings, spirits, and souls and their relationship to all around them. Consequently, the content of the outward activity, of the life of those beyond the grave, will consist of the union, bond, relationship, and communion of souls with those abiding on earth and of souls between themselves in the first period of life beyond the grave; while in the second period, the bond will be only between those in the kingdom of heaven, in the kingdom of glory, because only that will be united. The union, bond, mutual relationship and communion of souls beyond the grave make up their mutual action in the first period of life after death; but in the second period, when there follows the final separation and loss of connection between the saved and the lost, then there will be an end to any mutual action between them. Interaction in paradise will continue for all eternity, for without it bliss is impossible to picture; whereas in hell it ceased from the time of the Resurrection of Christ and the leading out of the righteous from there. In Hades there is no interaction; the dwellers in Hades are deprived of this bliss, they do not see one another, but see only the evil spirits.

Spiritual-moral beings, spirits (good and evil), and souls, both on earth in the body as well as those separated from the body and dwelling in the world beyond the grave, in a realm fully appropriate to their nature, interact with one another wherever they may be in relation to one another, as we said in the second part of this book. The spiritual world beyond the grave and the present world interact with each other. Consequently, spiritual-moral beings, souls abiding in the next world, also interact with one another. The word of God has revealed to us that God's angels do not live apart, but are in communion with one another. The same word of God, specifically the witness of the Lord Jesus Christ, assures us that beyond the grave, the souls of the righteous will live in the kingdom of God like angels; consequently, the nature of the soul is like unto that of the angels, and therefore the souls also will be in a spiritual communion amongst themselves.

Sociability is an inborn, natural state of the soul, without which the soul's existence does not reach its purpose: bliss. Only with personal contacts, interaction with others, can the soul come out of a state unnatural to it and of which the Creator Himself said, "It is not good for man to be alone" (Genesis 2:18), and this at a time when man was in paradise where there was nothing but bliss. This means that only one thing was lacking for bliss to be perfect: a being like unto himself with whom he could live together and associate. God Himself bore witness to this truth in paradise, and later the Holy Spirit repeated it through the lips of the Prophet King David: "What is good or what is beautiful, but for brethren to live together" (Psalms 132:1); in other words, for there to be fullness of bliss there must be devout souls living together, according to the witness of the same David who commands us not to withdraw from the society of people in general, but only from that of people who are not pious: "Blessed is the man that walketh not in the counsel of the ungodly, nor standeth in the way of sinners, nor sitteth in the seat of the scornful" (Psalms 1:1). Hence, one can see clearly that bliss demands specifically interaction, communication. As we have said, interaction is communion, based on a bond, union, and mutual relationship.

The soul, though it has given up its body, continues its activity as a live and immortal being. If society constitutes an essential need of the soul, without which bliss for the soul is consequently impossible, then this need is fulfilled in the most perfect way beyond the grave in the society of the chosen who have been pleasing unto God, in the kingdom of heaven. After these evidences from Holy Scripture concerning the righteous living together and enjoying one another's society beyond the grave in paradise, our reason itself comes to the same conclusion on the society of the chosen of God in the next life. The Lord Jesus Christ Himself depicts this interaction of souls in the first period after death in the parable of the Rich Man and Lazarus.

5. The Bond and Communion of This World with That Beyond the Grave

In the second part of this book, we set forth the teaching of the Orthodox Church on the union, bond, co-relationship, and communion of the two worlds, the present, visible world and the invisible world beyond the grave, where for the most part our attention was directed to what that bond entails for the living. In the third part, on the other hand, those outward means were shown which the living use to express a bond with the world beyond the grave. The present chap-. ter has the subject of showing wherein lie the union, bond, mutual relationship, and communion primarily from the side of the world beyond the grave towards those still abiding on earth, and specifically of those in the indeterminate state with the living. In the present chapter, for the sake of internal continuity of the various parts of the book and full treatment of the subject, it will be necessary to repeat what has already been said earlier in various places.

In the previous chapter the inner life of the soul beyond the grave was shown, along with the activity of its various powers, as well as how for the fullness of the soul's being, as God the Creator has said, "It is not good for man to be alone," a bond and communion is needed with spiritual and moral beings like themselves in spiritual-moral realm. At present this realm extends on earth and beyond, so that souls in an undetermined state have an interaction with souls still remaining on earth and also with souls likewise in the world beyond the grave that are among the saved. Those in the state of the lost have no bond and communion with either the saved or with those whose condition is undetermined, because the lost souls, even while they were on earth, had nothing in common, no bond or communion, with the good souls, those that are in the condition of the saved and those that are undetermined.

The external life, the activity of the world beyond the grave for those in the state of the saved or the undetermined, is based on and guided by one general law which joins all spiritual-moral beings with their Creator, God, and among themselves: the law of immortality, which is eternal love.

The external life of the saved with regard to those still on earth is a higher and more perfect degree of the same external activity as in the unresolved category. The souls in both states of the world beyond the grave, the saved and the undetermined that were joined on earth, and in particular if they were for some reason close to the heart, who were joined on earth by the close bond of relationship, friendship, acquaintance, continue also beyond the grave to love sincerely and with a pure heart even more than they did during their life on earth. If they love, then this means they remember their own who yet abide on earth. Remembering their own that have remained on earth, those that have passed into the world beyond the grave think of them. Knowing the life of the living, the dwellers beyond the grave are concerned over it; they sorrow and rejoice with the living. Having one and the same God, those that have passed into the world beyond the grave hope on the prayers and intercession of the living and desire salvation both for themselves and for those still living one earth, awaiting their joining them hour by hour in the peace of the homeland beyond the grave. Hour by hour, because they know the obligation of all those living on earth to be ready to depart for the other world at any hour.

"God is love" (I John 4:8), as the Apostle John teaches. And the Saviour says of Himself that He is life; therefore, life is love and the reverse: love is life. Since life is everlasting because God is everlasting, so also is love everlasting; for this reason, St. Paul taught that love never fails, that is, love never dies but passes on together with the soul to whom it is inborn, for whom love, like life, is a necessity, because the soul is undying. Consequently, love for a living soul is an essential belonging, without which the soul is dead, as the word of God itself bears witness: "He that loveth not [his brother], abideth in death" (I John 3:14). And so, love passes together with the soul beyond the grave into the kingdom of love where no one can be without love. Love is a divine quality, essential, inborn in the soul, according to the teaching of the holy Apostle; and together with the soul it is undying, still belonging to the soul in the next world. Love, planted in the heart, hallowed and strengthened by faith, burns beyond the grave towards God, the source of love, and towards those near to it that remain on earth, with whom it was joined by God Himself in a firm bond of love in various relationships. If we, as Christians, are all bound in various ways by strong, sacred links of undying love, then the hearts that are filled with this love, it is to be understood, beyond the grave also burn with this love toward God and toward those especially with whom they were united by the blessing of God, by special, individual, familial bonds of love. Here, besides the general commandment of Christ the Saviour, "Love one another, as I have loved you," a commandment given not to the body but to the immortal soul, and to which are joined other forms of holy, familial love. "He that dwelleth in love dwelleth in God, and God in him" (I John 4:16), as St John, the Apostle of love, teaches. This means that the dead who abide in God love us, the living. Not only those that abide in God, the perfected ones, but those also who are not entirely removed from God, the imperfect, retain love towards those that are still on earth. Only the lost souls alone, as being completely foreign to love, those to whom even on earth love was burdensome, whose hearts were constantly filled with spite, are also foreign beyond the grave to love for others. What the soul masters on earth, love or hate, that is what it passes over with into eternity. That the dead, if only they had true love on earth, continue to love us, the living, after their passing over to the other world, on this we have the evidence of the Rich Man and Lazarus in the Gospel. The Lord clearly expressed that the rich man, when he was in Hades, despite all his miseries, still remembers his brethren on earth, is concerned for their lot beyond the grave, and therefore, he loves them. If so, then what tender, parental love must parents who have passed on have for their children, orphans, who are still on earth! With what flaming love must departed spouses love their widows and widowers who remain on earth! What angelic love must departed children have for their parents who remain on earth! With what pure-hearted love must departed brothers, sisters, friends, acquaintances, and all true Christians love those that remain on earth, their brethren, sisters, friends, acquaintances, and all those with whom they are united by the Christian faith! The holy Apostle Peter, departing from this earthly life, promised his contemporaries that he would remember them after death: "Moreover I will endeavour always to remember you after my decease, ever to make remembrance of you" (II Peter 1:15).[13] And so, they that are in Hades love us and are concerned for us, and those in paradise pray for us. If love is life, which is undoubtedly the truth, then can one suppose that our dead do not love us? It often happens that we judge others, ascribing to them what we find in ourselves; we ourselves do not love our neighbor and think that all others fail to love one another, when in fact the loving heart loves all, not suspecting anyone of hostility, hatred, bitterness, and sees and finds friends for itself in the most malevolent people. Therefore, he that doubts the love of the dead for the living reveals his own cold heart, foreign to the divine fire of love, estranged from the spiritual life, far from the Lord Jesus Christ, who has joined all the members of His Church, regardless of where they be, on earth or already beyond the grave, with an undying love.

I do not love all that I remember; but I remember all that I love, and I cannot forget, so long as I love; and love is immortal. Memory is a power, an ability of the soul. If, for its activity on earth, the soul had need of its memory function, then the soul will also not be deprived of memory beyond the grave. The memory of life on earth will either soothe the soul or commit it to the judgment of conscience. If one were to suppose the absence of a memory beyond the grave, then how could there be self-knowledge or self-reproach without which reward

---

[13]The author gives chapter and verse, but quotes this passage in his own words, even though in Slavonic. Therefore it has been translated as it appears in the Russian text of this book, so as to preserve the sense the author had given it.

or punishment for the earthly journey would be unthinkable beyond the grave. Companions in earthly life therefore cannot be erased from memory, as they were participants in the soul's activity. That the departed remember their close ones who remain on earth, we know from the parable of the Rich Man and Lazarus and from good sense. The rich man in Hades, despite his painful state, remembers his five brothers still on earth. Therefore our departed who are dear to our heart remember us who abide still for a certain time on earth.

The mental state of a man consists of thought, desire, and feeling; this is the activity of the soul. The immortality of the soul also makes its activity unending. The activity of a good or a bad soul towards those close to it continues beyond the grave as well. The former, that is, the good soul, thinks of how to save those close to it and to save all in general; while the latter, the evil soul, thinks of how to ruin them. The good soul thinks: "How sad, that those still on earth believe only poorly, or else they do not believe at all; they think, but too little, or else they do not think at all of what God has prepared for man beyond the grave." The rich man in the Gospel, loving and remembering his brethren in Hades, thinks of them and is concerned about their life. The resurrection of the dead at the moment of the death of the Lord Jesus Christ on the Cross is an example of the concern taken by the dead in the life of us, the living.

If our departed ones love us, remember us, think of us, then naturally their love is vitally concerned for us who are alive. The dead now clearly see the fruits of life on earth, and therefore are vitally concerned for us, the living. They sorrow and rejoice together with the living.

Can the dead indirectly or directly know the life of those who remain on earth? Why then does the rich man in the Gospel ask Abraham to send someone from heaven to his brothers, to keep them from a bitter lot beyond the grave? From his request it is evident that he definitely knows his brothers are living as he himself lived, carelessly. Why does he know this; perhaps his brethren are living virtuously?

The Saviour Himself teaches us in this parable that our life on earth influences the state of our departed ones beyond the grave. How concerned the rich man was for the life of his brethren! He was distressed over their wrongful way of life. How strongly it moved the unfortunate rich man in Hades! The Lord says nothing on whether or not the living brothers cared about the one who had died; but their concern for the dead would be needed. Perhaps two reasons moved the unfortunate rich man to ask Abraham to dispose them towards a moral life, pleasing unto God; he had never thought, while on earth, of his own salvation or that of his brethren; loving himself, he lived for himself. But here, seeing the beggar Lazarus in glory and himself in denigration and sorrow, it may have been that his offended pride and feeling of envy were why he asked Abraham for an emissary to earth from the other world; in saving his brothers, he also may have hoped to obtain his own salvation through them. Of course, if they had changed their way of life, they would have remembered him, and in remembering would have involved themselves in his condition beyond the grave by offering prayers and sacrifices for him to God. The piety of the living brings joy to the dead, while wickedness brings sorrow. That the unfortunate rich man knew in his state beyond the grave, in Hades, the life of his brethren on earth witnesses the Scripture: the repentance of one, and with him also the correction of a sinner (that is, on earth) brings joy to the angels; and therefore, all the host of angels and with them all the other-worldly throng of the righteous, rejoice and are glad in heaven. This was the reason for rejoicing in heaven: the amelioration of a sinner on earth. The heaven-dwellers are in bliss, but to their bliss yet a new joy is added in our salvation when we, while still on earth, begin to turn away from that which is vain, passing, and carnal and begin to be aware of how far we have distanced ourselves from our destination, how far from God. Setting a boundary to our iniquities, our wrongs, we enter into a new activity, based on the teaching of Christ. And so, when our life on earth is in Christ and for Christ, a life pleasing unto God, moral, it brings joy to those in heaven. Not only those in heaven will have joy, but also those dead that have not attained perfection, and even those under judgment, as witnessed by the skull of one pagan priest to St. Macarius of Egypt, rejoice in the life of the God-fearing living whose prayers the Lord accepts. The dead will find their benefactors in us, the living, who constantly improve their state beyond the grave. Now one can understand that there was no joy in heaven over the earthly life of the unfortunate rich man's brethren, and his own lot was without joy in Hades, according to the witness of the Gospel, because there was no reason for joy beyond the grave; there was no repentance or improvement in his brothers who, however, could have improved the state of their unfortunate brother beyond the grave. That the rich man in Hades knew the life of his brothers on earth, can be confirmed by the conversation of St. Macarius of Egypt with the skull of the heathen priest. The skull bore witness: "When thou makest prayer for us, then we receive a certain comfort . . ." Consequently, the rich man in the Gospel could know the state of his brethren on earth from his own state beyond the grave, not seeing any comfort in the other world, as the Gospel tells us, he therefore could conclude that they were living carelessly. If only they had led a life that was more or less pious, then they would not have forgotten their deceased brother and would have helped him in some way; then he too could have said, like the skull of the heathen, that he received some comfort from their prayers on his behalf. But receiving no consolation beyond the grave, he concluded straightway that they were leading a careless life and therefore asked Abraham to send someone to them from beyond the grave. This is the first and main reason that the dead know our life on earth, be it good or evil, based on its effect on their own condition beyond the grave. Second, the activity of the soul, while it is in the body, is greatly limited by the latter as by something crude and material. The horizon of the soul's activity, from its close tie with the body, subordinate to the law of space and time, depends on the same law of space and time, and therefore the activity of the soul usually consists of that of a man living in the flesh. Having left the body, the soul, becoming free and no longer subordinate to the law of space and time, as a subtle, ethereal being, enters into an activity that goes beyond the limits of the material world. It sees and knows that which was concealed from it by the rude body. The soul, having entered into its natural state, now acts according to its nature; and its senses enter into their natural function, because the present state of the senses is an unnatural, unhealthy state, the result of sin. Certain dream visions, to be sure not all, ecstasy, somnambulism, confirm what has been said. Consequently, after death separates the soul from the body, the soul enters into its natural extent of activity for which space and time do not exist. If the perfected know (see, feel) the state of the imperfect in the next world, despite the immeasurable space that exists between Abraham and the rich man and enter into contact with each other, then they know our state on earth as well despite the indefinite space that also exists between paradise and earth. But if those that are imperfect also know the state of the perfected, then why cannot the former who are in Hades know the life of those on earth in the same way, since the unfortunate rich man in Hades knew the condition of his five brothers who were still on earth? Third, can the departed, remaining in spirit with us, the living, not know our life on earth? And so, there are three bases by which the imperfect departed know the life of the living: 1) their own state beyond the grave, 2) the perfection of the senses beyond the grave, and 3) sympathy.

That which is called true and beautiful we recognize in God's creation. The Creator, God Himself, says of His creation that all is "very good" (Genesis 1:31).

The spiritual world, the moral world, the physical world, make up one well-constructed and harmonious whole. Something in discord could not have come from the hands of God the Creator. In God's creation, all came about and comes about not by chance, as according to the materialists who recognize only matter, but by a definite plan, in a harmonious system, for a specific goal, according to unchanging laws; everything has its part in the whole, everything is mutually serving, everything is mutually dependant. Consequently, everything exerts a mutual influence, and the state of the one is bound and related to the state of another and the state of the whole. The life, the development of the spiritual, moral, and physical worlds, goes along parallel lines, hand in hand according to the laws of life, given once and not subject to change. The state of the whole is reflected in the state of its parts, and any change in the state of the parts is reflected more or less in the state of the whole. The state of the interacting parts of the whole brings them to agreement, to harmony. Agreement, harmony in the state of spiritual-moral beings is known as sympathy, that is, feeling the state of another, one involuntarily comes to be in the same state. In the kingdom of God, in the kingdom of spiritual-moral beings, such as the spirits and souls of men, there is one nature, one goal of being, and one law of concord following from the law of love that unites all spiritual-moral beings, spirits, and souls. Existence, the life of the soul, is not only for itself, but also for its Creator, God, and for others. Eve was created for Adam, and her soul came into being not for itself, but also for the fullness of Adam's being. And so, the state of a soul is conditioned by the state of the souls that surround it and with which it is in various relationships. Soon Adam reflected the fallen state of Eve. Pride is unnatural to the soul; the fullness of the soul's life is determined by its relationship to God and to beings like unto itself. The life of the soul is closely tied to that of beings like itself in various relationships, and therefore it is impossible for one and the same spirit that enlivens them not to be a guide leading souls to agreement, oneness of mind in various states, especially in joy, sadness, and in similar conditions. The feeling of joy, sadness, and of any state of the soul that is taken close to heart by another soul, constitutes sympathy. To the heart belong: feelings, forebodings, sympathies, and therefore joy and sadness belong to the heart. There is among the people a saying not without truth that "one heart gives news to another." Does this not mean sympathy? Sympathy is a natural quality of the soul; both weeping with others and rejoicing with others are characteristic of the soul. Man's moral fall distorted the natural qualities of the soul, and inborn love and hatred came to work perversely. The lessening of faith and love, the sophistries of the flesh, the depravity of the heart, these have turned sympathy into uncaring. Man knows so little in comparison with what he could know, insofar as God permits him to, that present knowledge is almost the same as no knowledge; this is a certain truth, confirmed by common sense and expressed by the holy Apostle Paul, the chosen vessel of the Holy Spirit. How many mysterious things there are in human nature which consists of flesh, soul, and spirit? The soul and body are in sympathy with each other, and the mental state is always reflected in the body, while the condition of the body is reflected in the state of the soul. And so, for spiritual-moral beings, sympathy is a natural quality, since they comprise one body and one spirit. From the sympathy of the parts of a lesser body such as ours, we can without error conclude about the sympathy of the parts, the members of the greater body: the Church of Christ, the kingdom of God, which is "very good" because only in it is there righteousness, peace, joy, that which is exalted, splendid, and good.

Death at first brings about sorrow, because of the seeming separation from a loved one. The strength, the degree of sorrow depends on the strength of the love that binds two people and on the mutual relationships between them. A like mental anguish is expressed outwardly, visibly, in weeping, in tears. They say it is easier for a sorrowing soul after tears. Sorrow without weeping oppresses the soul heavily. And since the soul has a close, mysterious bond and relationship with the body by means of which, as by an instrument, the soul can make its various mental states known visibly, therefore tears express mental sorrow. Weeping, tears are for this reason demanded by nature, while faith prescribes only restrained, moderate weeping. And so, nature calls for weeping and tears, while faith consoles us that the spiritual bond with the dead is not broken by death, that the deceased is with us, the living, remaining in spirit, that he is alive.

The law of sympathy consists in the weeping, the tears of one producing a state of sorrow in the soul of another, and not infrequently we hear, "Thy tears, thy weeping and sorrow, thy dejection, bring pangs to my soul"; or one who is leaving for some time and for a far destination asks the one he is parting from not to weep, but to pray to God. The deceased, in this case, is quite like someone who has thus set off, gone away; only with the difference that this parting with the person who has died may be of the shortest duration, and every coming hour may bring a joyous encounter according to the commandment given by God, to be ready for departing into the world beyond the grave at every hour. Therefore, immoderate weeping is not useful, but harmful to those that are separated; it interferes with prayer, through which all is possible to him that believes. Prayer and grieving for sins are beneficial to both of those separated. Souls are cleansed from sins by prayer. The Lord Jesus Christ Himself bore witness to this truth, saying on one occasion, "Weep not!" and in another place he gives indulgence to weeping: "Blessed are they that weep!" As love for the departed cannot be extinguished, and as therefore sympathy for them is commanded—to bear one another's burdens, to intercede for the dead, as if for one's own sins—there is weeping for the sins of the departed, through which God is moved to mercy towards the dead, according to His immutable promise to hear those that ask in faith; and, at the same time, bliss comes also to the one who intercedes for the dead. This psychic truth—sympathy of the soul—must refer to the souls of the departed. They, in dying, have already asked us not to weep for them as if they had ceased to exist, but to pray to God for them, not to forget them, but to love them. And therefore immoderate bewailing of the departed is harmful to both the living and the dead. Your weeping, not because we have passed over to what is better, but for our sins, this is pleasing to God, and brings us benefit, as well as preparing an everlasting reward for you beyond the grave.

If the living can help the dead greatly in the matter of their salvation, then what benefit does the deceased get from our unwise tears? But how can God grant mercy to the dead, if the living does not pray for him, is not of good spirit, but gives in to immoderate weeping, dejection, and perhaps to railing against God? And so, not feeling God's mercy towards themselves, the departed sorrow at our lack of caring.

The departed through their own experience have learned the purpose of man, and for us who yet remain on earth it remains only to strive to better their state, to a betterment that was commanded us by God: "Seek ye first the kingdom of God and His righteousness," and "bear ye one another's burdens." Our life will afford much help to the condition of the departed if we are concerned for their condition. So that man might picture the state of the dead beyond the grave clearly—even in the Old Testament—to hold man back from evil, the word of God postulated constant memory of death, the passing over into the world beyond the grave. Having eternal life constantly before our eyes, we seem not to have been separated from the dead, and at the same time, in avoiding all that is worldly and sinful, we seem to have joined the state beyond the grave. And since all are sinful before God, both the dead and the living, then we must needs share in the lot of the departed, a lot that will equally be ours after death. The state of the departed is our future state, and therefore it should be close to our heart. Anything that can better this sorrowful state beyond the grave is pleasing to the dead and beneficial to us. Jesus Christ commanded us to be ready for death at any time, which means to be in a constant bond and communion with those who have gone on before us to the life beyond the grave. One cannot fulfill this commandment of remembering death and the concepts of judgment, heaven, hell, and eternity without touching upon thoughts of those who dwell in the world beyond the grave; consequently, remembrance of the dead is closely tied to this commandment. One cannot conceive of judgment, heaven, and hell without people, among whom are our relatives, acquaintances, and all that are beloved to our heart. Therefore, what heart can there be that would not be touched by the state of sinners in the life beyond the grave? Seeing someone drowning, perforce one hurries to stretch out a helping, saving hand. Vividly picturing the state of sinners beyond the grave, perforce one will seek ways of saving them. And so, if it was commanded us to be mindful of death, that means it was commanded us to remember the departed.

If when I saw someone perishing, I were only to weep at the sight and did not use any of the means available to me to save him, but only stood there weeping, in what way would I be helping him? And the Saviour, regarding such useless tears shed by the widow of Nain as she buried her only son who was to have been the support of her old age and consolation of her widowhood, said to her, "Weep not!" St. Paul the Apostle also confirmed this truth for Christians who weep for their dead: "Mourn not!" he taught. Therefore, we should understand that we are forbidden only what is useless, and that which is useful is enjoined. Weeping is forbidden, but magnanimity is enjoined. Jesus Christ Himself explained why weeping is useless, having said to Martha, the sister of Lazarus, that her brother would rise, and to Jairus, that his daughter had not died, but slept; and in another place he taught that God is not a God of the dead, but of the living; therefore those who have passed over into the world beyond the grave are all alive. Why should we grieve for the living whom we shall join? Chrysostom teaches that honor is shown the dead not by wailing and cries, but by hymns and singing of Psalms and upright living. Wouldst thou honor the dead? Give alms, do good, and offer the Divine Liturgy. What is the use of much wailing? Such weeping the Lord forbids when he says, "Weep not." The Lord praises weeping for the sins of the dead which can bring him everlasting joy, and for the salvation of the dead He promises bliss: "Blessed are they that weep!" Inconsolable weeping, without hope, without faith in the life beyond the grave the Lord forbade, as did the Apostle Paul; but weeping that expresses sorrow at parting with a companion on earth, weeping such as the Jesus Christ Himself manifested at the tomb of Lazarus, such weeping is not forbidden.

Chrysostom entreats us, the faithful, not to imitate the unbelievers who do not know, as the Christians do, the promised resurrection and life to come: not to rend our garments, not to beat our breasts, not to tear out the hair of our head, or to commit any such unseemly thing, offensive to the dead as well as ourselves (Homily of St. John Chrysostom on Meatfare Saturday). From these words of

Chrysostom, one can understand the sympathy of the dead for the state of the living, and how useless and even harmful and distressing the unwise mourning of the living is for them that have passed on beyond the grave.

The appearance of the deceased wife of the widower priest in a dream showed how burdensome our bad life is to our departed ones and how heartfelt is their desire for us, the living, to live as befits Christians, having the promise of resurrection and eternal life beyond the grave (see the section "Appearances of Souls from Hades."

And so, if souls even in Hades, whose lot is still unresolved, despite all their pitiful situation, remember those close to their heart who are still on earth and are concerned for their fate beyond the grave, then what is to be said of those who are enjoying the foretaste of bliss and their solicitude, their care for those dwelling on earth? Their love, now no longer diverted by anything earthly or by any troubles or passions, burns ever stronger, and their repose is broken by a loving concern for those wanderers who abide on earth. "They," as St. Cyprian says, "having been assured of their own salvation, are concerned about the salvation of those who are still on earth" (*Exhortation on the Martyrs,* Chapter 12).

The spirit of man, having a divine origin, reassures him that he will certainly obtain from God what he asks, what he yearns for, which gives him a salutary hope on God. And so, hope is the resting of the human heart in God, the assurance of receiving what is asked, desired. Consequently, hope is a concept held by all humanity, as a state of the soul, based on faith, an essential belonging of the soul, and therefore of all mankind. There never has been a people without some beliefs, but with the difference that for wild, uneducated tribes religion does not constitute a science as it does for us. If faith is natural to man, then "hope" is a concept shared by all. The assurance of the heart that something will be attained, in general, constitutes hope. People on earth have such relationships to one another, as to place their hopes on one another in various situations, for example, as to defense, help, consolation, intercession; thus, for example, children place hope in their parents, husbands in wives and wives in husbands, relatives in relatives, in acquaintances, friends, subordinates in those in authority, societies in societies, subjects in their ruler and rulers in subjects, and states in states; and such a hope is in agreement with the will of God, if only hope in man does not exceed hope in God. Love is the foundation of hope and, joined by love, we have hope in one another. Thoughts, desires and feelings make up the content of the invisible activity of the soul, an activity that bears on it the stamp of the immaterial. It is natural for the soul to hope in God and in beings like itself with which it has various relationships. Parting with the body and entering into the life beyond the grave, the soul keeps all that belongs to it, including hope in God and in those close and dear that remain on earth. The blessed Augustine writes: "The departed hope to receive help through us; for the time of doing has flown by for them." St. Ephrem the Syrian affirms the same truth, that the dead hope on the living: "If on earth, when we move from one country to another, we have need of guides, then this is just as needful when we pass over into life eternal."

Hope belongs to the immortal soul. We hope on the Saints, that through their intercessions we may have God's blessing and obtain salvation, and therefore we have need of them. So also the dead, if they have not yet attained bliss, need us, the living, and put their hope in us.

As has already been said, the soul, passing on beyond the grave with all its powers, its abilities, habits, inclinations, and since it is alive, undying, it continues its spirituell activity beyond the grave as well: the combined activity of all its individual powers. Consequently, desire too, as one of the soul's powers, continues its activity beyond the grave as well. The object of desire's activity is the truth, the striving towards the exalted, the beautiful and the good, the desire for righteousness, peace and joy, the desire for life, the striving for further development, for perfection of life. The desire for life, the striving towards the source of life, is a natural property of the human spirit. The desire for self-preservation alone is something common to all that is alive.

The desires, the wishes that the soul has found for itself here on earth, will not leave it beyond the grave either; we desire now, while we are still alive, for others to pray to God for us; by the same token we do not wish them to forget us after we die. If we desire this now, what is to prevent us from desiring it after death? Surely we will not be without this mental power? Where would it go? In the Saviour's parable of the rich man and Lazarus, is there not the desire of the rich man, for example, to slake his thirst and to inform his brethren who are still living on earth? And having been in paradise, St. Paul, as his death approached, asked the faithful to pray for him (Ephesians 6:18–19). If the chosen vessel of the Holy Spirit, St. Paul, asked that prayers be said for him, then what is to be said of the imperfect departed? It is to be understood, that they too desire us not to forget them, to intercede for them before God, and insofar as we are able, to help them. They desire our prayers exactly as we, the living, wish the Saints to pray for us, and the Saints desire salvation for us, the living, as well as for the imperfect departed.

Desiring our prayers and in general our intercession before God, the imperfect departed at the same time desire for us, the living, salvation, and the correction of our earthly life, which is shown by the concern of the rich man in Hades for his brethren remaining on earth. In this desire of the departed for our prayers lies first and foremost their relationship to us. The holy Church, knowing their state beyond the grave and knowing that we are all sinners before God, and desirous of having the most effect on the hearts of the living, directs the following words to them on the state of the departed beyond the grave: "Pray for us; never were your prayers so needed by us as in these minutes. Now we go to the Judge where there is no acceptance of persons. We ask all and entreat you to pray for us to Christ our God, lest we be taken down by our sins to the place of torment; but may He establish us where there is the light of life, where there is neither sadness nor disease nor sighing, but life eternal." This is the common need of every soul that departs the earth, and the Church expresses it for us, the living, so that we might have sympathy for them. For our sympathy, for our prayers for them, they will send us their blessing from the other world, as Archpriest Putiatin put it (in his *Sermon No. 264,* p. 263). Loving us with a pure heart, they are frightened, troubled for us, lest we be traitors to faith and love. And if one can so express it, then all their desire consists in our following the Lord Jesus Christ, in imitating the life of good Christians.

We are pleased when our desires are fulfilled. One departing, desirous of acting on earth even after his death, entrusts another who remains to carry out his will. The deceased, in this way, acts through a living person just as a senior does through a junior, a master through a servant, a sick man through a healthy, one leaving, or equally one dying, through one who remains. In this activity two persons take part, one who commands and one who performs. The fruits of activity belong to the one who produces the activity, wherever he may be; to him belong the glory, the thanks, and the reward. The carrying-out of the Christian will bring its testator repose, since prayers are offered to God for his eternal rest. Non-fulfillment of such a will deprives the testator of repose, since nothing is heard of him, as one who is no longer active for the general good and that of his neighbor. He that fails to carry out the will is liable to the judgment of God as a murderer, as one who takes away the means that can snatch the testator from Hades and deliver him from eternal death. He has stolen the life of the deceased, he has taken away the means that might have brought him life, and he has not distributed his goods to the needy! But the word of God affirms that alms deliver from death, therefore he is his murderer. True, he is guilty as a murderer, but here for some reason there was no good will of God towards the soul that had gone into the world beyond the grave, the sacrifice was not accepted, it was rejected and not without reason, for God's will is in everything.

The last desire, it is to be understood, if it was not contrary to the law, the last will of the dying man is performed piously, for the repose of the departed and for the executor's own peace of conscience. Through the fulfillment of the Christian will, God is moved to mercy towards the dead, according to His immutable promise to hear those that ask in faith, and at the same time He grants bliss also to the one who intercedes for the dead.

All our wrongs towards the dead do not go without their sad consequences. There is a popular saying, "The dead man does not stand at the gate, but will take what is his." In all likelihood, this expresses those unfortunate consequences that come of the living not keeping a faithful relationship towards the departed. One cannot ignore this saying, as a proverb always has a bit of truth in it.

At the present time, until the final judgment resolution, even the righteous in paradise are not without sorrow that comes from their love for sinners who are still on earth and to sinners who dwell in Hades; and in the same way, the sorrowful state of undetermined sinners in Hades is increased by our sinful life. The deceased, wherever he may be, in paradise or in Hades, desires that his will be carried out exactly, in particular if its fulfillment can improve the state of the departed beyond the grave. But if the departed are deprived of that through our negligence, the taking of their property rights, then they can cry out to God for vengeance, and the true Giver of rewards will not be slow. The punishment of God will soon catch up to such wrongdoers. The stolen goods of the deceased and the property of the thief, as they say, "All went into the fire, all went to dust." For the honor, the property, the rights of the departed many have suffered and still do. The sufferings can be various to infinity. People suffer and do not understand the reason or, one might better say, they do not want to admit their guilt in not keeping love towards their neighbor.

Like the living, those that have gone on before us by passing into the world beyond the grave, loving us, being concerned about us, naturally expect us to join them. Our fathers, brethren, sisters, friends, spouses in the next life, enjoying immortality, await us, desirous of seeing us again. What a multitude of souls await us there! We are wanderers, how shall we desire to reach our homeland, the end of our wanderings, and rest at last in an untroubled haven where all that have gone on ahead of us await. And we shall sooner or later join them, and be together forever, face to face, in the words of St. Paul: "We shall always be with the Lord" (Thessalonians 4:17) and, therefore, together with all that have been pleasing unto God.

All infants that die after holy Baptism will doubtless receive salvation in the strength of the death of Jesus Christ; for if they are pure of sin, both original sin as they are cleansed by Divine Baptism and of their own sin, for as infants they have as yet no free will and therefore do not sin, therefore without doubt they are saved. Consequently, parents at the birth of their children are obliged, insofar as they are able, to lead them as new members of Christ's Church into the Orthodox faith, through holy Baptism, and thereby to make them heirs of life everlasting in Christ. If without faith salvation is impossible, then clearly the lot of unbaptized infants beyond the grave is not enviable.

Here are the words of St. John Chrysostom on the state of infants beyond the grave spoken to the consolation of grieving parents: "Weep not: our departing and passage of the aerial toll booths, in the company of angels, were without pain. The devils found nothing in us, and by the mercy of our Master, God, we are where the angels and all Saints abide, and we pray to God for you" (*Homily on Meatfare Saturday*). And so, if they pray this means that they know of the existence of their parents, remember, and love them. The degree of bliss of infants, according to the teaching of the Fathers of the Church, is more splendid than that of Virgins and Saints; they are children of God, nurslings of the Holy Spirit (*Writings of the Holy Fathers*, Part 6, p. 207). The voice of infants in the other world to their parents, by the lips of the Church, cries out: "Weep not for me; I am not lamentable: for unto infants the joy of all the righteous is given" (Order of the Burial of Infants). "I died early, yet had no time to blacken myself with sins, as did ye, and I escaped the danger of sinning; for which cause weep ye better for yourselves who have sinned." Parents with Christian humility and commitment to the will of God should bear the sorrow of separation from their children, and should not give themselves up to inconsolable sorrow for their death. Love for dead children should be shown in prayer for them. The Christian mother sees in her dead child her closest intercessor before the Throne of the Lord, and moved to piety, she blesses the Lord both for the child and for herself. Our Lord Jesus Christ has proclaimed that for such (that is, children) there awaits the kingdom of heaven (Matthew 18:3, Mark 10:14; Luke 18:16), a blessed eternal life.

The same belief on the death of children we meet with among the ancient Peruvians; the death of a newborn was even considered an occasion for joy among them, to be celebrated by dances and drinking feasts, since they were convinced that the deceased child was turned directly into an angel (Helwald, *Natural History of Tribes and Peoples*, Part I, p. 481).

6. The Bond and Communion Between Souls in the World Beyond the Grave

The soul, while it WAS in the body, acted on earth by means of all its powers amid the society of beings like unto itself; passing beyond the grave, it continues to live, since it is immortal and, according to the teaching of the holy Church, is again among beings like itself, spirits and souls, and therefore acts by means of all its powers, its abilities, as it lived and acted on earth. If life on earth should be a preparation for life beyond the grave, according to the teaching of the Lord Jesus Christ, then activity beyond the grave will be a continuation of earthly life: good and righteous or evil and sinful. Some wrongfully attribute to the soul some sort of slumberous inactivity, which is not in agreement with the teaching of the Church and the characteristics of the soul. To take away the soul's activity would make it cease to be a soul, to change its eternal, unchanging nature. An essential quality of the soul is immortality and unceasing activity, development, eternal perfection, and endless passing from one consciousness, or mental state, to another more complete one, be it good (in paradise) or evil (in Hades). Thus the state of the soul beyond the grave is active, that is, the soul continues to act, as it acted before on earth.

If here on earth there is interaction between souls, that is, despite the many obstacles and difficulties that the body causes the soul, despite the close bond of the soul with the body and their interaction, the effect of souls upon souls, according to the natural purpose of their action, is fulfilled: and the soul achieves its desire in acting upon another soul, so far as is possible here with a soul weighed down by the body and a mind burdened by an earthly tabernacle (Wisdom of Solomon 9:15); then what is to be said of the activity of the soul beyond the grave, when it will be freed from its body that so held it back in its earthly activity? If on earth it discovered and sensed only in part, according to the words of the Apostle, incompletely, then beyond the grave its activity will be much more perfect; and souls, interacting, will know and sense one another perfectly, and will see, hear, and speak together, in a way incomprehensible to us now; just as on earth we cannot understand fully the activity of the soul, which is a primary, basic activity, invisible, not material, consisting of thoughts, desires, and feelings, and which, nevertheless, was seen, heard, and felt by other souls, though they were in the body, but leading a spiritual life according to the commandments of God. The earthly life of all the Saints is the proof of what has been said: from them, the secret, hidden, inner, spiritual life and invisible activity of others was not kept back. The Saints answered the thoughts, wishes, and feelings of some with words and deeds. Is this not the most convincing proof that even beyond the grave, bodiless souls will interact amongst themselves, having no need for visible organs, just as the Saints of God saw, heard, and felt the inner state of others, with no help from outward organs? The life of the Saints on earth and their interaction is the beginning of preparation for life beyond the grave. They sometimes interact completely without the help of outward forms, but sometimes by means of such. This, incidentally, is one of the reasons why they cared so little, and often neglected, the body in general, considering this organ even extraneous to the spirituell life. If knowledge of the truth of some situation is based on and proven by one's experience of that situation, then based on the experience of living according to the law of the Lord (which is subordinating the body to the spirit and making the mind and heart obedient to faith), you too will be convinced that the present life of the soul and its activity on earth is the beginning of life and activity beyond the grave. Is there not convincing evidence of the interaction of souls beyond the grave, for instance, in the fact that a man, having told someone in advance that he would like to speak with them indicated a time for this: during sleep? And indeed, independently of the bodies resting on their beds, the souls carried on a discussion whose subject was known to them before sleep. They say that sleep is the prototype of death. But what is sleep? A state of man in which the activity of the body and of all the external senses ceases; therefore, all communication ceases with the visible world, with all that surrounds one, aside from organic life, which leaves the body only at its actual death. But life, the eternal activity of the soul, does not leave it in the sleeping state; the body sleeps, but the soul works, and the extent of its activity sometimes is far broader that when the body is awake. In this way souls, carrying on an intensified discussion during sleep, as was just mentioned, interacted with each other. And since the souls are mystically united with their bodies, a definite state of the soul in sleep was reflected in the body as well, although the interaction of souls in sleep took place without any involvement of the bodies; but in a waking state they put the decision of their mental sleeping discussions into effect. If on earth souls interact with each other without any participation of their bodies, then how and why should one not accept the interaction of the same souls beyond the grave after their separation from their bodies? True, in sleep, for the most part, the action of the soul, though unconscious, nevertheless is activity not depending on the body, if sometimes under its influence. Here we have spoken of the activity of souls that takes place in full consciousness, for which exclusively there was assigned in advance a time of sleep. There are other examples (somnambulism, clairvoyance) that confirm what we have said and prove that the activity of the soul during sleep is much more perfected when it is freed from the body, as Solomon bears witness (Wisdom of Solomon 9:15). Thus, it is known that many exalted thoughts first appeared in the souls of brilliant people during sleep, with the full activity of the soul, that is, with all its powers. The Apostle also teaches that the activity of the soul, that is, the activity of all its powers, attains perfection only beyond the grave in the absence of the body in the first period, and in the second period with the body which no longer interferes with the activity of the soul, but helps it; for the body and soul in the second period will be in perfect harmony between themselves, not as before on earth when the spirit fought against the flesh and the flesh rose up against the spirit.

As for all the conversations of the risen Lord with His disciples, are they not a direct evidence of recognition, meeting, and communication by souls in the life beyond the grave as in the first and in the second period? Not the body, which in the disciples of Christ was not yet glorified, and therefore not the external senses, but the internal which belong only to the soul, were opened, as stated in the Gospel conversation of the Lord with two disciples. What then is to prevent souls also in the first period beyond the grave from seeing, hearing, feeling, and being in communion with one another, just as His disciples saw, heard, felt, and were in communion with the risen Lord on earth? The Apostles and all that saw the Lord ascend into heaven were witnesses to the bond and communion of souls in the world beyond the grave. Were not all the examples of communion between the visible and invisible worlds, of souls still on earth with spirits and souls already in the next world, a reliable and undoubted proof that in the next world we shall see and recognize one another, will be together, if only we are worthy of it; that we shall interact; and joy or sadness, depending on the sort of life we have led on earth, will have no end?

And so, if the interaction of souls that are still in the body on earth and of those that abide in the next world without bodies is possible, then how can one deny this beyond the grave when all will be either without crude bodies, in the first period of life beyond the grave, or in new, spiritual bodies, in the second period?

Now let us go on to the description of life beyond the grave, of its two states: life in paradise and life in Hades, based on the teaching of the holy Orthodox Church on the two conditions of souls after death, in the world beyond the grave. But the word of God bears witness to the possibility of delivering certain souls from Hades, by the prayers of the holy Church. And where are these souls until they are delivered when there is no middle ground between heaven and hell? They cannot be in paradise, consequently, their life is in Hades. The significance of Hades and of the undetermined state is evidence of what has been said, that Hades has in it two states: the undetermined and the lost. Why are some souls not given a final decision at the individual judgment? Because they are not lost for the kingdom of God, therefore they have hope for life eternal, life with the Lord.

According to the witness of the word of God, the lot, not only of man, but even of the evil spirits is still not resolved finally, as can be seen from the words said by the demons to the Lord Jesus Christ: "Why art thou come to torment us before the time?" (Matthew 8:29) and their petition: "Send us not to Gehenna" (Luke 8:31). Only at the time of the worldwide judgment of Christ will there be revealed two eternal, definite, states beyond the grave: eternal life and eternal torment. In the first period of life beyond the grave, the Church teaches that some souls will inherit paradise and others Hades; there is no middle. In the Old Testament, although there were two states beyond the grave, paradise and Hades, nevertheless all the people of the Old Testament, including the righteous at death, went down to Hades. In the New Testament there are two states of souls, passing into the other world: paradise and Hades. The righteous, those that have been pleasing to God, pass from earth directly to paradise, joining the Old Testament righteous whom the Lord Jesus Christ transferred from Hades to paradise at the time of His glorious Resurrection, leaving there (in Hades) only those condemned from the ages whose number will grow continually, those not believing in Christ, until the great judgment. Not only those who did not believe in Christ, but also all the faithful who did not heal themselves on earth in a lawful order, that is, in active repentance, and therefore all the sinners, regardless of their degree of guilt, pass after death into Hades.

But where are those souls beyond the grave whose lot has not been finally decided at the individual judgment? In order to resolve this question, let us look at what the unresolved state in general and Hades mean, and for a graphic image of the resolution of this question let us take something similar on earth: the prison and the hospital. The former is intended for those that break the law, the latter for the sick. Some criminals, depending on the type of crime and degree of guilt, are sent for a limited prison incarceration, others to one that is permanent; so also the hospital in which the sick are received and enter, not being able to function in life and activity. Some have an illness that can be cured, others are mortally ill; therefore the former get well and are released from the hospital, while others remain permanently, do not leave, but die there. The sinner is morally diseased, a breaker of the law; his soul, after passing into the world beyond the grave, as being morally unwell and bearing the stains of sin, is not capable of being in paradise where there can be no impurity; and therefore, being sick and sinful he enters Hades as a spiritual prison and, as it were, a hospital for moral infirmities. Therefore some souls, depending on the nature and degree of sinfulness, are kept in Hades longer, while others are kept less. These are the souls that have not lost the desire for salvation, but have not managed to bring fruits of true repentance on earth; they are doctored by temporary punishment in Hades, from which they are freed only by the prayers of the Church, not by suffering punishment as the Roman Catholic Church teaches. But all the other souls in Hades remain there till the general judgment, after which they enter that place prepared for the devil, and not for man: they enter Gehenna.

And so, in the first period both paradise and Hades, depending on the nature and degree of virtue and sin (vice), present various degrees of bliss and torment and therefore the various habitations of paradise and Hades. As there are many habitations in the house of our heavenly Father, so there are many prison cells and many hospital rooms, sections of one and the same hospital. But since there has not yet been a final judgment and no final separation of the righteous from the sinners, the Lord Jesus Christ Himself shows this first period of life after death in the parable of the rich man and Lazarus, bearing witness that there exists a union, bond, relationship, and communion between those in paradise and those in Hades.

Those destined for salvation, but temporarily abiding in Hades along with the dwellers in paradise, bend their knees in the name of Jesus Christ. This is the third unresolved state of souls in the world beyond the grave in the first period, that is, the state of those who are to be in bliss, who therefore are not completely foreign to angelic life, as mentioned, for example, in one of the Paschal hymns: "Now all is filled with light: heaven, and earth, and the nethermost abyss . . . ," as well as in the words of St. Paul: "That at the name of Jesus every knee should bow, of those in heaven, and those on earth, and those in the uttermost abyss" (Philippians 2:10). Here the expression, "uttermost abyss," may be understood as the transitory or undecided state of souls destined for salvation, who alongside of the dwellers in heaven and on earth bend their knee before the name of Jesus Christ; they bow, because they are not deprived of the grace-filled light of Christ which enlightens and shines upon souls. Naturally those in Gehenna, who are foreign to the light of grace, do not do this. The demons and those with them do not bend the knee, those that do not believe in the Son of God, Jesus Christ; they do not bend the knee, as they are completely lacking in grace and therefore lost to life eternal. And so, in Hades there are those that bend the knee before the name of Jesus Christ, and there are those that do not, but who are destined for condemnation even on earth, being dead for life eternal.

Jesus Christ gave a pictorial representation in his parable of the rich man and Lazarus, of the bond and communion of three states: those living on earth with those who have been pleasing to God in paradise, and with those in Hades in the first period of life beyond the grave. The three states are represented by Abraham and Lazarus in paradise, the rich man in Hades, and the five brethren on earth. If between those that bend the knee before the name of Jesus—the dwellers in paradise and the lost—who do not bend their knees in Hades there is a bond and communication in the first period, according to the witness of Jesus Christ Himself, then a closer and unbroken bond and eternal communion exist between those that worship Jesus Christ in paradise and temporarily in Hades. There is not yet a state of the kingdom of heaven or of Gehenna in this period—they will be revealed after the judgment—but places for them have been prepared since the foundation of the world. A similar picture of communication in the world beyond the grave is painted by St. Dimitri of Rostov. The righteous rebuke the sinners who offend them and are in Hades (read further on this in the section "Life and Activity in Hades and in Gehenna").

In the Roman Catholic Church there is also a special state beyond the grave, resembling what the Orthodox Church teaches on the unresolved state. The Catholics call this state "purgatory," and it is not dealt with in the same way by all Catholic theologians. Our undecided state is in Hades, according to the teaching of the Orthodox Church, while purgatory according to the teaching of Roman Catholic theologians, has its own place, independent of heaven (paradise) and the innermost parts of the earth (hell). Some place it near heaven; others, in the air; still others, next to hell, in the innermost earth; and some think in agreement with Orthodoxy, taking purgatory in the sense of a state whose souls can purify themselves in the same place as those that are doomed to eternal torment are located, that is, in Hades, just as in the same prison there can be people of two sorts: those sentenced to confinement only for a time and those sentenced to permanent confinement. There is both similarity and divergence in the dogma of the Roman Catholic Church on purgatory and the Orthodox dogma on the unresolved state. The similarity of the teachings lies in the souls of this state, that is, which souls belong to this state beyond the grave, while the divergence lies in the method or means of their purification. Among the Roman Catholics, purification specifically demands that the soul undergo punishment beyond the grave, if it did not do so on earth; while in Orthodoxy, Christ is the cleansing of those who believe in Him, for He took upon Himself both the sins and the consequence of sin: punishment. Those souls that were not perfectly cleansed on earth, but are in the unresolved state, according to God's ineffable providence, are healed and fulfilled by grace, moved to this by the intercession of the Church Triumphant and the Church Vigilant for the imperfect dead, in other words, for those in Hades. The Spirit of God Himself, in this intercession, intercedes for His own temples (people) with sighs beyond human speech; He intercedes for the shortcomings of His creatures, fallen but not turned away from their God—the Lord Jesus Christ. And those who die at holy Pascha, during the days of its celebration, receive a special mercy from God; if they repent of their sins, then their sins are forgiven them, even if they have not brought the fruits of repentance (*Instructions on the Burial of the Dead at Holy Easter*).

7. Life and Activity in Paradise

a) The Beginning of This State While on Earth — Various Names for the Dwelling Place of the Saints

Man, having moral freedom and while living on earth, can change his character, his mental state: good to evil and vice-versa, evil to good. But after death this is impossible to do; good remains good, and evil, evil. The life beyond the grave, as was already said, is only a continuation of the soul's moral development—good or evil—a development having no end, an unceasing development; and the soul beyond the grave is no longer an independent being, for it cannot now change its course of development even if it wanted, as witnessed by the words of Jesus Christ: "Bind him hand and foot, cast him into the darkness," and also by the words of Abraham, spoken to the unfortunate rich man, that between paradise and Gehenna there is a great gulf, and it is impossible to pass over it from Gehenna to Paradise or from Paradise to Gehenna.

The condition of the soul after death, beyond the grave, is not independent, that is, the soul cannot freely begin a new type of activity. The soul cannot begin a new mode of thought and feeling and cannot change itself at all or become different, opposite to its life on earth; but what was begun by the soul on earth can only unfold further. That the state beyond the grave has life on earth as its foundation, is witnessed by the word of God which gives life on earth the meaning of a time of sowing, while life beyond the grave is the time of harvest. As ye sow, so shall ye reap. Such is the significance of earthly life as the foundation of life beyond the grave—happy or unfortunate. Even in ancient times, in the pagan world, a moral law of self-knowledge and attention to oneself was known: by what path dost thou walk? The lack of independence of souls beyond the grave unfolds from the fact that full independence of the soul involves the body as a basic part of man, and that otherwise the present life would have no purpose and no value in relation to the life to come, as St. Paul teaches: "He that soweth to the Spirit shall of the Spirit reap life everlasting" (Galatians 6:8). If a man's earthly activity is not based on and governed by Christian faith, then no exploits, nothing will save him. The holy Christian faith, shown by one's life and deeds, is the state of the soul that is the beginning of a life in paradise beyond the grave, according to the words of Jesus Christ: "He that believeth shall live and be saved forever."

Good begins to develop more and more in eternity. This development is the reason for bliss, because bliss is the effect on the feelings of incessant, gladsome activity. But one and the same sensation, if kept up, dulls the senses, and the soul becomes indifferent, insensate towards the feeling experienced which is inconsistent with its immortality. One and the same pleasure eventually ceases to bring any joy. And if there is no joy, then there is no bliss. The Saviour taught, "The kingdom of God is within you." Those that subordinate the flesh to the spirit, who serve God with fear, rejoice with a joy not of this earth, because the object of their life is the Lord Jesus Christ, heaven, bliss, and the life to come with Christ and with all those that have received mercy and with all those dear to them that have been redeemed by the Lord. Their mind and heart is in God and in heavenly life; for them all that is earthly is nothing. Nothing can mar their unworldly joy; here is the beginning, the foretaste of a blessed life beyond the grave. The soul, finding joy for itself in God, on passing into eternity has the object that sweetens its feelings, face to face.

And so, in conclusion to all we have said on the beginning of this paradisia-cal, blessed state on earth, let us close with the witness of God Himself, that whoever abides in charity with his neighbors on earth, that is, in Christian charity—pure, spiritual, heavenly love—abides in God and God abides in him. Abiding in communion with God on earth is the beginning of that abiding and communion with God that will follow in paradise. Jesus Christ Himself said to those that would be heirs of the kingdom of God, that during their time on earth in the body, the kingdom of God is already within them; that is, bodily they are still on earth while mind and heart have already taken on a state that is not of earth (which is full of passions), but spiritual, impassionate, a condition appropriate to the kingdom of God, a state of righteousness, peace, and joy. This spiritual-moral state of the soul on earth must have its corresponding state beyond the grave in the spiritual-moral kingdom. If the soul whilst still on earth was strongly bound to Christ, then beyond the grave it will be still more blissful in being with Christ (Philippians 1:23). Will not the end of the world consist in eternity swallowing up time itself, destroying death, and unfolding before humanity in all its fullness and limitlessness?

The peoples of antiquity and our contemporary primitives join the concept of a Higher Being, of immortality of the soul, and life in heaven with the idea of a reward beyond the grave for the earthly journey. The thought of recompense after death is common to humanity, met with as soon as man is aware of his rights and obligations. Having come to awareness, he then feels the need for a "paying of wages" for the fulfillment or the breach of rights and obligations.

For doing that which is evil, according to the understanding of all mankind, beyond the grave there is a special place, a place of punishment, a place of retribution, a particular moral state of the soul; whereas for doing good a different place exists: a place of reward, a special moral state of the soul different from the former. In general, the concept of life beyond the grave and of recompense after death has not always been the same among various cultures and at various times; however, the dominant, fundamental thought of reward and punishment has been at the base of all beliefs. Wherein consisted reward and punishment beyond the grave, depended on the degree of the culture's mental and moral development and on the circumstances that accompanied their earthly life. And so, the awareness of the need for recompense beyond the grave is a result of the moral law, hidden in the depths of human nature, the law of the spirit, and as the law of the spirit it is expressed among all of humanity, only in different conceptions: crude (sensatory) and spiritual.

In the period of time before the second coming of Christ to judge the world, there exist the following states of souls: 1) those still on earth, and 2) those already in the world beyond the grave: a) in paradise and b) in Hades, where there are two states: the undetermined and the lost.

The place where the righteous go after the individual judgment, or their state, has various names in the Holy Scriptures; the most usual and frequently met name is paradise. The blessed state of the righteous is called also the bosom of Abraham, the kingdom of heaven, the kingdom of God, the house of the heavenly Father, the city of the Living God, the heavenly Jerusalem. The Lord Jesus Christ Himself called the place of the righteous in the next world "paradise," when He said to the wise thief on the cross, "Today shalt thou be with Me in paradise" (Luke 23:43); and St. Paul calls the place of the righteous in heaven "paradise" (II Corinthians 12:4). The word "paradise" properly means "a garden," and, in particular, a good garden filled with shady and splendid trees and flowers. In the hot lands of the East, during the heat of the day, such a garden was a place of true enjoyment and repose, and therefore the word "paradise" became a figurative expression for the place of bliss of the righteous in the world beyond the grave.

In another place, the Lord uses another expression to signify the place of the righteous beyond the grave: the bosom or lap of Abraham (Luke 16:22). The Hebrews were firmly convinced that Abraham, the friend of God, dwelt in paradise, and that the angels carried the souls of the righteous after death to heaven; the Lord confirms this belief of the Hebrews in His parable of the rich man and Lazarus. To be and to recline with the friend of God is a blessed state for those found worthy of it.

The Lord Jesus Christ, offering a teaching on the bliss of the righteous in the life beyond the grave, and enumerating, as it were, the virtues that bring a blessed life beyond the grave to those that practice them, says that the poor in spirit, and also those banished for righteousness, are heirs of the kingdom of heaven. Here is the third name for the state of the righteous or the place of their abode in the world beyond the grave. So as to do away with the proud idea of the Jews who thought that only they would enter the kingdom of the Messiah, along with those of the Gentiles who adopted their faith, the Lord said that all those who believed in Him, from the whole world, would come and recline with Abraham, Isaac, and Jacob in the kingdom of heaven (Matthew 5:3–10; 8:11).

Sometimes the Lord called the place where the righteous abide in heaven the kingdom of God, for example, in His words addressed to the condemned: "There will be weeping and gnashing of teeth, when ye see Abraham, Isaac, and Jacob, and all the Prophets in the kingdom of God, but yourselves cast out. And they shall come from the East, the West, the North, and the South, and recline in the kingdom of God" (Luke 13:28–29). St. Paul also calls the abode of the Saints the kingdom of God, when he says that flesh and blood will not inherit the kingdom of God (I Corinthians 15:50). Further, in the commandment given to Christians, "Seek ye first the kingdom of God and His righteousness, and all these things shall be added unto you" (Matthew 6:33), that is, seek, take concern, try for your mind and heart to be occupied with the heavenly, eternal striving to gain the kingdom of heaven, for the heavenly to be preferred to the earthly; then, with such a concern for the eternal life beyond the grave, with such a commitment to becoming a true member of the kingdom of the Messiah, the kingdom of Christ, with such a commitment to satisfying first of all the needs of the soul, all that is of earth will be added as if of itself. To such a seeker of the kingdom of God, as if in reward for this, everything needful, useful, palpable is added. For those that seek the kingdom of God, not much of the palpable is needed on earth; they are happy with little, and a seeming lack, as the world would see it, is quite enough for them. In another place the Lord Jesus Christ calls the habitation of the righteous the house of the heavenly Father, with many mansions (John 14:2), which expresses the state of the righteous beyond the grave where God, in a special way, manifests His presence to the Saints and where the Lord Jesus Christ abides in glory with His glorified body—in heaven. The holy Apostle Paul calls the state of the righteous in paradise after death the city of the living God, the heavenly Jerusalem (Hebrews 12:22, Galatians 4:26).

All these names, and others—such as the treasure that abides in heaven (Luke 12:33: Matthew 19:21; Hebrews 10:34), the third heaven (II Corinthians 12:2–4), life eternal (Matthew 18:8–9; 19:29; John 5:24; 11:25), the city to come (Hebrews 13:14), the Sabbath of the people of God (Hebrews 4:9–10), the seeing of the face of God (I Corinthians 13:12; I John 3:2; Hebrews 12:14), living with Christ (II Timothy 2:11–12)—are only various names for one and the same subject, the state beyond the grave of the blessed spirits and angels, and the Saints and souls of the righteous (Archbishop Makary of Kharkov, *Theology*, Volume II, p. 547).

Of the various names that belong to the state of righteous souls beyond the grave, some constitute the names of places or of the blessed state of the righteous in the first period, to wit: paradise, the lap of Abraham; while heaven and other designations refer to the place or state of the saved in the second period. St. Paul's words bear witness to the two periods of the life of the righteous beyond the grave; he, rapt up to the third heaven, heard there speech which is not for man to utter—this is the first period of life in paradise, blessed life, but not yet perfect; and further he continues that God has prepared such perfect bliss for the righteous beyond the grave, as never on earth did the eye of man see nor the ear hear and which man on earth cannot imagine—this is the second period of life in paradise, that of perfect bliss. Thus, according to the words of the Apostle, the second period in paradise is not the third heaven, but another more perfect state or place—the kingdom of heaven, the house of the heavenly Father.

What we have said here—that some names refer to the first period of life beyond the grave in paradise and others to the second period—certain of the ancient Fathers and Doctors of the Church also confirm. St. Athanasius the Great, St. Ambrose, the Blessed Augustine, St. Gregory the Dialogist all expressed this in such words: "The souls of the righteous were assigned, at once after the individual judgment, to the lap of Abraham, to paradise, which they considered only the threshold of Heaven (Archbishop Makary of Kharkov, *Theology*, Volume II, p. 550).

The places of eternal life and repose or of death and torment, according to the witness of the Lord Jesus Christ, were prepared by God before the foundation of the world; the former for those that serve God, the latter for the devil and those that serve him. The heirs of eternal life or the kingdom of heaven, according to the word of Scripture, are called earthly angels, heavenly men, and citizens of heaven.

b) The Place and Description of the Habitation of the Blessed in the First Period — The Dwellers in Paradise — When They Enter There — The Character of the Saved — The Nature of the Sexes — The Number of the Saints

If on earth the good only very, very rarely enter into any sort of contact with the evil, and indeed such is not possible due to the different character of the souls themselves, then it is not natural for there to be contact beyond the grave between the saved and the damned, and only love causes the former to have sympathy for the latter. The states of the Saints, the unresolved, and the lost are divided from one another spatially by a great chasm, according to the teaching of the Lord Jesus Christ Himself; therefore, paradise must have its own definite location, separated from Hades and Gehenna. Where is paradise according to the teaching of the word of God? The future dwelling of souls will correspond to their spiritual nature. Thus, the Church teaches that the nature of paradise fully corresponds to the nature of good souls. Just as water has in itself all the conditions needed for fish to live in it, so does paradise have all that is needful for life, that is, for bliss. But where is this place of bliss, paradise? Where is that place in which the righteous live after death? The very word of God leaves this question unresolved, and the answer to it unrevealed as concerns the location of paradise in the universe. Paradise, according to the teaching of the Church (*Longer Catechism of Metropolitan Philaret*, p. 22), is a special, definite place in heaven, where God manifests Himself in a special way to the blessed spirits and His chosen ones, manifests Himself to them in all His eternal glory where the Lord Jesus Christ is present with His glorified body. But where is paradise in heaven? Heaven is big! We find a written answer in Divine Revelation, in the Book of Genesis. Moses writes that God planted a paradise of sweetness in the

East (Genesis 2:8). Paradise is the first heaven, the closest of the higher lands to earth, after which the other heavens follow.

The place of paradise is indicated by Holy Scripture as being in the East. Paradise is in this direction from the earth. The venerable St. Theodora recounted that, after her departure from the body, she went to the East with her accompanying angels to reach the heavenly habitations (Life of St. Basil the New, in the *Lives of the Saints* for March 26); the great Saint of God Simeon of the Wondrous Mountain saw paradise in the East (*Lives of the Saints* for May 24); it was in the East that St. Euphrosynia of Suzdal in her wonderful vision (MS. Life of the Saint). The teaching of the Veda (the sacred writings of the Hindus) in many respects agrees with the Books of Moses, in placing paradise in the East.

And indeed the East, before all the other directions of heaven, has its mysterious peculiarity, by which it imparts something not of this earth to the soul of man, making the heart rejoice with a spiritual joy. The daily rising of the sun has brought gladness to mankind, and there is not a heart on earth that has not felt a ray of spiritual joy at the rising of the sun. Christians, feeling the action of the invisible sun on the soul, turn to the Lord Jesus Christ, Who enlightens and brightens His creation, with a prayer of thanksgiving: "Glory to Thee Who hast shown us the light!" If on earth there still pours joy from the East to peoples' souls, then probably that is where the blessed dwelling is that was prepared by God from the foundation of the world for spirits and souls. Presentiment has not misled man!

The Orthodox Church, not concerned with seeking out the location of paradise in the universe, in her prayers, especially on Holy Saturday and the Resurrection of Christ, does express her opinion of the place of paradise in heaven. Thus, for example in the praises[14] for the forty-sixth and forty-seventh verses[15] of Psalm 118: "Of Thine own will descending as one dead beneath the earth, O Jesus, Thou leadest up the fallen from earth to heaven. Even though Thou wast seemingly dead, yet alive as God, O Jesus, Thou leadest up the fallen from earth to the heavenly places."[16]

On Holy Easter, at Matins in the Synaxarion reading after the Sixth Song of the Canon, again a view is expressed regarding the place of paradise, in the

[14]In this case, the term "praises" refers to verses of ecclesiastical origin that are inserted between the verses of Psalm 118 (119), at Matins of Holy Saturday.

[15]There is a typographical error in the Russian edition which says, "the sixteenth and seventeenth" instead of "the forty-sixth and forty-seventh verses."

[16]See *The Lenten Triodion,* Faber & Faber: London, 1978, p. 628. The second part of the above text has been modified here to agree more closely with the Greek and Slavonic, especially as to "heavenly *places.*"

words, "ancient heritage," that is, paradise, which is indicated as being in heaven: "By Thy Resurrection, O Lord, Thou hast opened paradise once more, and hast renewed the way up unto the heavens."

Thus, according to the teaching of the Church, paradise is in heaven.

The word of God and good sense bear witness that the word *paradise* first of all is the name of a place prepared by God from all eternity for the spirits and souls of the holy. Only God alone is not subject to the law of time and space, as being eternal and unlimited; everything else, as His creation, is under the law of time and space, that is, exists in a specific time, occupies a definite place in space; otherwise it could not be. Therefore, spiritual-moral beings—spirits and souls—are subject to the law of time, as having received their existence in a specific time, and to the law of space, as creations that must take up specific room in space. Consequently, there must be definite places for souls in the life beyond the grave. As regards the location of paradise, we must conclude from the answer of St. John Chrysostom that it is far more useful and needful for man to know that paradise does indeed exist, than to know only where it is located. For salvation it is enough to know that there is a paradise. You ask, where will paradise be? I suppose that it will be outside of this world. Let us ask, not where it is, but by what means we may obtain it. Chrysostom, disapproving of curiosity as to the whereabouts of paradise, nevertheless does not forbid those beneficial reflections and searches for paradise that lead to the fear of God and turn away from evil, but he also calls upon us always to exercise ourselves in them, having paradise ever before our eyes.

Paradise is obtained only by virtue. Only the virtuous obtain a reward beyond the grave. The deprivations and sorrows of earthly life in the consciousness of savages lead to satisfaction and joy in a happy life beyond the grave. Thus, the Eskimo, the dweller in Polar regions, marked for a life amid ice, snow and frost, and under the heavy yoke of the elements round about him, is led by his undying spirit to dream of something better beyond the grave. In the conception of the Eskimo, his life beyond the grave is a blessed, ever warm country—paradise, with a sun that is always shining, there, beyond the ocean which on earth is his only source of existence. The lack of foodstuffs on earth is fulfilled beyond the grave by their abundance; just as here on earth he did not have entirely enough fish, his only food, therefore his dwelling place beyond the grave, there, far beyond the ocean, abounds in fish and wild game. The main spiritual truth, that life beyond the grave is better than that on earth and that for magnanimous patience on earth there is a recompense after death, is expressed in the Eskimo's understanding in palpable forms; both sorrows and all the deprivations of life on earth, the Eskimo treats with the hope of something better beyond the grave.

The paradise of the Kamchadal[17] is filled with palpable things. Here there is no lack of food—of fish and game. In the Kamchadal's paradise there are no volcanoes, bogs, Cossacks, or Russians. His traveling companion in earthly life, the dog, in paradise never dies. Many dogs will be there. The majority of primitives suppose paradise to be in heaven, and they consider the Milky Way to be the path to heavenly paradise. The polar natives see in the Northern Lights, in the mysterious quivering and play of colors, heavenly spirits, flying in the sky.

From the words of Jesus Christ, "But the children of the kingdom shall be cast out into outer darkness: there shall be weeping and gnashing of teeth ... And cast ye the unprofitable servant into outer darkness: there shall be weeping and gnashing of teeth" (Matthew 8:12; 25:30), which define the character of Gehenna, one can see that for a blessed life there must be a place with light and warmth, for without them there is weeping and gnashing of teeth.

What are light and warmth in the habitation of the righteous?

Light and warmth are two physical manifestations (powers), with which alone life is possible, and therefore activity. Where there is no light and warmth, there is no life; there, everything is dead, lifeless.

Just as physical light and warmth are needed for the physical nature of the soul and body, so for the moral, spiritual nature of the soul, for bliss, there must be spiritual light and warmth, which enlighten and warm the soul with grace.

And so, if the soul too has its bodily side, then its place must be of physical nature, bodily, palpable, ethereal, and therefore physical light and warmth are also necessary. For eternal physical light there is no need for our visible sun; for the ethereal nature of the place and for eternal light, electricity[18] is sufficient, which was in the beginning of the creation of the earth before the sun, concealed in the thickness of the atmosphere, was revealed. If, as science bears witness, life was so strong on an earth not yet lighted by the sun, but by electricity, then what is to prevent such a light as that of electricity in the place of the righteous, where life and development do not cease.

The Bible (Genesis 2:8–9) presents paradise as a wonderful and vast garden in the East, and for that reason the East has a great significance in the Christian Church. Thus, churches are built with the altar facing East; the dead are placed facing East; the Orthodox pray towards the East. Many Saints of God

[17]Native of the southern Kamchatka peninsula.
[18]Here the author refers not to artificial electric lighting, but rather a natural primordial phenomenon.

in the New Testament Church saw paradise as a garden. Indeed it is such; but its composition and nature correspond to the nature of its inhabitants—spirits—and therefore paradise is inaccessible to our senses, crude as they have become through our great fall. At the burial of the Mother of God, St. John the Theologian carried a branch from paradise, brought to earth from paradise by the Archangel Gabriel. St. Macarius the Great writes that after death those who inherit paradise are met and led away to special gardens prepared as habitations for them, and precious garments are put on them (Homily 16:8). St. Gregory of Sinai writes that paradise is the lower heaven; that the trees of the gardens are always covered with flowers and fruits; in the midst of paradise, there flows a river which waters it and divides into four streams. Moses tells of this river in his Book of Genesis (2:10).

All the Holy Fathers and Doctors of the Church represent paradise as a garden of wonderful, indescribable beauty whose nature fully corresponds to the fine, ethereal nature of the soul, inaccessible to our blunted senses. Nevertheless, the inaccessible nature of paradise was accessible to some through the cooperation of the Holy Spirit: for those whose bodies had become temples, vessels of the Holy Spirit, and whose senses therefore were cleansed, that is, brought by the action of the Holy Spirit to their natural state, a state corresponding to that of the first parents before their fall.

Like St. Paul, who was rapt up once to paradise, one devout ascetic, the abbot Vlasy was also swept up to paradise. He began serving God from his early years and was decorated with all virtue. Vlasy was seized by an insurmountable desire to know where, beyond the grave, the souls of monks who had been ascetics during their earthly life dwelt. After prayer for two or three years in his cell every night, one night as abbot Vlasy was standing in prayer as usual, all at once he was swept up to paradise. Here he felt that he was walking along some sort of field; on the field was the paradise of God. Blessed Vlasy entered paradise, which took the form of a flowering garden filled with sweet fragrance and with various fruit trees. In paradise he saw the monk Ephrosimus (Euphrosinius known as "the cook") of his monastery, sitting under a tree on a throne of gold. Seeing Ephrosimus, Vlasy went up to him and asked, "Is it thou, my son Ephrosimus? What dost thou here?" "I was put here by God as a watchman," answered Ephrosimus. "But canst thou give me something, if I ask thee?" continued Vlasy. "I can. Ask." Then Vlasy pointed with his hand to an apple tree and said, "Give me three apples from this tree." Ephrosimus picked three apples from the tree and gave them to the abbot. The abbot put them in his mantle and at once came to himself; he was again in his cell and had three apples in his mantle. The bells for Matins rang. After the service, the abbot ordered the brethren that no one leave the church. Calling Ephrosimus from the kitchen, he asked him, "My son, where wast thou this night?" Ephrosimus, with downcast eyes, stood silently. The elder did not cease asking him. Then Ephrosimus answered, "I was in that place, abba, where thou sawest me." "And where did I see thee?" retorted the elder. Ephrosimus replied, "Where thou didst ask of me three apples, in God's holy paradise, and I gave thee them, and thou tookest." "Here are these three apples which I obtained in God's paradise," continued the abbot, and showed them to the brethren. "This night God granted me to be in paradise and to see it." The apples, as a blessing, were divided up between the brethren, and those among them that were sick, after tasting the fruits of paradise, became completely well *(The Alphabetical Patericon).*

From all that has been said it is evident that Ephrosimus and Vlasy were in paradise only in their souls, in which they had full consciousness, that the appearance of the soul was that of the outer man in his body, and that the souls had fully active sensory organs, such as, for example, vision. The souls engaged in conversation, using words; the souls had mental ability.

Let us conclude our description of paradise in the first period with the words of St. Paul who was there and saw it and heard there ineffable speech "which it is not for man to speak" (II Corinthians 12:3–4).

Western teaching on the heavenly paradise is quite vague; the better Western theologians (Bergier) seem to come involuntarily to the conclusion that paradise is in heaven.

The souls of the righteous and of truly repentant sinners go to paradise after the individual judgment of Christ, on the fortieth day after the separation of the soul from the body. According to the teaching of the Lord Jesus Christ Himself, only the faithful inherit paradise—those who believe in the Lord Jesus Christ and therefore are baptized, as a visible sign that bears witness to their faith: "He that believes and is baptized shall be saved: (Mark 16:16). Consequently, there is no other way to salvation other than active faith. Only those who believe in the Lord Jesus Christ become heirs of the kingdom of heaven. However, not all that believe and are baptized will receive salvation, but only those who live according to faith, who live according to the law of Christ (Matthew 25:31–46), as Jesus Christ Himself bore witness: "And those that have done good, will depart into the resurrection of life" (John 5:25), that is, those that have justified their faith by deeds. The teaching of Jesus Christ on the beatitudes indicated those who can be inhabitants of paradise; they are the poor in spirit, those that weep for their sins, the meek, those that hunger and thirst for righteousness, the merciful, the pure in heart, the peacemakers, those that have suffered persecution, abuse, and exile for righteousness, and so on (Luke 6:20–21). St. Paul writes that only those shall enter paradise who have lived on earth according to the spirit of Christ, as expressed in the following nine virtues: in love, in joy, in peace, long-suffering, in piety, in mercy, in faith, in meekness, and in temperance (Galatians 5:22). Whoever has these virtues is an heir of paradise. Those who do the works of faith, of love, obtain paradise; consequently, those that are gentle and merciful on earth will receive mercy at the judgment and become dwellers in paradise. To paradise will go the pure in heart, the merciful, the compassionate, the temperate, the chaste, those that fast, the strict keepers of their own and others' devoutness and good morals. God will judge the lechers and adulterers (Hebrews 13:4). Neither lechers nor adulterers will inherit the kingdom of God (I Corinthians 9:10), unless they offer proper repentance. Therefore, virgins and those who keep their marriage vows holy, as well as widowhood as if an unbroken marriage bond, inherit paradise. The beauty of virtue and the grace of God shine on the faces of the good angels; this character is also stamped on the faces of the dwellers in paradise.

The representatives of both sexes on earth—Adam and Eve before falling into sin—were immortal in both soul and body. Consequently, the body after the resurrection, joined with its soul, will again yield a new spiritual human being of a given sex. The incarnate Son of God and the Mother of God are representatives of the two sexes in the life of paradise beyond the grave. The manifestation of Saints to people on earth confirms the truth of what has been said about the existence of the two sexes beyond the grave. The life beyond the grave is no longer that of earth, but angelic, where there is no need for marriage—indeed it is impossible; it was necessary on earth for the continuance of the human race. The spiritual relationships of people begun on earth are maintained, and it could not be otherwise in the world beyond the grave for which these relationships were designed. Brother will remain brother there also towards his sister, if only she was on earth and if she too is a participant in the life of paradise; a wife remains the wife of her husband, her right to this remains with her; her spiritual relationship to her husband was determined by God Himself. If the existence of the soul does not end with bodily death, if it is to give answer for its actions, for example, in fulfilling or not fulfilling the duties of a wife, then in giving answer the soul must retain its gender. It is not in agreement with good sense that an undifferentiated being, a soul, should give answer for actions not belonging to it or not proper to it.

The word of God teaches us that in the resurrection bodies will be united to their souls; consequently, every soul is once more joined to its body for all ages. The body is an organ of the soul, its instrument for visible manifestation. One should not think that the difference of the sexes was only in the visible body. The character, the quality of one or the other sex belongs not to the body, but to the soul. With these essential characteristics that set one soul apart from another, the soul passes from earth into the world beyond the grave. Even without a body, the unfortunate rich man in hell recognized the bodiless Abraham and Lazarus. Obviously, this means that he in no way confused them with Sarah, Rebecca, and the other women who were in paradise. They are right in saying on earth that such and such a man has a woman's character, or that such and such a woman has a man's character; however, the man is not a woman and the woman is not a man. Here only a certain similarity in character is spoken of, just as it happens that men may have feminine faces or women may have mannish faces, retaining, nevertheless, their own gender which is an essential character of the soul.

On the existence of the sexes in the life beyond the grave, the Blessed Augustine writes as follows: "Then only that which is inadequate will be driven out of the flesh, but its nature will be kept. But the sex of a woman is in no wise a shortcoming (as some medieval theologians taught, denigrating the female sex); but her nature—which of course will then neither conceive nor bear children, and there will be no marriages—but she will continue to exist in her female members, not for their former use, but as a new decoration; and never will she arouse passions in those that look upon her ... On the contrary, she will serve as a new reason to glorify the wisdom and the goodness of God, Who created once that which had not been, and then delivered from corruption that which He had created. He that in such wise created both sexes, the Same will also maintain them."

The number of the saved—the righteous, the Saints, is far less than that of the lost, which can be seen from the words of the Lord Jesus Christ Himself: "Fear not, small flock ... Many are called, but few are chosen" (Luke 12:32; Matthew 22:14). Sacred history also bears witness to this truth for us: Lot with his family out of the whole condemned city; Noah with his family out of all humanity of that time. And it is always evident that the sons of God are far fewer than the sons of man. At the second and glorious Advent, according to the words of Jesus Christ, few will be found faithful.

c) The Basis and Definition of the Blessed Life, of Bliss — The Makeup of Bliss
— Incomplete Bliss

The basis for bliss in paradise, in the first period, is the presence of Jesus Christ, seeing His face, and being in contact with Him, as He Himself taught regarding this, that those who believe in Him will be participants in His glory. Having said that the faithful will abide with the Lord, He continues further on their seeing of His face: "Blessed are the pure in heart, for they shall see God" (Matthew 5:8). Therefore St. Paul said from impatience, "[I am in a strait betwixt two], having a desire to depart, and to be with Christ" (Philippians 1:23), abiding with Christ and seeing God "face to face" (I Corinthians 13:12). The seeing of God is given only to the Saints alone. Besides them, none shall see God (Hebrews 12:14). At the same time, the same Apostle bears witness that our bliss beyond the grave will be made complete by dwelling with all the angels and souls of the righteous, and consequently with those close to our heart, if only they are of one mind with us: "And so we shall be always with the Lord" (I Thessalonians 4:17).

St. John the Theologian writes to the faithful, "Beloved, now are we the sons of God, and it doth not yet appear what we shall be: but we know that, when he shall appear, we shall be like him; for we shall see him as he is" (I John 3:2).

The holy Disciples and Apostles of Christ consoled and delighted themselves and all the faithful with the heavenly hope of always being united with Jesus Christ and with each other (I Thessalonians 4:13–18).

In the first period the glorification of the righteous is twofold: in heaven, in the Church Triumphant, and on earth in the Church Militant.

The Lord Jesus Christ Himself expressed the first truth about the bliss of the Saints that is to be at once after death, in heaven, in paradise, in the parable of the Rich Man and Lazarus, where Lazarus, immediately after death, was carried by angels to the bosom of Abraham; or, in another passage, "In my Father's house are many mansions: if it were not so, I would have told you. I go to prepare a place for you. And if I go and prepare a place for you, I will come again, and receive you unto myself; that where I am, there ye may be also" (John 14:2–3). By the preparation and reception of the Apostles is understood the departure or death of each of them, for which there is the promise of being ever with the Lord. Here is the witness of the Lord that the Saints, those that have been pleasing unto God, and the righteous enter in their souls, at once after death, into the foretaste of eternal bliss by means of direct and bodily union with the Lord and by means of partaking in His glory.

These words of the Lord, directed to the troubled Disciples and Apostles, as the time of their (visible) parting with the beloved Lord Jesus Christ drew near, and carrying faith in the spiritual, invisible bond brought about by the descent of the Holy Spirit, Who would bring the Apostles and all those faithful to Christ into a close union and unbreakable bond with the Lord Jesus Christ, gave them strength in the work of preaching. "Today thou shalt be with Me in paradise," said the Lord to the wise thief, who repented on the cross; this means "from the moment of our passing into the world beyond the grave, thou shalt be in paradise with Me, and therefore a participant in My glory."

Before His passion on the cross, Jesus Christ, in His prayer as High Priest to God the Father, for Himself, for His holy Disciples, and in general for all those who truly believe in Him, asked, "Father, I will that they also, whom Thou hast given Me, be with Me where I am; that they may behold My glory, which Thou hast given Me" (John 17:24). This desire, or will, as it were a testament, the prayer of the Lord Jesus Christ, which is fully in agreement with the will of the Heavenly Father, is a clear proof for all of the Church of Christ—that is, for all her true, living members—that immediately after death, after passing over into the world beyond the grave, they will be with the Lord in heaven, in paradise, and will be participants in His glory. Those worthy of the kingdom of heaven, after passing into the world beyond the grave, will at once be where the Lord dwells, as God-man, with His glorified body.

The world beyond the grave, life after death, have been revealed to man while yet on earth by the Lord Himself; they have been revealed insofar as the mind's limitations can take in. And so, here is the state of the righteous in paradise, in the first period of life beyond the grave—they are with the Lord Jesus Christ, coheirs of the kingdom of heaven, and with Him in glory.

The holy Apostles were convinced of the truth of the Lord's teaching on the faithful abiding with Him in the world beyond the grave, at once after the parting on earth of soul and body, which last is committed to the ground, as a seed for the growth of a new body, while the faithful soul goes to the Lord. They bore witness to this their faith in the certainty of this truth in both word and writing. The holy Apostle Paul, who burned with love for the Lord, wrote concerning himself as follows: "For I am in a strait betwixt two, having a desire to depart, and to be with Christ; which is far better: Nevertheless to abide in the flesh is more needful for you" (Philippians 1:23–24). In another place, he confesses this truth about the faithful abiding with Christ in the first period of life beyond the grave, in the name of all the Apostles: "For we know that if our earthly house of this tabernacle were dissolved, we have a building of God, an house not made with hands, eternal in the heavens ... We are confident, I say, and willing rather to be absent from the body, and to be present with the Lord" (II Corinthians 5:1,8). Here the holy Apostle expresses that thought: we know that after death, after the destruction of our earthly tabernacle, our body, we have at once a tabernacle not made by hands, in heaven, that is, after death the soul, departed from the body, will at once go to the Lord and abide forever with Jesus Christ. Thus he consoles all Christians, lest they sorrow over the death of those close to their heart, assuring them that they will be with the Lord in the mansions of the heavenly Father.

The reality of what the Lord promised, that the righteous, after leaving the earth and after the individual judgment, remain with Him, the Apostle St. John saw in revelation: in heaven, round about the throne there were twenty four seats: and upon the seats were elders sitting, in white garments, with crowns of gold on their heads (Revelation 4:4); further, he "saw under the altar the souls of them that were slain for the word of God, and for the testimony which they held" (6:9). "After this I beheld, and, lo, a great multitude, which no man could number, of all nations, and kindreds, and people, and tongues, stood before the throne, and before the Lamb, clothed with white robes, and palms in their hands; And cried with a loud voice, saying, Salvation to our God which sitteth upon the throne, and unto the Lamb" (7:9–10).

The teaching of the holy Orthodox Church on the blessed life of the righteous beyond the grave, immediately after death, in the closest bond and communion with the Lord Jesus Christ, was expressed in the writings of the Holy Fathers and Doctors of the Church. In their works (writings) on this subject of the life of the righteous beyond the grave in the first period, the main thought is one and the same for all, as a truth no longer needing any substantiation, stated by the Lord, repeated by the holy Apostle Paul and its actuality revealed to St. John the Theologian.

The good things of life in paradise, both inner (boons for the spirit and soul), as well as outward (for the body), constituting the state of the righteous in paradise, or simply their bliss, have as their main foundation God, Who is the Source of all that is true, good and beautiful, with Whom, according to the teaching of St. Paul, the righteous will live forever and so be always with the Lord ... living and seeing Him face to face. Thus living and forever seeing the God is the state of man in which all our desires find their gratification, so that man has nothing more left to want; all feelings, both inward and outward, are completely satisfied. And as the first period of the soul's condition beyond the grave, according to the teaching of the Church, is a continuation of the soul's existence without the body, therefore the bliss of the soul in this period consists only in the gratification of inner feelings—inner spiritual enjoyment of spiritual good things, the action of inner feelings, an activity bringing joy, but still not perfect, since the body will take part in bliss only after its union with the soul. Concerning this state of life in paradise, the Prophet David wrote: "As for me, I will behold thy face in righteousness: I shall be satisfied, when Thy glory shall appear to me" (Psalms 16:15). On earth, when our desires are fulfilled, with all Thy blessings, always something is lacking; but beyond the grave, when I shall be with Thee, I will see Thee face to face, as it is: then I will be satisfied with my existence—I shall be filled, all my feelings satisfied. The blessed state of the soul, or its bliss, is its definite state in certain conditions, as expressed in certain actions, inward and outward, without which bliss is impossible.

Part of bliss, which allows not the least shade of sadness, is joy, from being together and in communion with those who are one's own, and especially with those close and dear to our heart. Thus St. Dimitri of Rostov wrote on this subject: "When the righteous see themselves glorified in the kingdom of their heavenly Father, and not only themselves but also those close to them glorified, their hearts are filled with eternal joy, not to be explained in words. The father will rejoice in the salvation of his son, the son in the salvation of his father, the mother in that of her daughter and the daughter in that of her mother; the husband will rejoice in the salvation of his beloved wife, and the wife in that of her husband. Brothers and sisters will rejoice in the salvation of their siblings; relatives will rejoice for relatives, neighbors for neighbors and acquaintances for acquaintances and for those they are not acquainted with, for all will love God and one another with one soul and one heart, with a love that cannot be destroyed and cannot fail" (Writings of St. Dimitri of Rostov, p. 111, Part 5). All will rejoice in the mutual joy of the sympathy they feel for one another. And it cannot be otherwise; the fulfillment of the natural psychical law of sympathy is to rejoice with them that rejoice and to weep with them that weep.

The life, condition, and activity of the soul are one and the same. Where there is life, there is a condition or activity that can be either bliss or torture. The natural purpose of life and activity, in the achieving of which bliss is found, lies in the constant attainment of all the exalted, not earthly but heavenly, thoughts, desires and feelings, to which the soul, with all its powers, is linked. Eternal bliss is found in the attainment of an eternal succession of natural desires, and that bliss, according to the teaching of St. Paul, is twofold: inward and outward.

In the first period of life in paradise, only the soul enjoys bliss. Only by means of the senses is the soul either in a state of bliss or a state of grief. Without senses, there is neither bliss nor torture. And since the senses are both internal and external, so bliss itself, and torment, will be both internal and external. The soul is in bliss when all its desires are gratified by inward and outward good things. The use of internal boons constitutes internal bliss, and that of external boons, external bliss. And so, into the composition of bliss there enter, first of all, inward bliss, and second, outward bliss. The makeup of internal and external blessedness is as follows: inward bliss is made up of a) the relationship of the soul to God, or its activity towards God, and b) its relationship to its own self, or its inward activity—profound self-knowledge, penetrated by the completely joyous action of a conscience that rewards and justifies it. Outward bliss is made up of the relationship of the soul to all its surroundings, or its activity with regard to all that is outside it, namely: a) its relationship or activity towards the spiritual-moral beings that surround it, the blessed spirits and holy souls, and b) its relationship to all the nature of paradise.

The reward of the righteous in the first period is still not complete, not full, as our holy Orthodox Church teaches (*Theology* of Archbishop Makary of Kharkov, Vol. 2, p. 543). The righteous in the first period enjoy sweetness only in their souls alone. In this period of life beyond the grave in paradise, the righteous shine only in the glory of their souls, as St. John the Theologian, the seer of mysteries, bears witness: "And white robes were given unto every one of them; and it was said unto them, that they should rest yet for a little season, until their fellowservants also and their brethren, that should be killed as they were, should be fulfilled" (Revelation 6:11). Their glorification in heaven follows at one after the individual judgment and will continue till the Last Judgment, when there will follow the full recompense to every human being, consisting of spirit, soul and body. If the righteous and the sinners, immediately after death, received at the individual judgment their final recompense—full bliss or total punishment (torment), then what would the general judgment be for? To judge what had already been resolved finally? But if, as our Orthodox, true Church teaches, Christ will come again to judge the living and the dead, this means that the dead who had gone into the world beyond the grave before His coming still have not been subject to a final judgment and their lot beyond the grave has not been finally resolved. Consequently, until the Dread Judgment, both those that are in paradise and those that are in Hades have not yet received their final reckoning. And, since in man's earthly activity the full man takes part, that is, soul and body, therefore the recompense must be to the soul and body, as the holy Apostle Paul bears witness, that each one will receive for the deeds in which the body also took part: "which he has done with his body," that is, both soul and body will receive recompense, and this will be after the resurrection of bodies and their joining to their souls, and after the universal judgment. The full man receives a full reckoning: either complete bliss or complete torment. Thus the Apostle teaches regarding all people: "For we must all appear before the judgment seat of Christ; that every one may receive the things done in his body, according to that he hath done, whether it be good or bad" (II Corinthians 5:10). And in another passage he repeats the same thought, mentioning also the personal recompense that he will receive on the day of the general judgment: "Henceforth there is laid up for me a crown of righteousness, which the Lord, the righteous judge, shall give me at that day: and not to me only, but unto all them also that love his appearing" (II Timothy 4:8). Here the Apostle clearly speaks of another, special reckoning, besides the first, when he says, "Lest they obtain perfection without us" (Hebrews 11:40). They obtain recompense at once after the individual judgment, but perfection of recompense they receive not without us, but in the presence of all, which will be at the Last Judgment, before which all shall stand.

Good and evil are developed, and those who plant and tend them must receive their recompense for all the fruits that have come about on earth down to the last possible limit of their development. This is why the workers of good and evil can receive a full reckoning only when earthly activity, earthly life has ended. Only then will each see for himself, to what awe-inspiring degree good or evil has grown in his posterity, for which he is the cause. And then we shall see for ourselves, that we who were the first cultivators of good or evil have been the cause of the salvation of some and the ruin of others. This is why the Apostle says, "Lest they obtain perfection without us."

And so, the absence of the body and unfinished moral development make the first period of life beyond the grave incomplete. Thus taught St. Gregory the Theologian and St. John Chrysostom.

Not only for our own deeds, but also for the life of others who continue to develop our concepts and who imitate us are we to receive reckoning. And this earthly life and development of thought will end on the last day of the world.

And then, how many curses will some hear from those who perish for following their concealed evil, which they have sown! But others will meet with the blessing of those who were saved by following their good life. Only then will good and evil be revealed in full and complete degree before all, if only it was not erased in due time by true repentance and life, the good and evil of each will be unfolded with all the endless good and evil consequences, and those that planted must taste their fruits first of all. Thus have all the Holy Fathers and

Doctors taught, concerning the incomplete bliss of the righteous in paradise in the first period of life beyond the grave, as well as on the incomplete torment of the damned in Gehenna.

d) Inward and Outward Incomplete Bliss, or the Activity of the Soul in Paradise

In the first period of life after death in paradise, the soul alone enjoys bliss. Since the activity of the soul is composed of its individual powers, of which we spoke above in the article on the activity of the soul and its individual faculties on earth and beyond the grave, it is necessary for the bliss of the soul that all its powers also act in such a manner as brings joy. Corresponding to the three main mental faculties: the mind, the will, and the feelings, inward bliss consists in the action of these faculties: to love, to come to know, and to glorify God its Creator, the Lord Jesus Christ, the Source of bliss, the Truth whence all truths flow—the One Who bears witness of Himself, that He is "Truth." Our Lord Jesus Christ is He Who becomes the object of life and activity for the soul, according to the teaching of the Apostle Paul: "In Whom we live and move," that is, in Him and for Him is all our life, both on earth and beyond the grave as well. Consequently, the object of the soul's life and activity beyond the grave remains the same: to love, to know and to glorify God; here is man's bliss. Love, knowledge and glorification of God are the content of life beyond the grave in paradise, a content that presents the entirety of the function of the three main mental faculties: the mind, the will and the feelings. Never ceasing, perfect, and forever developing the function of the mind, will and feelings in striving towards truth—this comprises the inner activity of the soul in the blessed life of paradise. This is internal bliss, or the inward activity of the soul towards God. Thus teaches the holy Orthodox Church (*Longer Catechism* of Philaret, First Article of the Creed).

From the source of bliss, of which we spoke above, that is, from being together and in communion with God and seeing His face, there derives an action of all the mental faculties producing joy. One action being replaced by another, more perfect, will develop further and further through all eternity. Desires and their corresponding satisfaction will go on forever. All the faculties of the soul attain their purpose in striving towards that which is true, beautiful and good. In this way, here too love towards God and God's love toward man have been the foundation for all bliss. Without man's love for God there is no salvation, and there is no happiness. Love naturally strives towards knowledge of the beloved. Loving and knowing, we thereby glorify the beloved and the known, and the soul in such a mood is in bliss. "I will not die, but live," full of love for the Lord, writes David: "I will not die, but live!" (Psalms 117:17), alive on earth, I will be alive beyond the grave. He assigns the living to sing of God, while yet in this life. "We, the living, bless the Lord from henceforth and forever more" (Psalms 113:26). Both here and beyond the grave there is one thing to do—to glorify God, to praise His name. The inner state of the soul is expressed in outward signs, and inner bliss in God is expressed by the following spiritual boons: standing before the Lamb, glorifying and serving Him (Revelation 7:9–17), living with Him (John 14:3; Philippians 1:26), reigning with Christ and sharing His eternal glory (II Timothy 2:11–12) and, finally, seeing the face of God and having a more perfect knowledge of God. On earth there was an incomplete knowledge, to be understood as "in part," along with seeing God on earth, which is demanded of all that believe in Him, and of which David bears witness: "I have seen the Lord before me always" (Psalms 15:8); this vision on earth, according to the teaching of St. Paul, is imperfect "as if in a glass, darkly," we now see God; but in paradise we shall see "face to face" (I Corinthians 13:12; II Corinthians 5:8; Hebrews 12:14).

All this will constitute: being, living, being in communion, in the closest bond with the Lord Jesus Christ, in Whom we live, move at first on earth, and them beyond the grave in His kingdom. This union, bond and eternal communion with the Lord is the main foundation of the bliss of the righteous, the first foundation of the good whence all else that is good flows—boons internal and external, without which bliss is impossible. Enjoyment of God brings forth a constant, joyous action of all the mental and physical faculties, as has already been said in general about the activity of the soul and its individual faculties on earth and beyond the grave.

Since evil is the source of all grief and suffering, and it is not natural to man—to man, good and bliss are natural, and he was created for them—therefore in paradise, evil is no more, and the state of the souls of the righteous in this period is completely free of any sorrow: "They shall hunger no more, neither thirst any more; neither shall the sun light on them, nor any heat. For the Lamb which is in the midst of the throne shall feed them, and shall lead them unto living fountains of waters: and God shall wipe away all tears from their eyes; ... And there shall be no more death, neither sorrow, nor crying, neither shall there be any more pain: for the former things are passed away" (Revelation 7:16–17; 21:4). Just such a description of the state of the souls of the righteous beyond the grave is found in Isaiah (25:6–9). But the Saints' seeing the hellish condition of sinners beyond the grave, and their vital concern for their calamity, brings about an age-long sorrow, one that is beneficial both to them and to those that suffer in Hades; a sorrow that moves the Saints to prayer for the captives of Hades, and therefore brings salvation to these last as well.

Rest, or eternal repose from labors, performed on earth for the sake of the kingdom of heaven (Revelation 14:13; Hebrews 4:3,11) constitutes the distinctive character of blissful activity in paradise in this period. Here the word "rest" should not be understood as inaction or inactivity. The concept of the soul is always joined with that of its activity, for activity expresses the life of the soul, and as the soul is immortal, its activity is unceasing. Therefore the word "rest" characterizes a specific sort of condition or activity of the soul, in contradistinction to disturbance. The activity of the soul, bringing it pleasure and enjoyment, puts the soul at peace. The natural state of the soul, foreign to passions, according to the witness of the Lord Jesus Christ Himself, brings the God-loving soul peace even while yet on earth: "Be meek and humble in heart, and ye shall find *rest* for your souls,"—the foretaste of heavenly rest while yet on earth, the expectation of one's final lot, which will come into effect after the last judgment of Christ, and the foretaste of the fullness of that ineffable bliss, which they will enjoy forever.

The hearts of the righteous, filled with true love, take a vital interest in the fate of those souls in Hades, whose lot has not yet been decided, and for whom the Church Militant intercedes, and this intercession, to which the Church calls all those that have been pleasing unto God, is not without effect in this case. The members of the Church Triumphant have a vital bond and communion with the members of the Church Militant through the concern they have for their brethren yet wandering on earth and carrying on the battle in the Church Militant, helping them by their prayers before God and active assistance unto salvation. The former is without doubt revealed in the Apocalypse, where it is stated that the Saints cry out to God and ask Him for a judgment soon, and a reward for the righteous who are oppressed on earth (Revelation 6:10; 11:18). The latter is evident from countless cases in which the Saints of God appeared and offered miraculous protection—cases that fill the history of the Church of Christ. As on earth the name of God was hallowed in their activity, so they also continue to do good works after death in paradise. This good work is an extension of that done on earth. Concerning the life of the Saints, Jesus Christ taught thus: "For in the resurrection they neither marry, nor are given in marriage, but are as the angels of God in heaven," that is, they will be like angels, and consequently the life of the Saints is completely angelic, since on earth they were earthly angels with heavenly activity, which, in the words of Jesus Christ Himself, will continue after death, for all eternity.

Since the life of the soul consists in self-knowledge, life in paradise will consist in true knowledge of self—perfect self-knowledge, full awareness of the past and the present, which (that is, true self-knowledge) very few achieve on earth, despite strict and attentive self-examination.

Outward bliss consists of: a) mutual, eternal communion with all the Angels (Hebrews 12:22–23; Luke 16:22); b) dwelling together with, and having the closest communion with all the Saints (Matthew 8:11; Luke 13:28–29) and finally c) the beauty of paradise itself, which St. Paul saw, when he was rapt up to the third heaven. He saw all the beauty of paradise, but could find no words in human language to describe it to earthlings. And if he had been able to tell, at least to some extent, of the endlessly splendid beauty of paradise, then those who heard would not have comprehended, would not have been able to grasp, just as children do not grasp many things that grownups understand. Not having understood or grasped the beauty of paradise, the carnal intellect, which accepts only what it can know by experience, would reject it, as usually has been the case with the wise men of this world, who reject all that is supernatural, spiritual, miraculous. And so, external bliss consists of the actual dwelling place in paradise, with its unimaginable splendors, and the society of Angels and holy souls. This is the internal and external blessedness that awaits every holy soul, immediately after the individual judgment.

It now remains to show the evidence of the word of God about that inexpressible blessed life of the Saints in paradise, in a bond and communion amongst themselves.

The Patriarch Jacob was willing, in his sorrow over the loss of his favorite son Joseph, only so as to be with him and to see him, to go to Hades, that is, willing to die if only he could be with him (Genesis 37:35). And the holy Prophet David had a living faith in meeting beyond the grave, when he spoke of the death of his son who was born of her that had been with the wife of Uriah: "I will go to him" (II Kings [Samuel] 12:23). The holy Apostles Peter, James and John on Tabor recognized at once the dwellers beyond the grave, Moses from Hades and Elias from paradise, when before they had never seen them anywhere, but only known of their existence. But here they knew at once who they were, and without mistake recognized them as Moses and Elias; they knew them at sight, and they knew their names. Further, the lives of the Saints also give us evidence, that the Saints, for example, without knowing certain individuals beforehand, saw their mental state when they encountered them, saw their civil position that they occupied in society, saw their family life, and as if seeing how they were called, addressed them by name; and they knew all this at once, at the moment of first meeting. Everything was accessible to their purified senses, and all that was secret, was evident to them. Hence it is natural to conclude, on the basis of the evidence of Holy Scripture, that these souls, gifted while yet on earth with such perfection of the senses, do not lose these abilities after passing into the world beyond the grave, and the activity of the senses will gain even more strength, being freed from the body of death, as St. Paul expresses it. Consequently, all those found worthy of a blessed life in paradise will see and recognize one another; all those beloved of our heart, while on earth, and if only they obtain this life, will at once be recognized by us, and equally they will know us. The holy Apostle Paul thus consoled the Christians of the Thessalonica, who had been parted from those close and dear to their hearts by death: Your parting is only for a time! Ye shall doubtless soon meet your departed friends, so as never again to be parted from them. "And so we shall always be with the Lord" (I Thessalonians 4:16–17). These last words indicate an eternal abiding together in the bond and communion of all true Christians and especially those, whom the Lord joined yet on earth by a bond of family and friendship. Consoling the Thessalonian Christians in this way, the holy Apostle commands "with the same," that is, with the fact that we shall meet and remain together, for all of us also to console one *another:* "Console ye one another with these words" (Verse 18). Consolation for mourning Christians who have been parted from those close to their heart is found in these two dogmas of our Orthodox faith, as expressed in the eleventh and twelfth articles of the Creed. Only we must believe without doubt in these two truths: 1) the resurrection of the dead and 2) a blissful rejoining of those who have departed from us.

Only there, in the life beyond the grave—in paradise, will the significance of man be fully evident: what man is (I John 3:2).

And so, if those in paradise will be together with the Lord, as St. Paul taught and as did the Lord Himself, in abiding with the Lord we will all be together; and being together in society, as living, moral beings, we will necessarily be in communion with one another.

God, having created man on earth, said, "It is not good for man to be alone" (Genesis 2:18), which bears witness to man's purpose as one who should live in society. For a life in common, corresponding to that of the angels in heaven, people are joined with God by an unbreakable, holy bond of divine love. Joined to God, they are joined amongst themselves as well, by the will of God, also by an unbreakable bond of love. God does not join people on earth by a spiritual bond of love so as, having joined them here, to part them there. Consequently, the disjoining of souls is unnatural beyond the grave too. In the words of the unfortunate rich man, as witnessed in the Gospel parable, it can be seen that Abraham and Lazarus were not separated from each other in paradise, but together, and therefore they had a bond and communion between themselves. The faithful will live eternally with the Lord, as the Lord Jesus Christ Himself teaches (John 14:2–4; 17:24); the faithful will be with Him, and therefore they will have interaction among themselves, and will see one another, as St. John bears witness (Revelation 4:4; 6:9, 11).

Two truths—the unity of the nature of souls, and the love inborn in souls, which serve as the basis for social life, bring us to the conclusion that man has a natural striving to live in society, that is, he has a striving by all means to be with beings like himself, while the purpose of the soul is to live in heaven, and consequently, social life beyond the grave will not be contrary to the soul's nature. There has never been a people that did not believe in a life in common beyond the grave, except for those who think that all ends with death, for example, those that follow the teaching of Buddha with its Nirvana, the present Nihilists,[19] materialists and others that are in the diabolical beguilement of unbelief and carnal thinking.

The human mind cannot imagine such a society of people as the Saints constitute in paradise. Joined by an everlasting love and continuous communion, in this very way they fulfill one another's blissful state. On earth it is sad to part with good people, with a moral society, because in being together with them our soul has found joy, cheer; and since in paradise this parting will not take place, the soul's bliss will be eternal. All spiritual-moral beings, the holy souls and spirits of the righteous, will enter into a close bond and communion amongst themselves.

The state of those beyond the grave in the first period, both the righteous and the sinners, before the resurrection of the dead, is represented by the Lord Jesus Christ Himself in the parable of the Rich Man and Lazarus. From this parable, St. John Chrysostom draws the conclusion that, however great the chasm between the two, the righteous and the sinners will know one another, whether or not they were acquainted in life. This is demonstrated by the fact that the unfortunate rich man in the Gospel, while in Hades, recognized Abraham even though he had never seen him anywhere before. This means that after the separation of the soul from the body, its senses regain their nature and their action is far extended. The dwellers in paradise see and know the denizens of

---

[19]This was written in the nineteenth century.

Hades and the inhabitants of the earth, while those in Hades see and recognize those that live in paradise and on earth. If the rich man had not seen and known the state of his brethren, who were still on earth, then he would not have asked Abraham to send Lazarus to them. This means that our departed, regardless of where they might be, in paradise or Hades, know our state, so to speak, hear and see us and all our life, and what we hide is no longer concealed from them. For this knowledge of one another the inner, mental eye will do service. In order to see, one must have the sense of vision, of which the Apostle John writes in the Apocalypse: "Behold, the Saviour cometh . . . and every eye shall see Him" (Revelation 1:7). Consequently, seeing the Lord, we shall see also the whole world beyond the grave, along with all its inhabitants: spirits and souls.

Here is how the blessed Theodora recounts her meeting in paradise: "All that saw me, rejoiced in my salvation, came forth to meet me, embraced me, and praised the Lord Who had delivered me from the snares of the enemy" (Life of St. Basil the New, March 26).

St. Pimen the Great said of his aged mother, who had sought to see him, as follows: "Wilt thou see us (thy children) here, or in the next world?" She answered, "If I do not see you here, will I indeed see you there?" Pimen replied: "If thou resolvest not to see us here, then thou wilt certainly see us there."

Once the Abba Joseph, who had taken sick, sent to tell the Abba Theodore: "Come to me, so I can see thee before parting with my body." This was during the week. The elder did not go, but sent word: "If thou livest till Saturday, I will come; but if thou departest, we shall see each other in the other world" (*Sayings on the Lives of the Saints*, p. 339).

St. Basil the Great spoke as follows of future encounters, in addressing himself to various unjust people: "Dost thou not have the judgment of Christ before thine eyes, when round about thee, those thou hast wronged cry out against thee? For wherever thou castest thine eyes, there appear the images of thy wrongs. Here are the orphans, there the widows; yonder, the beggars thou hast cast aside, the servants whom thou hast beaten; the neighbors thou has offended, and so on."

St. John Chrysostom offers two consoling truths to them that weep over the death of those close to their heart: "If the body is given over to corruption, one should not weep, but rejoice, because death goes to corruption, and what is mortal perishes, not the essence of the body. Remember that these closed lips one day will speak better, and these closed eyes will then see better and greater things, and these feet will walk on clouds, and this perishing body will be decked in immortality, and thou shalt receive thy friend." Dost thou hear, that weepest?

Thou shalt again have thy friend, but one better and brighter. Weep not, says God Himself, the deceased has not died, he is alive, and sleeps! Sorrow not, says St. Paul: but believe without doubt, and thou shalt meet again, and remain together for all ages! And finally, Chrysostom adds, Thou shalt again receive thy friend.

And in another passage he says, "For we shall recognize not only those we have known here; but we shall see those who never came before our eyes, for thou hast not seen Abraham, nor Isaac, nor the first Forefathers, nor the Prophets, Apostles and Martyrs; but having seen them at that great, universal and fearsome gathering, thou shalt say: 'Behold Abraham, and Isaac, and all the Apostles; behold David, and the choir of Ancestors of God and Prophets; here is John the Forerunner, and Stephen the first martyr, and the multitude of Saints'."

The great universal Doctor St. Gregory the Theologian, in his funeral homilies for his brother Caesarius and his sister Gorgonia, recounts all these internal and external good things, which make up the bliss of the righteous in heaven in the first period. Thus he says to his brother Caesarius, "Enter thou into heaven, take rest at the bosom of Abraham; behold the choir of angels, the glory and magnificence of the blessed, or better, be of one choir with them, and be joyous!" Here can be seen: repose, joy, paradise and dwelling with all the Angels and Saints—outward bliss. Further he continues: "May thou stand before the great King, filled with higher light!"—inner bliss, standing before God, seeing the face of God and partaking in His glory. And to his sister Gorgonia he says, "I am certain that thy present state is beyond comparison more excellent than the former, visible state; the voice of them that celebrate, the joy of the angels, the heavenly orders, the seeing of glory, and more than anything else the most pure and perfect glow of the Holy Trinity, no longer concealed from the mind, as when it was bound and distracted by the senses, but wholly perceived and accepted by the entire mind, and brightening our souls with the full light of divinity. Thou enjoyest all these good things, whose streams reached thee whilst thou wast yet on earth, for thy sincere striving towards them."

St. Ephrem the Syrian speaks thus of future encounters: "Parents will judge their children, as those that have done good deeds, and as sinners will see those they know at that time, some of them placed at the right side, and those that have been cut off will moan for their place".[20]

---

[20]It appears as if one or more words may have been left out of the Slavonic text as printed. It is also possible that this quote is not attributable to St. Ephraim.

St. Athanasius the Great, in his "Homily on the Departed," says: "For this reason God granted it to the saved, to be with one another even before the general resurrection, and to rejoice in expectation, that the future divine gifts are to be given them. But sinners are deprived of this consolation, for they do not have knowledge of one another. But at that universal spectacle, when the deeds of all are revealed, all faces will be thus made known, until the final parting shall be, and each shall be sent to the place he has prepared for himself. For the righteous shall be with God and with one another, but the sinners, estranged of God and their fellow into eternal torment, still together but not knowing one another; for they are deprived, as it has been said before, of this consolation. For what shall be the shame of them, when all shall see? For shame is great and bitter when one knows and is known. For everyone that is shamed, is ashamed before those that know him: if he is unknown and others do not know him, the shame is less. This is indeed without doubt, that we shall all manifestly know one another; and then the rebuke of them that have lived in a fallen manner, will be before the eyes of all."

St. Cyprian says: "A great number of beloved ones—parents, brethren, sons will receive us there; a numerous and dense throng of those who are already certain of their own immortality, but who still had been concerned for our salvation, will strive towards us. What a great general joy it will be, for them and for us, to attain unto seeing them and greeting them!" (*Exhortation on the Martyrs*, Chap. 12).

St. Ambrose of Milan writes: "What consolation is left to me, except that I hope soon to come to thee, beloved brother; I hope that our parting will not be for long, and indeed thou thyself by thine intercession canst call me, who am willing, the sooner; for who would not desire for himself, 'That this which is corrupt be clothed in incorruption, and this which is mortal be vested in immortality'?" (*Writings of St. Ambrose of Milan*, Book 2, p. 113).[21]

St. John of Damascus in his *Homily on the Departed* speaks of our future encounter thus: "Let no one think that there will be no mutual recognition at that dread judgment; yea, indeed, each will know his neighbor, not in a bodily manner, but by the clear vision of the mental eye."

St. Dimitri of Rostov writes concerning meetings beyond the grave: "All will see one another," that is of course in the first period of life beyond the grave, on the basis of the teaching of the Lord Jesus Christ on this subject in the parable of the Rich Man and Lazarus, and equally on the dread Judgment Day all will see one another only until the final separation of the righteous from the sinners.

---

[21]In a nineteenth-century Russian edition.

If all is to be made manifest on Doomsday, uncovered for all the spiritual-moral world; if earthly life with the manifest and concealed deeds of each person is to be self-evident for all the holy Angels, the Saints of God, and for all sinners (Luke 12:2–3), then of course all will recognize one another. After the soul's passing beyond the grave, regardless of where it is to be—in paradise or in Hades—at once it will be recognized by the Saints, and on Doomsday by the sinners. Further St. Dimitri writes: "Not only our brother sinners will look at us, but all the choirs of Saints as well: the Prophets, Apostles, Martyrs, Hierarchs, Ascetics and Righteous."

"Beyond the grave," continues the Hierarch, "kings will see their subjects and subjects will see their kings; lords and magnates will see their servants and slaves, and servants will see their masters; those who have been wronged will see their offenders, and the offenders their victims; friends will see friends, and enemies, enemies, as the word of God bears witness: 'This is he, whom we, the foolish, have had in derision' (Wisdom of Solomon, 5:3). Unrighteous judges will see the innocent that they have condemned and wrongfully committed to death; torturers will see those whom they have tormented without mercy, will see them glorified and crying out to the Lord: 'Judge, O Lord, them that have wronged us, and take vengeance, O Lord, on them that have ill used us!'—Parents will see their children, and children their parents; brothers, sisters, relatives, spouses shall meet; the righteous shall see the sinners, and sinners the righteous. There, beyond the grave, Cain will see Abel, and Herod, John the Forerunner, and the persecutors will see the Christians: Nero, Diocletian, Maximian and other persecutors will see glorified those whom they martyred, the confessors of the name of Christ." (*St. Dimitri of Rostov's Works*, Part I. Homily on the Sunday of the Last Judgment).[22]

St. Tikhon of Zadonsk writes as follows on the recognition of one another, and therefore on meeting one another beyond the grave: "They see those whom on earth they slandered, abused, persecuted, mocked, treated ill, trampled upon; they see them in great glory and joy." (*His Complete Works*, Vol. I, Chap. 1, p. 45).

In this way the Holy Fathers and Doctors of the Church depicted the life of the righteous in paradise in the first period beyond the grave; they depicted it in a bond and communion with the full activity of the soul and its individual faculties.

And so, the word of God assures us that in the world beyond the grave, whither we too shall go, soon, very soon, the souls that abide in a bond and

---

[22]This is the alternate name for Meatfare Sunday.

communion with God meet with one another and are in communion with one another even before the general judgment, and that much more will they have communion with God and with one another after Judgment Day. God grant only to be in paradise, where bond and communion are unbreakable; for in Gehenna this is not, since there, the state of souls will be deprived of every joy.

The true believer, dying without any sense of discouragement, parts with his family and friends in the hope that soon he will again be united with them in the house of the heavenly Father, if they too live by faith and hope on the Divine mercy. The word *if* signifies that for some there will be an eternal, joyous joining of relatives and friends, while for others—an eternal and bitter separation. What circumstances bring about separation?—An active faith joins us in the future, while the lack of it divides us for eternity.

If parents bring up their children in the fear of God, then it will be well for the parents even on earth, for the soul of a parent rejoices in a wise son (Proverbs 23:24), and it will likewise be well with them in heaven, where good parents will rejoice doubly when they stand before the face of God together with their children, and say: "Behold us with our children, whom Thou hast given us, O Lord."

If the wisest and best of the pagans, guided only by reason and inner feeling, recognized it as a truth that in the life to come they would see other wise men and those who had done good in all times and places, would be joined to them and enter into friendly ties and relationships. The assurance of this, that is, that all would encounter one another and live together eternally, was like a consoling ray of light amid the darkness of paganism for all those who, in their mode of thought and action, rose above the usual milieu. Here, for example, is what Socrates said to those who sat in judgment on him: "The death to which you sentence me I consider more a gain than a loss. It is either a sleep without awakening or dreams, or else a means of moving my abode to where I can speak with the shades of the famous dead. I go to death, you remain to live; but whose portion is more to be envied, the gods alone know." In fact, for whom was man put here in such a close relationship to others, that without them he cannot continue his life, or at least, enjoy it? Was it so that, being joined to them by the closest bonds, suddenly to break them, and to forget forever about those with whom he had enjoyed his existence together? Or was it so that, through nature at his physical birth, or through God's Law at his spiritual birth, or through the development in him of mind and will, being bound by special ties of love to certain people, knowing on earth the sweetness of friendship, the pleasure of doing good for others and of feeling gratitude, of paternal and filial love—that having experienced these feelings and their sweetness, he then would renounce them for all eternity, and break all ties which bind people here together? Thus reason guesses rather accurately about the future communion between people, depending on the form and agreement of their feelings and actions.

And so, the word of God itself gives us witness and affirms an immutable truth to us, a doctrine of Orthodoxy, that beyond the grave, the righteous will be together and the Lord will be with them, while the sinners will be with sinners, distanced from the Lord. The former will be together, will see one another, recognize one another, will enter into contact among themselves, and, according to the witness of the Old and New Testaments, they will speak with one another. The captives of Hades met the king of Babylon who had come to them, and said to him, "And thou also art come hither" (Isaiah 14:10–11). Abraham, who was in paradise, spoke with the rich man who was in Hades. St. Paul, rapt up to the third heaven, heard speech there and for this reason in another passage mentions the speech of heaven, of angels. From the stories of the blessed Theodora, of St. Andrew the Fool for Christ, the holy Apostle Thomas and many other Saints, we see that souls, after parting from their bodies, and already in the world of spirits, have conversed with angels and among themselves on various subjects. All this bears witness that the souls will not remain in silence among themselves, but will have a mutual exchange of thoughts, feelings and desires, an exchange corresponding to the spiritual nature of souls.

In order to understand to any extent how bodiless beings speak in the world beyond the grave, let us recall that to speak means for one to convey his thoughts, his desires and feelings, to another. We convey invisible thoughts, desires and feelings, which belong properly to the unseen soul, and we convey them by means of visible and audible signs, sounds and letters. And this is necessary so long as the soul is in the body. The Lives of the Saints give us no small number of examples where the thoughts, desires and feelings of some were known to the Saints without palpable conversation. The secrets of the mind, the will and the heart were seen by the Saints, and the latter answered in words, rebuking the former for their thoughts, desires and feelings. If while yet on earth, cleansed souls have the ability to see or read the thoughts, desires and feelings of others, then what would prevent the righteous souls in the world beyond the grave from seeing or reading one another's thoughts, desires and feelings? From the time that animated flesh, as were Adam and Eve before the fall, was made earthly by the ancestral falling, direct communication of the invisible soul with the invisible world ceased, and for the communication of soul with soul, an

instrument was needed—visible signs. As a prison deprives its inmates of communication with those not incarcerated in it, so the body prevents the soul from
having direct communion with another soul. But having given up the body, the
soul regains the perfection of its senses, and there is no obstacle to the soul's
seeing and, as it were, reading the thoughts, desires and feelings of another soul,
and thus exchanging such, which make up the inner activity of the soul.

How else did Abraham and the unfortunate rich man engage in conversation at such an immeasurable distance from each other? Therefore one can correctly conclude that souls, regardless of where they are, in paradise or in Hades,
though only in the first period of life beyond the grave, have the ability proper
to their nature and new life, of sharing thoughts and desires. But this ability to
speak in the world beyond the grave is not an earthly one, by means of sounds
and signs, as shown by the conversation of Abraham with the unfortunate rich
man, when they were separated by an immeasurable space. This is a special,
spiritual ability of the soul to see and read thoughts and desires and in general all
the mental state of another soul. The word of God ascribes only to the righteous
mutual communion, which is one of the conditions for the bliss of man's soul
on earth and beyond the grave.

The truth that is revealed to us, and especially to Christians who lead a life
on earth in the spirit of Christ, according to His holy commandments, this truth
assures the Christian of being an heir of the kingdom of God, prepared from
before all ages. The life of the spirit on earth is manifested in man, in his family
life first of all, and then in public life—in that of the state; and the members of a
family or the members of a state, of a society, beyond the grave become members
of blessed life in paradise. The members of a family—spouses, parents and their
children, then relatives, acquaintances, after a righteous life on earth, entering
into a new life beyond the grave, as the holy Orthodox Church teaches, are not
separated, but live together, like angels of God. Spouses and their children and
relatives have a mutual relationship to one another—they act upon one another
and are not parted for eternity. Christian marriage is not that of the Old Testament, this is the matrimony of a new spiritual man, it is the close spiritual bond
of spouses, of which Jesus Christ Himself bore witness, that those whom God
has once joined together, cannot be parted either on earth or beyond the grave,
according to the Apostle, because love is undying. Those conjoined by love on
earth are not parted beyond the grave either; because the love that never fails,
joins forever those once bound together on earth. The Lord, having established
the Sacrament of Matrimony on earth, bound spouses together by such a firm
bond, that nothing is strong enough to break it; therefore, he joined them with

an eternal, indissoluble bond both on earth and beyond the grave. As He did not break the marriage bond, the Lord invited to the dinner in His parable, among the other guests, spouses as well, by this proclaiming to Christians that devout spouses will inherit the kingdom of heaven, if, serving God with fear and trembling, they fulfill also the Christian obligations that the Lord gave to married couples. This is the teaching of Jesus Christ Himself about the life of spouses in paradise. Having shown in this parable that spouses also are called to eternal life, He shows the truth of this teaching in very deed; entering the house of Zaccheus, He says, "Today salvation is come to this house" (Luke 19:9), a house which obviously is made up of parents, children, relatives and servants. Spouses beyond the grave remain spouse-angels, burning with the purest, heavenly, divine love for God and between themselves. A husband and wife, says St. Peter, are heirs of the grace-filled life of the kingdom of heaven (I Peter 3:7). To this end, that is, so that spouses could achieve their purpose, the holy Apostles defined rights and obligations for them on earth, so that indeed they would constitute one spiritual human being, able to inherit eternal life. Breach of their marriage obligations would bring them, yes, a life beyond the grave, but a life filled with weeping and suffering.

The word of God has given us assurance that death will not part us, and therefore will not part spouses. The Church, confessing this dogma, glorifies Christian spouses, proclaiming their life beyond the grave to us in her songs of praise, for example, in two Kondaks for Jan. 26, for the venerable Xenophon and his wife Maria with their children: "Thou wast vigilant in the Master's commandments, quietly scattering thy riches to the needy, O blessed one, with thy spouse and children, therefore ye[23] inherit divine delight." "Having fled the sea of life, Xenophon the venerable with his honorable wife, rejoice in heaven with their children, glorifying Christ."

Spouses never are separated, just as Christ is not separated from those faithful to him: "I am with you for all ages" (Matthew 28:20). St. Paul repeats the same thing: "We shall always be with the Lord," when he spoke of life beyond the grave. The same Apostle compares the sanctity and firmness of the marital bond, as a Sacrament, to the highest and most inscrutable of Mysteries—the eternal and unbroken bond of Christ with His Church. Hence it is understood that Christian spouses in Christ are not separated even beyond the grave, but, according to the Lord's teaching, live there like the Angels of God.

---

[23]There is a misprint here in the Russian edition, which gives "he inherits" instead of "ye inherit."

The soul's very nature, according to the witness of God its Creator, needs to dwell with beings like unto it: "It is not good for man to be alone." What was lacking for Adam in paradise, with his perfect and full bliss, perfect and full because it had a close bond and communion with God, the Source of blessedness, not to mention his outward bliss in paradise? And yet God the Creator Himself says that it is not good for man to be alone, and creates and gives him a helpmeet on his path of life. The mysterious origin of Eve from Adam shows how close spouses should be, and this closeness could not be limited to the earth: God did not join spouses together, only to separate them beyond the grave! Likewise all mankind, descended from spouses, is joined by immortal love, and not only for its time on earth. No! The immortality of souls, their existence beyond the grave, according to the witness of the Lord Jesus Christ Himself, is revealed in the dwelling together of souls. The parable of the Rich Man and Lazarus and the parable of the Marriage Feast give the teaching of the Lord on dwelling together beyond the grave. "It is not good for man to be alone" is shown also in the words of Jesus Christ, demonstrating that all the righteous will be together in the kingdom of heaven, and the damned will also be together, in eternal torment.

And so, if on earth the existence of souls is conditioned by living together— by a bond and mutual relationship with other souls—then it is obvious that the life beyond the grave, far exceeding that on earth in all things, demands a bond and communion of souls between themselves, as expressed in dwelling together, in tasting the fruits of immortal, divine love in the kingdom of love, whither no one enters without love. Consequently Christian spouses also pass from this world without parting, because it is not good for man to be alone, and they live joined by an angelic, spotless love, like the Angels of God.

However, there are cases when Christian spouses, despite their firm bond on earth, unfortunately are separated and their former tie is dissolved forever beyond the grave. The reason for this is difference in faith, the lack of concord between spouses.

Only oneness of mind, oneness of faith of spouses, who abide in Christ Jesus our Lord, Christians of one hope, one joy on earth and beyond the grave, can make for a living together of spouses that is not to be broken apart beyond the grave. But if this condition, necessary for salvation, is lacking in one or another of the spouses, then despite all the piety of the other, the life beyond the grave divides them, and only to the faithful one will it be adjudged to enter into the joy of the Lord. The unrighteousness and unbelief of the other, alien to the lot of the faithful, will draw him into the land of eternal mourning and weeping for his wickedness and unbelief.

In general, the Christian becomes a participant in a blessed eternity by fulfilling the obligations imposed on him by the Holy Church; consequently, Christian spouses also, as members of the Church of Christ, by carrying out their obligations devoutly, are made heirs of the kingdom of heaven. Those spouses, however, who do not fulfill their obligations, as well as their children and all family members, and every Christian individual, reap bitter fruits beyond the grave; but those who carry out their obligations are set apart after death from those that break and despise the Law of God; "And the righteous will go into life everlasting, but the sinners into everlasting torment," as Jesus Christ Himself bears witness.

If it is so, then Christian spouses also either remain together beyond the grave without parting, in paradise or Gehenna, or else they are parted from each other for all ages. The holiness of married life, filled with the Spirit of Christ, is the basis for their salvation. Devout Christian couples inherit eternal crowns in the next world for their virtuous life, as St. John Chrysostom says (*Commentary on the Gospel of St. John*, Homily 69). And so, truly Christian spouses and the children raised by them in the fear of God, and their wise, God-fearing servants and all members of the family on earth, joined by the firm bond of Christian love, remain together beyond the grave as well. What has been said here about spouses applies also to entire families, great-grandparents, grandparents, parents, children, grandchildren and the entire extended family, whose members are either together beyond the grave in heaven or hell, or apart, depending on the character of their family life.

But a meeting beyond the grave can be either blessed in the highest degree, or agonizing in the highest degree. Being together eternally, and continuous society in paradise are blissful to such an extent that that there are no words to express the bliss that truly devout Christian spouses inherit, together with their children and all members of the family for their piety, which was first and foremost seen in the main family members (husband and wife), and which they encouraged in all the other members of the family. What joy in the Lord will bring sweetness to the souls that served Him on earth in fear and love! And, on the contrary, what awaits impious spouses and their children and family members beyond the grave, if in that family there developed only wickedness, unbelief, and indifference to all that is holy? Hades is their inheritance! Will there not be eternal weeping for what is lost and can never be restored? Will not rebuke and indignation, and even curses, be heard against those who caused the ruin of the unfortunate? The absence of devotion by spouses cannot give children guidance on living in the fear of God. Depending on the first members of the family, the others permit themselves to follow their life example without fear. And thus, beyond the grave there will flow curses against the first culprits of misfortune. Will not the wife curse the day she was born, who was led by her husband into a sinful life? Will husband and wife not curse each other eternally, as culprits of their ruin? Will the same rebuke not be heard from the perished children as well, for the carelessness of the parents in the matter of their salvation?

Not only will we recognize and see one another, but according to the spiritual character of our soul, free in the first period beyond the grave from the heaviness of the body—the prison of the soul, but we shall see as well all the heart's secrets. It will be splendid, if we were joined on earth by a true, pure, unspotted, heavenly love—then the meeting will be without reproach, full of heavenly joy in the kingdom of peace and love! But what if love was hypocritical on earth? Woe to the hypocrite after death! With contempt, the heart will be turned away from him whom, on earth, it had loved without reproach. Christian spouses, so as to be together beyond the grave, you must preserve to the grave the promises you gave at your marriage.

Frightful and pitiful will be the first meeting beyond the grave with those who loved us on earth, and who, departing this life, placed their hope in those who remained, not knowing their pretended love, hoping on their prayers and intercession, on a rightful carrying-out of their spiritual will! But, having been deceived in their hope, how will they meet the culprits of their misfortune? Will there not be tears of reproach shed for their lack of piety, their careless life and indifference for their salvation and that of others? St. John of Damascus in his *Homily on the Departed* writes: "At the last judgment, and even before the last judgment, as the rich man saw Abraham and Lazarus, we shall see one another, shall recognize one another, and a close meeting before on Doomsday will not be a joyous one for those who are not devout. Reproaches, curses, tears—that will be the meeting of the indifferent." Friendship and family relationship between the damned will forever cease. Parents will not defend their lost children, and neither will children help their condemned parents. Evil children will curse their parents for not teaching them faith and good works, and the torment of impious parents will be augmented by the suffering of their children in Hades. The flock that has erred will be indignant at its pastors for not having taught them a life that is pleasing unto God, not having corrected their vices, not having filled their hearts with the fear of God, having been indifferent to their unforgivable weaknesses. No easy obligation, and a fearful responsibility lies on the pastors of the Church. They must be vigilant in their concern for the salvation of their flock, their spiritual children, concerned to prepare them gradually for their departure from this life, to direct their mind and heart towards eternity! And woe, woe to that careless pastor if even one of his flock should perish through his lack of attention, when their salvation depends entirely on the priest, and when, not cleansed of sins by the priest's administration of confession and communion of the Body and Blood of Christ before death, one of them should stand with his sins at the judgment of the impartial Judge. Will not such a soul curse its pastor eternally? Will not eternal anguish weigh upon the soul of the careless pastor? The awareness and conscience of pastors as to the ruin of those people on earth entrusted to their care by God will bring about eternal anguish. The meeting of friends with friends who have drawn them into a sinful life on earth will be mournful, filled with curses at the culprits of their eternal ruin. But those who did not follow their bad example on earth will be forever parted from those who transgressed the Law of God. And so, ruined husbands, wives, children, brothers, sisters, acquaintances, relatives and all members of a family will look with such shame and reproach of conscience at the saved, with whom they were on equal terms on earth, and who, nevertheless, despising a sinful life on earth and cleansing themselves by true repentance, after death are among the saved. In the first period of life beyond the grave, on the basis of the teaching of the Lord Jesus Christ in the parable of the Rich Man and Lazarus, it is evident that the dwellers in paradise see the denizens of Hades, and vice-versa, those in Hades see the saved. And so, one spouse can be in paradise, and the other in Hades, unbelief having brought the latter to ruin. In the first period of life after death, and on Doomsday itself, while all are still in communion with one another until the final parting:—"And these depart unto eternal torment, while those go into life eternal"—encountering one another is for the saved filled with inexpressible joy, while the for damned, meeting is mixed with indignation, weeping and eternal cursing. Their state beyond the grave is such, that neither disavowal of their deeds, nor attempts to excuse, to justify themselves, have any place either before God or before the entire spiritual-moral world. Between the lost there is no more help or intercession for one another.

Concerning the beatific life of the righteous in paradise and the beauty of paradise itself in the first period of paradisiacal life, we may draw a conclusion in the words of him who saw all this himself, being rapt up to the third heaven, but could not convey on earth what he had seen and heard there: first, because of the lack of words in human language to describe the state of the righteous

beyond the grave, and second, because every age in the life of man has its corresponding level of understanding, and therefore, even if the Apostle were to
tell of the bliss of the righteous after death, those on earth would not be able
to receive what they heard—they would not understand, just as children do
not understand those things that adults do; how could one teach those truths
in the lower grades of school, that are taught in the higher classes? That which
is understood by the students of the higher classes cannot be comprehended
by the pupils in the lower grades. To each age there is a corresponding level of
understanding, and knowledge of what is beyond the grave far exceeds earthly
knowledge, according to the witness of St. Paul.

If Jesus Christ Himself, so as to depict the life beyond the grave to the Jews,
took images and symbols from earthly life and visible objects, then one should
truly conclude that the nature of earth and her beauties, all that is true, exalted,
beautiful and good can serve us as an image, a symbol of the blessed life to come,
the beginnings of which are here on earth. If every virtue on earth, reflected
in the conscience, brings joy to the soul, filling the heart with some mystical,
unearthly joy, then what will be the mental state of virtuous people in paradise
on account of their righteous life on earth, when the earthly by comparison with
the heavenly is counted as nothing? If on earth the soul found joy in virtue, then
what will be the bliss of that soul beyond the grave—in paradise?

8. Life and Activity in Hades and Gehenna

a) The Beginning of These States Beyond the Grave — Of Hades and Gehenna on Earth

If on earth there is a state of soul that distances one from the kingdom of
heaven, and yet is completely alien to the state of Hades, then this is man's
falling due to his weakness, ignorance and other reasons, a falling and rising,
a striving of mind and heart towards heaven, by their non-earthly destination,
and at the same time the pull of the flesh to earth; at times a joy which is not
of this earth, which gladdens the soul, especially after any virtuous act, and the
gnawing of conscience, that comes after a falling: such a state of souls on earth
is the beginning of the undetermined state after death, where the conscience
reproaches, but faith and hope strengthen. But the rejected sinner, who was
once redeemed by Jesus Christ, is healed here, in Hades, for not carrying out
the proper repentance, contrite in his having offended the Lord. Contrition
is natural for the undetermined state; it is impossible in the state of the lost.

Feeling, while on earth, a repugnance to evil, and yet contrary to desire, doing that which is forbidden, and for some reason not succeeding while on earth in erasing their sins by prayers, tears, good deeds and other signs of repentance, after death, they go to Hades and, not having renounced the Lord Jesus Christ, there too they bend the knee at His name, as they had worshipped Jesus Christ on earth. If, according to the witness of God Himself, only to him that asks is it given, then understandably the choice between a blissful life beyond the grave or torment depends on our earthly life. If there was no Christian life whatever, then the lot beyond the grave is Gehenna; but if life on earth was completely in the spirit of Christ, according to His commandments, then the lot beyond the grave is paradise. The indeterminate state, Hades, corresponds to a Christian life on earth that is distracted, inattentive, as a result of which a man passes into the world beyond the grave without having brought forth the fruits of a true, active repentance while on earth.

The state of the soul after death, beyond the grave, is not independent, that is, the soul cannot freely begin a new type of activity. The soul cannot begin a new mode of thought and feeling, and in general cannot change itself and become another, opposite to its earthly life, but can only continue to develop what it began on earth. That the state of the soul beyond the grave is based on earthly life, this can be seen from the word of God, which gives life on earth the sense of a time of planting, but that beyond the grave—of a time of harvest: "As ye sow, so shall ye reap"; such is the sense of earthly life, as the foundation, the beginning of life beyond the grave, happy or unhappy. Even in antiquity, the pagan world knew a moral law of self-knowledge and attention to oneself, *on what path are we walking?* The lack of independence of the soul beyond the grave is revealed by the fact that full independence requires the body, as a basic component part of man, and that otherwise the present life would have no purpose and no value with regard to the life to come, according to the teaching of St. Paul, that "He that soweth to his flesh, shall of the flesh reap corruption" (Galatians 6:8). The Lord Jesus Christ Himself taught that every unbeliever is already condemned; therefore the state of his soul, so long as it remains in unbelief, is the beginning of an eternal life in Gehenna, and such an unbeliever, after death, as being already condemned on earth for his unbelief, does not fall under the individual judgment of Christ, but goes directly to a state appropriate to him beyond the grave, a state of eternal death, to the beginning of eternal torment—to Gehenna.

Evil will begin to develop more and more in eternity. This development explains the torment, because it is the result of an incessant, sorrowful effect on the feelings. But the same constant sensation dulls the feelings and the soul becomes indifferent, without awareness of that which is sensed, which is not in agreement with its immortality. And with sorrow, and one and the same punishment, the soul becomes accustomed and the feeling does not bring sorrow. If there is no sorrow, then there is no punishment. From the words of Jesus Christ one can see that Gehenna can be within us, just as the kingdom of God can be within us. Are many at peace, who serve their passions? Pleasure from the passions is momentary, the passion is gratified, but then it flames up again with new strength. It is well if it is satisfied, but if not, as for example with greed for money and the like, then the unsatisfied passion brings grief, spite, hatred; this is the beginning, or the foretaste, of Gehenna within us. The soul that finds pleasure in the gratification of passions will not find, beyond the grave, the object that pleased it on earth. If while on earth the soul acted without Christ and not according to His most holy will, then, in the next life, this alienation from Christ will be its ruin and hopeless fate.

Let us conclude all that we have said about this afterlife in Gehenna beginning on earth with the witness of the very word of God, that its foundation is laid on earth. He that does not love his neighbor remains in death, that is, in a state of mind when one is far from God, and therefore not in communion with Him; and such a state, as being completely opposite to that of paradise, and is already the start of an afterlife in Gehenna, a state of enmity, bitterness, hatred; a state completely foreign to love. But if within us there is not the kingdom of God, this means there is Gehenna, while yet on earth. This spiritual-moral state of the soul on earth naturally must have a corresponding state beyond the grave, in the spiritual-moral kingdom. Such a truth is found also in the words of Jesus Christ: "He that believeth not on earth is already in a state of condemnation." The condemned state on earth has a correspondence beyond the grave: Gehenna.

1) THE VARIOUS NAMES FOR THE PLACES OF THE SOULS IN THE
UNDETERMINED AND CONDEMNED STATES — THE PLACE AND
DESCRIPTION OF THE DWELLINGS OF THOSE IN THE UNDETERMINED STATE
— HADES

Immediately after the individual judgment, as our Orthodox Church teaches (*Orthodox Dogmatic Theology*, by Archbishop Makary of Kharkov, Vol. 2, p. 589), the state, or place in the world beyond the grave, of the souls whose fate has not been finally resolved, is given various names in the Holy Scriptures. Thus, more often than other names, the following are encountered: Hades, the abyss, the prison of spirits, the nethermost regions, the heart of the earth—synonymous names for the painful, still indeterminate, state of souls beyond the grave.

Lost souls, however, condemned while yet on earth as having perished for the kingdom of God, go directly from earth to special places beyond the grave—the cells of Hades, which in the first period are a sort of threshold of the Gehenna to come, the state of the damned in the second period, just as the state of the righteous souls in the first period is only a threshold of heaven, the blessed state of the second period, as some of the Holy Fathers of the Church taught, such as St. Ambrose of Milan and others.

The general name of the state of sinners after death, or of their place, is Hades. All other names, such as Gehenna, where the worm dies not and the fire is not extinguished, the fiery furnace, where there is weeping and gnashing of teeth, the lake of fire and brimstone, the outer darkness, the pit that is frightful even to the evil spirits, Tartarus, the land of eternal darkness, where there is no light—all these names, met with in the Holy Scriptures, are the names of sections or cells in Hades. Hades in the second period is no longer the same as in the first, and therefore Hades and the other names have differences between them, as can be seen from the words of the Apocalypse (Revelation 20:13–14). And indeed, what in the first period constituted a punishment only for the souls in Hades, the same can no longer be a punishment for a complete man, consisting of soul and body, in the second period. Therefore the word of God gave a new name to this new state of soul and body, a name that more or less defines this state by means of comparison, image and symbol, seen in the description of this state as something completely different from the state of the first period. Thus, one section is called Hades, a second—Gehenna, a third—Tartarus, a fourth—the Lake of Fire, and so forth (*Theology* of Archbishop Makary of Kharkov, Volume 2, p. 593).

Hades and Gehenna must have their specific locations, separating one state from the other. But where are Hades and Gehenna, according to the word of God? Where are the boundaries of the world? When and how will the end of the world come about? These age-old questions have interested people from the creation of the world down to our time, and mankind has made every mental effort to solve them. The Bible itself leaves this question unresolved and the answer to it veiled, as to the whereabouts of Hades and Gehenna in the universe. However, from many places in the Holy Scriptures of the Old and New Testaments, it can be seen that a place for Hades is given in the interior of the earth. After the fall of our first ancestors, God, angered at the breach of the law He had given, designates a punishment for sinners—death for man, who consists of body and soul, consequently, death for both the soul and the body. But, being created immortal for eternity in soul and body, man could not be destroyed after the fall, just as the fallen angels were not destroyed. Therefore, death is only a punishment for man, a punishment for the soul and a punishment for the body, but not a destruction, and the immortal man nevertheless remains immortal. It is a truth that the goal of punishment is correction, the wiping away of the crime, the righting of the offender and stopping the further development of evil. Consequently, punishment is beneficial for those who have transgressed the law. All this is included in death, but only for those that have wept for their sins and hated them. But what is death and wherein does it consist for the soul and body? For the former, that is, for the soul, death consists in its drawing away from God, while for the latter, that is, for the body, death consists in its parting from the soul, with which it had been so closely and mystically bound, and in its reverting to the earth from which it was crated. One lot befell both the soul and body, as being inseparably bound to each other, their distancing from God, which was the basis for the punishment that extends to the state after death. "To the earth thou shalt return" (Genesis 3:19), in both soul and body, which means that the earth gives asylum to both soul and body; therefore a place of abiding, and a place of punishment, is given for the immortal soul that has moved God to anger.

Awareness by man of his guilt, guided by the spirit, determined a place for the guilty soul to be confined—a place that would be lacking everything joyous, far from the living, hidden in the depths of the earth. The words of God, the Creator of man, "Thou shalt go into the earth," buried themselves deeply in human nature, and the peoples of all times and places envisioned hell as being inside the earth.

In the opinion of the ancients, Hades is underground, and as they pictured the earth as being flat, it was as far beneath the surface of the ground as the earth was from heaven. There existed an opinion, that for those who found themselves in Hades, there was no way out again; but Plato says that after a year of torment, the waves carry us away to another, more peaceful place. Not only the Cabbalists, but all Jews put Sheol (Hades), as a state of souls temporarily located there, in the inner parts of the earth. But the Jewish simple folk assign Hades a place in the air. Here are the words of popular philosophy: "The soul, after the death of the body, remains immortal, and does not at once attain heavenly joys; it wanders for a whole year in this world, and especially near its body, suffering much from demons, which are in the air; here it is cleansed of vices, and this is the higher Gehenna. The unbelieving will be kept in Hades forever, but Jews only for a time. Hades is twofold: one is higher, and the other, lower." It is hard to say who borrowed the idea from whom, the Greeks from the Jews or vice versa, that Hades is in the air, because the later Greeks also put their Hades in the air, as witnessed by Plutarch, who, without himself assigning a place for Hades, quotes his contemporaries' explanation of the words of Homer: "The soul, having flown from the body, came to Hades," taking Hades for a dark, unseen place, regardless of where it is, in the air or under the ground.

All of the Old and New Testaments represent Hades as being in the interior of the earth. All the righteous of the Old Testament are representatives of the popular belief, and confess Hades as being inside the earth. Thus, the Patriarch Jacob, struck with sorrow at the death of his beloved son Joseph, wishes to go down himself to Hades to him, thinking him dead. The much suffering Job, amid his trials [temptations], reflects on his place beyond the grave, which he calls a dark earth without light, an earth of eternal blackness, where there is neither light nor human life (Job 10:21–22). The fate of Chore and his companions, according to the prophecy of Moses, came true: the earth swallowed them up, and they went down alive into Hades (Numbers 16:29–35). The holy prophet-king David calls the state of souls after death Hades, the nethermost region, that is, located inside the earth (Psalms 85:13). The holy prophets Isaiah and Ezekiel see Hades as being in the interior of the earth (Isaiah 14:15; Ezekiel 31:16–18).

The Founder of the New Testament, our Lord Jesus Christ bears witness Himself, that the Son of man must be three days and three nights in the heart of the earth (Matthew 12:40), showing His descent into hell, which was needful in order to lead out from thence all those who awaited Him in faith, the Old Testament righteous ones, according to the Prophecy of Hosea: "I will deliver them from the hand of hell" (13:14).

Chrysostom sets forth his opinion on the location of Hades in his solemn prayers for Holy Saturday and the Resurrection of Christ. At Matins of Holy Saturday, after the reading of the Six Psalms and the Great Litany,[24] the proper part of the service begins with two profoundly moving, and at the same time splendidly poetic chants, the first of which sings of the burial of the Lord, and the second of His descend into Hades. "The Noble Joseph, taking down Thy most pure body from the Tree, wrapped it in clean linen with sweet spices, and he laid it in a new tomb." "When Thou wentest down to death, O Life immortal, Thou didst slay Hades with the dazzling light of Thy Godhead; and when Thou didst raise up the dead from the nethermost regions, all the Powers of heaven cried out: O Giver of Life, Christ our God, glory to Thee." After this, all the

[24]These form a regular part of Matins during most of the Church's year.

clergy, and in monasteries the entire community as well, come out carrying lighted candles to the center of the church, stand before the Shroud[25] and begin the Praises of the Lord, as they are called in the Church's rubrics, joining them with the verses of Psalms 118 (119). Of these Praises, we quote those in which there is an especially clear mention of Hades as being in the innermost part of the earth: "Thou art gone down beneath the earth, O Morning Star of righteousness, and hast raised up the dead as if from sleep, dispersing all the darkness of Hades" (Praise to the 96th verse of Psalms 118).[26] "He that holds the earth in the palm of His hand, put to death according to the flesh, is now held under the earth, delivering the dead from the grasp of Hades" (Praise for the seventeenth verse). "Thou camest down to earth to save Adam; and not finding him on the earth, O Master, Thou didst go down even to Hades, seeking him" (Praise to the twenty-fifth verse). "O that joy! O multitude of sweetness, which Thou hast brought to those in Hades, shining as light in its gloomy depths" (Verse 48). "Willingly, O Saviour, Thou hast gone down beneath the earth, and Thou hast restored the dead to life, leading them back to the glory of the Father" (Verse 53). "In obedience to Thine own Father, O Word, Thou hast descended to dread Hades and raised up the race of mortal men" (Verse 59). "Thou art gone down beneath the earth, Who by Thy hand didst create man, to raise up the throngs of fallen men by Thine almighty power" (Verse 80). "Adam was afraid when God walked in Paradise, but now he rejoices when God descends to Hades. Then he fell, but now he is raised up" (Verse 88).[27] "Without leaving Thy Father's side, O merciful Christ, Thou hast consented in Thy love to become a mortal man, and Thou hast gone down to Hades" (Verse 117). "Arise, merciful Lord, and raise us from the depths of Hades" (Verse 166). "Of Thine own will descending as one dead beneath the earth, O Jesus, Thou leadest up the fallen from earth to heaven" (Verse 46).[28] "Though Thou wast seen to be dead, yet art alive as God, and Thou leadest up the fallen from earth to heaven" (Verse 47). In the last two Praises, the Church proclaims for all to hear, not only the place where Hades is located, but also where paradise is. In the Canon of Matins on Holy Saturday the following is proclaimed in hymnody: "To fill all things with Thy glory, Thou didst descend to the nethermost parts of the earth" (Song 1, Third Tropar). Further on it is said that the Lord revealed Himself to those who were in Hades, that He associated Himself with them, that "Hades, O Word,

[25] The Shroud, or Epitaphion, is a painted or embroidered depiction of Christ in the tomb.
[26] The Russian text has a misprint here, and gives "verse 56" in place of "verse 96").
[27] There is a misprint in the Russian text, which gives "verse 58" instead of "verse 88."
[28] The Russian text gives "36" in place of "46."

was grieved in seeing Thee," that "Thy soul was not left in Hades" that "Hades below moans," that "Hades was pierced, receiving in its heart Thee, Who wast pierced by a lance in the side," that "the Lord descended even to the storehouses of Hades." In the Synaxarion[29] of Holy Saturday we read that on this day, the Church observes the burial of the Lord and His descent to Hades, that He went down to hell in His incorrupt and Divine soul, which had separated from the body in death. Expressions are used regarding Hades as a deep abyss, which, as can be seen from the entire service, is seen as being underground, and located in the innermost part of the earth (*Triodion*).[30]

We can see the same opinion as to the location of Hades and paradise in the service for Easter Sunday. This view is especially clearly set forth in the *Eirmos*[31] of the Sixth Ode of the Canon: "Thou didst descend into the nethermost parts of the earth, shattering the eternal bonds which held the captives, O Christ." In the Synaxarion after the Sixth Ode the following is said: "The Lord, now snatching human nature from the storehouses of Hades, has led it up to heaven, and brought it back to its incorrupt heritage of old. But in descending to Hades, He did not resurrect all, but [only] as many as would believe in Him. And the souls of the Saints from all ages, who had been held by force, He freed from Hades, and granted all to go up to heaven." Here once again the "inheritance of old," that is, paradise, is mentioned as being in heaven.

Everywhere that the Church uses the word Hades, it is represented as being inside the earth, for example in such expressions as: the nethermost parts of the earth, the womb of the earth, the nethermost lands of Hades, the last [uttermost] parts of earth, the nethermost Hades, the land of weeping, the place of darkness, and others. The teaching that Hades is inside the earth is a teaching of the Orthodox Church: all the Holy Fathers and Doctors of the Church thought thus, and so they taught: St. John Climacus,[32] St. Athanasius the Great, St. Basil

---

[29]The *Synaxarion* is a reading at Matins, describing what is commemorated on a given day. In the Greek books this term is used more broadly than in the Slavonic, where it refers to texts in the Triodion—the other readings, for fixed dates, being called, in Slavonic, the *Prologue* for a particular day.

[30]The *Triodion,* in two volumes, is a service book with texts for the Lenten and Paschal cycles of the year.

[31]*Eirmos* is a Greek word meaning, literally, a musical "sequence," because it gives a melody repeated in the following stanzas of a "Song" or "Ode" [a Canon has nine Odes]. In Russian Orthodox practice, the Canon of Pascha or Easter still is sung in its entirety, and makes up the heart of the Resurrection Matins; the stanzas of most other Canons are only recited, the *Eirmos* [plural: *Eirmoi*] always being sung.

[32]Also called "St. John of the Ladder," from his book *The Ladder of Divine Ascent.* "Climax" means "ladder" in Greek, and "Climacus" means "of the Ladder."

the Great, St. Cyril of Alexandria, St. Dimitri of Rostov, St. John Chrysostom, St. Patrick, St. Epiphanius of Cyprus and others. For convincing evidence of this, we present below several reflections from the writings of the aforementioned Fathers and Doctors of the Church.

St. Epiphanius of Cyprus indicates, with all clarity and definiteness, Hades as being in the inner part of the earth, as he describes the salvation of mankind by the God-Man in his homily on Holy Saturday. Here we include this homily with a few omissions: "Why is there such silence on earth? What does this silence and great quiet mean? The silence is great: the King is deep in sleep. The earth was afraid and fell silent, because God in the flesh had fallen asleep. God fell asleep in the flesh, and Hades was struck with awe. God slept for a short time, and raised up those who had slept from the ages, beginning with Adam. Now is salvation for those on earth, and those who have been under the earth from all ages; now is salvation for all the world, visible and invisible. Now is the redoubled coming of Christ, redoubled providence, redoubled visitation of man: God comes from heaven to earth, and from earth to the underworld. The gates of Hades are opened, and ye that have slept from the ages rejoice. Ye that sit in the darkness and the shadow of death, receive the great light: the Lord is with the servants, God is with the dead; life is with the dead, with them that were in darkness is the Light that never dims, with the captives is the Deliverer, and He that is above the heavens is with the nethermost regions. Christ is among the dead: let us go down thither with Him, so that we may know the secrets of this land, and know the secret of God under the earth, and understand the Lord's miracles; let us learn what sermon the Lord proclaims to those in Hades, and what He that hath power commands to those in fetters. Go forth, He announces, ye that are in darkness, and be enlightened: go forth, and rise up, ye that lie. And to thee I command, O Adam: Rise up, thou that sleepest. I did not create thee to remain bound in Hades; arise from the dead. I am the Life of men, and the Resurrection. For thee, thy God became thy son. For thee I, thy Lord, took on the form of a servant. For thee I that am higher than the heavens came to earth, and went under the earth. Arise and depart from hence. Arise ye all, and go from here: out of the darkness into eternal light, from sufferings to rejoicing. Arise, go hence: from servitude to freedom, from prison to the higher Jerusalem, from fetters to God, from the underground to heaven."

St. John Climacus also mentioned the location of Hades in the innards of the earth, in passing, as if speaking of something generally known. He advises the devout ascetic to bear constantly in mind the bottomless abyss of the nethermost flame, and the frightful underground places and pits, the narrow passages, so as by such reflection and such memory to restrain the soul from its acquired love of pleasures (*The Ladder of Divine Ascent,* Step 7, "On the Weeping that Gives Rise to Joy").

In the first days of Christianity, when the harsh and blind zeal of the idolaters to preserve idol worship on the earth shed rivers of innocent Christian blood, in Broussa,[33] the main city of Bithynia [in Asia Minor], the bishop of the city, St. Patrick,[34] suffered torture and martyrdom. The chief torturer took baths at the warm healing springs near the city; here he interrogated the bishop and put him to death. Concerning these hot springs, whose temperature and healing qualities the commander ascribed to the action of the images he deified, St. Patrick said the following to him: "Most splendid commander, if thou wouldst know the source of the waters and their warmth, then I can reveal it to thee, if thou wilt patiently hear me out. Everyone who confesses holy Christianity and worships the One True God seeks to have a mind filled with understanding of the Divine secrets; and I, as a servant of Christ, though sinful, can explain the truth about these waters. God, foreseeing that the human beings He had created would provoke Him to anger—God, their Creator—and, rejecting true worship of God, would set up lifeless idols for themselves and worship them, prepared two places for humans after their life on earth. The first place He brightened with eternal light and filled with abundant and ineffable good things, but He filled the other with impenetrable darkness, a flame that is never extinguished, and eternal punishments. He designated the first place for those who try to please Him by fulfilling His commandments, while the other, the dark place, is where those are cast who anger their Creator by their evil life and who deserve punishment. Those found worthy of the bright place will live an immortal life in unceasing and endless joy, but those cast down into the dark place will be tormented without ceasing, endlessly. The Creator, separating fire from darkness, placed each of them, as he had created them, apart in a special place. There are fire and water both above the firmament of heaven, and below the earth. The water that is above the surface of the earth, gathered into its gathering-places, is called the sea, and the water that is underground is called the abyss. From this abyss, for the needs of the men and animals that inhabit the earth, waters rise through the depths of the earth, as if through pipes, and, coming out at the surface, form springs, wells and rivers. Of these waters, those that come near the underground fire are warmed by it, and flow out as hot water; but those

[33] Also called Prusa.

[34] The date of his martyrdom is usually given as ca. 100 A.D., though some place it in the third century. He should not be confused with St. Patrick of Ireland.

that flow far from the flame, retain their original coolness. In certain places of the abyss there are very cold waters that form ice, being very far from the fire. The underground fire is meant for the torment of wicked souls. The nethermost water, forming ice, is called Tartarus. In Tartarus, your gods and their worshippers are subjected to endless torment, as one of your poets sang: "The ends of the earth and sea are nothing else than the last limits, where Iapetus[35] and Saturn[36]—thus are your gods named—are not consoled by either the shining of the sun, nor the cooling winds." This means: your gods, incarcerated in Tartarus, are not lighted or warmed by the sun, and as they are cast into the fire, there is no wind to cool them. Tartarus is deeper than all the other abysses under the earth. That under the earth there is a fire prepared for the wicked, at least let the fire that is belched up from within the earth in Sicily convince thee." Thus did this holy bishop of Christ's Church in the first ages speak of the underground flame (Lives of the Saints for May 19).

St. Dimitri of Rostov says, "At the Last Judgment, when Christ our God says to the sinners, "Depart from Me ye cursed, into fire eternal," at that moment the earth will open under the sinners, as it did under Cor•,[37] Dathan and Abiram in the time of Moses, and then all the sinners will fall into Hades, after which the ground will again close up. The sinners will be in Hades under the earth, as in an iron vessel, tightly sealed and without exit for all ages" (2nd part of his 2nd homily on Palm Sunday).

In conclusion, one can say that the location of Hades has never been defined exactly. The ancients were as little in agreement in this case as are the most recent writers.

"Hades" first of all signifies a place for the souls in the undetermined state, prepared by God from before all ages. God alone, as has already been said, is not subject to the laws of time and space, while His creation, which falls under these laws, must occupy a specific place in the universe. Consequently spirits and souls must be in certain places outside of the earthly world. Chrysostom says that Hades is outside of this world, while St. Augustine teaches that it is not possible to know the place where Hades is.

Hades is a particular, definite place, a place of sadness and sorrow; it is a specific, painful state of souls, and as anything painful, it is therefore abnormal,

---

[35]In Classical Greek mythology, Iapetus was one of the Titans, son of Uranus [Heaven] and Ge [Earth], and the father of Atlas, Prometheus and Epimetheus, and was supposed to be the progenitor of the human race. He was imprisoned with Cronos in Tartarus.

[36]Roman name for the Greek Cronos, who was the father of Jupiter, Neptune, Pluto and Juno.

[37]The name Co-re is spelled "Korah" in the King James Version [Numbers 16:6].

contrary to their nature—a state, not in agreement with the will of God, into which state spiritual-moral beings have placed themselves. Hades, as a place or painful state of spiritual-moral beings of a fine, ethereal nature, is above palpable fire, which can act only on our crude bodies. *Hades* is a Greek word,[38] to which correspond the Hebrew *Sheol,* the Slavonic and Russian *preispodnjaja* —names synonymous with the meaning of a deep, dark place in the bowels of the earth; but in Christian teaching a spiritual prison, that is, the state of souls alienated for their sins from seeing the face of God, and therefore deprived of light and bliss (fifth article of the Creed). Hades is not a tollbooth, as some think. Hades is a recognized state of the soul, whereas a tollbooth is also a state, but one that brings the soul to awareness of its moral deserts, be they of paradise or Hades.

Jesus Christ descended, in His soul, not to Gehenna, but to Hades, and from thence He led forth all of the Old Testament captives. Hades, being a state of disease, and also a spiritual prison, rather than a state of condemnation, according to the teaching of the Orthodox Church, has also its New Testament captives, who bow down at the name of the Lord Jesus Christ, and who consequently also benefit from the means of grace granted to Christ's Church interceding for such dead. At the time of the Second Coming of Christ to judge, Hades and death will be abolished, that is, the state of undetermined souls will enter paradise, according to the Prophecy of Hosea, "I will ransom them from the power of the grave; I will redeem them from death: where is thy penalty, O death? O Hades, where is thy sting?" (Hosea 13:14).[39] St. Paul, telling of the resurrection of the dead, refers to these words of the Prophet Hosea, as to a prophecy on the redemption of the souls of the dead from death and Hades: "When this corruptible shall have put on incorruption, and this mortal shall have put on immortality, then shall be brought to pass the saying that is written, Death is swallowed up in victory. O death, where is thy sting? O grave, where is thy victory?" (I Corinthians 15:54–55). And St. John the Theologian in the Apocalypse saw that after the universal judgment, death and Hades, that is, the unresolved state of souls, will cease to exist, and for the second period of life beyond the grave there will remain only the eternal existence of the kingdom of heaven and Gehenna. St. John the Theologian sees how, on the day of the dread, final judgment of Christ, Hades will be cast down into the lake of fire: "And the sea gave up the dead which were in it; and death and Hades delivered up the dead which were in them: and they were judged every man according

---

[38] An earlier form was "Aïdas." Possible derivation is *a-* [non, not-] and *idein,* "seeing"; thus "a place of not seeing." Hades was also personified as the ruler of the underworld.

[39] This is the Septuagint reading, which is also quoted in I Corinthians 15:55.

to their works. And death and Hades were cast into the lake of fire. This is the second death" (Revelation 20:13–14).

In this manner the Prophecy of Hosea, the Revelation of St. John the Theologian, and the words of St. Paul bear witness that there is an end assigned to the existence of Hades, beyond which it will not continue. The same meaning was also ascribed to the Prophecy of Hosea, that is, that the souls of the dead of the unresolved state will be freed from death and Hades, by St. Cyril of Jerusalem, St. Basil the Great, St. John Chrysostom, St. Jerome and others. Here are their own words on this subject.

St. Cyril of Jerusalem writes, "As Jonah was in the belly of the whale, so Jesus willingly descended to that place where the spiritual whale of death was. And He descended willingly so that death would release those it had swallowed, as it is written: I will deliver them from the hand of Hades, and I will redeem them from the hand of death."

St. Basil the Great writes, "Having laid aside stubborn disbelief, let us show obedience and subordination to the commandments. Flaming in spirit, let us glow. Let us free ourselves from the power of darkness, which draws towards death, so that in us there might be fulfilled that which was said by the Apostle, 'Death is swallowed up in victory. Where is thy sting, O death? Where is thy triumph, O Hades?'"

St. John Chrysostom writes, "The Apostle spoke of the great and unusual, but proved the truth of his words from the Prophecy. Death, he said, is swallowed up in victory, that is, utterly exterminated. There is no trace of it, no hope of its return, when corruption has been swallowed by incorruption. Where is thy sting, O death? Where is thy victory, O Hades? Dost thou see the manful soul? For as one that offers a victorious trophy, and as one inspired of God, and seeing the future as already accomplished, he treads on death which lies prone, and over its prostrate head he sings a triumphant song, crying out and saying: Where is thy sting, O death? Where is thy victory, O Hades? It is gone, it has perished, and completely disappeared, and in vain didst thou do all these things."

St. Jerome writes: "The Lord has promised deliverance from the hand of death, and redemption from death, to Ephrem and the ten tribes, and the heretics, when pains come as of a woman giving birth. The deeds by which he kills, he calls the hand of death, as it is written: Death and life are in the power of the tongue.[40] But the Lord has delivered all, and redeemed them by His suffering on the cross, and by the pouring out of His blood, when His soul descended to

---

[40] *Proverbs 18:21*. In the Hebrew, and also in the Greek and Slavonic, the expression is "in the *hand* of the tongue"—"hand" signifying "power."

Hades and His flesh did not see corruption, and to death itself, and to Hades, He said: "O death, I will be thy death. For this I died, so that thou mightest die in My death. O Hades, I will be thy wound, for thou didst devour all as thy fodder."

9. The Dwellers in Hades and Gehenna — When Souls Enter This State Beyond the Grave

a) Distinctive Character of Souls in the Undetermined and Condemned States — The Basis, Definition and Makeup of Torment — Incomplete Torment, Internal and External — Life in Hades and in Gehenna

Members of both sexes, male and female, enter Hades or paradise after the individual judgment of Christ, on the fortieth day after death. Those Christians souls also go to Hades who have fallen into mortal sins, who have offered repentance, have not despaired of their salvation, but have not managed to offer the fruits of repentance. Sinners go to Hades if their fate has not been finally decided at the individual judgment. The souls incarcerated here remain temporarily.

Besides fallen, evil spirits, for whom eternal torment was prepared from the ages for their apostasy, those people who while living on earth constantly remained in a bond and communion, not with good angels, but with evil spirits, become heirs and members of Hades. Thus, according to the teaching of the Lord, associates of the fallen, rejected spirits are all the merciless, the cruel-hearted, foreign to works of love and mercy, those who cannot therefore be in the kingdom of love beyond the grave, and who inherit a state after death that corresponds to the disposition of their souls—they inherit Gehenna (Matthew 25:31–46). According to the teaching of the Orthodox Church, the following enter Gehenna immediately after death, as they have been condemned while yet on earth: unrepentant sinners (the hardened, those in despair), unbelievers, free-thinkers,[41] blasphemers, haters of mankind; they are cast directly and without return into Gehenna, as being hopelessly and definitely lost for the kingdom of God; the wicked, that is, those who do not believe in Christ, impious heretics, and those Orthodox Christians who have spent their lives in sins or have fallen into some mortal sin and not healed themselves by repentance—these inherit eternal torment together with the fallen angels.

The distinctive character of the indeterminate state of souls is similar to that diseased state of souls on earth, in which life predominates over destruction. In

---

[41]By "freethinkers" is meant those who reject the teachings of the Church, as did the followers of Voltaire.

the same way, souls of the undetermined state, despite their pull towards sin, are full of faith and hope in God their Redeemer, Who has taken their sins upon His shoulders, and in such a disposition of the spirit, together with the dwellers in heaven, they bend the knee before the Lord Jesus Christ and His Most Pure Mother, singing the triumphal song "Alleluia." They are in Hades until the time assigned for their salvation. They are there now, as they were before, to whom John the Baptist went down after death to preach to them the Saviour Who had come to earth. Thus the Orthodox Church says in the Tropar composed in his honor: "The memory of the just is celebrated with hymns of praise, but the Lord's testimony is enough for thee, O Forerunner, for thou wast shown to be the most honorable of the Prophets, as thou wast granted to baptize Him in the streams, Whom thou hadst preached: therefore having suffered rejoicing, thou didst preach the tidings unto them that were in Hades, that God had appeared in the flesh, Who takes away the sin of the world, granting us great mercy" (Tropar of St. John the Baptist). It was to such souls of the undetermined state that, finally, the Lord Jesus Christ Himself descended in His divine soul. "The divine soul went down to Hades," writes St. John of Damascus, so that, as on earth the Sun of truth had shined, so also underground light might shine on those that sat in darkness and the shadow of death; so that, as on earth Christ had proclaimed peace, remission of captives and restoration of sight to the blind, and therefore He was the cause of eternal salvation for those that believed, and the Reproach of the unbelief of those that did not believe, so also in Hades; that every knee might bend to Him, of those in heaven, those on earth, and those in the abyss, and in this way having released the captives of the ages, at last He rose from the dead, showing us the path to salvation" (*Extensive Exposition of the Orthodox Faith*, Book 3, Chapter 29). He descended to those souls that had faith and hope; but to those that knew Him not, and that stubbornly rose up against faith in Him, He did not go down into Gehenna, just as, while on earth, He did not go where He saw no possibility of faith. Here is the distinguishing characteristic of the dwellers in Hades, who are to be dwellers in paradise; a characteristic consisting of faith and hope, brought by these souls from earth to Hades, something that in Gehenna there is not.

In the first period of life in Hades, as the soul exists without the body, so there is torment only for the soul. The distancing of sinners from God, Who is the Source of life, light, joys and of bliss in general, is the first and main basis of torment. As the soul in the first period exists without the body, this distancing from God constitutes its internal, spiritual torment.

It has been said earlier that in Hades, where there are many cells, in the first period there are two states of souls: the undetermined and the condemned; for this reason they have differing torments. The inward, spiritual torment of souls in the undetermined state is mixed with hope on God, Who desires not the death and ruin of sinners; these souls, even in Hades, recognize themselves as guilty, and before the name of Jesus Christ, along with all the dwellers in paradise, they bend the knee and thereby, more and more, they receive grace, which heals that which is infirm and completes that which is lacking. Therefore the souls of the undetermined state cannot be said to be completely distanced from God, as those in Gehenna, condemned for their unbelief, are distanced. Cast down into Gehenna, as unbelievers, they do not bow their knees before the name of the Lord Jesus Christ.

Torment is a state of soul that is completely opposite to bliss, it is an abnormal state, and therefore a diseased, pathological state, in which the soul with all its faculties and feelings suffers a particular, unceasing pain, one that grows ever more and more. According to the teaching of the Orthodox Church, (*Theology* of Archbishop Anthony, p. 247), the lives of the Saints are opposite to the life of those who are not found worthy of bliss at the individual judgment. The state of the souls incarcerated in Hades and in Gehenna, or their activity regarding God and themselves—this activity or inner, spiritual torment; or their activity towards all round about them, and towards other moral beings, such as good Angels, Saints, towards those together with them in Hades or Gehenna, and finally towards those still on earth—this is external activity. Consequently, for a soul in Gehenna, torment even in the first period will be both internal and external. As in the evil activity of man, in his sinful deeds, both the soul and body took part, the recompense must be for both soul and body. Therefore in the first period the torment is not complete, imperfect; but in the second period, it will be complete, utter. Incomplete torment in the first period, but complete torment in the second, will be both inward and outward. A parable (Luke 16:24–28) represents the state of souls beyond the grave in the first period (the unfortunate rich man,[42] Lazarus and Abraham), and of the brethren of the rich man who are still on earth; consequently, here the afterlife of the first period is represented. If the rich man, according to the words of Jesus Christ, suffers in the flame (verse 24), then what is had in mind is that fine ethereal heat which corresponds to the fine ethereal nature of the soul, and of evil fallen angels, since God is only spirit, while all of His creation is not spirit, but matter; and to this ethereal

---

[42]This rich man is sometimes called "Dives" in English. This, however, is not his name, but only the Latin term for "rich man." Therefore it does not appear in Russian-language writings.

matter, that is, to the soul and the evil angels, there corresponds the fine nature of Gehenna fire (Matthew 25:41); but to the body of man, as being palpable, after its reunion with the soul in the second period, there will correspond a palpable fire, of crude nature.

As concerns the souls of undetermined status, that, although they died in sins, and therefore are adjudged torment, but at the same time made a beginning of repentance while on earth, and had, in the depths of their souls, the seeds of good, albeit not altogether unfolded—as to these, the Holy Scripture has not seen fit to reveal anything definite to us. Be that as it may, the mercy of God and the strength of the merits of Christ the Saviour, which extend to people up to the Last Judgment, as well as God's righteous judgment, which, while punishing for evil, cannot leave good without any reward, give us the right to believe that the torment of such will be mixed with some consolation. These souls are not without hope, and although they cannot rise out of their situation by themselves, still they thirst and await the help of others, and are able to make use of it. Thus our Orthodox Church confesses: "The souls of those that have fallen into mortal sin, and at death have not fallen into despair, but have repented before departing this life, yet who have not managed to offer any fruits of repentance, such as: prayer, tears, bending of the knee, contrition, consoling of the poor and expression in acts of love for God and neighbor—which the Church Catholic has from the beginning recognized as pleasing unto God and requisite—these go down to Hades and suffer punishment for the sins they have committed, without, however, being deprived of the hope of relief." Concerning the internal and external life and activity of the souls of unresolved status, St. Paul bears witness, when he says that their activity towards God is expressed in adoration of the name of the Lord Jesus Christ; but adoration involves also standing before God, and to some degree as well, the seeing of God. All this is tied together with hoping on God, and consequently to some degree with joy in the Lord, consolation, comfort. And since, according to the Church's teaching, these souls after repentance, not having fallen into despair, have passed into the world beyond the grave in the hope of God's endless mercy towards repentant sinners, therefore beyond the grave the state of these souls, even though suffering, nevertheless is mixed with hope, as it bears down the soul with the weight of sin, yet at the same time comforts it with hope. The unceasing alternation of contrition and consolation—this is their inner activity as concerns themselves. Adoring God, they are therefore not foreign to respect and piety towards all that is holy, they offer up honor to the servants of God—to the holy Angels and the souls of the righteous. To their activity towards God, the holy Angels and

Saints of God, there is joined also their activity towards those yet on earth, and it is expressed in desire and hope for their help to improve their state beyond the grave. And so, if the undetermined souls have some comfort, then one can admit also the seeing of those who are with them in Hades, as co-worshippers of the Lord Jesus Christ. This is the internal and external activity of the souls of the unresolved state. Thus exactly do the Eastern Patriarchs confess regarding such souls, in their Confession of the Orthodox Faith (Article 18).

The activity of the lost sinners in Gehenna, like that of the souls of the righteous in paradise, is of three kinds: towards God, towards others, and towards the self. In regard to God their activity consists in hatred of Him, blasphemy against Him, and desire of that which is contrary to His will. The inner torment of the soul in itself consists in: clear and detailed knowledge of its sins, by which the soul has offended God in this life; in the gnawing of conscience, which will awaken beyond the grave in full strength; an agonizing languor and anguish from the soul's attachment to the earthly and fleshly, which now cannot find gratification for itself; while towards the heavenly and spiritual, its taste and desire has not unfolded, and now cannot unfold. And finally, it consists in despair and a desire to cease their existence.

Self-awareness, which makes the soul a personal being, will not leave it even in Gehenna. The activity of the soul's faculties continues in Gehenna. The functions of thought, of knowledge, of feeling and desire have a character distinct from that of these faculties in paradise. The qualities of the soul, its inner activity, of self-awareness are completely opposite the state and internal activity of those in paradise. The objects of activity in Gehenna, both internal and external, are falsehood and the father of lies—the devil. Everything sinful, contrary to God, was the object of thought while on earth; evil will be the object of thought's activity beyond the grave as well. Free-thinking,[43] which strives to destroy moral order on earth, and such thinking beyond the grave, not being in agreement with the will of God, belongs to the kingdom of the enemy of God and man, to the kingdom of the devil.

The God-given faculty of knowledge can, through man's evil desire, be turned aside from its natural, true purpose to one that is unnatural, when the object of knowledge is the perversion and ruin of oneself and one's neighbor, the spreading of what is amoral. The knowledge of evil, according to the law of incessant development, passes over to the state beyond the grave, into the kingdom of evil, and here it continues to develop for all eternity. And here, in Gehenna, there are

---

[43]Note the definition of this term above. "Atheist is an old-fashioned word," wrote Addison: "I'm *a freethinker* [that is, infidel]."

no few subjects for the function of knowledge—for perfection in that which is contrary to all that is true, good and beautiful.

As on earth the action of feeling became the opposite of what was true, good and beautiful, and the senses constantly were exercised in the unnatural, the unlawful, so also beyond the grave their action will correspond to what it was on earth; their action will be mixed, not with joy, but with inexpressible bitterness. The habit of feeling for that which is sinful will not find its gratification here; and deprivation of what is desired is not bliss. Despite the intent striving of the senses for gratification, due to the lack of objects of desire, the action of the senses remains forever unsatisfied.

The abnormal state of the soul, which is contrary to its nature, a diseased state, is called a state of passion. Passions are sores, illnesses, which on earth are healed by holy Baptism, by penitence, communion, prayer, fasting, and attention to oneself. Here on earth, grace, which heals all that is infirm, heals passions. Everyone knows how strong the pull, or action, of the passions is, and how much effort it takes to overcome them. On earth, passions are either overcome by grace, or else gratified by the individual. In the first case, he is the victor; in the second, he is the vanquished. Since the soul is firmly and mystically joined to the body, and they have a mutual effect on each other, the state of the soul is reflected in that of the body, and vice versa; by the same token, mental and physical passions have a mutual action with both the soul and the body. A passionate state of soul is not only manifested in man's visible actions, but also in the state of the body; a particular paleness, trembling, gnashing of teeth—these are the expression of envy, of malevolence, of anger. To what do man's passions lead on earth? To forgetfulness of self, if they are not gratified and at the same time not healed; but the constant gratification of passions also upsets all faculties and abilities of the soul, and causes one to act unnaturally.

The soul that has passed beyond the grave with unhealed sores, with its passions, remains there in a passionate, diseased state. As it was not healed on earth, here it can no longer free itself from its passions. And as an illness when not healed develops more and more, so it is beyond the grave with a passionate state of soul—its passions, according to the law of life, will develop more and more, until they reach frightful dimensions. Here there is no healing, there is no deliverance from the passions, there is no more grace for sinners and there is no gratification of passions, but rather the anger of God. A passion that is not and cannot be gratified is a state of soul that fully corresponds to Gehenna. A continually unsatisfied passionate state of soul brings it, finally, to despair, to embitterment, and then to the state of the evil spirits themselves—blasphemy against God and hatred for the Saints. Here are life and development, and at that, life eternal, development that goes on and on, development to infinity. The development of passions cannot stop according to the law of life. If in earthly life the object of mind and heart was God and the kingdom of heaven, then after death the soul will attain its desire in reality. On the contrary, if the object of the soul on earth was the world with all its glamour, then here beyond the grave there will be no such object for the soul. The habit of sin, of fulfilling one's passions, turned into nature and having made the passionate state of the rejected seem normal, will unceasingly, for all eternity tear at the soul. The object of desire of the Saints constantly develops and is gratified, but the desires of the damned (passions) develop, only without an object upon which they could be realized. This is the internal torment of the sinners in Gehenna. Passions that cannot be overcome by anything, whose hopeless, useless, never eradicated, powerful striving for the unattainable preys upon the soul for all eternity, and one can positively conclude that the action of the passions beyond the grave is much stronger than it was on earth. That all the soul has acquired on earth, be it good or evil, passes with it beyond the grave, characterizes it there, defining its state, which corresponds to the qualities of the soul, on this we have the witness of St. Gregory of Nyssa: "If anyone has fully plunged his soul into the carnal, then such a man, even if he is no longer in the flesh, nonetheless will not be free from carnal desires. Just as those who have spent their life in unclean places, even though they be moved to clean and fresh air, nevertheless cannot at once free themselves from the odor that clings to them, so also those who have soiled themselves in the flesh will always carry with them a carnal odor." In this way, death, according to his teaching, in destroying the bond of the soul with the body, by itself does not cleanse the soul that has been soiled in sensuousness from its carnal passions and habits. These passions and habits continue to exist, and, as a result of their being unfulfilled, are a source of torments for the soul. Wherein one has sinned, therein is he tormented, if only he has not been healed while on earth. St. Paul bears witness: "God is not mocked: for whatsoever a man soweth, that shall he also reap. For he that soweth to his flesh shall of the flesh reap corruption; but he that soweth to the Spirit shall of the Spirit reap life everlasting" (Galatians 6:7–8). Weeping is a visible, outward expression of a spiritual state, penetrated by real joy or sorrow; hence some weep for joy, and all for sorrow. Awareness of one's sinful state, the gnawing of conscience, mourning for what is lost forever, bring about the state of the soul known as despair. This internal torment of sinners in Gehenna is called in the Scriptures weeping and gnashing of teeth: "Then the King said to the servants, bind him hand and foot, take him and cast him into the outer darkness: there will be weeping, and gnashing of teeth." The place of the confinement of sinners is not only a place deprived of all light, but it also contains unbearable torments. Similar mental states on earth are shown by these signs: weeping, and gnashing of teeth.

Man, consisting of spirit, soul and body, is a spiritual-moral being, whose image and likeness of God his Creator show his destination. Man's purpose is the imitation of God: "Be ye merciful, as your Father, which is in heaven, is merciful," or: "Let this mind be in you, which was also in Christ Jesus" (Philippians 2:6). Man was created for eternity. A spiritual-moral being must lead a moral-religious life. So that man could fulfill his purpose or the will of God for him, God gave him a conscience, as the beginning of a moral-religious life, a spiritual life, which was to continue beyond the grave into eternity. Therefore, conscience is an inseparable companion of the soul, a property of the human spirit.

Conscience is contemporary with man and has the purpose of constantly reminding him what man should be on earth and beyond the grave, according to the purpose for which he was created. If the spirit is a necessary, basic part of man, then conscience, according to the words of St. Paul, belongs to every person. But why then does it appear among various peoples at various times and in various degrees of intellectual development in one and the same people, and even in persons of completely like intellectual development—as a completely different internal and external activity? The answer to this we see in the word of God and in actuality. Some live by the spirit, others by the flesh; the former recognize the demands of conscience as binding for them, the latter do not! A demand of conscience is a demand of man's spiritual nature itself. Fulfilling the demand of conscience, man fulfills his purpose; if he does not fulfill it, if he does not consider himself obliged to follow the inner voice and acts contrary to nature, he rejects his purpose, he does not recognize the goal of his existence. The word of God bears witness of the conscience, as belonging to the spirit, which the first humans had. If the first people had had no conscience immediately after the fall, then why would they have been frightened and hidden themselves from God, why would they have covered their nakedness? Shame—the expression of conscience—moved them to this.

Shame, embarrassment, is a feeling that belongs to the spirit of man. The meaning of shame is a desire, a striving to cover one's nakedness, one's weakness, disgrace; to cover that which is unnatural to him: vice, passion, in short, his evil.

At the Last Judgment and in the second period of life beyond the grave, man will again be complete, consisting of spirit, soul and body; and since weakness, infirmity is both spiritual-moral and bodily, physical, man's striving to cover his unnaturalness from the sight of the people round about him, or the shame of one condemned, reaches extremes. According to the two natures of man, there are two shames: physical and moral; however, spiritual and moral shame is the essence of the shame that determines the worth of a deed contemplated or carried out. Shame is the expression of the conscience, and as belonging to man's spirit, it moves in step with man. Shame belongs to all, to children, to the aged, to the coarse and to the educated, to the stupid and to the intelligent, only in various degrees, and all are subject to this shame, only in varying degree, at the Judgment and in the second period of life beyond the grave. Spiritual-moral shame is an expression of the offended conscience, or the broken internal law. In the Holy Scriptures, the conscience is called the inner law, written in the heart of every human. Shame is the inseparable belonging of the spiritual nature of man, and as only man is gifted with the spirit, therefore shame is proper only to man and constitutes an inseparable belonging of his spirit, as it were showing the spirit's awareness of its imperfection, its weakness. Shame holds man back from bad acts and punishes for committed evil. Conscience, as the beginning of religious-moral life, is a higher, moral power in man; it is a need, concealed in the essence of the spiritual nature, and shown in our aware-ness, a need for what man should be according to his purpose. Lack of shame is the highest degree of spiritual depravity, consisting in the rejection of truth and the embracing of evil. Such a moral state is characteristic of fallen spirits and condemned sinners.

The activity of the mind, will and heart clearly show how we carry out our assignment—life in God—as expressed by our conscience; its demand that man live according to the Law of God is the main object of conscience. Conscience directs the whole life and activity of man, the activity of the mind, will and heart. Life, the activity of man on earth, should be in agreement with the demands of conscience. Why do life and works according to the demand of conscience give man, while still on earth, so to say, a foretaste of unearthly joy, gladness, calm, peace, which are the first fruits of eternal, blessed joy beyond the grave? If on earth, amid all that is hostile to man, while he is in constant battle, virtue brings joy to the soul, then what is to be said of that state beyond the grave of the virtuous, already free of everything hostile? Truth, peace and joy—here is the blessed lot of life in paradise!

The action of the conscience on the soul, and therefore on the man, is two-fold: a preliminary effect here on earth, and a complete effect beyond the grave; inward bliss or torment, repose or the gnawing of the conscience. If every deed on earth is reflected promptly in the conscience, if every wrongful act is followed by the reproach of conscience, then what will the reproach be in Gehenna, where there is development only of evil alone? Life is development, and as experience shows, evil can develop in the human persona to such a dreadful extent, that one can say, as of habits in general, that it becomes second nature. Having made evil his own, beyond the grave one is in the state of the fallen angels. Life in Gehenna is an endless development of evil. Life, as the development of good and evil, can change only on earth. A bad, vicious man becomes a good Christian, or a good man becomes bad. Penitence, with the aid of the grace that heals that which is infirm, changes an evil way of life to one that is good; but a good life, through self-assuredness, forgetting of God, and pride, is imperceptibly forsaken by grace, and the man goes along the path of increasing evil; eternal evil is followed by the eternal rebuke of conscience, which punishes those who break the law.

The conscience, through the fulfillment or non-fulfillment of its demands by the will, is either satisfied or offended. In the former case, it regards the man as deserving merit; in the latter, as being guilty. For merit, as a free act, in agreement with the law, it promises reward; but for guilt, as a free act not in agreement with the law, it promises punishment. The action of the conscience extends not only to merit or guilt, but also to the degree of reward or punishment. To the obedient, the conscience promises good things, but to the disobedient, evil things. St. Paul ascribes such action of the conscience even to the pagans (Romans 2:15; 8:16), and in general to each and every man, as belonging to the spirit. The conscience, having determined reward or punishment for a men, at once carries out its decision, that is, it indeed rewards or punishes. "Thoughts," according to the teaching of the Apostle, "rebuke or excuse each other" (Romans 2:15).

According to the degree of sin, or breach of law, the conscience, darkened by passion, at once after the commission of the crime, seeing itself offended by disobedience to truth, by its clawing brings about, yet on earth, a dreadful mental state. The conscience rewards or punishes: 1) by joyous or bitter awareness of merit or guilt, an awareness conjoined with the judgment of conscience (John 8:9; Matthew 27:3; Acts 23:1); 2) by foretelling a particular reward or punishment for obeying or disobeying it, and 3) it rewards with the hope of good beyond the grave, and punishes with the terror of torment after death, by means of hope or horror, which are brought about in the soul of man; this is a foretaste of what is to come, this is the action of the conscience on earth. Consequently, beyond the grave there follows either a repose that no one and nothing can disturb, or else a never-ceasing, bitter awareness of one's guilt.

St. Dimitri of Rostov writes: "The weight and harshness of torments includes the fact that they, being in torture, will see those whom in this life they had hated, treated with bitterness, hurt, tortured and killed. Then the righteous man will stand with great boldness before the face of those who mistreated him. Every righteous one will say to his oppressor, 'Why didst thou abuse me, persecute me, torture and kill me without mercy?' The persecutors will find no answer to make to the righteous ones; but seeing them, they will be troubled by a great fear, and will say to themselves, repenting and moaning, 'Those whom we had once in derision and as an example for mockery, how have they changed into the sons of God? Indeed their lot is with the Saints'" (St. Dimitri of Rostov, Homily on the Sunday of the Last Judgment). And so, the condemned, being in Gehenna, and seeing the saved in paradise, though only in the first period of life after death, according to the witness of St. Macarius of Egypt, do not see the other inmates behind their back. And St. Athanasius the Great, in his homily on the departed, says, "Until the Last Judgment, the sinners in Gehenna will not know one another, despite the fact that they abide together." They are deprived even of this consolation. Outward torment consists in being together with other, similarly unfortunate souls, and especially with the evil spirits, and in other actual tortures of Gehenna, which, however, only serves as a beginning and foretaste of future, eternal torments. This foretaste of torments to come is so great, so horrible, that one who saw and experienced it, if only such were to occur with anyone, that he would not be able to recount what the damned undergo in Gehenna in the first period, could not retell it, just as St. Paul was not able to tell those of earth about paradise, whither he was rapt up. The activity of the perished souls in Gehenna bears the character of evil spirits. Just as on earth these souls were completely alien to love, overflowing with evil, hatred, malice and spite, so with this mental disposition, the opposite of love, they remain beyond the grave in Gehenna, and their activity towards those remaining on earth is identical to that of evil spirits towards earth-dwellers. As a result of their voluntarily falling away from love towards God, they become more and more hardened in hatred for God and man. Their natural gifts of vision (mind), and free choice (will), even though they remain to them, nevertheless have taken on a perverse direction. The goal of all their mind's activity is evil, while that of the will is the fulfillment of evil intentions, and consequently mind and will do not depart even from the souls of sinners, marked for eternal torment. The desire for the ill and destruction of those still on earth—this is what all the activity of the perished souls strives towards, in regard to the living.

Section III

1. The Second Coming of Christ to Earth. The Resurrection of the Dead. The Final Judgment of Moral Beings, and the End of the Age

a) The Time and Speed of These Events

1) SIGNS AND EXPECTATIONS OF THE END OF THE WORLD

"Ye know not the day, nor the hour, on which the Son of Man shall come" (Matthew 25:13): this is proof that the time of the Second Advent is unknown. In another passage, the Lord Jesus Christ Himself bears witness that the end of the world is unknown (Matthew 24:36). On the day and at the hour predetermined by God before all ages, there will take place the Second Advent of Christ (Luke 17:24; I Corinthians 1:8), the resurrection of the dead (John 5:25; 6:54), the last, final Judgment over moral beings (John 12:48; Romans 2:5–6), and the end of the world (Matthew 13:39; I Corinthians 15:24). All these actions of the might of God are joined by an inner, unbroken link, and therefore take place almost at the same time, or the time of one action of God's omnipotence is correlative to the time of another. Knowing the time of one, we also know the time of the others. But this time remains a Divine secret which no one among mortals knows, and the angels themselves do not know the time of the end of the world; "But of that day and hour knoweth no man, no, not the angels of heaven, but my Father only" (Matthew 24:36).

When will the resurrection of the dead be? The Lord Himself taught us that the resurrection is to be at the end of the world, and the end of the world is at the end of the day, that is, at midnight, at twelve midnight, which Chrysostom confirms when he says that the resurrection of the dead will be like the Resurrection of Christ. And the Saviour rose at twelve midnight. "And at midnight there was a cry made, "Behold, the bridegroom cometh; go ye out to meet him" (Matthew 25:6), as the Gospel tells us. And the Church in her moving hymn proclaims the Second Coming of Jesus Christ to judge, which is to be at midnight: "Behold the Bridegroom cometh in the middle of the night . . ."[44] Since midnight is ordinarily followed by the morning, so after this midnight, so fearsome for the whole world, there will dawn the fateful morning of an eternal day

---

[44]This is a Tropar sung on the first three days of Holy Week, and it also is found in the daily *Mesonycticon* (Polunoschnitza) service [the Mesonycticon, held—in the Russian tradition—for the most part in monasteries, is the first in the daily cycle of public services: Mesonycticon, Matins, First, Third, Sixth, and Ninth Hours, Vespers and Compline.]

of bliss or of torment. Christians sometimes take leave of the departed with the words, "Until the joyous morning!" which they write on the tombstones of those close to their hearts. With the resurrection of the dead, naturally there must unfold a new life for the whole world. The new begins when the old ends, which is indicated by midnight, the division between one day and another, between the present and the future. Midnight is the end of one day and the beginning of another. Not making known the time of these events, the Lord nevertheless taught and left us a commandment to be ready at every hour. This time may still be very far away, but it may also be very close—this hour that has begun. This hour may be that of the resurrection of the dead, the hour of my death and resurrection, the hour of Christ's Advent, the hour of the definitive judgment, and, finally, the hour of the end of the world. The first and last hour: the last hour of the Kingdom of Grace, the first and eternal hour of the Kingdom of Glory in the kingdom of heaven, and the first and eternal hour of damnation and eternal torment in Gehenna. This is the fateful hour for the visible and invisible world which Christians were commanded always to keep in memory and, indeed, from the first days of the Church of Christ, it has been the object of special attention as we shall see further.

It was by leaving such a commandment that the Lord concluded His words to His disciples at the Mount of Olives concerning the end of the world: "Be vigilant, for ye know not what hour your Lord cometh" (Matthew 24:42), that is, unexpectedly, at a time ye did not think this would occur; therefore do not sleep spiritually, do not be careless, but be attentive to the signs of the time, and be always ready to meet the Lord; and in order to be ready, one must lead a virtuous life. And in another passage, the same Evangelist bears witness of the same thing (Matthew 25:13). The Evangelist Mark also writes of the same (Mark 13:34–35). Hearing from their Teacher and Lord such a prophecy of the end of the world (Matthew 24:2) which was, in their opinion, to follow immediately after the destruction of Jerusalem, the Apostles could not resist asking the Lord to tell them when His second advent and the end of the world would come and what would be the signs of His coming and the end of the age? (Matthew 24:3).

In order to correct their erroneous impression that the end of the world would be at once after the destruction of Jerusalem, the Lord fulfilled the disciples' request and revealed the signs of His second coming and thus also of the end of the world; at the same time He added that all this would not be that soon after the destruction of Jerusalem.

The signs of these events, according to the Lord's teaching, are the following: the preaching of the Gospel to all people, the decrease in faith and love between people, the multiplication of vices and misfortunes as a result of the decline of faith and love. There will be great wars, a terrible famine will overtake people, pestilence, and other troubles unheard of before, as is written in the Gospel: "For then shall be great tribulation, such as was not since the beginning of the world to this time, no, nor ever shall be" (Matthew 24:21), and, finally, the coming of the antichrist. Jesus Christ often made use of imagery in speaking, and for matters in the spiritual, invisible world would take objects in the visible world, and the most recent events served at times as images of distant events, as, for example, in Isaiah (Chapters 40 and 56), the recent event of the Hebrews' delivery from Babylonian captivity is a symbol of a distant event, the coming delivery of all humanity from the realm of darkness through Jesus Christ. The Lord used this very form of speech in His talk with the disciples on the Mount of Olives concerning the end of the world and, consequently, concerning His Second Coming which is to be at the end of the world. The approaching fulfillment of this prophecy, namely the punishment of Jerusalem for murder of God, which came about in the thirty-sixth year after the Ascension of the Lord, the Lord takes as an image of the distant event of the end of the age, of the world. And so, the prophecy of the fall of Jerusalem and the destruction of the temple and the kingdom of Jerusalem is an image of the end of the world, and, according to the concepts of that time, these events were perceived, even by the Apostles themselves, as being very near. With the fall of Jerusalem were connected, in thought, the Second Coming of Christ, the resurrection of the dead, the Last Judgment, and the end of the world. The Evangelist Matthew (24:1–43) depicts the prophetic conversation of the Lord Jesus Christ on the Mount of Olives with His disciples regarding His second, glorious advent and the end of the world. Jesus Christ, pointing out the temple to the Apostles, said, "See ye not all these things? Verily I say unto you, there shall not be left here one stone upon another, that shall not be thrown down" (verse 2). Indeed, thirty-six years later, after the fulfillment of this prophecy (in 70 A.D.), when Jerusalem was taken by the Romans, the temple was destroyed and turned into a ruin, and some time later (under Trajan), the very traces of it were destroyed. Titus, the leader of the Roman army, had wanted to save the temple when the city was taken, but nothing could change God's judgment and purpose. The Jews themselves burned the porches of the temple, and one of the Roman soldiers, despite the orders of the military leader, threw fire through a window into the temple itself, which was instantly seized by flames. In vain did Titus give orders to put out the fire, it was not carried out; the soldiers threw themselves into pillaging the burning sanctuary, and neither commands nor threats nor blows could stop them; the temple was burned and sacked.

The disciples, struck by the prophecy of the fall of Jerusalem, found a time to approach the Lord and asked Him to tell them when these things should come to pass, that is, when the destruction of Jerusalem would be and what would be the sign of the Second Advent and the end of the age, of the world? Jesus Christ, without at this time correcting the disciples' misconception about the time of these events, gave a definite answer on the time of His Second Coming and the end of the world, as follows: "It is not for you to know the times or the seasons, which the Father hath put in his own power" (Acts 1:7). Nevertheless, He told the disciples that the end of the world would not be immediately after the destruction of Jerusalem and the temple when He spoke of the signs of this destruction; this fall of Jerusalem and of the kingdom of Judea is not yet the end of the world (Matthew 24:6), which will not be that soon; and specifically at that time when the Gospel will have been proclaimed to all mankind on earth: "And this Gospel of the kingdom shall be preached in all the world for a witness unto all nations; and then shall the end come" (Matthew 24:14).

The holy Apostles saw this sign of the nearness of the end of the world and, therefore, of the coming of Christ for judgment even in their own time. Indeed, the Gospel at that time was preached to the entire world but to the world of that time, for at that time the world was spoken of as the broad Roman Empire (Luke 2:1). Here is the witness of St. Paul that the Gospel in his time was preached to all the world: "Their sound went into all the earth, and their words unto the ends of the world" (Romans 10:18); and in another passage, "The gospel, which ye have heard, and which was preached to every creature which is under heaven" (Colossians 1:23). If St. Paul alone carried his teaching from Jerusalem to Spain, then how much could all together do to spread the good tidings, and what space must they have covered? Thus Chrysostom concludes.

And so, from the prophecy of the Lord one can see that His Coming to earth is not to be until the Gospel has been preached to the whole world, when His holy will has been completely fulfilled—the commandment He gave His disciples and their successors before His Ascension to heaven: "Go, teach all peoples" (Matthew 28:19); "Go ye into all the world, and preach the gospel to every creature" (Mark 16:15). There shall not remain on earth a single place or people or tribe where the Gospel has not been proclaimed; that is, the glad tidings of salvation for those who accept and believe with all their heart: "And only then shall the end come" (Matthew 24:14). But this time is not yet come; it could perhaps be nigh. After the unusual success of good on earth has reached its extreme limits, there will follow a gradual fall in morality according to the witness of St. Paul: "In the last days perilous times shall come. For men shall be lovers of their own selves, covetous, boasters, proud, blasphemers, disobedient to parents, unthankful, unholy, without natural affection, trucebreakers, false accusers, incontinent, fierce, despisers of those that are good, traitors, heady, highminded, lovers of pleasures more than lovers of God; having a form of godliness, but denying the power thereof" (II Timothy 3:1–5). Immorality draws with it a reduction of faith and love among people: "When the Son of man cometh, shall he find faith on the earth?" (Luke 18:8); "And because iniquity shall abound, the love of many shall wax cold" (Matthew 24:12), as a result of this multiplication of vices; and, at last, the appearance of the antichrist.

The Lord's teaching on the end of the world was deeply imprinted in the hearts of the Apostles, the more so when they heard on the Mount of Olives from the angels who had appeared to them that the Lord Who was now ascended up to heaven would come again to earth, and therefore the Apostles zealously proclaimed the end of the world. Thus the Apostle Peter, who was already in his own time so close to the prophecy of the end of the world, found those who doubted this would come true and was obliged to write to them as follows: "The Lord is not slack concerning his promise, as some men count slackness; but is longsuffering to us-ward, not willing that any should perish, but that all should come to repentance" (II Peter 3:9). Here is the reason why the time is not yet come, though it was predetermined from eternity and is known to God alone Who holds times and years in His power. Sooner or later that fateful day and hour will come that God once determined: "But the day of the Lord will come as a thief in the night" (II Peter 3:10). The Apostle Paul also writes: "For yet a little while, and he that shall come will come, and will not tarry" (Hebrews 10:37). St. John the Evangelist writes in the Revelation: "Behold, I come quickly; and my reward is with me, to give every man according as his work shall be" (Revelation 22:12). He also writes in another place, "Blessed is he that readeth, and they that hear the words of this prophecy, and keep those things which are written therein: for the time is at hand" (Revelation 1:3). Further developing the thought of the nearness of the end of the world and therefore of the resurrection of the dead, of the Second Coming of Christ to earth for judgment, he writes thus: "Little children, it is the last time: and as ye have heard that antichrist shall come, even now are there many antichrists; whereby we know that it is the last time" (I John 2:18). That the time is coming to an end, the circumstances of life, and the morality of Christians bear witness. In the days of the holy Apostles, the expectation of the Messiah and therefore of the end of the world was strongly excited; and, indeed, around that time there were many false Messiahs, deceivers. The country, as the historian Flavius writes, was filled with deceivers and wizards who led the people into the desert so as to demonstrate miracles there, brought about supposedly by the power of God. Among these false Messiahs were: Dositheus the Samaritan, who called himself the Christ, Simon Magus,[45] another Samaritan who called himself the son of God, and Theudas (Acts 5:36). Chrysostom writes concerning the end of the world: "Not much time remains till the close. But the world already is leaning toward the end; let us be ready." According to the Church's teaching, antichrist is the opponent of Christ and tries to extirpate Christianity. But since there are now already many antichrists, according to the words of St. John the Theologian, the Blessed Augustine writes in explanation of these words: "Everyone who lives unrighteously and rebukes good is an antichrist." Therefore, St. Dimitri of Rostov concludes, "If the corrupt behavior of Christians turned them into antichrists, then what more have we to await except the end of the world? From this we understand that it is the last hour" (*Homily on the Sunday of the Publican and Pharisee*).

The Second Coming, the resurrection of the dead, the Last Judgment, and the end of the age or world are concealed from human knowledge with the purpose that people be constantly ready for all of this, having God in heaven as the object of mind and heart. The Second Coming of the Lord, mentioned by the Apostle, along with the resurrection of the dead, the Last Judgment, and end of the world, these truths which, as St. Basil the Great says, are the true philosophy were so deeply imprinted in the souls of the first Christians that their fulfillment, for example, the end of the world, was seen as extremely near. Beginning with the Apostles themselves, the first Christians saw the fulfillment of Christ's prophecy about the destruction of Jerusalem and the end of the world as very close; for the signs of the end of the world, pointed out by the Lord Himself, in some degree coincided with the circumstances of their times.

In the first ages of Christianity, belief in a near end of the world was spread everywhere among Christians. The Acts of the Apostles (the teaching of John, Peter, and Paul) and the Revelation hint, as it were, that the end of the world will take place in the time of the current generation. The Lord's commandment on the end of the world, on attention to the circumstances of the time, had gone, one might say, into the flesh and blood of the Christians and caused them to

---

[45]"Magus," his usual title, is the Latin for "sorcerer, wizard."

see in anything unusual a sign of the coming of the antichrist and thus of the end of the world. The teaching of the Lord, the Apostles' preaching on the end of the world, accepted by good sense and science, caused thinkers during all of this period of Christianity to keep an eye out for antichrists and therefore for the end of the age, of the world.

The concept of the antichrist includes all that is contrary to Christianity, and therefore in the person of the antichrist they saw Nero, according to the witness of the Blessed Augustine, the Gnostics,[46] and finally the papacy (the pope or Roman pontiff), a thought which arose and became rather widespread in the middle ages in the West among many sectarians. (Archbishop Makary, *Theology*, Part II, p. 624). Inseparable from the idea of the antichrist is that of the end of the world, and therefore there did not pass a single century without its prediction of the end of the world. With the end of the first millennium the entire West expected the end of the world. The Latin Church, so to say, planted the idea of the end of the world in the minds, hearts, and fantasy of the people and thus kept them in constant fear. Awaiting the end of the world on November 2, 998,[47] it established this date as one of commemoration of all the departed.

The expectation of the end of the world increased even further under the influence of general misfortunes: famine, plague, wars, superstition, and so on.

"The thought of the end of the world," wrote the French historian Michelet,[48] "is sad, just as all earthly life was sad, and served as the hope and terror of the Middle Ages. Look at these old statues of the tenth and eleventh centuries—dumb, emaciated, with contorted facial features expressing vivid sufferings joined with the convulsions before death; see how they pray for the coming of that yearned for yet fearful moment when the last day of the Lord's judgment will free them from all sorrows and restore their nothingness to being, from the grave to God. The Middle Ages are ages of miracles, romanticism, and fear. The tales of hermits, miracles in monastic cells, the visions of anchorites, the trembling excitement that accompanied the Crusades, and other similar influences, made the world a continuous mirage. The eruption of volcanoes was considered the work of troubled Hades; demons were beside

[46]The Gnostics represented a trend of thought already present in pagan religious circles that led to the formation of heretical sects in all of the centers of Christianity by the end of the second century A.D.

[47]At this time, Rome was still in communion with the rest of the Orthodox Church.

[48]Jules Michelet (1798–1874) headed the historical section of the national archives, was a professor at the College de France, and wrote numerous historical books, often in collaboration with his wife Adele.

everyone, nocturnal apparitions made their appearance everywhere. Attila's Huns, who had laid waste southern Europe, were literally seen as the children of Hades, who had burst out of the abyss. Belief in the Messiah and in witchcraft was universal."

Let us permit ourselves also to quote the predictions of the end of the world from Flammarion's[49] book *History of Heaven.* Here is what the author writes: "With the approach of that time (the year 1000 A.D.), we encounter the most frequent and earnest admonitions of preachers. Thus, for example, Bernard of Thüringen began to preach publicly around the year 960 that the world would soon be destroyed, and he claimed that the Lord Himself had revealed this to him. For the theme of his sermons he took the following words of the Revelation; 'after a thousand years the devil will escape from his prison and will deceive the nations of all four corners of the earth. The book of life will be opened; the sea will cast up its dead; everyone will be judged for his deeds by Him Who sits on the great glowing throne, and there will be a new heaven and a new earth.'

"Bernard of Thüringen assigned a day for the end of the world: the world, according to his view, was to have been destroyed when the feast of the Annunciation fell in Holy Week. This occurred in the year 992, and nothing unusual happened at the time.

"During the tenth century, royal charters began with the following characteristic words: 'Since the end of the world approaches . . .'

"In the year 1186, the astrologers frightened Europe by proclaiming that all the planets would be joined together. Rigor, a writer of the time, says in his *Life of Philip Augustus:*[50] The astrologers of the East, Jews, Saracens, and even Christians sent letters to all ends of the world in which they positively announced that in September there would be great storms, an earthquake, mortality among the people, troubles and disturbances, revolutions in all governments, destruction, and ruin of everything living. But, adds this writer, nothing took place to justify their predictions.

"Several years later, in 1198, there spread a rumor of the end of the world, but this time the world was supposed to have been destroyed without the involvement of heavenly manifestations; they predicted that in Babylon the antichrist would be born, and through him the whole human race would perish.

---

[49]Nicolas Camille Flammarion (1842–1925) popularized the study of astronomy in his writings.

[50]Philip II or Philip Augustus (1165–1223), the son of Louis VII, was a Capetian king of France and Crusader who made France a major political power in Europe.

"Vincent Ferrer,[51] the famous Spanish preacher, asserted that the world would exist as many more years as there were verses in the Psalter, that is, about 2,537 years.

"The sixteenth century presents, perhaps, an epoch when men were more and more preoccupied with the ruin of the human race. Here, for example, is the announcement inserted by Simon Guillard in his *Treasury of Amazing Histories:* the great commander of Malta ordered the publication in 1532 of a miracle that took place in Assyria. Around the seventh of March, a woman named Rachienne brought into the world a splendid baby boy with bright eyes and gleaming teeth. At the very minute of his birth, the heaven and earth were shaken; the sun came out at midnight and was as bright as at midday, while in the daytime it was so dark that in that region one could not see one's hand before one's face. Then the sun once more came out but in a completely new manner, accompanied by new stars that wandered hither and thither in the sky; and the sun appeared over the house where this baby had been born, and besides several other wonders, fire fell from heaven and killed many persons. After the darkening of the sun, there was a frightful storm in the air; then pearls began falling from the sky. On the following day, a flaming dragon was seen running about the entire country. A new mountain, higher than all those before it, suddenly appeared, cracked into two parts, and in the middle there was found a pillar on which was a Greek inscription saying that the end of the world was approaching, and a voice was heard in the air warning each and every one to prepare for this.

"Since the prediction did not come true this time either, it was transferred by Leovicius, the famed astrologer, to the year 1584. Louis Guyon tells that the fright was so great that the churches could not accommodate all those that sought refuge in them, that many made out their wills, not reflecting that this would be quite pointless if the whole world were to perish.

"One of the best known mathematicians in Europe by the name of Stoffler, who flourished in the sixteenth century and for a long time worked on the calendar reform proposed at the Council of Constance,[52] predicted that in 1524 there would be a worldwide flood. This flood was supposed to take place in the month of February because then Saturn, Jupiter, and Mars would be joined into the sign of Pisces. All the peoples of Europe, Asia, and Africa, having heard of this prophecy, were struck with fear and discouragement. Despite the rainbow, everyone expected a flood. Many writers of that period tell how the inhabitants

[51](1350–1419); Dominican friar, born in Valencia; itinerant preacher from 1399.
[52]This council, which took place in 1414–1418, is usually reckoned by Roman Catholic theologians as their sixteenth ecumenical council.

of the seaside provinces of Germany hurried to sell their land at the lowest prices and that people with money, less confident in the prophecies, bought up these lands. Everyone equipped himself with a boat in the manner of an ark. A doctor of Toulouse named Oriole had an ark of unusually large proportions made for himself and his family and friends. Similar precautions were taken in the greater part of Italy. Finally the month of February came and not a single drop of rain fell. Never, not in any month, was there such a drought, and never had the astrologers been so confounded. However, these worthy people did not fall in spirit, and others continued to believe in them. The same Stoffler, corresponding with the noted Regiomontanus,[53] again made a prediction, this time that in 1588 would be the end of the world, or at least that there would be some dreadful events which would lead to disorder and upset the world.

"A new prediction, and a new disappointment! The year 1588 was not marked by any unusual event. In 1572, to be sure, there was a most unusual occurrence which could justify all concerns. An unknown star suddenly was lit up in the constellation of Cassiopeia; this star was distinguished by its blinding light and was visible even in the daytime. The astrologers declared it to be the star of the Magi which had now returned to announce the second and last coming of Jesus Christ.

"The seventeenth and eighteenth centuries were filled with new predictions, and extremely contradictory ones, as to the end of the world.

"In a little work on religions, printed in 1826, Count de Salmar Montfort sincerely tried to prove that the world would continue to exist only for another ten years: the world, said he, was growing old, and soon its end would come. 'I am certain that this dreadful event will not be slow in coming. Jacob, the forefather of the twelve tribes of Israel, and, consequently, the high priest of the Old Testament Church, was born in the year 2168 from the creation of the world, that is, in 1836 B.C. The ancient Church, the prototype of the new, therefore existed 1836 years. Now, as I write these lines, we are still in the year 1826, and since, according to the word of the Lord, the new Church is to exist until the end of the ages, and if the Old Church exactly prefigured the New (which is beyond doubt), then from this it is clear that the world will continue to exist only another ten years.'

"Mme. Kruedner, friend of the Emperor Alexander, also prophesied the destruction of our planet. She assigned this event to the year 1819.

---

[53]This was the name assumed by Johann Müller (1436–1476), German mathematician and astronomer.

"The world was also to have perished in 1832 and 1840. The prediction for 1840 served as the object of widespread expectations and fears. The year 1840 was marked as fated. The most terrible and dread predictions were scattered from all sides. January 6 was assigned as the last great denouement of the human drama. Very many prepared themselves for a fatal event, settled their affairs entirely, and, with firmness, awaited the final destruction.

"A work written in 1840 by the priest Pierre-Louis in Paris and dedicated to Pope Gregory XVI includes a commentary on the Revelation that assigns the end of the world to the year 1900. Here are the grounds on which Pierre-Louis designates that year:

"The Revelation says that the pagans occupied the holy city for a period of forty-two months.

"The Holy City is Jerusalem, taken by Omar in 636 A.D.

"42 months = 1260 days, or symbolically, 1260 years.

"The total is thus 1896 years.

"Daniel foretells the coming of the antichrist 2300 days after the accession of Artaxerxes[54] to the throne of Persia, which was in 400 B.C.

"2300 − 400 = 1900.

"The following omens have already appeared:

"A white horse appeared (in the Prophecy of Zacharias; horses served as emblems of empires); he that sat on this horse held an onion—this is the Corsican Napoleon ('Ye shall hear of wars and the sound of weaponry'); he was given a crown.

"Enoch and Elias are to return in 1892. In 1896, the Israelites will reenter Jerusalem. Finally, according to the new prophecy, Jesus Christ should appear on April 11, 1900 on the clouds" (pp. 513–518).

If all the predictions and expectations of Christians of all ages have not come to pass in their time, one still cannot conclude, as do some in our enlightened nineteenth century, that this prophecy, perhaps, will not be justified. To them the Apostle Peter says even now that the Lord will not be slow in fulfilling that which has been determined and promised; by the assurance of Jesus Christ Himself, His words "will not pass away" (Matthew 24:35). If the Christians of all the preceding ages were mistaken in their predictions, nevertheless, they have honor and praise for their attentiveness to the circumstances of the time and for their sincere concern for their future lot and life beyond the grave.

---

[54]Name of three Persian kings: Artaxerxes I (d. 424 B.C.), Artaxerxes II (d. 359 B.C.) and Artaxerxes III (d. 338 B.C.).

Let us close this chapter with rumors from our time on the end of the world. The truths of the spirit never have departed from man and never will, regardless of what height of development he may stand on. Truth itself will be made known to men in one or another form. Thus, for example, our present nineteenth century, calling itself enlightened, is told in newspaper announcement of the end of the world. Is this not the foreboding of mankind?

Here is the news from the gazette *Novoye Vremia* in which among other things the following was published: "The end of the world, according to predictions, should occur in the year 1881. At least, the Italian papers quote a passage from the article 'Aquila Volante,'[55] in which the author, Leonardo Aretino, who lived in the fourteenth century, announces the end of the world for November 15, 1881. The destruction of the earth and those on it will take fifteen days. The misfortune will begin with the rising of all seas over their banks; the physicists, indeed, see the possibility that the firmament, in the fatal minute, will be flooded by the seas" *(Novoye Vremia,* June 20, 1881).

The same newspaper, on August 19, 1884, informed us of a new prophecy on the end of the world which was to take place in 1886. Here is what it says: "Colonel Delonais predicted that in 1886 there would be frequent and strong earthquakes; another French colonel, Brock, brings it to the information of all that in that year is the end of a sixteen-year period, at the end of which there is always a great change in magnetic currents, as was the case in 1854 and 1870. The engineer, Duponchel, in turn informs us that in 1886 the greater part of the sunspots will be visible. But St. Malachi,[56] who was Bishop of Armagh in 1148, prophesied that when Easter fell on St. Mark's day,[57] the Descent of the Holy Spirit on St. Anthony's day, and St. John's day on Corpus Christi (a Roman Catholic feast),[58] then all the world would cry out, "Alas!"—and such a coincidence of dates would take place in 1886. Already in 1878, American astronomers predicted a mass of fearful manifestations in the years 1880–1885, because then the planets Jupiter, Saturn, Uranus, and Neptune would all be at their closest distance from the sun, which happens with Jupiter, Saturn, and

[55]"The Flying Eagle."

[56]Malachi O'More (1095–1148) became Bishop of Connor and Archbishop of Armagh in 1132. He is said to have worked zealously to Romanize the Irish Church and to have replaced the Celtic Liturgy with the Roman. The prophecies ascribed to him were found in Rome over four centuries after his death. The Roman Catholic Church canonized him in 1190.

[57]That is, when it fell on April 25.

[58]However, there was no such feast in his day. *Corpus Christi* was only initiated around 1230 A.D. by the nun Juliana of Liege and was not a general observance until 1264 or more than one hundred years after the death of Malachi O'More.

Uranus every six hundred years, but if one includes Neptune as well, only once in several thousand years. At the same time, history bears witness that in the sixth and thirteenth centuries, that is, when the first three of the planets named above were at their closest to the sun, there were terrible misfortunes on earth: plagues, devastating earthquakes, volcanic eruptions, floods, and hurricanes. Astronomers ascribe this to the influence of the above mentioned planets on the earth, and the misfortunes they predicted are reminiscent of those ascribed to St. Malachi. And the pessimists appear to be right. Even the year 1879 was no normal year. Earthquakes followed one another then. On February 10 was the Dellinger catastrophe in Teplitz;[59] and on the same day in Neufchatel it was noted that the water level suddenly rose and then went down again, a spectacle unseen till then. In the same year, there were many hurricanes, cyclones, floods, and in Persia a strong earthquake destroyed forty-five villages. Volcanoes were constantly active and caused a mass of troubles. Then in October, followed the catastrophe in Murcia.[60] In the following years, things were no better for humanity. Let us remember only the dreadful catastrophe in Manila (June 20, 1880), the earthquake in Zagreb (1881), the catastrophes on the island of Ischia[61] (1881 and 1883), the earthquake on Chios in April 1881, and so on. And this year there were no few catastrophes."

On April 30, 1887, the same paper carried the lecture of a certain English scholar on the end of the world. William Thomson,[62] professor of Glasgow University, in his public lecture stated the following: "The colossal sphere of the sun gradually, but constantly, is cooling. Although such a cooling and the resultant compression of the sun's mass are not so great as to be evident in a relatively short period of time, nevertheless, the dynamic theory of heat leads to the conclusion that the sun's emanation of colossal heat energy into space is accompanied by a reduction of its diameter by thirty-five meters per annum, and this, in turn, every two thousand years lowers the strength of the photosphere rays by one percent of the amount of heat that the sun now gives off. It would seem that such a fateful time must come that this amount of heat given off will be reduced so much as to be insufficient to support life on earth." According to Thomson's calculations, based on the preceding and similar considerations, this time of universal deadly cold will arrive on our planet in ten million years.

[59] A resort in northern Bohemia, now the Czech Republic.
[60] A city and province in southeast Spain.
[61] An Italian island in the Tyrrhenian Sea, west of Naples: earthquake 1883.
[62] William Thomson, first Baron Kelvin (1824–1907), professor at Glasgow University, 1846–1899, proposed the absolute, or Kelvin, scale of temperature and the doctrine of the dissipation of energy as well as the theory that the earth is not more than one hundred million years old.

Consequently, the conclusion of this lecture brings us to the words of Jesus Christ, that finally there will come a time when "The sun will darken and the moon will not give light" (Matthew 24:29; Mark 13:24; Luke 21:25).

II) THE SECOND COMING OF CHRIST TO EARTH

Concerning His second, glorious coming to earth, Jesus Christ Himself says: "The Son of man shall come in the glory of His Father with His angels; and then He shall reward every man according to his works" (Matthew 16:27). Jesus Christ will come to earth now not in lowly form, as He came the first time for the salvation of men, but now He will come in all His glory, by which God Himself is surrounded, and He will come to judge. And in another place the Lord spoke in detail of the Second Coming (Matthew 24:27–31; 25:31–42; Mark 8:38; Luke 12:8–9; John 14:3). At once after the Ascension of the Lord Jesus Christ to heaven, angels appeared to the Apostles who stood wondering, looking up at the sky, and said to them: "This same Jesus, which is taken up from you into heaven, shall so come in like manner as ye have seen him go into heaven" (Acts 1:11). The Apostle Judas quotes in his Epistle the prophecy of Enoch[63] on the Second Coming of the Lord: "Behold, the Lord cometh with ten thousands of His holy angels, to execute judgment upon all, and to convince all that are ungodly among them of all their ungodly deeds which they have ungodly committed, and of all their hard speeches which ungodly sinners have spoken against Him" (Jude 1:14–15). The other Apostles often reminded Christians of the Second Coming to confirm them in faith and piety (I John 2:28; Titus 2:12–13) or to discourage Christians from judging others (I Corinthians 4:5) or to move the faithful to vigilance and constant readiness to meet the Lord (I Thessalonians 5:2–6) or to console them in their sorrows (I Peter 4:13).

The second, glorious coming of our Lord Jesus Christ to earth so as to judge mankind is a teaching of the Christian Church, is one of the dogmas of Orthodoxy, is the seventh article of the Symbol of Faith (the Creed): "And He shall come again to judge the quick and the dead. Whose kingdom shall have no end."

When will the last hour of this world's existence come? This hour will be midnight, since the beginning of the day is considered to be twelve o'clock midnight, and the Church therefore teaches us thus about this truth in her hymn: "Behold the Bridegroom cometh at midnight . . ." At midnight there will follow the glorious Second Coming of the Lord to earth in His glorified Body so that

---

[63]From the "Pseudepigraphic" Old Testament Book of Enoch, the rest of which was not accepted by the Church into the Canon of Holy Scripture.

all will see Him, as His disciples saw Him for forty days after His Resurrection. But what His Second Coming to earth would be like the Lord Himself said: "My advent will be as lightning on the horizon: appearing in the East, it shines in the West also." Such will be the rapid advent of Christ, and, like the glowing of glory, it will be visible everywhere and to all. After the sorrows of those days, the days of the antichrist, and all the misfortunes, which according to the teaching of Jesus Christ will not be of long duration "for they shall be shortened for the sake of the elect"—there will be a change in the laws of nature, a new arrangement of the world, corresponding to the new order that is to come about in the kingdom of Christ. The Lord Jesus Christ Himself revealed that before His coming there will be changes, wondrous turnabouts visible and invisible in nature: "Immediately after the tribulation of those days shall the sun be darkened, and the moon shall not give her light, and the stars shall fall from heaven, and the powers of the heavens shall be shaken: And then shall appear the sign of the Son of man in heaven: and then shall all the tribes of the earth mourn, and they shall see the Son of man coming in the clouds of heaven with power and great glory" (Matthew 24:29–30). In general the expression "the sun shall be darkened" is does not mean that it will be destroyed, but what is its light before the light of Christ's advent? The moon will not give light, the stars will fall from the sky; this signifies a change in the laws of nature, a new arrangement of the world corresponding to the new order that is to be in the Kingdom of Christ. For with the appearance of divine light, the sun, moon, and stars will necessarily darken. The day will dawn, the eternal day, the light of Christ which enlightens the faithful. What will the role of the sun be, the moon, and stars when there is no night? The unseen, spiritual world will be moved, that is, all the powers of heaven—the angels, like a heavenly host, will form ranks to accompany the King of glory, the Lord Jesus Christ, going to judge the universe—they will be moved, seeing such a change. For if they were so awe-struck and amazed, when the stars were created (Job 28:7), then how can they not be awed and shaken more than before, seeing that all is transfigured and their co-servants, the humans, must give answer for their deeds. The visible world will also be moved before the coming of Christ unto its change, as St. Peter bears witness concerning this change, that heaven and earth will be new: "But the heavens and the earth, which are now, by the same word are kept in store, reserved unto fire against the day of judgment and perdition of ungodly men ... But the day of the Lord will come as a thief in the night; in the which the heavens shall pass away with a great noise, and the elements shall melt with fervent heat, the earth also and the works that are therein shall be burned up. Looking for and hasting unto the coming of the day of God, wherein the heavens being on fire shall be dissolved, and the elements shall melt with fervent heat? Nevertheless we, according to his promise, look for new heavens and a new earth, wherein dwelleth righteousness" (II Peter 3:7,10,12–13), so that there will be "a new heaven and a new earth," and the present heaven and earth will be changed by means of fire. The actual coming will be preceded by the appearance of the sign of the Cross in the sky, so as utterly to rebuke the shamelessness of the Jews; for Christ will come to judge, having a great justification—the Cross—showing not only His wounds but his shameful death. They will weep with fear at the glorious coming of the Lord, seeing this worldwide turnabout, the new order of things, the breaking and transformation of all the relationships in the former life. All the tribes of the land of Judea will weep, bewailing their disobedience; all those also will weep who follow earthly wisdom, even though they be Christians: "The wicked shall not see Thy glory, O Christ, but we keep vigil unto Thee from the night, O Only-begotten One, the glow of the Father's Godhead, and we hymn Thee, O Lover of Mankind" (Tone 4, Song 5).[64] But the glory, with which Christ will come, will be manifested in the grandeur of His Advent, surrounded by throngs of angels (Matthew 25:31).

b) Resurrection of the Bodies of the Dead

1) THE BASIS FOR THE RESURRECTION OF THE BODIES OF THE DEAD — THE IMMORTALITY OF THE BODY — THE TEACHING OF THE OLD AND NEW TESTAMENTS ON THE RESURRECTION OF THE DEAD — THE RESURRECTED BODIES, THEIR GENERAL CHARACTERISTICS FOR THE SAVED AND THE DAMNED — THE HISTORY OF THIS DOGMA

God created man immortal both in soul and body. The law and the word of God are unchanging; the soul and body are immortal, that is, once created they are never destroyed—and the soul and body remain forever. The death of the soul and body to which man is condemned for disobedience to the Law of God is only a particular abnormal state of soul and body—the punishment of an immortal man. Death is a great, hidden mystery; it is man's birth out of temporal life into eternal; it is a mystery, a mysterious process of decomposition and, at the same time, of a liberation from corpulence to restore that new, fine, spiritual, glorious, strong, and immortal body that was given to our first parents and which they lost for themselves and their descendants, for mankind. And so death is necessary, inescapable for the rehabilitation of the primeval man,

---

[64]From the *Octoechos* or Book of Eight Tones.

immortal in soul and in body. The body, being left by the soul which gives it life, decays; and the elements (component or constituent bodies) that form it, according to God's laws, return to the material mass that makes up the visible world.

One of these laws known to us from Divine Revelation is that every human body will retain, in this general mass, the materials for its restitution; and that all human bodies, restored by the action of God's omnipotence, will once more be joined with their souls so as to live an eternal life jointly.

The Romans, too, in distant antiquity, recognizing the existence and immortality of the soul, thought the body also immortal; left by the soul, the body, buried in the ground, is not destroyed but continues its being; but where, how, and in what did the immortality of body and soul consist? It was Christianity that resolved this question.

And so, the body, placed in the ground, like a sown seed, in its very vegetating has life; otherwise the grain would not yield a plant if there were no life in corruption itself. Consequently, the decomposition of our body is necessary, inescapable, so that there could be a new body, appropriate to the new, eternal life beyond the grave at its second union with the soul. And therefore, if the body has been given immortality, according to its purpose, then assurance of the resurrection in its time is hidden in the depth of the human spirit. The thought of burying the body is common to all humanity and therefore is a property of the spirit. The meaning of "burial" is to hide, to save up, to keep, to lay away;[65] and these actions are always associated by the mind with objects that constitute a belonging and in due time will be needed again. It is not with such a basic conviction that funerals are conducted by all humanity? And so, besides the evidence of Holy Scripture on the resurrection of bodies, we have also the evidence of common sense: 1) as we have just said on the purpose of man in eternity, and this, God's purpose, is unchanging; therefore beyond the grave also there must exist a soul and body in the very same close, mystic union, just as there was before on earth; 2) in the activity of the soul, both good and bad, the body was always a participant in everything, as an instrument of manifesting the soul's activity; therefore, it is natural in God's perfect jurisprudence that the body take part in the life of the soul beyond the grave, and St. Paul bears witness of this: "that which it has done with the body"; and 3) the very concept of man brings us to the conclusion that beyond the grave, man would not be man unless the soul is joined with the body. The nature itself of the soul, according to its destiny

---

[65]The English word *bury* and the Russian *beregu*, *berech'*, (to guard, save, keep) which is used here in the text, seem to go back to a common Indo-European root meaning "to hide, put away."

of being with the body, cannot be in a state abnormal to it without the body. By death, man is painfully cut into two component parts, and after death there is no more man, his soul exists by itself and so does his body. Therefore, for the soul's full existence beyond the grave it needs to have the flesh, the instrument of its visible manifestation. Man's nature is a spirit incarnate, or a flesh made spiritual. This is why, for the soul to exist fully beyond the grave it needs the flesh, without which there is no man. Man beyond the grave lives an immortal life, either in a state of bliss or else in a state of torment, but in both cases he *lives*.

One and the same spirit, which enlivens the soul beyond the grave and gives life to the process of vegetating of the body in the earth, makes an inter-relationship inescapable between the soul abiding in the world beyond the grave and its body vegetating in the grave; and this inter-relationship cannot be without consequences for the former.

St. Paul revealed all that man is able to understand about the state of the soul beyond the grave, that is, about life after death, in his First Epistle to the Corinthians, in the fifteenth chapter: "Christ died for our sins" (verse 3). He died for our sake, having cleansed us of sins, which He took upon Himself, and by His death destroyed, annihilated our eternal death which we deserve for our sins and "rose again" (verse 4). If He rose, this means that all the other dead will rise as well. And so, the resurrection of Christ serves as the basis of our resurrection. If Christ rose from the dead, and we preach His resurrection, then how is it that some of you have come to deny the resurrection of the dead? (verse 12). He first rose from the dead and laid the foundation for our blessed resurrection. "Now Christ, risen from the dead, is become the first fruits of the dead" (verse 20). But you, by the insinuation of the enemy of the human race, have taken it into your heads to doubt or not even to believe the resurrection of the body. If, as you suppose, there will be no resurrection of the dead, then our preaching is false that Christ rose from the dead; whereas this is such a proven truth, of which the Prophets foretold, in which all the disciples of Christ and many of the followers came to believe, even by speaking with the Risen (verses 4–10). Here is the consolation offered by the Apostle to those who sorrow over the death of those close to them (hearken, O Christian!): "Christ, being risen from the dead, is become the first fruits of the dead"; this means that I too, and my deceased friend, as believers in Christ, will also rise. This is a doctrine: this is the Eleventh Article of the Creed, the Symbol of our true Faith. John Chrysostom says on this subject: "Jesus Christ, having died for our sins, rose, and is the First-born of the dead. Of whom will He be the First-born, if there are none who are to rise? How can He be the First-born, if those of whom He is the First, do not rise?" (Homily 39). If there were no resurrection, then there would be no reason to call the Risen Lord the First fruits and the First-born of the dead.

In the Old Testament there is evidence of the resurrection of the dead in the books of Isaiah, Ezekiel, Job, and Daniel. Isaiah wrote: "The dead shall rise again and they that are in the tombs shall stand once more, and those on earth shall rejoice" (Isaiah 26:19); Ezekiel; "The hand of the LORD was upon me, and carried me out in the spirit of the LORD, and set me down in the midst of the valley which was full of bones, And caused me to pass by them round about; and, behold, there were very many in the open valley; and, lo, they were very dry. And he said unto me, Son of man, can these bones live? And I answered, O Lord GOD, thou knowest" (Ezekiel 37:1–3). And further, the Prophet continues: "Behold, O my people, I will open your graves, and cause you to come up out of your graves, and bring you into the land of Israel. And ye shall know that I am the LORD, when I have opened your graves, O my people, and brought you up out of your graves, And shall put my spirit in you, and ye shall live, and I shall place you in your own land: then shall ye know that I the LORD have spoken it, and performed it, saith the LORD." "A new heart also will I give you, and a new spirit will I put within you: and I will take away the stony heart out of your flesh, and I will give you an heart of flesh. And I will put my spirit within you" (Ezekiel 37:12–14; 36:26–27). Daniel prophesied: "And many of them that sleep in the dust of the earth shall awake, some to everlasting life, and some to shame and everlasting contempt" (Daniel 12:2). Here the dead state of the body is likened to the state of sleep. The body in both cases retains physical life: in a sleeping state the powers are restored, while in the state of death the process of vegetation takes place. Just as, after sleep, the body his its strength new and restored for life, so exactly after the state of death the body, resurrected, is a new, better, spiritual body for a new life. Job writes: "I know that my redeemer liveth forever: on earth he shall raise up my skin, which has borne these things, for from the Lord these things have taken place with me" (Job 19:25).[66]

The Church bases its teaching on the resurrection of the dead, which is in direct connection with the teaching about the resurrection of the Church's Founder, the Lord Jesus Christ, on Him alone. Before His resurrection, Jesus Christ taught of the general resurrection of the dead (John 5:28–29); the teaching of St. Paul on the same subject (I Thessalonians 4:16; I Corinthians 15), the witness of the Old Testament, and, finally, the conclusion of good sense on the need for the resurrection of the body—this is the basis of the Church's teaching.

[66]This is the Septuagint version of the text.

Jesus Christ taught that the time of the future, general resurrection is coming, and indeed already is come (John 5:25), because the foundation of the resurrection of all is in Christ; and with His appearance there began the last epoch of the building of the salvation of humanity, an epoch that certainly will end with the general resurrection and judgment. Therefore, this time, in the inner, close connection of events, not only is arriving but has already arrived. In the same Gospel (John 5:28), it is stated quite definitely that all the dead (without exception) will rise from their tombs: "There will come the time when all those that are in the tombs will hear the voice of the Son of God and having heard, will come to life." They will come to life in exactly the same fashion as the friend of Christ, Lazarus who, four days dead and already decaying in the ground heard the voice of the Son of God. The resurrection of Lazarus serves Christians as a proof and image of the resurrection of all mankind. At the general resurrection, the dead will hear the voice of the Son of God in the sense of a divine command at which they cannot refuse to rise from their graves to stand before the judgment seat in the way that they could refuse a spiritual-moral resurrection: for they had heard the voice of the Son of God, but they did not accept it, they did not believe His teaching about His redemption of all believing humanity; and they remained dead in spirit as before the preaching of Christ. Verse 25 reveals to us the Lord's teaching on the moral, spiritual resurrection of the dead spiritual world (of the unbelieving souls). In the Gospel of St. Matthew (24:31), the teaching of the Lord Jesus Christ on the resurrection of the dead is expressed in the following words: "And he shall send his angels with a great sound of a trumpet, and they shall gather together his elect from the four winds, from one end of heaven to the other." "And they shall gather out of his kingdom all things that offend, and them which do iniquity, and shall cast them into a furnace of fire: there shall be wailing and gnashing of teeth" (Matthew 13:41–42). Here is the meaning of these words: not angels will blow trumpets, but there will sound the one last trumpet, the trumpet of God, the voice of the Son of God, His will, desire; there will arrive the hour predetermined from eternity for the might of God to be manifest, the bodily resurrection of all humanity, except for the bodies of the Mother of God, Elias, and Enoch, whose bodies are in paradise. Then at the sound of this trumpet, with the arrival of the fateful hour of the universe, the Lord Jesus Christ will send angels, and after the sound of this trumpet there will follow the almighty (and inscrutable for the human mind) act of God: the resurrection of the dead.

For the time of the universal judgment, at the sound of the trumpet, all the dead without exception who have ever lived, both the righteous and sinners, the saved and the condemned, will come to life, will rise. All will rise, regardless of what type of death befell them: the drowned, the burned, those eaten by beasts, by birds, those murdered by evil people, the suicides. All those who were born and who died, from Adam down to the hour of the end of the world, will arise. All will rise in one equal age and condition with only the difference of their earthly life and works. The risen bodies will again become the garment of their souls, and they will not be parted again for all eternity. The Apostle Paul writes in some detail of the general resurrection to the Corinthians. At the moment when the dead arise, we who are still living on earth will be changed instantly, according to the new, spiritual life beyond the grave, that is, we shall die and at once rise again with bodies like those of all the other people: "For the trumpet shall sound, and the dead shall be raised incorruptible, and we shall be changed" (I Corinthians 15:52). The same teaching is in these words: "The dead in Christ shall rise first: then we which are alive" (I Thessalonians 4:16–17). The book of the Acts of the Apostles also bears witness to the universal resurrection of the dead, that is, of the dead bodies, both of the righteous and sinners: "And have hope toward God, which they themselves also allow, that there shall be a resurrection of the dead, both of the just and unjust" (Acts 24:15).

Regardless of how our body was destroyed, nevertheless its elements were not annihilated: and for God's almighty power it is possible to resurrect a body from existing elements, even if it had been burned or eaten by beasts. The elements, hearing the voice of their Creator, will gather to carry out their assignment of forming a human body; they will gather at once in the same way as the fish heard the voice of the Son of God and immediately gathered into the nets that the holy Apostles at the command of Jesus Christ had lowered into the sea.

The resurrection of dead bodies is an action of the might of God, an action possible for Him alone, an action by which the bodies, having decayed and turned into invisible particles, separated into their component elements, by the same will that created the body of the first man from the earth, now are restored as the same bodies from the same elements—the body of Adam is raised up again as it was before the fall. The resurrected bodies are joined to the souls that belong to them, and the new man stands immediately before judgment. We all will rise, and our bodies will all be of the same fine nature, immortal, incorrupt, but not all alike in quality. The bodies of the righteous will be distinguished from the bodies of the condemned. "The resurrection of the dead," as St. John Chrysostom writes, "will be like the resurrection of Christ."

The second period of life beyond the grave for the soul will open with its being joined to its resurrected body. Conjoined now forever, the soul with its body will stand before judgment after which it will enter a state either of eternal bliss or of eternal torment. The Church's teaching on the resurrection of dead human bodies so that they can be joined to their souls forever is an Orthodox doctrine, and every true Christian confesses his faith in this doctrine by word and deed, saying: "I await (expect) the resurrection of the dead"; this is the Eleventh Article of the Creed. The world saw the heavenly truth of the resurrection of bodies and their being rejoined to their souls in actual fact, that is, people resurrected in the Old Testament were seen; thus the Prophet Elias raised up the son of the widow of Sarephtha, and Elisseus raised the son of the Sunnamitess. The Lord Himself showed His teaching of the resurrection of the dead in deed when He raised the daughter of Jairus, the son of the widow of Nain, and the four-days dead Lazarus. And did not the resurrected righteous at the hour of the Lord's death bear witness to the universal resurrection? The seven resurrected youths of Ephesus and a multitude of examples of the dead being raised up by the prayers of Saints; is all of this not a visible proof that we too shall all be resurrected for eternal life? God's creation of the invisible (the spiritual world of angels, the world of beings like unto the souls of men) and all the visible is an action possible for God alone and beyond the limits of the human mind, accessible only by faith. To these wondrous acts of God's creation, which constitute the glory of God, belongs also the resurrection of dead bodies which were originally designed by God to be immortal. Adam and Eve were once also immortal before their fall in both soul and body: man as created, consisting of spirit, soul, and body was immortal. And so, the resurrection of dead bodies is necessary for man to be immortal in spirit, soul, and body, which also is designed for immortality, that is, to have an eternal being, to exist forever. The awareness of eternity and immortality which naturally belongs to the spirit of man gave, as it were, a foretaste of the life to come beyond the grave for all mankind of all times and places, except for those individuals that were darkened by carnal reasoning. Consequently, the resurrection of bodies, necessary for the new life beyond the grave was something all humanity was aware of and was fulfilled in our Lord Jesus Christ Who made a beginning for the resurrection of man—the righteous as well as the sinners and the condemned. All the bodies will rise and be united with their souls, and all will stand before judgment, both Christians and non-Christians. The bodies of all dead people will rise, righteous as well as sinners and the wicked, and will be joined by God's almighty power with their souls. Then there will be a new man with all three component parts: spirit, soul, and body, only no longer as in his time on earth. He will now receive completely new qualities with which he could exist in the new spiritual world beyond the grave, in paradise or in Gehenna. The general quality of the risen bodies is that now they will have lost that heaviness that they had on earth, a heavy corpulence that Adam and Eve received immediately after their fall. The body of the new man will have, as before, flesh and bones, as evidenced by our resurrected Lord Jesus Christ Himself Who after His rising from the dead had flesh and bones and ate fish and honey with the Apostles. "Why are ye troubled?" said the Lord Jesus Christ, having appeared to His disciples after His resurrection, "Behold My hands and My feet, that it is I myself: handle Me, and see; for a spirit hath not flesh and bones, as ye see Me have" (Luke 24:38–39). To show that He was not a spirit, the Lord allowed Himself to be touched, and even ate with His disciples baked fish and honey (verses 40,43). This means that the body of Jesus Christ even after His resurrection consisted of flesh and bones and was the same as it had been before His resurrection; but now it was a heavenly body, glorified, and could float in the air, pass into closed places, be invisible, and ascend to heaven. Just such a spiritualized body will belong to everyone after their souls are united with their risen bodies. However, the bodies of the righteous will have qualities distinct from those of the sinners. The family species is the same, man; but the forms of the members are different: the righteous and the sinners. Just as plants from various seeds are unlike, so the future bodies of righteous and sinners will be unlike. The risen bodies, on the basis of their eternal purpose and that spiritual sphere in which they will live eternally, taking into consideration also their earthly life, will have completely new qualities different from those they had on earth. The Apostle Paul speaks clearly of the resurrection of our dead bodies, that is, of the general resurrection, in the Epistle to the Romans: "But if the Spirit of Him that raised up Jesus from the dead dwell in you, He that raised up Christ from the dead shall also quicken your mortal bodies by His Spirit that dwelleth in you" (Romans 8:11). If the Spirit of Him Who raised Jesus from the dead lives in us—since the body is a temple of the Holy Spirit—then the same One that raised up Christ will bring our dead bodies to life by means of His Spirit living in us. The whole fifteenth chapter of the First Epistle to the Corinthians reveals the mystery of the resurrection of the dead and of life beyond the grave. And to the Philippians the Apostle wrote concerning the resurrection of the dead: "For our conversation is in heaven; from whence also we look for the Saviour, the Lord Jesus Christ: Who shall change our vile body, that it may be fashioned like unto his glorious body, according to the working whereby he is able even to subdue all things unto himself" (Philippians 3:20–21). As to how the human body, having been corrupted and turned to dust, again is to come to life with all its faculties, members, and joints, this is a question that cannot be resolved by human knowledge and therefore it has been a temptation, a stumbling block for certain theoreticians. Since it was not within their ability to explain this in the ordinary manner that they could explain all the manifestations of visible nature, they came to doubt, to disbelief, unbelief, and other unnatural conclusions, contrary to Christianity. St. Paul, in order to explain this mystery of the resurrection of dead bodies, takes an example, an image from visible nature: the seed. The body is likened to a seed which is put into the ground, disintegrates, and, in falling apart, brings forth a plant. Just so, the body, disintegrating, brings forth in due time a new body: "But some man will say, How are the dead raised up? And with what body do they come? Thou fool, that which thou sowest is not quickened, except it die: And that which thou sowest, thou sowest not that body that shall be, but bare grain, it may chance of wheat, or of some other grain: But God giveth it a body as it hath pleased him, and to every seed his own body" (I Corinthians 15:35–38). And so, "to every seed, God giveth its own body," every seed brings forth a plant proper to itself, and thus exactly the bodies of the righteous and the sinners will, after the resurrection, possess different qualities. The difference in deeds brings forth a difference in the bodies themselves. Bodies in whose activity the name of God was hallowed and glorified will shine in the kingdom of heaven through their good works as by the undimmed lamps of the wise virgins; we say that these bodies which were the instruments of devout activity will be bright as the sun, that is, they will be made holy by glory in the kingdom of glory, as the sun, the moon, and all the stars glow with light. Thus also, distinguished by their righteousness, the just will not all have the same glory, on the basis of the words of the Apostle: "There is one glory of the sun, and another glory of the moon, and another glory of the stars: for one star differeth from another star in glory. So also is the resurrection of the dead" (I Corinthians 15:41–42).

But what will the bodies be like after the resurrection? Here is the question that occupied the carnal intellects of the Corinthian Christians. The warfare of the spirit and flesh caused them to think: what sort of bodies will there be in the afterlife? The same ones as on earth: corrupt, feeble, abased, pulling the soul down to sin—no small obstacles in attaining moral perfection and the knowledge of truth, bodies distancing one from glory and blessed living? Or after the resurrectio will the bodies possess new qualities, opposite to the former? St. Paul resolves this question also, saying: "It is sown in corruption; it is raised in incorruption: It is sown in dishonour; it is raised in glory: it is sown in weakness; it is raised in power: It is sown a natural body; it is raised a spiritual body. There is a natural body, and there is a spiritual body" (I Corinthians 15:42–44). And so, after the resurrection, the bodies will be incorrupt, glorious, strong, spiritual, immortal, light, nimble, fine, adroit in motion, and transit from place to place, so that no bounds are able to hold them; and, finally, they will retain flesh and bones, as Jesus Christ Himself has assured us in His glorified body which consists of flesh and bone. These are common properties of the new bodies after resurrection, common to righteous and to sinners. We have noted that the bodies of the righteous will be distinguished from those of the sinners; what then is this difference? As on the body of the Lord Jesus Christ there forever remained the marks of the wounds, to bear witness to the moral world of the work He had done in redeeming mankind, so also on the body of a man, as in a mirror, his earthly life is reflected, not excluding even one idle thought. The bodies of the righteous have their qualities that distinguish them from the bodies of sinners. The bodies of the former shine like the sun. On the resurrected bodies of the righteous, the Lord Jesus Christ Himself taught that "they will shine like the sun in the kingdom of their Father" (Matthew 13:43). This is the state of the bodies of the righteous in paradise in the second period of life beyond the grave or simply the highest bliss of the righteous, in the words of St. Paul regarding the stars: "there is another glory of the sun . . ." These glorified bodies will feel neither illness, nor suffering, nor chagrin, nor exhaustion, nor yearning. Consequently, the sons of God, holy by grace, will receive after the resurrection the same body in which they were vested during their earthly life, only glorified, made spiritual, like the body of Christ which He had after His resurrection, with qualities distinguishing it from earthly bodies and from the bodies of the condemned. The blessed Augustine and St. Ambrose find the following four qualities in the bodies of the Saints: 1) absence of feeling of external, harmful influences which during their earthly life evoked painful, unpleasant sensations in the body; 2) the shining of such bodies like the sun; 3) inscrutable speed in moving from one place to another, and, finally; 4) a complete subordination of the body to the soul, hence there will be a full harmony in the human being. In order to show his hearers more strikingly the difference between the future bodies of the righteous from their present ones, St. Paul takes a comparison and example from visible nature, saying: "There are both heavenly and earthly bodies; but there is a different glory for the heavenly, and a different glory for the earthly." Comparing the resurrected bodies of the righteous with those of the present, he concludes that the resurrected bodies will be marked by such clarity, glory, and light as our mind cannot now imagine.

These stars, quotes the Apostle, in the present case, serve as it were to foretell the bright bodies of our future. The special qualities given to the bodies of the Saints will make them glow with glory, as the sun shone on the earth; but the bodies of the condemned will be dark and unsightly, reflecting in themselves all the foulness of their activity and moral ugliness.

It never occurred to any of the pagans that dead bodies, having turned into dust, could ever come to life again: rise for a new, eternal life, although immortality of the soul and its eternal existence beyond the grave, be it a happy or unhappy one, was something that belonged to the spirit of man. For some peoples, the concept of the resurrection of the body was a dim idea, while others did not know it at all; but for the wise men, it was a puzzling thought. However, the keeping of the remains of human bodies existed in various forms among all peoples in all times and places. Love and respect for them, as if subconsciously, expressed the thought of the spirit which was hidden in the depths of human nature: the foreboding that this ruined body would exist at some time beyond the grave. All of man's activity is directed more or less by his immortal spirit, and it is a truth that man preserves and seeks to preserve that which will at some time be needed. This thought concerning the resurrection of dead bodies was revealed in all its fullness only by the resurrection of Christ. From the very first days of Christianity, the thought of the resurrection of the dead was a stumbling block, a fatal thought for many thinkers, and brought those who followed carnal wisdom to frightful errors. The Hebrews believed in the resurrection of the dead, and this truth is inseparable from their history. The Judeans at the time of the Lord Jesus Christ pictured life beyond the grave and, in general, everything spiritual in too crude and physical a way. They looked upon the Messiah as a great political warrior-king who would deliver them from the yoke of the Romans, would give them freedom, form a Hebrew kingdom to which he would subjugate all their enemies, and under whom there would follow the resurrection of the dead and the judgment. And Martha, the sister of Lazarus, said to the Saviour: "I know that my brother will rise in the general resurrection" (John 11:24). The Sadducees did not believe in anything spiritual; neither the existence of angels, nor the existence of the soul, nor life beyond the grave; they did not believe in the resurrection of the body. The Athenian philosophers, the Stoics, and Epicureans, called the doctrine of the resurrection of the dead "madness" (Acts 17:18); however, despite this, in their teaching they admitted the possibility of the resurrection of dead bodies. The ancient Greeks had a special sect of philosophers who were marked by their strictness of morals and whose teaching consisted in an unshakeable firmness of spirit in the face of all trials, misfortunes, and sufferings. An unshakeable firmness of spirit in all things was the subject of this school's teaching. These were the Stoics; they taught that the universe is made up of four elements: fire, water, air, and earth. Four hundred years before the birth of Christ, there existed another sect of philosophers, founded by Epicurus,[67] whose followers called themselves Epicureans. The teaching of this school (Epicureanism) was that the goal of life is attained by using all that is requisite to gain every mental pleasure; they taught that the universe is made up of atoms and space. Finally, the Platonics[68] taught that the universe consists of matter and God. In the teaching of these three schools there are common tenets recognized by all of them. These common tenets are: 1) what exists cannot come out of nothing, nor can it resolve itself into nothing and disappear; 2) there are elements that cannot be destroyed from which everything comes. And so, according to these positions, which are common to all these schools, there is the possibility of carnal restoration for, according to the teaching of Plato, God and matter exist eternally and cannot be destroyed. Thus, from the teaching of Plato which shows God as the eternal Creator, creating from eternal matter the various objects of the visible world, for example the human body, we conclude that these objects, like the body destroyed in death, return to the same eternal matter from which God if only He wills it can again make the same objects, including the human body, entirely like the first. The teaching of the Stoics leads us to the very same conclusion, since for them, everything including the human body is made up from a certain combination of the four elements: fire, water, air, and earth; and therefore, if God wishes, He can again bring forth the human body which was destroyed and returned to its elements, just as it had been before. And according to the teaching of Epicurus, everything was made up of atoms, including the human body. But when it is destroyed and turned into atoms, then perhaps the same atoms in a given combination can once more bring forth the body as it was before under specific conditions, with the same mixture of these atoms. Thus did the pagan philosophers conclude as to the resurrection of the dead (Chistovich, *Concerning the Immortality and Future Life of Man*, p. 205).

Among the first Christians there soon appeared people who did not believe in the resurrection of the dead, and this was the case in Corinth, in the Corin-

---

[67]Epicurus (341 or 342–270 B.C.) was born on the island of Samos and in 306 B.C. took up residence in Athens where he established the philosophical school named after him in a garden he had purchased.

[68]Plato (429–347 B.C.) was a disciple of Socrates and the teacher of Aristotle and in Athens founded the Academy, named for a grove dedicated to Academus, where he taught. His followers were therefore called the Academicians, or Academic philosophers.

thian Church, and where, for this reason St. Paul entered into battle with a false teacher to affirm the dogma of the resurrection of the dead. St. Paul, after the Stoics and Epicureans, names the founders of the false teaching: "Hymenæus and Philetus, who concerning the truth have erred" (II Timothy 2:17–18), in that they denied the resurrection of the body. Striving towards a spiritual under-standing of the resurrection of the dead, they thought that the work of redemp-tion related only to the soul, as the Gnostics later taught, and at the present time so do the followers of Swedenborg.[69] The Gnostics, a religio-philosophical sect of the second century whose teaching on faith was derived from Christian and Jewish teaching, denied the resurrection of the dead and claimed that Jesus Christ did not have a human body but only appeared to.

According to Swedenborg's view, people immediately after they die are in bodies, dressed, in dwelling-places, so that they are ashamed of those false notions they had held of the afterlife before experiencing it. Those people whose death found them inclined towards truth and good, live after death in magnifi-cent chambers, surrounded by splendid gardens and so on ("Strannik," 1873, Volume 1, p. 14). To protect the thoughtless from the errors of such heretics, let us point out briefly certain elements in their false teaching. Relating redemption to the soul alone, Hymenæus and Philetus taught that the faithful have already been raised from the dead and live with Christ. Their followers taught that the soul, immediately after separating from the earthly body, forms from it a fine, spiritual body for itself—a spiritual organism—with which it passes into eter-nity, having it as its vestment (the teaching of the Spiritualists[70] on this subject is the same). Thus the followers of Hymenæus and Philetus affirmed that from an earthly, crude body there will instantly arise a new, fine, ethereal, spiritual body. Not having the possibility of explaining the inexplicable action of God's omnipotence over the process of bodily life on earth, the proud mind makes its false conclusion, vesting truth, the spirit, the immortality of the body, in an imaginary form of development. The arrogant mind explains the truth which belongs to the spirit, that the soul will in due time need a body appropriate for its destiny, by saying that this new body will arise from the earthly, old body. If

---

[69]Emmanuel Swedenborg (1688–1772) original surname Svedberg: Swedish scientist, phi-losopher, and mystic. He began having visions circa 1743. His doctrines combined elements of Christianity with those of pantheism and philosophy and were taken up by his followers, especially five former Wesleyan preachers who, on May 7, 1787, founded the "New Jerusalem Church" or "New Church," in London.

[70]In its present form, Spiritualism or Spiritism dates from the occult activities of the Fox family in America in 1848, and it spread to England and the Continent as a reaction against materialism.

the mind could not explain the resurrection of the body, then let it explain its conclusion: How does a new, spiritual body grow? This means that the mind, with all its conceit, could not distance itself from the truth of the resurrection of the body nor could it refute this truth.

The law of immortality belongs to the soul and body, as man was created for eternity. The resurrection and growth can only be seen as the omnipotent and inscrutable action of God. The proud, deeply fallen mind cannot explain the former nor can it explain the latter: how does a spiritual body grow from the earthly. Man can distort the truth, but he has not the strength to exterminate it, destroy it, put an end to it, and so it, wherever necessary, expresses itself. The eternity of the body's existence, as a truth, gives expression to itself even in their error. What is true, true for all ages, for all eternity remains the truth.

The teaching on the resurrection of the dead (that is, of the body) is not *madness*, as the Athenian philosophers expressed themselves, but a true teaching based on true faith in the Originator of our resurrection and on good sense about the purpose of man, created by God for eternity; and man, after his creation, does consist of body, soul, and spirit.

c) God's Final Judgment on Moral Beings

1) THE UNIVERSAL JUDGMENT — JUDGMENT ON CHRISTIANS AND NON-CHRISTIANS

Eventually there will come a day, the last day for this human race (John 6:39); as there is a last day for each man by himself, the end of the age and the world (Matthew 13:39), so it is with the day of a person's death—the day will come, set by God, on which He will judge the universe in righteousness (Acts 17:31), that is, to make a universal and firm judgment. This day therefore is called in the Scriptures the Day of Judgment[71] (Matthew 11:22,24; 12:36; II Peter 2:9); doomsday (II Peter 3:7); the day of wrath and revelation of the righteous judgment of God (Romans 2:5); the day of the Son of man (Luke 17:22,24,26); the day of the Lord (II Peter 3:10; I Thessalonians 5:2); the day of Christ (II Thessalonians 2:2; Philippians 1:10; 2:16); the day of our Lord Jesus Christ (II Corinthians 1:14; I Corinthians 1:8; 5:5), because the Lord Jesus Christ will then appear on earth in all His glory to judge the quick and the dead; the great day (Acts 2:21; Jude 6), according to those great events, which will then take place (Archbishop Makary of Kharkov, *Theology*, Volume 2, p. 618).

---

[71]These are not necessarily the same words that appear in the King James translation.

The second Coming of the Lord Jesus Christ to earth is a doctrine of Orthodoxy and is found in the seventh article of the Creed. In the same article the doctrine of the coming dread Judgment of God over mankind for his earthly life, for his deeds, is set forth.

Of course, before the court is opened, the judge arrives, and then the humans and demons who are to be judged appear. Consequently, all the evidence of the Holy Scriptures about the second, glorious coming of the Lord Jesus Christ to earth, about the resurrection of the dead, remain evidences of the reality of the universal judgment. Here is the witness of the Lord Jesus Christ Himself about the Last Judgment, the witness of the holy Apostles, and of the holy Fathers and Doctors of the Church.

Jesus Christ teaches: "For the Father judgeth no man, but hath committed all judgment unto the Son ... And hath given him authority to execute judgment also" (John 5:22, 27); and in another passage He says: "For the Son of man shall come in the glory of his Father with his angels; and then he shall reward every man according to his works" (Matthew 16:27). The Apostles also preached of the judgment: "Because [God] hath appointed a day, in the which he will judge the world in righteousness by that man whom he hath ordained; whereof he hath given assurance unto all men, in that he hath raised him from the dead" (Acts 17:31); "Behold, the Lord cometh with ten thousands of his saints, to execute judgment upon all, and to convince all that are ungodly among them of all their ungodly deeds which they have ungodly committed" (Jude 1:14–15); the Apostle Paul more than once bears witness of the universal, final judgment (Romans 2:5–7; 14:10; I Corinthians 4:5; II Corinthians 5:10; Ephesians 6:8; Colossians 3:24–25; II Thessalonians 1:6–10; II Timothy 4:1) and finally, St. John the Theologian writes of the same (Revelation 20:11–15).

The Holy Church has always confessed this doctrine of the universal judgment. In the Nicene (Constantinopolitan) Creed there is read, "And He [Christ] shall come again with glory to judge the quick and the dead." In the Athanasian Creed: "He [Christ] shall come to judge the quick and the dead, at Whose coming all men shall rise again with their bodies, and shall give account for their own works." This dogma is witnessed by all the holy Fathers and Doctors of the Church in their writings.

Here is a staggering picture of the Last Judgment over mankind, a picture that the word of God presents us (Matthew 25:31–46), and which is confirmed by good sense. Parts of this picture are: 1) the Judge—God; 2) the participants in the judgment—the angels and Apostles; 3) those who are to be judged; 4) the subject of the judgment; 5) the separation of the righteous from the sinners;

and 6) the final decision concerning both. In the first place in the picture of the Last Judgment, according to the witness of Jesus Christ Himself, is the Son of God as God, King, and Judge seated on the throne of His glory, surrounded by the holy angels and Apostles. "Sitting on the throne" is a figurative expression taken from the custom of kings to ascend the throne on especially important occasions.

Further, there is the representation of those who carry out the will of God or, as it were, those who take part in the judgment—the angels and Apostles: "And he shall send his angels with a great sound of a trumpet, and they shall gather together his elect from the four winds, from one end of heaven to the other" (Matthew 24:31), "and they shall gather out of his kingdom all things that offend, and them which do iniquity" (Matthew 13:41); "and [they shall] sever the wicked from among the just" (Matthew 14:49). Here is the participation, the activity of the angels at the Last Judgment. The Jews were customarily summoned to meetings by means of trumpets (Leviticus 25:9; Numbers 10:2; Judges 3:27), which served Jesus Christ as a symbol for speaking figuratively of all humanity gathered for judgment by angels with a great trumpet sound. This is imagery in speech, and one should not think that the angels will be sent with trumpets. No, there will sound one last trumpet (I Corinthians 15:52), the trumpet of God (I Thessalonians 4:16), at whose sound the holy angels will be sent by the Son of God; at the same time, at the sound of this trumpet there will follow the resurrection of the dead as well. The cardinal points (the East, the West, the North, and the South) were usually called the winds by the Jews. The angels, being sent, will gather all people from all the lands of the earth for judgment; they will gather the righteous and the evil and will separate the former from the latter.

Then the participation that the Apostles will take in the judgment was expressed thus by the Lord: "Verily I say unto you, that ye which have followed me, in the regeneration when the Son of man shall sit in the throne of his glory, ye also shall sit upon twelve thrones, judging the twelve tribes of Israel" (Matthew 19:28). Here the Apostles' thrones do not signify their seats but the glory and honor with which they will be dignified specially before all, and they will reign with the Lord and be partakers of glory. The Messiah will judge all, for to Him alone God gave all judgment (John 5:22); but the Lord says that the Apostles also will judge in the same sense as all the faithful, participants in the glory and rule of the Messiah, will also be participants in the judgment of the world, as St. Paul also wrote: "Do ye not know that the saints shall judge the world?" (I Corinthians 6:2).

Here, too, the Apostles' judgment, represented by the Lord, had for its imagery or symbol the judgment of counselors, courtiers, who surrounded earthly kings and helped them in matters relating to judgments. The Twelve Tribes of Israel is a name for the people of God, once chosen and beloved of God; but in the present expression of the Lord, this takes on the meaning of the whole people that are beloved of the Lord and redeemed by Him, namely all Christians, who are under judgment. Thus, the Apostle James (James 1:1), calls all Christians the Twelve Tribes.

Paradise will bring forth its heavenly dwellers to the place of judgment: the souls of the righteous; while Hades will bring forth its dead: the souls of sinners; and there will follow the joining of the souls with their bodies. Then, the fateful sentence will be pronounced to the righteous and the sinners, and each will receive his full recompense for the deeds of his earthly life.

The unbelievers, as not having accepted redemption, will, at the dread, universal judgment seat of Christ, be condemned to a deprivation of eternal, blissful life in Christ; and with them also, the believers and the baptized who led an earthly life contrary to the law of Christ. At the time of the last judgment all will arise, without exception, who ever lived, and they will be subjected to the last judgment, as attested by the words "They shall look upon Him, Whom they pierced" (Zacharias[72] 12:10). All those who arise shall look upon Him, among them also those who crucified the Lord Jesus Christ, which means that the unbelievers will be at the judgment, all the believers and the unbelievers: in short, all humanity. Not only people will stand before judgment, but also the evil fallen spirits whom, according to the Apostle's witness, "God spared not [the angels that sinned], but ... delivered them into chains of darkness, to be reserved unto judgment" (II Peter 2:4). The Apostle Jude also writes: "And the angels which kept not their first estate, but left their own habitation, he hath reserved in everlasting chains under darkness unto the judgment of the great day" (Jude 1:6).

Since man consists of spirit, soul, and body, therefore the visible, outward life and activity of man is nothing else than an expression, a manifestation of the life and activity of the soul. Thoughts, desires, feelings—these are objects of the immaterial world and constitute the invisible activity of the unseen soul, and, when expressed by words and actions, they make up the visible activity of the body as the organ of the soul: the activity of a person. And so, at the judgment, both the inner, spiritual and the outward, bodily activity of a man will be judged. According to the dual nature of man and his dual activity which will be judged

---

[72]Spelled *Zechariah* in the King James Bible.

at the universal judgment, there will follow both dual reward and dual punishment: spiritual and inward for the soul and outward, palpable, corresponding to the new body of man.

Every person will, at the last judgment, give a strict and very full answer for all thoughts, desires, feelings, words, and deeds, for all his earthly life. Of course, sinful thoughts, desires, feelings, thoughts, and words will not be brought to mind at the judgment if in due time on earth they have been washed by true repentance.

The soul's activity is manifested in man's outward activity, in his words and deeds, so that words and deeds always reliably characterize the soul's moral state, good or bad. The very name given by the Saviour to the word "idle" (uncharacteristic, inappropriate, unbecoming to Christian activity) will be judged on Doomsday: "But I say unto you, that every idle[73] word that men shall speak, they shall give account thereof in the day of judgment" (Matthew 12:36). Words are expressions of man's thoughts and feelings and in general of his inner, moral condition; through them a person is known, as a tree is from its fruits. If a man's words are just, honorable, pious, edifying they show a good person, and such a one will receive justification at the judgment; if his words are false, wicked, they are indicative of a man's evil heart, and such a person cannot be justified, but will be fall under condemnation. Justification or condemnation at the judgment depends on faith and deeds, while words only signify the inner, moral state of the soul. An idle word is such as contains a lie, slander, evokes indecent laughter, a disgraceful, shameless, empty word, one with no relation to the matter at hand.

St. Paul writes concerning the invisible, secret activity of the mind as follows: "Therefore judge nothing before the time, until the Lord come, who both will bring to light the hidden things of darkness, and will make manifest the counsels of the hearts: and then shall every man have praise of God" (I Corinthians 4:5). Of these Apostolic words, Chrysostom writes: "For He is the Judge not only of works, but He also brings forth into the midst those things which are unknown." And so, at the judgment everyone will give the most strict and full account of all his activity, be it internal and spiritual (Matthew 12:36) or visible and external, that is, for every word and deed the Lord will recompense each one (Romans 2:6; II Corinthians 5:10).

[73]The word in the Greek New Testament is argós, which means "unemployed, idle, with nothing to do; neglectful, careless: a careless word, which, because of its worthlessness, had better been left unspoken" [compare A Greek-English Lexicon of the New Testament and Other Early Christian Literature, University of Chicago Press 1957, p. 104].

At the last judgment in full view of all the moral, spiritual realm of spirits and souls there will unfold the entire life, earthly activity, of each soul, both good and evil activity; not one hidden thought, not one sigh or glance, nor yet the least bodily action will be concealed. Every right and every wrong that was not cleansed in due time by proper repentance, everything will be seen by all, by the angels and the Saints and all people. It is not without reason, says John Chrysostom, that for such a long time there is no judgment; it is not without purpose that the general, final judgment of humanity is so long postponed; time has been given for intercession for one another before God. But with the arrival of the decisive hour for the fate of mankind, this intercession will be broken off; then, neither prayer, nor petition, nor friendship, nor kinship, nor tears, nor good intentions and desires, nor virtue will help us. At that fateful hour neither the prayers of sinners to the Saints nor the prayers of the Saints to God for the pardon of sinners will be effective. The prayers of the Saints will not help the condemned; nor will the intercession of a father lighten the lot of a condemned son, nor will the tears of children free their unfortunate parents from eternal torment; neither will the husband help his careless wife, nor the wife her husband. Indeed, even love for the truth will not permit intercession for those that have forever rejected the truth; it would be contrary to nature to ask for the kingdom of heaven for one who had absolutely no desire for it, and who therefore has no affinity for a life full of peace and love, no affinity for the life of the Saints. Then love, kinship, friendship, acquaintance will lose their significance for souls that hated them; and every relationship between souls that love truth and righteousness with those hostile to these qualities will forever vanish; and the memory of sinners will be consumed without any influence on the state of the souls of the Saints, those that have been well-pleasing to their Lord.

At the dread judgment, when every secret is revealed, all, both the righteous and the sinners, will see and recognize one another. The sinners, who in Hades up to this time see the Saints in paradise but do not see one another, now will see and recognize each other, as Athanasius the Great writes in his *Homily on the Departed.* But their encounter will not be a joyous one! Why? Because we ourselves were the cause of eternal damnation, along with those close to us on earth with whom we now must meet. Surely we will not hear gratitude from those close to us when we who remained on earth after them led a life like that of the brethren of the unfortunate rich man in the Gospel?

St. John of Damascus, warning us of such a frightful encounter with our own people on Doomsday, writes: "We must try with all our powers, that on that dread and terrible day our relatives should not reproach us for neglecting them;

especially those of us to whom they entrusted concern for their property and to whom they left it. For let no one think that we shall not know one another at that fearful gathering. The penetrating eye of the mind is the organ of sight and knowledge, as the Lord Jesus Christ Himself bears witness in the parable of the rich man and Lazarus.

True, the rich man while on earth knew Lazarus and saw him, perhaps more than once, and therefore it is not surprising that he recognized him; but how did he recognize Abraham, according to the witness of the Lord Jesus Christ, for he recognized Abraham whom he had never before seen? Thus, we can conclude and attest as truth, that at the judgment all will know one another, both those acquainted and those unacquainted. St. John Chrysostom writes thus of this truth: "We shall recognize not only those with whom we were acquainted here, but also those whom we never saw."

St. Ephrem the Syrian writes: "Then children will rebuke their parents for not having done good works; on that day the unfortunate will see many of their acquaintances, and some, seeing them placed at the right hand, will depart far from them, tearfully taking leave of them."

"Then," says St. Gregory the Theologian, that is, on the day of the general judgment, "I will see thee, my beloved brother Caesarius, bright, glorious, joyous, exactly such as thou hast often appeared to me in dreams."

St. Dimitri of Rostov, addressing a parent who wept over the death of a son and, as it were in consolation, says: "Thou wilt see him (that is, the deceased son) in the grace of God among the righteous, in a place of brightness and coolness."

Thus do all the pastors and teachers of the Church instruct us, that we shall all see one another at the time appointed. Consequently, all humanity will stand before judgment, from the first to the last human being: "And before him shall be gathered all nations" (Matthew 25:32); "He shall judge the quick and the dead" (II Timothy 4:1); "it is he which was ordained of God to be the Judge of quick and dead" (Acts 10:42).

What could be more dreadful and disgraceful than that state of souls when, before the gaze of each, all of our secret and manifest deeds are uncovered, words, thoughts, and desires; when everyone will clearly see all the activity of another? Then, indeed, our love and our hypocrisy, our righteousness and unrighteousness, will be made evident to all. St. John of Damascus says: "This will be a great, heavenly shame, when everyone recognizes one another and will be known to everyone" (*Homily on the Departed*). And then the Lord "shall set the sheep on his right hand, but the goats on the left" (Matthew 25:33), that is, the Lord will separate the righteous from the sinners; then unbelief will cut off father from son, daughter from mother, and spouses must go separate ways forever. Faith will save some, and unbelief will ruin others.

"And he shall separate them one from another, as a shepherd divideth his sheep from the goats: And he shall set the sheep on his right hand, but the goats on the left." Since at the judgment there will be Christians and non-Christians, one part of the judgment is a judgment on Christians, evident from the questions of Jesus Christ and the replies of those under judgment which relate directly to Christians; and this is affirmed by the chosen vessel of the Holy Spirit, the Teacher of the Gentiles, when he says: "We must all (that is, Christians, righteous, as well as sinners) appear before the judgment seat of Christ; that every one may receive the things done in his body according to that he hath done, whether it be good or bad" (that is, for his thoughts, desires, feelings, words, and deeds)—a full recompense: either a reward or a punishment (II Corinthians 5:10; Romans 2:6). The other part of the judgment on non-Christians is briefly depicted in the words of Holy Scripture: I Corinthians 6:2; Matthew 19:28. Jesus Christ Himself will bring judgment on the Christians; the faithful will be judged for their deeds, and therefore our works either judge us or justify us. The works of love [charity] and mercy put at the judgment by the Lord before the Christians, as having known His all-holy will, will bring some the kingdom of heaven which was prepared for them before all ages; but a punishment will be declared to others, to those on the left who also knew the will and commandments of God but scorned them—these will go into eternal torment.

All Christian activity, all our mutual relationships, must be based on eternal, divine love. In accordance with the degree of love of Christians, some will be placed on the right hand and others on the left. The right side is more a place of honor than the left and is usually assigned to higher persons, kings, and in general those senior, very close kinfolk, friends, and, according to the word of the Lord Jesus Christ, it is the place for the blessed, the place for all the children of God, the heirs of the kingdom of heaven; while the left is the place of the damned, those cast out, because they themselves willfully cast aside the good things prepared for man in his life beyond the grave.

Then Jesus Christ will turn to those standing at the right side and pronounce the sentence of their eternal lot, indicating the reason for it: Come, ye blessed of My Father, inherit the kingdom that was prepared for you from the foundation of the world, for your good works on earth. They (the works) relate directly to Me because ye did them for My lesser brethren. Ye fed the hungry, gave drink to the thirsty, took in wanderers, gave clothing to those in need of it, visited the sick, and did not forget those in prisons (Matthew 25:34–36). God, Who knows all things, foresaw the actions of people before all time, therefore accordingly determined rewards and punishments for them from before eternity. For good works, life, and the kingdom of heaven; but for evil works, death, eternal torment.

True Christians, as His true followers, Jesus Christ calls His brethren, because they are close to Him in spirit, in inclination, and in sufferings; "For whosoever shall do the will of my Father which is in heaven, the same is my brother, and sister, and mother" (Matthew 12:50). St. Paul also bears witness of this recognition by Jesus Christ of His faithful servants as brethren: "For both he that sanctifieth and they who are sanctified are all of one: for which cause he is not ashamed to call them brethren, saying, I will declare thy name unto my brethren" (Hebrews 2:11–12). The union of the Lord with His true followers is the closest union, the unity of faith, love, spirit, and actions. For this reason, all that we do unto others the Lord relates to Himself and rewards as if for something done unto Himself: "Ye have done it unto Me," or: "He that receiveth you, receiveth Me."

Then He will turn to the Christian sinners who stand on the left side and say: "Depart from Me ye accursed, into the eternal fire prepared for the devil and his angels" (Matthew 25:41), because ye did not have living faith and active love. The Saviour, in His speech to the righteous and the condemned, says nothing more about faith, because faith here is shown by deeds; consequently, the works of faith justify some but condemn others. The works of charity and mercy justify those that stand on the right side of the judgment, but the lack of these works condemns those on the left to eternal fire (Matthew 25:42–46).

The other part of the final judgment consists of judgment on non-Christians, judgment on those not believing in Christ. This judgment the Saviour gives over to the Apostles: "Verily I say unto you, that ye which have followed me, in the regeneration when the Son of man shall sit in the throne of his glory, ye also shall sit upon twelve thrones, judging the twelve tribes of Israel" (Matthew 19:28). How is this judgment to be understood? "The Apostles who were with you, with all the other Jews[74] (of one race)—having received the same education as ye did, brought up under the same laws and according to the same customs, and led the same way of life as ye did—believed in Me, but ye did not. What prevented you from believing in Me also? For this reason they shall

[74]Because of the way it is used in Russian, the word *Iudei* that appears in this passage could be rendered either "Jews" (in general), or else "Judeans" (that is, men of Judea; compare Acts 2:14).

be your judges!" The twelve tribes of Israel—this name of the people of God, the people once chosen and beloved of God—is here used in the sense of all mankind, whom God so loved that He gave His Only-begotten Son, so that everyone that believed in Him might be saved (John 3:16). Israel is beloved, and the whole world also is beloved: humanity, redeemed by the Lord Jesus Christ. But since redemption was made use of only by those who had come to believe, therefore those of the twelve tribes who did not believe correspond to the whole mass of people who do not know their Redeemer. The saved believers will be a clear reproach for the unbelievers; they will be evidence, judgment, and condemnation for their unbelief. "They (that is, the disciples of Christ) will be judges for you (those Jews who did not believe)." "In the rebirth" (see Matthew 19:28; *regeneration*) is understood to mean the future transformation of the world, the restoration of the primeval perfection of the world before the fall of Adam into sin—the restoration, the transformation that is to follow at the end of the world. The disciples of the Lord, the Apostles, in the new life beyond the grave, will reign with Him and be partakers of glory and will judge in the sense that all the faithful are partakers in the glory and lordship of the Messiah and participants in the judgment of the world—especially those persons closest to the Judge, His disciples, and Apostles. This expression uses imagery of the King and Judge Who is surrounded by counselors, fellow judges, helping Him in the work of judgment. Chrysostom understands the judgment of the Apostles in the same sense as Jesus Christ spoke of the judgment by the Queen of the South, of the judgment of the Ninevites (Bishop Mikhail, *Gospel Commentary*, on Matthew 12:42).

On that judgment by the Saints, not only upon unbelievers, but even upon evil spirits, St. Paul teaches thus: "Know ye not that the Saints shall judge the world? And if the world shall be judged by you, are ye unworthy to judge the smallest matters? Know ye not that we shall judge angels, and not only things that pertain to this life?" (I Corinthians 6:3). All the holy Fathers and Doctors of the Church recognized this depiction of the universal judgment as being undoubtedly true.

II) THE END OF THE AGE (OF THE WORLD)

After the universal, solemn, open, strict, dread, decisive, and last judgment over the spiritual-moral beings, at once that very day and moment there will follow the end of the world, the end of the kingdom of grace of Christ on earth, and the beginning of the kingdom of glory, the beginning of the new, blessed life of the righteous and eternal life of torment of the sinners. After the judgment there follows the end of the world, the end of the age. Jesus Christ Himself bore witness to this truth in His parable of the seed: "The harvest is the end of the world; and the reapers are the angels. As therefore the tares are gathered and burned in the fire; so shall it be in the end of this world" (Matthew 13:39–40,49). One should not understand the word end as meaning the destruction of the world; the existence of the world will not end, the world will not be destroyed, but it will only be changed in the way that man is not destroyed, changing only from corruptible to incorruptible, from mortal to immortal. With the change of man, there will follow a change in the whole world, a change in the laws of nature; there will follow a new arrangement of the world, corresponding to the new order that is to come in the kingdom of Christ. The change in the world will come about by fire, according to the witness of the word of God. Thus, the Apostle Peter says: "The heavens and the earth, which are now, by the same Word are kept in store, reserved unto fire against the day of judgment and perdition of ungodly men . . . But the day of the Lord will come as a thief in the night; in the which the heavens shall pass away with a great noise, and the elements shall melt with fervent heat, the earth also and the works that are therein shall be burned up . . . Looking for and hasting unto the coming of the day of God, wherein the heavens being on fire shall be dissolved, and the elements shall melt with fervent heat" (II Peter 3:6–7, 10,12). That sooner or later there will indeed come the end of the age, the end of the world; in this we have the assurance of Divine Revelation and science. Revelation ascribes the change of the world to fire, while science, besides fire, admits also other means that could put an end to the present state of the earth and, consequently, to mankind living on it.

Here are passages from the word of God witnessing the reality of the end of the world. In the Old Testament, the Prophet and King David wrote thus of the end of the world: "Of old, O Lord, hast thou laid the foundation of the earth: and the heavens are the work of thy hands. They shall perish, but thou shalt endure: yea, all of them shall wax old like a garment; as a vesture shalt thou change them, and they shall be changed" (Psalms 101:26–27). Just as nature corresponded favorably to the state of the souls of the first people before their falling, so it came to relate unfavorably to man after his fall: "For the creature was made subject to vanity, not willingly, but by reason of him who hath subjected the same in hope . . . For we know that the whole creation groaneth and travaileth in pain together until now" (Romans 8:20,22); that is, as a result of the fall of man, all creation unwillingly was subjected to the work of corruption and groans and is pained with us, something that was not the case with nature before the fall. After the falling of our first ancestors, according to the words of St. Paul and the Book of

Genesis, one can see that creation was "very good," that in all of spiritual and palpable creation there reigned peace—that is, an accord, a bond, a harmony, joy, bliss. Consequently, all that was created by God was in union, a bond, a mutual relationship, and communion with its Creator, God, and among itself. All was in peace and agreement until man himself—the king of nature—disrupted it. With the fall of man, the bond of all creation was upset, and out of a peaceful agreement there followed a hostile uprising, sown into God's creation by the enemy of peace and love. In the same way also, nature must correspond to the new, spiritual man. All the visible, material world, lying in evil, must be cleansed from the ruinous consequences of human sin and renewed to match the renewed man: "Because the creature itself also shall be delivered from the bondage of corruption into the glorious liberty of the children of God" (Romans 8:21). The renewal of the world will be accomplished on the last day by means of fire, so that in the new heaven and on the new earth there will remain nothing sinful, but there will dwell only righteousness. After the change of man there will at once follow the change in nature as well, and then there will be a new earth and a new heaven, according to the witness of the Creator Himself of heaven and earth, Who made them and is able to change them according to their purpose: "How long shall the world stand?" or: "Till heaven and earth pass, one jot or one tittle shall in no wise pass from the law, till all be fulfilled" (Matthew 5:18). "Behold, I am with you all days until the end of the age," (Matthew 28:20). From all the words of the Lord Jesus Christ Himself one can see that the present heaven and earth will only pass but will not be destroyed; and according to the words of David, like an old garment, they shall be changed into a new one (Psalms 101:26–27), which is confirmed by the Apostle Peter as well when he says, "We, according to his promise, look for new heavens and a new earth, wherein dwelleth righteousness" (II Peter 3:13). St. John the Theologian, indeed, also saw a new heaven and a new earth in the Apocalypse; "For the first heaven and the first earth were passed away" (Revelation 21:1).

Exactly thus did all the Doctors of the Church teach about the end of the world. St. Irenaeus:[75] "It is not the essence or the substance of creation that will be abolished (for He that made it is true and mighty), but rather the image of this world will pass away, that is, that in which the disruption took place . . . And when this image passes away and man is renewed and rises for incorruption, then there will appear the new heaven and new earth."

---

[75]St. Irenaeus of Lyons, circa 125–202 A.D., was a native of Asia Minor and a disciple of St. Polycarp, who in turn was a disciple of St. John the Apostle [St. John the Theologian, the Evangelist].

St. Cyril of Jerusalem:[76] "Our Lord Jesus Christ will come from the heavens, will come with glory at the end of this world, on the last day. For there will be an end to this world, and this created world will be renewed. So that this wonderful abode of creatures would not forever remain filled with iniquity, insofar as depravity, theft, and concupiscence and every sort of sin have poured over the earth: "blood toucheth blood" (Hosea 4:2) this world will pass away, so as to appear anew, better . . . The Lord will fold up the heavens, not so as to exterminate them, but so as to reveal them again in a better form. Hear the words of the Prophet David: 'In the beginning, Thou, O Lord, hast laid the foundation of the earth: and the heavens are the work of thy hands. They shall perish, but thou shalt endure' (Psalms 101:26–27). But someone may say, Why does he say definitely, 'They shall perish?' This is evident from what follows: 'Yea, all of them shall wax old like a garment; as a vesture shalt thou change them, and they shall be changed' (Psalms 101:27). For as it is said of man, that he perishes, in one place it is said, 'The righteous perisheth, and no man layeth it to heart' (Isaiah 57:1), while he awaits resurrection; thus equally a certain resurrection awaits heaven too." St. Basil the Great: "A forewarning of the dogmas on the end and change of the world is what we have now been given briefly in the first words of divine teaching: 'In the beginning God created . . .' What begins with time must needs end in time. If it has a temporal beginning, do not doubt the end . . . But they (the learned pagans) did not find one means out of all for understanding God, the Creator of the universe and righteous Judge, Who repays each worthily according to their deeds; nor did they find a way to compass in the mind the thought of the end based on the judgment; because the world must be changed if the state of souls is to pass into another kind of life. For just as the present life has its qualities, native to this world, so also the future existence of our souls will obtain a die, proper to its state."

St. Jerome: "It is clearly shown (Psalms 101:27) that the end and ruin of the world does not mean that it will be turned into nothing, but changed for the better. Equally so, what is written in another place: "The light of the moon shall be as the light of the sun" (Isaiah 30:26), means not the destruction of what was before but a change for the better. Let us reflect on what has been said: the image passes away, but not the essence. St. Peter expresses the same thing; he did not say that we would see a different heaven and earth, but the prior, old ones changed for the better."

---

[76]Circa 315–387 A.D.; a priest in 345 and Patriarch of Jerusalem from 350 till his death; he is noted for his instructions on Christian doctrine, addressed to the catechumens preparing for baptism.

Thus also taught Justin Martyr,[77] Athenagoras,[78] Tatian,[79] Theophilus of Antioch,[80] Minucius Felix,[81] Hippolytus,[82] Methodius,[83] and others. The Fifth Ecumenical Council, refuting various errors of the Origenists, solemnly condemned also their false teaching that the material world "will not only be transformed, but utterly annihilated" (Makary, Archbishop of Kharkov, *Theology*, Volume II, p. 645).

From the hands of the Creator—the source of love—all came forth according to His own witness, "very good," that is, perfect and as splendid as was needful the first time. If all had not been created perfect and splendid, then wherein would the disruption have consisted after the fall of our first ancestors? In God's creation we see a wonderful order in all things and a harmonious arrangement of each thing. Each thing is assigned for a higher or lower service in the realm of nature. In the kingdom of nature, as in the house of a wise and sensible master, all is arranged properly and in good order (I Corinthians 14:40), that is, the lower directly serves the higher, as being subordinated. Inorganic beings for the most part serve the organic, which in turn serve the sensible, and the sensible serve the reason-endowed; which last are intended for solemn, direct, and visible service to God Whom all serve indirectly and directly. As the Holy Spirit gives life to the whole world, and without Him all is dead, consequently, in God's creation, the main composite part is the spiritual and moral world on whose condition the state of the physical world depends. Thus it was in the beginning immediately after the creation. There was unity and agreement in the whole creation—all was "very good." All was subordinated to man, to the spiritual-moral being; all worked for him, and physical nature was in agreement with spiritual-moral nature. Then the earth and heaven, that is, the atmosphere and all its manifestations, were in good relations with man.

Damage came about in spiritual-moral nature, and the consequences of this were reflected at once in all of creation as well, in all visible, physical creation. Concord was disrupted, harmony fell apart, all was brought into a state foreign

---

[77]Justin the Philosopher or Justin Martyr (circa 100–165 A.D.) wrote *Apologies for the Christian Religion* and *Dialogue with the Jew Tryphon.*

[78]Athenagoras, in the second century, wrote an *Apology* on Christian beliefs addressed to the Emperor and later a work *On the Resurrection of the Dead.*

[79]Tatian (circa 160) is best known for his work *Diatessaron.*

[80]Theophilus, Bishop of Antioch (died 181) was an Eastern philosopher who became a Christian as a result of reading the Scriptures with the intent of attacking them.

[81]M. Felix (second or third century) wrote a work called *Octavius.*

[82]Hippolytus (circa 170–236) is best known for his *Refutation of All Heresies.*

[83]Methodius, Bishop of Olympus in Lycia (died 311) is known for his *Banquet of the Ten Virgins, Symposium,* and a treatise on the Resurrection.

to love; all rose up mainly against the culprit of the misfortune, man, from whom the poison spread, as it were, over the whole world changing its blissful state into one that was under the wrath of God. Now "the whole world lieth in wickedness" (I John 5:19), as witnessed by the Word of God as took place after the fall of our ancestors; consequently, before the falling in the moral world, the world did not lie in wickedness, but righteousness dwelt therein. The word of God reveals to us three periods of the existence of the world: 1) before the fall, 2) after the fall, and 3) after restitution. The first state of the world, or the first period of its existence, bears the character expressed by God Himself in which all was "very good." In the fulfillment of the law, as the natural purpose of creation, was its bliss. But the breach of the law placed creation in a state that was not normal for it and therefore contrary to bliss. According to the will of God the Creator, all things served one another, all things depended one upon another, and in the mutual relationship there was bliss for the whole and the parts; besides love and the fulfillment of the law, there was nothing. All things strove to fulfill their purpose, and in this striving there was life and bliss. There could be no disagreement, because it contradicts the words of God that all "was very good."

God is the Creator among His creation. The spiritual-moral world and the physical must fulfill their purpose, acting mutually on each other as they make up one, multipartite whole. The law of action is definite—fulfillment of the will of the Maker, achievement of the goal of one's purpose, striving towards perfection.

The representatives of God's works or of all His creation are the spiritual-moral beings: spirits and souls, angels and people, the family of the One Father, the kingdom of the One King; they live and were made for one goal: having one and the same law and one nature. Oneness of mind united the angels and our first ancestors and was to have united all humanity, if only the falling had not occurred. Man, mystically joined together out of a soul and body, definitely comprised only one whole; soul and body had a joyous effect on each other. This truth is revealed of itself in the present state of man, in which the spirit rises up against the body and the body against the spirit, and according to the word of Jesus Christ: "the spirit indeed is willing, but the flesh is weak" (Matthew 26:41); this is natural for the present state of the world and of man; therefore, this was not natural for the primal state of the world and man when all was "very good." If even now there is an obvious bond, a harmony or, as it were, a sympathy of visible and invisible nature between moral and physical nature—a mutual relationship and a mutual influence of one nature on the other—how can one not admit of a joyous, mutual effect of these natures on each other before the appearance of evil on earth; if now, when all sighs and is infirm, we see a beneficial relationship of bright sunny weather on the spiritual state of man and at the same time on his visible nature, the body. In sunny weather, they say, the soul is somehow more joyous, happier, and at the same time the body too enters a more active state; some gladness is reflected in the soul and body. And, conversely, overcast, foggy, rainy weather has a negative effect on the soul and body: the soul is somehow sad, depressed, disposing the body as well to inactivity. In short, good weather has a positive, joyful effect on the whole human system, while bad weather has the opposite effect: the soul is sad and the body lacks energy. Both the sick and the healthy, contrary to their will or desire, sympathize with the weather, the atmospheric conditions. A surfeited body interferes with the activity of the spirit, while a joyous state of the spirit brings about in the body an eagerness and zeal for labor, so that external activity itself is mixed with a certain unexplainable joy. In this way we can conclude without error from the present state of the world and man, with the support of Divine Revelation as well, that in the first period of the existence of the world "all was very good"; we come to a conclusion on the wonderful harmony of all parts of God's creation where alone is bliss possible. And so, the purpose of all that God has made, with man as its crown, is a purpose of bliss, of striving towards perfection, eternal life. But where is eternal life? It is in the kingdom of God, the Lord Jesus Christ, life in all His creation, the life of the whole world; life in paradise on earth, where all breathes agreement, bliss, where all serve each other with love and joy, where heaven and earth, that is, the earth with its atmosphere, the sky, in a bond and harmony with the spiritual-moral world (with the first ancestors), or physical nature in union with spiritual nature, as in man: the body with the soul. This is the first period of the world's existence in its innocent, sinless, blessed state with the character and distinguishing quality to which the Lord Jesus Christ bears witness: "all was very good." In the concept of "good" there is no "evil." But did this first period of the world's existence continue long? That is, was it long in its blissful state, and what was the measure and degree of bliss? The word of God has not revealed this. The breach of the law of God, of the moral law, was not followed by the destruction of the guilty ones and of the world but by a most just punishment. There followed punishment and not destruction, of that which was to exist forever. Punishment is not destruction, the ceasing of existence.

On the other hand, from the character of the second period there is revealed only that the bliss of the first period is lost; and evil, which was completely lacking in the first period, now is dominant in the world to the extent that good itself does not remain without an admixture of evil: "the whole world lieth in wickedness"! Here is the character or distinguishing quality of the second period of the world's existence. With the fall of our first ancestors, all visible nature at once changed in its qualities: 1) the body rose up against the spirit, 2) the earth changed its fertility, and with the change in the qualities of the earth which fell not under a blessing but a curse, the atmosphere also changed, heaven and earth changed, the beasts took arm against their former king, and so on. The second state of the world, or the second period of its existence, also has its distinctive character opposite to the first, as stated in Holy Scripture: "the whole world lieth in wickedness." Life, once given to the world, was not taken away, but life with bliss or blessed life changed to a life of weeping and sorrow. That which had constituted bliss was taken away for the breach of the law, just as we often fall into illness by ruining our health willfully. The spiritual-moral and physical natures of man are closely joined with each other, making up a spiritualized flesh or an incarnate spirit. But now it is not as before; now, according to the words of the Apostle Paul, the parts of man have risen up against each other; the spirit wages war on the flesh and the flesh against the spirit; and man often does not do what he wants but what he hates, fulfilling the will, the desire of the body, and subjecting the spirit to it. As the two natures in man have an effect on each other, so also the physical world is bound in harmony and a mutual relationship with the spiritual-moral world, that is, with its beings which are enlivened by one and the same Holy Spirit Who gives life to the whole world. The changes in the moral world did not remain without effect towards the visible, physical world. At the time of the suffering of the God-Man, the earth was shaken, the veil of the temple was rent in two, the stones fell apart, the sun was darkened, and many dead arose. The disordering of the moral world reached its limit and was reflected in visible, physical nature, in the worldwide flood, according to the witness of the word of God. With the falling of our first ancestors, there began the second period of the world's existence, with a disruption in the moral world (disobedience to God the Creator), and then changes came to follow more and more in physical nature which finally came to their completion in a worldwide event—the flood—which finally changed both the earth and the sky, that is, the atmosphere. After the flood, the former heaven and earth were no more; the water changed the earth, and the earth, always in relationship to the atmosphere, brought about a change in the heaven, the sky, and there appeared, according to the word of the Apostle, "the present heavens and earth": the state of the world lying in wickedness, alien to righteousness, concerning which one cannot say that the present heaven and earth are "very good," for the earth is deprived of a blessing, is accursed, and with the earth all the elements of the air are hostile. Man's life was very, very significantly shortened as opposed to the first period, and the conditions of life themselves were worsened. This is the second period of the world's existence in which heaven (the atmosphere) and earth, called "the present" by St. Paul, have been changed; this nomenclature is confirmed by the very fact that the heaven and earth of this time are not those that were before the flood. The word "present" corresponds to this present time; therefore, for the future or to express the transformed world to come, we find the word "new," both heaven and earth, according to the witness of St. Paul and St. Peter. And finally, there will be a third state of the world, or a third period of its existence, where all is new: man, and heaven, and earth, and where only righteousness abides, according to the witness of the Apostle Peter. And so, in the third period of the existence of the world, there will again be a new heaven and a new earth, different from the present ones. The heaven and earth that exist now will not be destroyed but will be changed into new ones by means of fire, as the first period of the world's and man's existence gave way to the second, by means of water. Water and fire have an important, mystical significance in religion in general. As gold is cleansed from outside admixtures by fire, so also the world (heaven and earth, that is, the earth with its atmosphere) must be purified from the evil in which they lie by means of fire, according to Apostolic witness. Then once more for the new, renovated man, there will be a new heaven and a new earth in which only righteousness shall dwell, and to the restored world and man once again it will be possible to apply the expression "very good." It cannot be otherwise.

To reconcile faith with science is, it seems, the direct purpose of contemporary knowledge. If every science is a systematic exposition of the truths relating to some subject, then it goes without saying that these truths obtained by science must be in agreement with the revealed truths made known to man by the Truth Himself, as the word of God bears witness: "I am the Truth, and without Me ye can do nothing"; consequently, without revealed truths, a correct scientific improvement is impossible. Only in the present time have revealed truths begun to be confirmed by modern knowledge and to come into agreement with science. The Apostles Peter and John the Theologian bear witness to us of the third period of the world's existence of the changed, new earth and heaven; and the study of the shape of the universe (science) admits this truth, that dead worlds—and therefore our planet also—can begin life again; and if they begin to live, this means to become the habitation of beings. The Word of

God does not speak of the death, the annihilation of the earth, but bears witness only to its being changed, as will be the case with the people living on it at the moment of the end of the world; that is, all will die and then at once be resurrected in a new, better form with all those who died before, and together the earth also will be changed. Science sees a cause that can call back the bodies of dead worlds to life. The collision of bodies can awaken life. All beliefs and good sense bear witness to man of the beginning and end of the world; and this belief, common to humanity, belongs to mankind at all levels of development; thus, for example, the belief of the Chinese on the end of the world consists in the following: a certain Feso, who first discovered salt in China, in time came to be recognized by them as a deity. Feso is to come to earth only to proclaim the end of the world. In the most ancient Greek mythology, there is a prophecy in one of the myths or, as it were, an indication of the dogma of the end of the world and of its transformation by means of fire: "With the victory of good over evil, of light over darkness, there will follow the end of this world, and for future life, this world will be transformed into a better one by means of fire, that is, the old world will burn" (*Writings of the Holy Fathers,* 1881, Book Four, p. 436). Concerning the end of the world which is to come sooner or later, not in the sense of ceasing, annihilation, but only of its transformation into a better world and specifically by means of fire, Heraclitus[84] taught five hundred years before Christ. He said outright that the world, carrying out eternal and endless circuits, finally will join the beginning—which in his teaching is primeval fire—and will burn, but will not be annihilated, but changed, for out of the ashes there will come about a new world. Democritus,[85] the creator of the first mechanical philosophy, taught: "If worlds can arise, then they can disappear"; but disappear not in the sense of ceasing to exist, as Democritus himself taught that "nothing that exists can be destroyed," and that means it can only change its form, appearance, its old existence for a new one.

Science says that our planet earth has many ways it can be destroyed, and the most likely of all is the fire that fills the inside of the earthly sphere. That the world will be destroyed by fire, this teaching came down to us from the ancient Jews and is the teaching of the Christian Church and of all her teachers and writers. The possibility of the world ending through fire is recognized by science as a view worthy of acceptance. It is known that every one hundred feet into the

[84]Heraclitus, of Ephesus, was a philosopher of the Ionian school. He considered fire to be the primary form of all matter.

[85]Democritus [460–361 B.C.] was born at Abdera in Thrace and was the founder of the "atomic theory."

earth, the temperature[86] rises one degree, so that at two and one quarter versts[87] (1.5 miles/2.4 kilometers) deep the temperature would be eighty degrees, at which water boils, while at a depth of twenty versts (13.25 miles/21.34 kilometers), the heat would reach eight hundred degrees, at which all mineral bodies turn into steam. What must the heat be at the center or at the very heart of the earthly sphere which is at a depth of six thousand versts (3977 miles/6402 kilometers) from the surface? Indeed, one can almost certainly suppose that the surface of the globe on which we build our cities and homes is no more than fifteen versts (10 miles/16 kilometers) thick, and that beyond this thin layer all minerals are in a melted form. On the other hand, it has been proven that this thin surface of the earthly sphere is constantly fluctuating, and that thirty hours do not go by without some greater or lesser earthquake. We, therefore, live on the thinnest float which at any moment could go to the bottom (Flammarion, *History of the Heavens*, p. 520), that is, into the abyss of fire!

Section IV

1. The Second Period of Life Beyond the Grave

a) Definition of the Second Period of Life in Paradise — Description of the Habitation of the Saints in the Second Period — Degrees of Bliss — Bliss of the Soul and Body — Perfect, Complete, Inward, and Outward Bliss — Distinctive Character of the Second Period of Life in Paradise

After the souls have been joined with their risen bodies and after the conclusion of the general judgment, there will come the second period of unending life beyond the grave, not only of the soul, as was the case in the first period, but eternal life of the full man consisting of soul and body. The second period of life beyond the grave reveals to us two states of souls, the saved and the condemned souls joined to their risen bodies for eternal life or for eternal death. The second period of life beyond the grave is the further and endless development of the moral state of the soul, either good or evil, which the soul acquired while yet on earth and with which it passed over into the world beyond the grave. That which the soul made its own while on earth determines both the character of

---

[86]Given here, not in Fahrenheit or Centigrade, but on the old *Réaumur* scale, where water freezes at o degrees and boils at 80 degrees.

[87]A *verst* is a traditional Russian distance measurement equal to .6629 miles or 1.067 kilometers.

life beyond the grave and the place where it remains, a place whose nature and all that surrounds it must correspond to the nature of the soul and its acquired qualities that make up its life on earth. As a life it will be eternal with its peculiar character of good or evil.

The concept of eternity is inseparable from the concept of eternal life. If life consists in development, then development can only cease with the ceasing of life. But since life is eternal, development is eternal: a development that never ceases, either of good or of evil. Consequently, life in paradise consists of eternal development of good alone. The object of the activity of the mind, will, and heart is good, truth, God.

After the completion of God's just judgment which is to be over the whole man (consisting once again of spirit, soul, and body), there will begin the eternal existence of the complete man whose image we see in our resurrected Lord Jesus Christ with His flesh and bones. Then our body too, which is now perishable, will after resurrection also consist of such flesh and bones as those of the New Adam, our Lord Jesus Christ.

To the innocent, blessed state of our first ancestors before their fall there corresponded the natural habitat that surrounded them (that is, earth). For the place where they lived—paradise—was on earth. Nothing disrupted their bliss; nothing will disrupt the bliss of the saved in the kingdom of heaven in the second period on the renewed and changed earth, since that evil in which the whole world lies will be exterminated, and the enemy will be incarcerated with the sinners in Gehenna. Everywhere that righteousness, peace, and joy prevail there is the kingdom of heaven which has no boundaries, just as God is unbounded, everywhere present. In Christ's kingdom of grace the earth was the habitation of Christians, so there is no doubt that in this very kingdom of Christ (II Peter 1:11; II Timothy 4:18; Revelation 1:9)—the renewed earth with the Christians and all the angels in heaven which constitute His own kingdom in the realm of glory—according to the witness of the Apostles Peter and John the Theologian, there will no longer be the former heaven and earth, but the new, where God reigns with His angels and Saints and where there is no longer anything but righteousness, peace, and joy as it was in the beginning before the fall of Adam and Eve. And so, if it was possible for there to be a blessed habitation for the first people in paradise on earth, then it is possible for there to be a habitation on earth for the saved in the new, unending age—the more so as the present heaven and earth with all their beauty are taken even by the word of God as an image, a likeness, a symbol of the coming, future joys of life in the kingdom of glory. Indeed, the very body of our first ancestors, taken from the earth and made spiritual, was intended for eternal life on earth with its soul; and paradise, the blessed abode of the sinless ancestors, was spiritual for the soul and palpable for the fine, light body. As man was created for eternity in both body and soul, just so his first and last eternal habitation—earth, paradise—was created for eternity. What happened with the soul and body of Adam and Eve after the fall, this same change followed in their habitat also: the paradise of sweetness turned into a land of labor and weeping, and the same beasts that had been mild and obedient became fierce, frightful, hostile towards man. With a moral change in man there followed a change of everything. Consequently, with the restoration of the primeval man, there will follow also the restoration of all of damaged nature, and the new man will be on a new earth under a new heaven in the kingdom of glory, of which we spoke earlier in the section on the end of the world.

Let us close our discussion with the words of Chrysostom that little spiritual benefit would be gained by knowing the exact place in the cosmos where the righteous will live an unending life: on the present earth or on some other planet or in some other place in the universe—a place so beautiful that we cannot imagine anything like it. It is enough for the Christian to know that there indeed is such a place, and he can see a shade of it within himself; but as to where exactly such a place is located, the answer to this question goes beyond the bounds of human knowledge, and therefore it does not constitute something needful for salvation. Knowledge has its bounds beyond which the mind of man is not yet able to pass. We will not seek the location of the kingdom of heaven—this is no obligation of ours—but we shall try to fulfill the law, the obligation of a Christian: first of all to seek the kingdom of God and His righteousness, that is, to try with all one's powers to gain, to deserve, to receive the kingdom of heaven regardless of where it might be. It is also within us and outside of us. It is in the sky, it is on earth, it is everywhere that God is. "He that abides in love, abides in God, and God abides in him." This is the teaching of the Christian Church on the location of the kingdom of God in the cosmos.

In the kingdom of heaven there is neither sun, nor moon, nor yet stars; the kingdom is lighted by the glory of God (Revelation 21:11), and the only universal luminary is the Lord Jesus Christ (verse 23). There neither the heat of the sun (Revelation 7:16), nor frosts, nor storms, nor bad weather, nor hunger, nor thirst, nor the darkness of night are to be felt (Revelation 22:5); in that place there is no dejection, no sorrow, no sadness, no moaning, no pining away, no temptations; there is no fear, nor despair, nor separation from those close to one, nor death. In that place there will be an eternal, unclouded day, ever-flowering, lightened by the Lord God Himself (verse 5); there the heaven and earth will be *new* (Revelation 21:1); there the kingdom of immortal and blessed life is, and this life is supported by the waters of life and the tree of life (22:1–2). The tree of life is the Lord Jesus Christ, and the waters of life are the inexhaustible abundance of the priceless and countless gifts of the Holy Spirit. With the assistance of such almighty means, the souls of the righteous will be made worthy of seeing the face of God (verse 4), on which, as its main source, depends all bliss, both internal and external. The kingdom of grace will end, and the kingdom of glory will begin, in which the righteous will inherit the kingdom prepared for them from the foundation of the world (Matthew 25:34), where human reason, neither subject to mistakes nor falling into error, will clearly see eternal truths and delight in knowing them; the will, not inclining to the stubborn paths of vice, will feel the highest enjoyment in complete submission to the will of God, the desires of the heart will be completely satisfied by the perception of the glory of God; the vision will delight in seeing our Saviour Jesus Christ face to face, as He is (I John 3:2; I Corinthians 13:12); the hearing will not cease to enjoy the singing of angelic choirs; the sense of smell will inhale ineffable sweet scents; the taste will have full pleasure; thus, everyone found worthy to inherit the heavenly kingdom will constantly feel every sort of delight in his state, as if immersed in uninterrupted joys and wonderful delights *(Homilies and Talks of Anatoly*, p. 246).

St. John Chrysostom writes thus of the new, blessed life of the righteous in the second period: "Picture such a life insofar as it can be pictured, for there is no word to depict it adequately; only from what we hear, as if from puzzles, can we get a certain vague conception of it. Disease, as [the Scriptures] say, has fled, along with sadness and sighing (Isaiah 35:10). What could be more blissful than such a life? There is no need there to fear poverty, nor sickness; there is no offender to be seen there and none aggrieved; nor is there any that irritates or anyone irritated; no one envies or burns with vile passion; nor is anyone tormented by concern for obtaining that which is needful for life or troubled over authorities and those in power; for all the storm of our passions will have quieted and ceased, and all will be in peace, happiness, and joy; all will be calm, in day and clarity and light; not this light that is now, but another, as many times brighter than this, as the light of the sun is brighter than that of a candle; for the light there will not be darkened by nightfall nor by the gathering of clouds; it will not cause heat or burns to bodies; for no night will be there, nor evening, nor cold, nor heat, or any other change of weather; but another state, such as only those worthy of it will know. There is no old age there nor those things that accompany age; but all that is subject to corruption is driven out, because everywhere incorrupt glory is dominant. But what is most important is uninterrupted enjoyment in association with Christ, together with the angels, archangels, with the higher powers. Now look at the heaven and pass mentally over to what is above it: imagine all creation transformed; for it will not remain as it is, but will be far more splendid and bright; and as much as gold is brighter than pewter, so will the situation then be better than now, as St. Paul says: "Because the creature itself also shall be delivered from the bondage of corruption" (Romans 8:21). Now it suffers much, partaking of corruption, and it is characteristic for such bodies to suffer in this manner; but then, having divested itself of all this, will present us with incorrupt splendor. Since it will receive incorrupt bodies, therefore it will itself be transformed for the better. There will be no troubles and battle then; for there will be a great harmony in the choir of Saints, because of the uninterrupted, mutual oneness of mind among them. It will not be needful there to fear either the devil or demonic snares, nor the threat of Gehenna, nor death—the present death or the other, which is more fearful than this—but every such kind of terror will have been ended."

To the bliss of the Saints in the kingdom of heaven there will be added this also that their virtues in this life—their faith, mercy, love for truth—will flower in the kingdom of eternal love, eternal truth, and eternal good. In the Revelation it is said that the deeds of the righteous will follow them into the kingdom of heaven: "Blessed are the dead which die in the Lord from henceforth: Yea, saith the Spirit, that they may rest from their labours; and their works do follow them" (Revelation 14:13). All their virtuous and devout feelings, strivings, and purposefulness, marked in this world by holy works, will remain inseparable from their souls in the other world. In the world here, how many sweet feelings do those that live in God experience from the fruits of the spirit which, according to St. Paul's enumeration, are: "love, joy, peace, longsuffering, gentleness, goodness, faith, meekness, temperance" (Galatians 5:22–23). These very fruits of the spirit will enter with the souls of the Saints into the kingdom of heaven and, of course, will obtain new perfection and redouble the bliss of the Saints.

The bliss of the righteous in paradise in the second period will be bliss for both the soul and body. They will delight, rejoice in both soul and body, as witnessed by the Prophet Isaiah in saying: "in their land they shall possess a double portion" (Isaiah 61:7), that is, then they will rejoice in the glory of both soul and body. Besides the spirit, man after the resurrection of his body will have two natures: the soul and the new, fine body. And since the spirit, soul, and body took part in man's works, therefore, according to the teaching of St. Paul, "every one [shall] receive the things done in his body, according to that he hath done, whether it be good or bad" (II Corinthians 5:10), that is, the reward beyond the grave must be for both soul and body, a spiritual bliss, inward and outward, corresponding to the new, fine, ethereal body. This external, so to say, palpable bliss consists of: 1) the nature of paradise, the like of whose beauty the soul never saw or heard anywhere and therefore cannot imagine, as witnessed by St. Paul, and 2) the society of the holy angels and of the holy souls.

The teaching of our Lord Jesus Christ about heavenly bliss is as follows: "In the house of My heavenly Father there are many mansions" (John 14:2). These words of the Lord should not be construed as indicating various degrees of bliss in heaven. As Archimandrite Michael writes in his Gospel commentary on this passage, they signify only the great number of habitations, the extensive space, which has room for much. The teaching of Jesus Christ on various degrees of bliss is based on other words of His: "Her sins, which are many, are forgiven; for she loved much: but to whom little is forgiven, the same loveth little" (Luke 7:47). Here is witness of a reward but not in the same degree: "For the Son of man shall come in the glory of his Father with his angels; and then he shall reward every man according to his works" (Matthew 16:27). Just as works differ, so the rewards are different, and as the same virtue (good works) can be in greater or lesser degree, so one and the same reward will have various degrees: "He that receiveth you receiveth me, and he that receiveth me receiveth him that sent me. He that receiveth a prophet in the name of a prophet shall receive a prophet's reward; and he that receiveth a righteous man in the name of a righteous man shall receive a righteous man's reward. And whosoever shall give to drink unto one of these little ones, a cup of cold water only in the name of a disciple, verily I say unto you, he shall in no wise lose his reward" (Matthew 10:40–42). And the parable of the talents (Luke 19:17–20) bears witness of the degrees of bliss. All receive a reward but not in equal degree. St. Paul writes of the same: "All flesh is not the same flesh: but there is one kind of flesh of men, another flesh of beasts, another of fishes, and another of birds. There are also celestial bodies and bodies terrestrial: but the glory of the celestial is one, and the glory of the terrestrial is another. There is one glory of the sun, and another glory of the moon, and another glory of the stars: for one star differeth from another star in glory. So also is the resurrection of the dead" (I Corinthians 15:39–42). Of the varied recompenses he writes also in another place: God will reward each according to his works (Revelation 22:12).

In bliss and also in torment both the soul and body take part. The Apostle compares the blissful state of the bodies of the righteous with bright stars. And since he says that the stars themselves do not have an equally bright light, he then concludes that there will be varied degrees of bliss for the righteous. All the various features in which Holy Scripture represents the future bliss of the righteous may be summed up in two main forms: inner bliss found within oneself and outer bliss from the various relationships of beings both spiritual and bodily. From the union of these two forms of bliss there is formed a full, perfect bliss.

Man, as a being with mental powers, moral, with self-knowledge, acting independently, opens within himself the beginning of his bliss. His nature is so constituted that he must find within himself the sources of pleasure, and in certain circumstances he cannot feel bliss; for in the whole makeup of creation he is only the smallest part, and other beings, both spiritual and physical, can and do have various relationships to him which, depending on whether or not they are in agreement with the direction of his own abilities and inclinations, may decrease or increase his inner pleasure; therefore man's full bliss will be when he feels inner delight and when from without he feels a pleasant attitude of other beings towards him. The word of God assigns both these forms of bliss in the highest degree after death to those who try here to obtain the right to them by purity of life and the holiness of their actions. They will enjoy inward bliss, for they will recognize and feel within themselves a high perfection and a superb mutual agreement of the active spiritual and mental faculties. They will enjoy outward bliss for they will be in the most pleasant and harmonious relationship with the other beings that surround them.

Man is made up of a soul and a body which is a permanent and inalienable inheritance of the soul, a necessary part of man, without which he would not be man. He that created man and intended him for bliss made him of soul and body; consequently, both for the fullness of his existence and for the fullness of his bliss, it is necessary that the body always exist together with the soul. Thus it was arranged in the beginning; man was immortal in the soul, and he was not mortal as to his body and his palpable part as intended by the Creator should in no wise have been subject to corruption, but gradually being perfected and refined, together with the perfection of the soul it was to have ascended, so to say, unto spiritualization. Only sin, poured out from the soul, harmed the essence of the body, so that it was made subject to corruption and ruin. However, the power of divine purpose for the body remained unchanged even in its present state of corruption. For despite all the change that it experiences constantly from the effect of various outward influences on it, despite all the effect of the power of death, as revealed in illnesses and weaknesses, in the depth of its being it always retains the imperceptible seed of immortality which develops and unfolds all the more as the present state of the body weakens and is corrupted. From this seed, together with this mortal frame, when it is put into the ground, at a certain time there will rise up a new body for the man. In speaking of the connection of this life with that to come, which is nothing other than a continuation of the present life, one must note the truth that the moral state of man has a corresponding state beyond the grave, either good or evil. A good mental outlook on earth has a corresponding state beyond the grave—one in paradise—a state of righteousness, peace, and joy. Such a state of the soul on earth, walking in the fear of God and according to His commandments, is the state that Jesus Christ Himself calls a state of moral resurrection. The soul is alive and will not die forever, and the visible death of the body is only a passing over by the soul into the state of blissful life. This is why all virtues fill the soul with a certain joy that is not of this world; the soul tastes in advance that which is prepared for those that love and fear God. On the other hand, all vices put the soul in a state not natural for it, a state of embitterment, of despair.

In general, the life of the soul consists in consciousness. According to the teaching of the word of God, the life of the soul consists primarily in a true, full awareness of its Creator, the source of life, of the One God in Trinity. This knowledge, joining man with God, constitutes eternal life, as the Lord Jesus Christ Himself teaches concerning this: "He that believeth in Me shall not die, but will live forever." The Lord Himself gave this definition of eternal life: "And this is life eternal, that they might know thee the only true God, and Jesus Christ, whom thou hast sent" (John 17:3). Eternal life consists in the knowledge of the heavenly Father as the One True God and in knowledge of Jesus Christ, or the Messiah, Whom He sent. True knowledge, based on faith, living, and active knowledge, and not only a cold and reasoning knowledge, embraces all the soul's abilities. Knowledge joined with faith obtains for those that know or those that believe the redemptive merits of the Saviour sent by the only true God. For this reason, such knowledge is life eternal, for it places man in a spiritual union with the source of eternal life—God and Christ (Archimandrite Michael, *Gospel Commentary on John 17:3*). Here is to be understood the knowledge of God and not merely scientific or theoretical but primarily the practical knowledge of God expressed in deeds. The content of the awareness or life of the soul as a life that constantly develops further and further is 1) love towards God, 2) perception of Him, 3) knowledge of Him, 4) experience of Him, and 5) glorification of Him on earth; for this is the life of the soul, as well as beyond the grave where life is nothing else than the further development of awareness of those very parts of life without which life is not life but death.

While still on earth man begins to live an eternal life. It is on man himself that this life depends, as a fruit of his faith. The believer, the one who has gained knowledge, does not die eternally, for he remains in God and God remains in him.

In Holy Writ, the bliss of the righteous is clearly called "eternal" and specifically:

a) *Eternal life:* "And I give unto them eternal life; and they shall never perish, neither shall any man pluck them out of my hand" (John 10:28; compare 3:16); "I am the resurrection, and the life: he that believeth in me, though he were dead, yet shall he live: And whosoever liveth and believeth in me shall never die" (11:25–26; compare 8:51; I Corinthians 15:26); "And this is the promise that he hath promised us, even eternal life" (I John 2:25; compare Titus 1:2); "And these shall go away into everlasting punishment: but the righteous into life eternal" Matthew 25:46);

b) *The eternal kingdom of Jesus Christ* "For so an entrance shall be ministered unto you abundantly into the everlasting kingdom of our Lord and Saviour Jesus Christ" (II Peter 1:11);

c) *Eternal salvation:* "Though he were a Son, yet learned he obedience by the things which he suffered; And being made perfect, he became the author of eternal salvation unto all them that obey him" (Hebrews 5:8–9);

d) *An eternal inheritance:* (Hebrews 9:15);

e) *Eternal glory:* (I Peter 5:10; II Corinthians 4:17).

The eternal quality of bliss is represented in the following ways:

a) An *everlasting treasure* in heaven (Luke 12:33; Matthew 6:20);

b) A *constant possession* in heaven (Hebrews 10:34);

c) An *incorruptible inheritance,* not perishing (I Peter 1:4);

d) A *crown of glory* that never fades (I Peter 5:4);

e) Always *abiding with Christ* (I Thessalonians 4:17; John 12:26; Romans 8:17–29).

Concerning the bliss of the righteous, all the holy Fathers and Doctors of the Church taught and wrote: Theophilus of Antioch, Ephrem the Syrian, Hilary, Clement of Alexandria, Cyprian, Ambrose, Gregory the Theologian, Basil the Great, and others.

From the concept of God and of the soul there emerges that of an eternity, either of bliss or of torment. Only God alone is eternal as One all-perfect and unchanging; but man, created by Him for eternity—and eternal as to soul and body—undergoes change, constantly moving towards perfection, in which his life consists. Change—further development—is life; consequently, life is unceasing further development, the uninterrupted passing from one mental state to another. Where there is no development, there is no life; since life beyond the grave, be it bliss or torment, is the fruit of earthly life, therefore, according to the laws of life, neither bliss nor torment can stop in their development for so much as a moment. The desires of the soul can never be satisfied; the desires of the soul are replaced with new desires, and this replacement of desires in the eternal existence of the soul constitutes an endless, eternal succession of desires and their gratification beyond the grave, in paradise—for the righteous eternal bliss or the eternity of blessedness—ever further and further developing into a whole eternity; therefore there is not and cannot be any measure, any boundary to bliss or, by the same token, to the torment of sinners. This is the conclusion of good sense based on the characteristics of God and the soul, concerning the eternity of bliss or torment; a conclusion supported also by the word of God and the witness of the holy Fathers and Doctors of the Church.

And so, bliss will constantly grow beyond the grave, constantly increase. Amid development, one moment of an unsatisfied desire is not bliss, which is in agreement with the law of life and with the witness of Divine Revelation as expressed by the holy David: "they will go from strength to strength" (Psalms 88:8). The soul of each righteous person, confirmed in good and holiness, will try without ceasing more and more to come close to God and, therefore, to seek a greater, inner perfection, and this desire of the soul is constantly gratified; otherwise there would be no bliss. The souls of the righteous, growing in perfection, become all the more wise and holy and will approach ever closer and closer to the limitless perfection of God—the Lord Jesus Christ—Whose image and likeness they bear in themselves.

The immortal souls of the righteous alone will inherit the kingdom of heaven and pass into a new eternal state of bliss beyond the grave or simply into a blessed eternity. This state of the righteous beyond the grave is for the most part called eternal life in the word of God, and the righteous will be ever with God and with one another, as the Lord Jesus Christ Himself revealed concerning this, saying that "Many shall come from the east and west and take up their place with Abraham, Isaac, and Jacob in the kingdom of heaven" (Matthew 8:11). This is the divine, heavenly truth about the common life of the righteous in paradise after the dread day of judgment, that is, in the second period of life beyond the grave in paradise in which many from all the lands of the earth will be partakers. The very words of the Lord on life in paradise bear witness that only those faithful to the Lord Jesus Christ, the faithful of all nations, times, and places will dwell in paradise; and not only the Hebrews alone, as the latter thought would be the case. The Hebrews who were contemporary with Jesus Christ pictured the kingdom of the Messiah in earthly terms,[88] and for this reason the Lord represents the kingdom of heaven to them as a feast where, in the Eastern manner, one did not sit but reclined. The Lord depicts the state of bliss in paradise as a wedding feast offered for the joy of those present at the wedding, to make it somewhat easier for their childlike understanding. Thus also in the kingdom of heaven there is nothing sad or sorrowful, but all is filled with spiritual joy and happiness. It is usual to remove from the celebration of a wedding all that can in any way spoil the pleasant festive atmosphere. Hence, one can see the inscrutable splendor of the kingdom of heaven, the concern of God for man, and the endless love of the Creator for His handiwork, providing His creation with perfect happiness. Just as Jesus Christ used symbols such as the Valley of Hinnom[89] or the Babylonian furnace, to make the state of Gehenna understandable for the Hebrews, so also, in order to bring them closer to the conception of bliss in paradise He used symbols—the dinner, the feast, the wedding, and the sun—to whose light the state of the righteous in paradise is compared: "Then the righteous shall shine like the sun in the kingdom of their Father" (Matthew 13:43). Under this image is understood the bliss of the righteous souls in paradise, in the future heavenly kingdom of Christ, or in the kingdom of God the Father to Whom the Son will commit the Kingdom after the universal judgment (I Corinthians 15:28). And—in the kingdom of peace and love—eternal goodwill, friendship, kinship, and perfect unanimity will reign among those who dwell there. Joy in God, the source of all happiness, will overflow in the hearts of the righteous, and there will be eternal joy, not disturbed by anything.

[88]In the Russian, *chuvstvenno,* literally meaning "palpably," "physically."

[89]Otherwise called the "Valley of the Son," or "Children/Sons of Hinnom," rendered "Ennom" or "Onom" in the Greek Septuagint (Joshua 15:8), and spelled *dolina Evnomova* here in the Russian. It was in this valley where there were sacrifices to Moloch, that Ahaz and Manasseh made their children "pass through the fire."

Every stage in life has its horizon of knowledge and its corresponding degree of understanding. Let us close this chapter with the words of St. Paul, that we who are still on earth will know the life in paradise of the first period only in part—we guess as it were; and as to the second period of life beyond the grave, be it in Paradise or Gehenna, we cannot even imagine anything like it. If the earth and all that is earthly was in some way still an image, a likeness, and symbol of the life beyond the grave of the first period, then the second period has nothing like it either on earth or in heaven, which is the forecourt of paradise, of the kingdom of heaven, of the bliss that none can imagine of those yet on earth, nor of those already in heaven. Childhood can never imagine what the life of the adult is or those pleasures, joys, and sorrows that accompany it. This state of adulthood remains a puzzle for the child, and the passage to it takes place gradually.

There is much, very much, that we do not know; we cannot picture or account for the "how, whence, why, whither." For example, we cannot picture or even imagine how two completely different natures, the spirit and the flesh, so closely and inscrutably are joined together in man, so that it can be said without error that the spirit has become incarnate or that the flesh has been given a spirit. Thus, the state of life in paradise with all its fullness cannot be pictured by any perfect mind. Only for the faithful here on earth is it revealed as the first-fruits of the life to come; and as the dawn precedes the day, so those enlightened by the light of Christ's grace are aware that all on earth is only dust, that it is as nothing before what is to be, and that what is most true, good, and splendid on earth is only a barely noteworthy shadow of the bliss that is to come; and only the faithful, and then only sometimes, have a foretaste of it on earth. But even he who was in the third heaven, that is, St. Paul, could not make a full description of the bliss that is prepared from before all ages for the righteous, not only in the second period, but also in the first period of life beyond the grave: "He was caught up into paradise, and heard unspeakable words, which it is not lawful for a man to utter" (II Corinthians 12:4). These apostolic words sketch the characteristics of life in paradise in the first period for us; they give an idea to those still living on earth of how the bliss of the righteous and the beauty of paradise cannot be expressed by one who has seen them, as St. Paul writes of himself who heard and saw all in paradise. What he saw and heard in heaven he cannot convey for lack of words in the language; and even if he conveyed it to those on earth, they would not understand it, just as children do not understand many things. Besides St. Paul, others who were pleasing unto God, for example, St. Andrew the Fool for Christ and others saw this paradise, heaven—the dwelling place of the Saints in the first period—while still on earth. Having seen the habitation of the Saints of the first period, they did not see that of the second period, that dwelling of the Saints whose beauty "Eye hath not seen, nor ear heard, neither have entered into the heart of man, the things which God hath prepared for them that love him" (I Corinthians 2:9) as St. Paul writes, that is, the mind of man cannot even imagine that there is nothing like it either on earth or in heaven and that the Saints themselves have not yet seen or heard—not excluding even himself—what has been prepared by God for those who love Him. This means neither we nor the Saints can picture that bliss that awaits the sons of God, the true Christians—bliss for both soul and body. These last words of the Apostle characterize paradise of the second period and its beauty which he himself could not even imagine.

b) Definition of the Second Period of Life in Gehenna — Life in Gehenna — Eternal Death — Description of the Abodes of the Lost — Gehenna — The Degree and Eternal Quality of Torture — Utter, Complete, Internal, and External Torment — Distinctive Character of Life in Gehenna in the Second Period — The Life of Suicides Beyond the Grave

After God's most righteous judgment, the condemned, having heard their final determination: "Depart from Me ye accursed, into the eternal fire, prepared for the devil and his angels!" will go to the place of their eternal ruin, to the place of eternal punishment—to Gehenna. From this moment, the second period of eternal suffering has come for these unfortunate souls, eternal torment of soul and body, full, utter torture for the sinful human being. The condemned, although they remain together both in the first and second periods, nevertheless are deprived of the possible enjoyment of seeing and knowing one another because the state of the condemned is deprived of even the shadow of joy. The state of Gehenna is utterly deprived of light, and there is moral and spiritual darkness because those who are to inherit it, that is, those who work wickedness (on earth), hate the light (John 3:20).

Unbelief is the reason for man's downfall. The concept of ruin belongs without doubt to the state of souls in Gehenna. This is where those go who seek to please the flesh, the belly, and themselves: "Whose end is destruction, whose God is their belly, and whose glory is in their shame, who mind earthly things" (Philippians 3:19) and "their heart is as hard as stone" (Job 41:15). Consequently, all will be the victims of Gehenna who do not believe in the Lord Jesus Christ, the Son of God, who for us men came down to earth, and as He

Himself taught: "He that hath not faith, will be condemned," and "the unbeliever is already condemned, while yet on earth." The complete separation of
these souls from God serves as the basis of eternal torment—"eternal," for as
science itself bears witness, there is time only on earth, but beyond earth's limits
there is eternity.

In everything without exception in Gehenna we find the opposite of Paradise. As night is the opposite of day, death of life, evil of good, darkness of light,
poverty the opposite of riches, disease of health, and so forth, on the basis of
what St. Paul has told us of Paradise and its splendors, everything that is opposed
to this must relate to Gehenna, to the state that was prepared by God not for
man, but for the devil. There, in Paradise, is reward; here, there is punishment;
there, there is joy; here, there is sorrow, and so on. In short, since man is quite
unable to form a conception of paradise and its bliss, in the same way he also
cannot picture Gehenna and all its horrors. If vice is repulsive and intolerable,
then to what degree must its father—the devil with his minions—be repulsive
and unbearable? What must association with him be like? After denunciation
of the sinners at the righteous judgment, they "will depart unto eternal torment"
so as to taste the fruits of their unbelief, for only active faith in our Redeemer,
the Lord Jesus Christ, can save man.

The state of the condemned soul, according to the teaching of Holy Scripture, is in general called the state of death, the death of the soul, which happens with every soul on earth after falling into sin until arising—the moral
resurrection that takes place with faith and the confessing of this sin; and, in
distinction from the death of the body, the condition of the uncleansed soul
beyond the grave is called the second death (Revelation 21:80), eternal death,
eternal dying.

From the concept of eternity, there follows that of eternal life, the never-
ceasing development either of good or of evil. An unceasing development only
in the direction of evil constitutes the life of those lost to the kingdom of heaven.
The activity of the mind, the will, and the heart is developed only in the direction
of evil, that is, the object of its development is evil. According to the teaching of
the Lord Jesus Christ Himself, this state of the soul is one of eternal weeping, of
the gnashing of teeth, a state of despair, and eternal ruin: "There shall be weeping and gnashing of teeth" (Matthew 8:12; 13:42–50; 22:13; 25:30).

Here is how Chrysostom speaks of the state of rejected souls in the second
period: "When we go there, then even if we show the strongest repentance, we
shall have no benefit from it; but, however much we might gnash our teeth,
however much we might wail and entreat a thousand times over, no one will

cast a droplet to us from the tip of a finger, as we are embraced by flame; on the contrary, we shall hear the same thing as the unfortunate rich man in Hades, that 'a great chasm has been formed between us and you'... We shall gnash our teeth from sufferings and unbearable torments, but no one will help. We shall cry out mightily when the flame catches onto us more and more strongly, but we shall not see anyone except the evil spirits tormented with us and besides a great emptiness. What shall we say of those horrors, which the darkness will bring our souls!"

"What will be the condition," said another of the holy Fathers, "of the body of those who are subjected to unending and unbearable torments there, where the flame is not extinguished, the worm undyingly tortures, the dark and awful depth of hell, the bitter moaning, the unaccustomed outcries, weeping and gnashing of teeth, and no end to the sufferings! From all this there is no more deliverance, there are no ways, no possibility of escaping the bitter torments" (Archbishop Makary of Kharkov, *Theology*, p. 659).

The state of the soul or life in Gehenna, opposite to the state of souls or life in Paradise, can be known exclusively by the inner and outer senses which bring about in the soul impressions that are without peace and joy, more than filled with sorrow, grieving, hardness of heart, embitterment, and frightful despair, turning into malice, envy, and hatred against God as well as against the holy souls and spirits.

There is awareness of one's past, the incessant gnawing of conscience, that is, self-knowledge and self-condemnation: "We are worthy of this because of our deeds and our life," as the self-knowledge and self-judgment of the wise thief was revealed on the cross. Darkness, gnashing of teeth, unbreakable bonds, the undying worm, the fire that never goes out, sorrow, oppression, and suffering—this is the eternal, future lot of the unrepentant sinner in Gehenna.

The Abbot Evagrius, among his other spiritual directions, advised monks to be mentally active when they were in their cells, picturing the terrible state of the souls shut up in Gehenna for all eternity. "Reflect on what situation the souls are in now that are cast down there! In what bitter silence they remain! How terribly they cry out! What fear and torment they are in, in what despair, in what sadness, in what endless tears! Confront thyself with the forms of eternal torments, the fire that is never extinguished, the darkness of Tartarus, the gnashing of teeth" (*Selected Sayings of the Monastic Saints*, edited by Bishop Ignaty, p. 103).

As concerns the place of Gehenna in the universe, let us resolve this question in the words of Chrysostom, that there is little spiritual value in knowing the specific location where the condemned will suffer or be tormented without end. It is enough for the Christian to know that there is indeed such a place, and we can discern its shadow within us. Let us not seek the location of Gehenna. This is no obligation of ours, but let us rather try to fulfill the law—the obligation of Christians: not to have anything in common with Gehenna and to hate all that belongs to it as being unnatural to man; to be concerned only with avoiding Gehenna after death and not with learning its place in the universe.

The teaching on hell in a broader sense, as a place for the condemned in general, is a dogma common to all mankind; evidence of this can be seen in the written texts that have come down to us from ancient, medieval, and recent times. Not only the Christians but even the pagans raised the teaching on hell to the level of a dogma. The religious conceptions of hell of all mankind in all times and places, the Greek and Roman poets and the philosophers of antiquity, the writers of the Middle Ages, the scholars of modern times, and the conceptions of hell of today's savages form a detailed picture of hell and life there as a state of souls condemned to eternal torment. Here is a picture of hell expressing man's awareness of this state beyond the grave in various times. Every tribe, every people, every person has a concept of good and evil, although this concept is relative and depends on many causes. Just as reward is promised beyond the grave for virtue, so for vice there is punishment. Hell, in the understanding of almost all the peoples of antiquity, is located under the earth (in the center of the earth). It is ruled either by a king or by a queen. Thus among the native inhabitants of Greenland, hell is seen as ruled by a queen reminiscent of the Proserpine[90] of antiquity sitting on a throne in the depths of a cave. Various sea monsters surround her. The soul either is punished by being fed to the demons or, continuing its unfortunate existence, is forced to live on snakes, insects, and lizards. Punishment for evil people after death, according to the conceptions of certain pagan beliefs, for example, those of the Greeks (Plato expressed this thought in *Phaedo*),[91] was to return to earth, where their souls were doomed to wander near their homes, and, because of the evil character they had acquired, they continued even after death to trouble the living and frighten them by

[90]Called Proserpina by the Romans and Persephone by the ancient Greeks, this goddess was believed to be the daughter of Zeus and Demeter. Homer describes her as the wife of Hades, the queen of the Shades, who ruled with her husband over the souls of the dead. She was also worshipped as *Coré*, meaning "the Daughter."

[91]Phaedon or Phaedo was a Greek philosopher of the early fourth century B.C., a native of Elis, on the west coast of the Peloponnesus. He was taken prisoner and sold as a slave, and after regaining his freedom, he became a disciple of Socrates. Plato's dialogue *Phaedo*, in which he is the principal speaker, treatise on the immortality of the soul.

haunting of various kinds. Some Negro tribes believe that evil souls are forced, under the influence of evil spirits as a punishment for their bad life on earth, to fill the air with noise and to disturb the sleep of the people they hated in life; hence the beginnings of the incantations (necromancy) to which the living resorted in order to move such wandering evil souls to mercy. Lactantius[92] says that the sun, moon, and many of the heavenly luminaries, in the opinion of the ancients, were considered dwelling places where sinners suffered for their sins. Such a view of life beyond the grave by the ancients bears witness that they were aware of the truth of moral development continuing after death and of the eternal nature of reward and punishment.

Here is a detailed picture of the ancient pagans' Hades as told by the eye witness Thespesius: "At the moment when I fell from a rather high place, I completely lost consciousness, and in such a state of senselessness I passed three days and nights. They were getting ready to bury me, but did not have time, because I came to, as if from a long sleep. The state in which my soul was during those three days is significant. As I was falling, it seemed vividly to me that I was thrown into the sea. After several moments without consciousness, I saw myself in a new world. The space in which I seemed to be was filled with luminaries of incredible size set apart from one another by great distances. They cast a blinding light, iridescent with incredible colors, and my soul, like a light boat, was carried swiftly and calmly along the ocean of light. Here I saw the souls of the dead, which took the form of fiery bubbles rising up in the air where they burst, and out of them emerged souls in human form of very small size. Some of these souls rose up easily and quickly in a straight line, while others rose less easily but circled around as they rose. Out of the multitude of souls I noticed one, and in it recognized one of my relatives who had died during my childhood. "Hello, Thespesius," this soul said to me at length. But I replied in amazement, "My name is Arideus, not Thespesius." "But that was your[93] former name," continued the soul, "and now you are called Thespesius,[94] since according to the will of the gods you are here in the intelligent part of your soul in the new world beyond the grave, while the other faculties of your soul remained with your body on earth." Traveling farther in the world beyond the grave, I saw a high mountain assigned for sinners. Finally I heard the voice of a woman who

[92]Lactantius Firmianus was an early Christian writer who went to Gaul circa 306 A.D. as Constantine the Great's son's tutor. He is considered the author of *De Mortibus Persecutorum* ("On the Deaths of Persecutors").

[93]Although one might have expected the *thou* form, here the Russian has the "polite plural" or "you."

[94]This is a Greek play on words: *thespesios* means "heavenly, divinely inspired, supernatural."

foretold the future in verses . . . This was the Sibyl. Between her prophecies she spoke of my death. My soul flew rapidly, but nevertheless I saw many lakes, one of which bubbled with liquid boiling gold, another with lead which was colder than ice, and a third with very hard iron. There were spirits guarding these lakes with pincers in their hands. In these lakes, greedy, grasping people suffered. The spirits that stood over these lakes used their pincers to pull souls out of the first lake which was red-hot, and threw them into the second lake where they became cold and hard as ice. From there they were cast over into the third lake where they became black. The spirits broke up the hard, blackened souls into small bits and again cast them into the golden lake. The unfortunate souls suffered inexpressible torments. I saw also that place beyond the grave from which souls are returned to earth. Here souls are forced to turn into all manner of animals. Here I saw the soul of Nero nailed with hot nails. The spirits turned it about, giving it the form of a viper in which it was to appear on earth."

Homer represented his Hades in two different forms: in the Iliad, Hades is a vast underground, and in the Odyssey, Hades is a distant land, mysterious, located at the ends of the earth, beyond the ocean, in the country of the Cimmerians.[95]

In Homer, Hades is the expression of most people's idea of hell in those times. Hades was seen as a copy of the earthly world, a copy that took on a special character. The philosophers deemed and taught that Hades was equally distant from any place on earth. Cicero, seeking to show that it did not matter where one died, said: "Regardless of where a man might die, it is everywhere the same distance to Hades."

Like the Christians, so also the pagans, placing hell in the innermost parts of the earth, had and have its description. The Greek poets and Roman philosophers left us a rather detailed description of this mysterious country, a country of eternal sorrow. Thus, the Greek poets wrote that the river Lethe[96] serves as the entrance to Hades from the direction of the Scythians;[97] in Laodicea,[98] Hades was entered from the Plutonic Pass;[99] near Lacedaemonia,[100] through the cave

---

[95]There was a *real* nation of Cimmerians, who lived by the Sea of Azov, but were driven out by the Sarmatians and migrated westward across Asia Minor. The *mythical* Cimmerians, mentioned by Homer, dwelt in a land of constant mists, darkness, and gloom.

[96]*Lethe* was a river in the lower world, from which the shades drank to obtain forgetfulness (the meaning of the word "lethe" in Greek).

[97]The name Scythia was applied to Southeastern Europe, and later to part of Asia.

[98]Laodicea was in Western Asia Minor.

[99]Pluto or Pluton was the giver of wealth, and also a name for the god of the lower world.

[100]Another name for Sparta.

of Tænarum.[101] From Epirus, the shades of the buried dead swam across the river Acheron to Hades with the help of the old, dirty boatman of the underworld, Charon, who received as payment for the ferry an *obol* (a Greek coin) which was put into the mouth of a dead person; and taking the souls down to Hades was the duty of Hermes, which is why he was called the conductor of the dead. From Egypt, the dead traveled to judgment across the lake Acherusia, near Memphis, under the protection of the god Anubis who, accompanying the soul to the underworld, sought to obtain for it a favorable sentence at the judgment of the dead.

Virgil's Aeneas reached Hades through Lake Avernus[102] where he descended together with the Cumæan Sibyl[103] in order to see his father there; Ulysses crossed the ocean to the land of the Cimmerians to get Hades; Hercules entered Hades through the Arechusiad peninsula. From Hermion the way to Hades was the shortest, and therefore the denizens of this region did not put a coin in the mouths of their dead to pay Charon for the passage. The accounts of travelers—Phoenicians undertaking distant sea journeys in search of tin and Baltic amber—were the main source of the Greeks' Elysian Fields and Tartarus. There, beyond the ocean, beyond the Pillars of Hercules, according to the Phoenicians, are the happy islands—the place of eternal spring—and beyond them the land of eternal darkness. These tales, vaguely passed down and, therefore, poorly understood by the people, gave rise in the popular imagination to the blessed land, the Elysian Fields, and to the land of punishment, Tartarus. In this way, the Greek poets and Roman philosophers gave a detailed picture of an underworld realm; they enumerated the rivers there, marked the location of lakes, forests, mountains, where the Furies[104] eternally torture sinners—those condemned to everlasting torment; they point out the fields of asphodel[105] stretching across the whole underworld and overgrown with an unpleasant, brooding form of the plant *asphodelus* (king's spear, day lily)—having the form of a lily and with small bulbs at the root—which, according to the popular belief, was the food of the dead. In these poems one can find the stories of certain notorious sinners and

[101]Through this cave, Hercules was supposed to have dragged Cerberus to the upper world.

[102]A lake in Italy filling the crater of an extinct volcano, once surrounded by a gloomy forest sacred to Hecate. The Greek name is *Aornos,* meaning "without birds," due to harmful vapors that rose from it. Near it was the cave of the Cumæan Sibyl, through which Aeneas descended to the lower world.

[103]Cumæ was the most ancient of the Greek cities in Italy, and the Sibyl there was the earliest of all. See Virgil's *Aeneid,* Book 6.

[104]The Furies, also called Erinys or Erinyes, were avenging spirits bringing retribution on those that violated the laws of natural goodness.

[105]Various southern European forms of flowers such as lilies and daffodils.

particular details of their torments: Sisyphus[106] eternally rolls his marble block uphill; Tantalus[107] cannot slake his thirst in the midst of the river; Ixion[108] has not a moment of peace on his wheel; the Danaides[109] are unable to fill a bucket, try as they might.

The word of God assures us that as there are two spiritual states that develop on earth there are also two states beyond the grave: a blessed one (Paradise), the state of good people who lived on earth according to the spirit of God's law, and a tormented state (Hades) which is abnormal, contrary to the will of the Creator, resulting from the willfulness of man who corrupted his own nature and, as a result, was deprived of his first designation since he was no longer apt for it. Hades became the lot of mankind. A deadly poison spread through all of man's nature, and sin, having infected our first ancestors, must naturally infect all of humanity descended from them. In death, both the righteous and the sinner's souls went down to Hades, which, with the resurrection of Christ, lost its significance and power and became only a place of temporary punishment for imperfect souls, that is, for those who have not attained bliss and not lost their salvation utterly.

Both the kingdom of heaven and Gehenna were prepared, through God's foreknowledge, from eternity. The former is for the angels and blessed souls and the latter for fallen angels—evil spirits—and, consequently, also for their cohorts: evil souls, unrepentant sinners. And so, primarily Gehenna is meant for evil spirits, fallen angels. According to its designation for spirits and souls, the nature of Gehenna corresponds to the fine, ethereal quality of its denizens. As in the house of the heavenly Father there are many mansions; so exactly in hell, according to the witness of the Third Book of Esdras, there are also many dwellings called cells, the keeping place of souls and not the place of corpses. "Did not the souls also of the righteous ask question of these things in their chambers, saying, How long shall I hope on this fashion? When cometh the fruit of the harvest of our reward? . . . In Hades the chambers of souls are like

[106]Sisyphus was the son of Aeolus, and the father of Ulysses. He was supposed to have built Corinth, where, as king, he was wicked and deceitful. In the lower world his punishment was to roll a large marble block uphill, and on reaching the top, it always rolled back down again. See Homer's *Odyssey*, Book 11.

[107]Tantalus, son of Zeus and the Nymph Pluto, supposedly divulged the secrets entrusted him by Zeus, and after his death was punished in the lower world with a thirst, while in the midst of a lake whose waters retreated from him as he tried to drink them.

[108]Ixion murdered his father-in-law, was purified of this crime by Zeus, but punished for later ingratitude, by being chained hand and foot to a wheel that rolled perpetually in the air.

[109]The Danaides, or the fifty daughters of Danaus, murdered the fifty sons of Aegyptus. They were punished in Hades by having to pour water forever into a sieve.

the womb. For like as a woman that travaileth maketh haste to escape the necessity of the travail, even so do these places hasten to deliver those things that are committed unto them" (III Esdras 4:35,41–42);[110] "And the earth shall restore those that are asleep in her, and so shall the dust those that dwell in silence, and the secret places shall deliver those souls that were committed unto them" (III Esdras 7:32).

While in the age of childhood, we cannot picture to ourselves or imagine the joys, pleasant things, and sorrows of adulthood, because this depends entirely on the state of the soul. Every state of the soul has its corresponding state of awareness; therefore the state of souls beyond the grave with its corresponding degree of awareness cannot be pictured during the present, earthly life. St. Paul, bearing witness to present knowledge, says that it is only "in part." And therefore the Lord Jesus Christ Himself, so as to bring the present concept of the life to come beyond the grave uses symbols, comparisons, likening the future life to that which is familiar in the present. The description of the kingdom of heaven and of Gehenna is in the form of a comparison: the former with a wedding feast and the latter with the valley of fire.[111] But this earthly comparison with that which is beyond the grave is almost nothing, according to St. Paul; man cannot imagine on earth what is prepared beyond the grave. Consequently, an exact description of Gehenna is impossible, unnatural to the present state of the soul. If life is an unending development consisting of a continuous change in the state of the soul from one state to another more perfect, regardless of whether it be in good or evil, passing, in the words of David, "from strength to strength," then from this we can understand the impossibility of forming a full conception of that state which is to be beyond the grave, be it good or evil. But since life beyond the grave is a further development of earthly life, then the characteristic marks of either life, according to St. Paul can be pictured "in part": bliss and torment as fruits of virtue and vice, are already tasted "in part" on earth by those who do these things. A joy that is not of this earth, a heavenly delight, an inner trouble, the gnawing of conscience are the beginnings of heaven and hell beyond the grave.

If, on earth, we encounter wicked persons ready for any villainy, then what will their mental state beyond the grave be? It will be such a state as we cannot even imagine; a state which is not possible on earth. This is the general human inability to achieve a purely spiritual life in general beyond the grave.

[110]Note that the Book designated in the Slavonic and Russian Bibles as Esdras III is called "Esdras II" in the Apocrypha of the King James Version, and also in the Oxford Annotated Apocrypha, but "Esdras IV" in the Latin Vulgate.

[111]That is, Hinnom. See Joshua 15:8.

Now one can understand why the people chosen by God, to whom the Law and Revelation were given by God, and even the righteous sect of the Essenes who devoted themselves exclusively to God and lived far from the world in the desert had a conception of life beyond the grave that was in many respects close to that of the pagans. Thus, according to Flavius[112] (Book 2, Chapter 12), the Essenes thought that the souls of the righteous go over the ocean to a place of repose and bliss where no concerns can bother them nor any change in the year. The souls of the wicked, on the other hand, are removed to a place subject to all the harshest changes of weather, and there they suffer eternal torment. If the Hebrews had been completely free from pagan views on life beyond the grave, then Jesus Christ would not have told them, "Ye do err"; and with error it is impossible to have a true conception of life after death. And at the present time, concerning the life to come, "Jewish tradition says that before the great day of the resurrection of the dead, the Archangel Michael will appear and blow the trumpet for the dead to arise, and the righteous dead of all ages, together with the living Jews, whom the Messiah will gather from all the countries of the earth, will exult in Jerusalem; the sinners will be deprived of this. The Messiah will make a most magnificent feast for the righteous Jews; he will slaughter a great whale and "Leviathan," *Levieson*.[113] After this they will be led into the kingdom of glory where Moses was brought while still alive and saw, as is written in the book Gdulath-Moshe,[114] various precious seats prepared by God in paradise for the holy ones of Israel and also for him—chairs in which they will take their place after the coming of the Messiah—and will celebrate eternally" (Alexeiev's *The Triumph of Christian Doctrine over the Talmud*, p. 126).

Dante,[115] in his great work *The Divine Comedy*, written in the beginning of the fourteenth century, gives us a detailed description of Hades, following the generally accepted views of the Middle Ages. In his hell he depicts everything that was known to him from religion, mythology, history, and personal experience. Lost in a wild, gloomy wood,[116] he reaches a hill, but three animals (a pan-

---

[112]Flavius Eutropius, better known simply as Eutropius: A Roman historian of the fourth century A.D., author of a compendium of Roman history in ten books called *Breviarium ab Urbe Condita*.

[113]*Leviathan* and *Levieson* are alternate pronunciations of the Hebrew spelling, in which the same letter can be rendered either as *th* or *s*, *a* or *o*.

[114]Hebrew: "The Greatness of Moses."

[115]Dante (or Durante) Alighieri (1265–1321) was the first important author to write in Italian. The *Commedia*, known from after the sixteenth century as the *Divina Commedia*, was finished in 1321.

[116]The poet finds himself lost in the Woods of Error on Good Friday, 1300. He meets the spirit of his idol Virgil who shows him Hell to free him of temptation, and then on Easter morn-

ther, a lion, and a hungry she-wolf) bar his way, and he is already descending back to the darkness of the deep valley when before him there appears a human shade having lost its voice through long disuse. This was Virgil sent to help him in all things and show him the way by the "divine" Beatrice,[117] the object of Dante's love, a real being and at the same time mystically ideal. "For thine own good," says Virgil, "thou must follow me. I will show thee the way, and lead thee forth through the lands of eternity, where to thine ear shall come disconsolate weeping and the gnashing of teeth; here thou shalt see the pale, dry, wandering shades of people who lived on earth before thy time and who seek to destroy themselves. Next thou shalt see lands quite opposite to the first, lands of light that purifies amid the cleansing flame, because here the souls hope through their sufferings to gain access to the places of bliss. As a conclusion to all, thou shalt see Paradise."

Virgil and Dante arrive at the gates of hell on which is inscribed a fearful motto: *"Abandon hope all ye that enter here."* They enter and see first the unfortunate souls that spent their lives with neither virtues nor vices. They reach the banks of Acheron and see Charon in his boat ferrying souls to the other bank; Dante suddenly falls into a deep sleep. He awakens on the opposite side of the river, and here is how hell appears to him: Hell is a murky, underground realm, inhabited by the wicked, condemned to eternal suffering. It is a crater-like abyss, located inside the earth, covered by the spherical vault or shell of the hemisphere we live in. This crater, going down towards the center of the earth, gradually narrows, and near the center it ends in a well. The inner wall of the crater is divided into ledges or steps which encircle the pit like ridges and on which the sinners are distributed according to the type of their sins. The closer to the center one gets, the more the circle of Hell narrows, and the more serious the offense, the less common it becomes, and, it would seem, the less space is needed for those party to it; thus the greatest sin—betrayal—is punished in the last circle, while the one responsible for sin, the leader of the rebellious angels, the king of the realm of woe, Lucifer, is held by Divine justice up to the breast in ice in the very center of the earth, in the well. In all, there are nine ledges or circles. Virgil also admits nine divisions: three times three—a sacred number. Dante goes down to the threshold which forms the first circle of Hades called Limbo.[118] There he finds the souls of virtuous pagans and innocent babes not cleansed by baptism.

---

ing they ascend the Mountain of Purgatory. Here Virgil must leave him, for without grace one can go no further.

[117]Beatrice Portinari (1266–1290) was the beloved of Dante. In the *Divine Comedy*, she is the symbol of Divine revelation through faith.

[118]The term Limbo has a somewhat different meaning in Dante, Milton, and scholastic (Roman Catholic) teaching. For Dante it was the outermost circle of hell (from the Latin expres-

Next, they descend to the second circle where Minos,[119] judge of Hades, is seated; here adulterers are punished. In the third circle gluttons are punished. In the fourth, he meets Plutus[120] who is set here as a guard; here, squanderers and misers are punished. In the fifth circle are punished those who give themselves up to anger. Dante and Virgil see a boat approaching, driven by Phlegyas;[121] they board it, cross the River Styx, and reach the walls of red-hot iron that surround the city of Dis,[122] the capital of hell; the demons that guard the gates refuse them entry, but an angel orders the demons to let the travelers through, and in the sixth circle they see heretics locked in coffins surrounded by flame. Then the travelers visit the circle of those guilty of persecutions, the circle of swindlers, and the circle of usurers where they see a river of blood guarded by a detachment of centaurs. All at once Geryon[123] approached them, personifying greed and deception; this beast set them on his back, so as to carry them across Hades. The eighth circle, known as Malebolge,[124] divided into ten valleys in which are incarcerated liars, simoniacs, those who steal from the Church, soothsayers, astrologers, warlocks, grafters, false saints, dishonest judges, hypocrites who go about covered with heavy leaden robes; thieves, eternally bitten by venomous snakes; heresiarchs, charlatans, and counterfeiters. Finally, the poets descend to the ninth circle divided into four sections where four types of deceivers[125] are punished; it is here that Dante relates the

sion *in limbo*, meaning "on the borderland"); for Milton, in Book III of *Paradise Lost*, it lay on the edge or confines of hell. In Roman Catholic teaching it is the place of those confined to hell through no fault of their own, but also "any intermediate state between heaven and hell" [*compare* Fathers Rumble & Carty, *Radio Replies*, Volume II, p. 176; St. Paul MN 1940; published with the imprimatur of Archbishop John Murray]. Thus, sometimes *Limbo* and *Purgatory* can be synonymous in Roman Catholic teaching.

[119]In the Eleventh Book of the *Odyssey*, Minos was the son of Zeus and Europa, king and lawgiver of Crete, and after death he became a judge of the shades in the underworld.

[120]Plutus [from the Greek *Ploutos,* meaning "rich") was the god of wealth or fertility. He was supposed to have been punished with blindness by Zeus.

[121]Phlegyas was the father of Ixion and Coronis, and when Apollo sired Aesculapius by Coronis, Phlegyas set fire to the temple of Apollo—who killed him and condemned him to punishment in the lower world.

[122]Dis was another name for Pluto and hence for Hades.

[123]Geryon, "the monster of fraud," was supposed to be a human monster with three heads whose oxen ate human flesh and were guarded by Orthrus [means "vigilant"), a two-headed dog. This is said to be an allegory meaning that Geryon ruled over three kingdoms [in what is now Spain], and was defended by an ally who reigned over two tribes.

[124]"The evil ditches," consisting of ten *bolgias,* or pits. This is the upper part of the hell of the fraudulent or malicious.

[125]The four are: treachery against blood ties, treachery to country, treachery against hospitality, and treachery against the Master.

tale of Count Ugolino.[126] In the last division, called that of Judas, Lucifer is chained. Here the center of the earth is located, and Dante, hearing the babbling of a brook, passes over this center and begins to climb up into the other hemisphere on the surface of which is the mountain of Purgatory surrounded by the southern ocean. Dante's hell is like Homer's Hades, with its crater-like (conical) shape.

In the poem *Orlando Furioso* of Ariosto,[127] written in the beginning of the sixteenth century, the place of Hades is also designated as inside the earth. According to the words of the author, at the foot of a high mountain from which the Nile flows forth there is an opening by which the Harpies[128] returned to the abyss; from here the author begins his journey through the realms of hell.

If a place for Hades was set apart in the center of the earth, then this was not hard to recognize. Hell could not occupy more than three thousand French miles (lieux) in width. Dexelius and Ribert calculated that the number of those condemned to eternal torment was as great as one hundred million and that hell was only one square German mile.

The teaching of Western theologians on hell, as the life of sinners beyond the grave in general, is very vague, and the contemporary Western theologian Bergier says without conviction that hell is inside the earth. Thus we have a general historical outline of the kingdom of death beyond the grave, the realm of the condemned—of hell, in the general sense of the condemned. Now let us look at the cells of Hades individually. Their significance, on the basis of Holy Scripture, is as follows.

The Hebrews call the state of the condemned beyond the grave, Gehenna (in Hebrew *Abaddon*),[129] as can be seen from the rabbinical books: "They will be gathered as the vanquished are gathered in the subterranean pit, and they that are subject to Gehenna will be incarcerated in Gehenna." Thus Gehenna was represented also by the ancient Hebrews. Thus the Prophet and King David depict the eternal lot of sinners beyond the grave and their state after death, in

---

[126]Count Ugolino was a plotter, betrayed along with his four sons, by a fellow-plotter and started to death.

[127]Ludovico Ariosto (1474–1533) is best known for *Orlando Furioso* ("Roland Gone Mad"), which is a continuation of Boiardo's *Orlando Innamorato* ("Roland in Love"), dealing with the adventures of Roland and other knights of Charlemagne, fighting the Saracens.

[128]These were supposed to be vultures with the head and breasts of a woman. Homer mentions *one* Harpy, Hesiod *two,* and later writers *three:* the names are Ocypeta ("Rapid"), Celeno ("Blackness"), and Aello ("Storm").

[129]"The angel of the bottomless pit."

these terms: "Upon the wicked the Lord shall rain snares, fire and brimstone, and an horrible tempest: this shall be the portion of their cup" (Psalms 11:6 [Septuagint 10]). To bring the people at least somewhat closer to an idea of the eternal punishment of sinners beyond the grave, the prophet represents the doom of Sodom and Gomorrah and the surrounding towns (Genesis 19:24). The prophet takes this punishment of sinners on earth as an image, a symbol of their punishment beyond the grave. The inescapability of retribution—the fate, the lot, the destiny of sinners, and their doom—the prophet expresses by the word "Gehenna." Regarding this cup of eternal punishment, the prophet writes in Psalm 74 [in the King James Version, Psalm 75], verse 9: "For in the hand of the Lord there is a cup . . . all the wicked of the earth shall drink." Thus also Jesus Christ Himself, in His prayer before death in the garden of Gethsemane before His passion, taking away the punishment of the world, calls it a "cup." Concerning this cup of eternal punishment, the Prophecy of Jeremiah also bears witness, who was ordered by God to take a chalice and to give drink to Jerusalem and the princes and the neighboring peoples: "For thus saith the Lord God of Israel unto me; take the wine cup of this fury at my hand, and cause all the nations, to whom I send thee, to drink of it" (Jeremiah 25:15–28). The Prophet Isaiah writes: "For thou shalt be required before thy time: hath it been prepared also for thee to reign? Nay, God hath prepared for thee a deep trench, wood piled, fire, and much wood: the wrath of the Lord shall be as a trench kindled with sulphur" (30:33).[130] And in another passage he writes again: "And they shall go forth, and see the carcasses of the men that have transgressed against Me; for their worm shall not die, and their fire shall not be quenched, and they shall be a spectacle for all flesh" (Isaiah 66:24). The composer of the Book of Judith writes: "Woe to the nations that rise up against my kindred! The Lord Almighty will take vengeance of them in the Day of Judgment, in putting fire and worms in their flesh; and they shall feel them, and weep forever" (Judith 16:17). Jesus the Son of Sirach[131] writes in his "Book of Wisdom": "Say not, God will look upon the multitude of my oblations, and when I offer to the most high God, He will accept" (Ecclesiasticus 7:9).

Gehenna is the name of that state of cast-away souls, where the worm does not die and the fire is never put out (Matthew 5:22,29,30; 10:28; 18:8–9; 25:41–46; Isaiah 66:24; Mark 9:45–48). Jesus Christ takes, as the symbol of the

---

[130]This is the reading of the passage according to the Septuagint Bible, which differs here from the King James Version.

[131]The extra-canonical *Book of Ecclesiasticus* is also referred to as "The Wisdom of Jesus the Son of Sirach," especially in Russian texts.

sinners' eternal state beyond the grave in Gehenna, an object of fear, horror, and repulsion for the Hebrews of His time. This is the Valley of Hinnom, which once was most splendid, to the northeast of Jerusalem; a small rivulet runs through it and then encircles part of the city. When the Hebrews were strongly given to idolatry, this valley was the site of the horrid worship of Moloch (IV Kings 16:3; II Chronicles 28:3). This Syrian idol was of bronze, with the head of a calf, crowned by a royal diadem;[132] the hands were extended as if to receive someone; children were offered to him in sacrifice as follows: a fire was lit inside the idol, and when it was hot, they cast poor children into the extended arms where they were burned at once. To cover up the cries of the children, during these sacrifices there was usually raised up a great shout and noise by means of various instruments. But after the Babylonian captivity, when the Jews had become completely repulsed by idolatry, they had a feeling of aversion to this place; it was deserted; all the impurities from the city were dumped there. It was also a place of execution; the air in this place was constantly contaminated; to cleanse it, a continual fire burned. The place became frightful and repulsive, and it became known as the valley of fire (Archbishop Michael, Gospel Commentary on Matthew 5:22). This is the place that was chosen by the Saviour as an image, a symbol of the eternal torments of sinners in the life beyond the grave.

St. Basil the Great describes in part the characteristic of the unsleeping worm and the undying fire: "When thou feelest the urge to commit some sin, then call up before thy mind's eye that dread judgment of Christ, which no mortal can withstand, when the Judge shall sit on His high and exalted throne; while all creation in fear and trembling will stand before His bright and glorious presence. All will stand before Him for examination, as to who did what during life. Those who did much evil during their lifetime will be surrounded by certain fearsome and terrible angels, gazing on the fire that is prepared, breathing fire because of their dread purpose, having an appearance like that of the night, because of sorrow and aversion to humans. Then picture the abyss, that impenetrable darkness and murky fire which has the ability to burn, but does not have light. Picture a breed of worm, innumerable, venomous, and carnivorous, which always eats but is never filled, and by its gnawing causes unbearable pains. Picture, finally, the most cruel punishment, that dishonor, and eternal shame! Fear this, also."

Incidentally, let us recall here the worm of which the Athonite monk told us.

---

[132]"Moloch" comes from a Semitic root meaning "king."

The word of God also calls the state of the lost a fiery furnace in which there is weeping and gnashing of teeth (Matthew 13:42,50). Here also, as in the first case, in defining Gehenna, the Lord Jesus Christ takes the Babylonian furnace, into which state criminals were cast, as a symbol of the fearful and everlasting torments to come.

Punishment by fire, burning, is the cruelest, and therefore the eternal fire to which sinners will be committed is without doubt the highest degree of torment. This fire was prepared for the devil and his angels; this torture was not intended for men, but for the evil spirits that rose up against God with their prince (Jude 6; Revelation 12:8–9). But, since sinners become through their sins, as it were, cohorts of the evil spirits, therefore they receive a like punishment with them—eternal fire.

The punishment of Sodom and Gomorrah and the surrounding towns by fire and brimstone serves as an image, a symbol of the eternal torments to come, represented by the lake of fire and brimstone.

What sort of place is it that the Saviour calls darkness? Darkness is the absence of light; therefore, darkness is a place deprived of light. Holy Writ refers to hope as light; consequently, darkness is despair. And so, the outer darkness is a place deprived forever of all hope. And without hope there is no life. Here there is no hope of dying, of being annihilated. Eternity and eternity—horror and despair. Here is a place bereft of any light and filled with weeping and the gnashing of teeth brought about by unbearable torments (Archbishop Michael, *Gospel Commentary on Matthew 22:13*).

The abyss signifies that place of eternal punishment, which has no bottom, a bottomless place, and a place of agony, according to the words of Scripture, fearful even for the devil. The evil spirits in the territory of Gadara[133] asked the Lord Jesus Christ not to torment them before the time, and not to send them away into the abyss (Matthew 8:29). The word "abyss" is used in the Revelation: Revelation 9;1–2; 11:7; 18:8; 20:1–2).

The Apostle Peter writes, "God spared not the angels that sinned, but cast them down to hell, and delivered them into chains of darkness, to be reserved unto judgment" (II Peter 2:4).

Just as there are many mansions in paradise, so exactly there are many dwellings of the condemned, depending on the character, the degree, and variety of

---

[133]Gadara itself is not mentioned in the Bible, but it is "the country of the Gadarenes and Gergesenes" [Mark 5:1, Luke 8:26,37]. The area was filled with ancient tombs, often inhabited by troglodytes, or "dwellers in the tombs," like the demoniac in the Gospel.

sins, habitations with different names: Gehenna, the fiery furnace, Tartarus, and others according to the nature and degree of sinfulness.

For every evil state of souls on earth, foreign to righteousness, there is a corresponding, condemned state beyond the grave. Such a sinful state of the soul on earth, according to the teaching of the Lord Jesus Christ, is a dead state, and moral judgment over it has already been pronounced: "condemned" (John 5:29). The dead state of the soul, as experience itself shows, is always foreign to it, lacking in meekness and humility, and heavenly joy is incomprehensible to it. With what is the mind and heart of those committed to vice constantly occupied? This everyone knows. With what is the lover of glory, the voluptuary, the lover of money constantly concerned? Do they ever taste that sweet peace that is not of this world?

As concerns the degrees of the state of Gehenna beyond the grave, here is the teaching of the Lord Jesus Christ Himself: "That servant, which knew his Lord's will, and prepared not himself, neither did according to his will, shall be beaten with many stripes. But he that knew not, and did commit things worthy of stripes, shall be beaten with few stripes. For unto whomsoever much is given, of him shall be much required: and to whom men have committed much, of him they will ask the more" (Luke 12:47–48). The sinner is not completely freed from punishment beyond the grave by ignorance of the will of God, since he could have learned it, if only he wished. To elucidate these words of the Gospel, we quote the words of Saints Basil the Great, John Chrysostom, Ephrem the Syrian, and others.

St. Basil the Great: "One must realize that the expressions 'shall be beaten with many stripes' and 'beaten with few stripes' signify not an end but a difference of torment. For if God is the Righteous Judge not only of the good but of the corrupt and recompenses each according to his works, then one may deserve the undying fire, either weaker or more caustic, while another may deserve the undying worm, but again causing greater or lesser pain, according to the merit of each. One may deserve Gehenna in which, without doubt, there are various kinds of torments, while another may deserve the outer darkness where some are brought only to weeping, but others, from intense torment, to gnashing of the teeth. The outer darkness itself, without doubt, shows that there is something internal in it. And what is said in Proverbs: "in the depths of hell" (Proverbs 9:18), lets us understand that some, although in hell, but not in the depths of hell, suffer less torment. This distinction can be seen now in physical sufferings. For one is sick with fever and attacks and with other infirmities, while another has only a fever and that not in as great a degree as the other; yet another has no fever, but suffers only a pain in some one limb and that, again, more or less than another does."

St. Ephrem the Syrian: "There are various kinds of torment, as we have heard in the Gospel. There is the "outer darkness" (Matthew 8:12): and from this we can see that there is also another, deeper darkness; "fiery Gehenna" (Matthew 5:22)—another place of torment; "the gnashing of teeth" (Matthew 13:42)—also a particular place; "the unsleeping worm" (Mark 9:48)—in another place; "the lake of fire" (Revelation 19:20)—again another place; "Tartarus" (II Peter 2:4)—again a place to itself; "the undying fire" (Mark 9:43)—a particular country; "the abyss" (Philippians 2:10) and "ruin" (Matthew 7:13)—in their own places; "the uttermost lands of the earth" (Ephesians 4:9)—another place; "Hades," where sinners abide, and "the depths of hell"—the most tormenting place. The unfortunate will be assigned to these places, each according to the degree of sin, be it of greater or lesser gravity, according as it is written: "[each] shall be holden with the cords of his sins" (Proverbs 5:22), "beaten with many stripes" or "beaten with few stripes" (Luke 12:47–48). Just as there are various punishments here, so will it be in the life to come. The adulterer, the voluptuary, the murderer, the thief, and the drunkard shall all be punished differently."

St. John Chrysostom: "Whoever shall receive more instruction must suffer through greater punishment for his crime. The more knowledgeable and mighty we are, the more seriously we will be punished for our sins. If thou art rich, a greater donation is expected than from the poor; if wise, a greater obedience; if vested in authority, show splendid merit. Thus, in everything else thou shalt give an answer according to thine abilities. He that departs to that place with a multitude of good and evil deeds will receive some lightening of punishment in the torments there; on the other hand, he that has no good works, but offers only evil ones, there is no saying how much he will suffer, being sent to eternal torment." Thus also St. Cyprian, the Blessed Jerome, and the Blessed Augustine taught.

Not only are there various states of the condemned, corresponding to their sinful state on earth; but, just as the sins themselves have their varying degrees, so also punishments of the same kind will nonetheless not be in the same degree. This is shown in the word of the Lord: "Verily I say unto you, it shall be more tolerable for the land of Sodom and Gomorrah in the day of judgment, than for that city" (Matthew 10:15). The Lord says that after the universal judgment the punishment of Sodom and Gomorrah will be milder than the punishment of those who have rejected the Apostles' preaching. This truth of the degree of guilt emerges from the moral law that guilt is greater, the more clearly and fully the will of God, against which the crime is committed, is expressed. Consequently, the greater the punishment for this; and so, those that have rejected the Apostles' preaching of Christ are more guilty of crime than those that rejected the demands of the natural law of conscience, by which the dwellers of Sodom were ruled, since the positive law of God had not been given. The extreme corruption of the dwellers in these cities was the reason for the righteous anger of God, and they ended their existence through volcanic eruptions and collapse. The cities of Sodom, Gomorrah, Admah, and Zeboim[134] were located in the place where now the Dead Sea is, in the southern part of Palestine.

"But I say unto you, it shall be more tolerable for Tyre and Sidon at the day of judgment, than for you" (Matthew 11:22).

Jesus Christ spoke thus on the degree of punishment, corresponding to the degree of guilt, in the works of the Pharisees: "[The Pharisees] devour widows' houses, and for a show make long prayers: the same shall receive greater damnation" (Luke 20:47; Mark 12:40). The Apostle St. Paul also teaches that retribution will be according to works.

The Lord Jesus Christ Himself bears witness of the eternity of punishment in Gehenna when He says: "And these (that is, the sinners) shall depart unto eternal punishment." This means that for the condemned after the universal judgment of Christ, life will consist of endless torment. The same teaching on the everlastingness of the torments of sinners is found in the Gospel of St. John: "He that believeth on the Son hath everlasting life: and he that believeth not the Son shall not see life; but the wrath of God abideth on him" (3:36). From this we can conclude that unbelief is eternal death. Unbelievers depart into eternity as sinners, consequently, they are under the wrath of God for sin and have not been reconciled; and the wrath of God remains upon them (Ephesians 2:3). The word "abides" signifies eternity, showing that the wrath of God will never again depart from such, and they will not see life: this means the unending torment of the unbelievers, eternal punishment (*Gospel Commentary* of Archbishop Michael). In one of His talks, Jesus Christ teaches thus about the eternity of punishment: "And if thy hand offend thee, cut it off: it is better for thee to enter into life maimed, than having two hands to go into hell, into the fire that never shall be quenched: Where their worm dieth not, and the fire is not quenched. And if thy foot offend thee, cut it off: it is better for thee to enter halt into life, than having two feet to be cast into hell, into the fire that never shall be quenched: Where

---

[134]The five "Cities of the Plain" were *Sodom, Gomorrah, Admah* [Adema], *Zeboim* [Seboim], and *Zoar,* formerly called *Bela.* The last-named was spared to afford shelter to Lot, and renamed Zoar (Genesis 19:22–23, 30).

their worm dieth not, and the fire is not quenched. And if thine eye offend thee, pluck it out: it is better for thee to enter into the kingdom of God with one eye, than having two eyes to be cast into hell fire: Where their worm dieth not, and the fire is not quenched" (Mark 9:43–48). The same warning appears in the Gospel of St. Matthew (18:8). Concerning the eternal, endless torment in Gehenna, as well as bliss, the Lord Jesus Christ spoke in another passage—in the reply of Abraham to the unfortunate rich man, condemned to eternal torment in Gehenna: "Between us and you there is a great gulf fixed: so that they which would pass from hence to you cannot; neither can they pass to us, that would come from thence." The words "great gulf," besides their literal meaning—that the space between Paradise and Gehenna is so great that neither will the righteous see and hear the sinners, nor the sinners the righteous after the universal judgment—it signifies the eternal nature of bliss and torment. The difference in the moral state of the righteous and the condemned is so great that those who have been confirmed in evil cannot become righteous or capable of life in Paradise; nor can the righteous now become evil or capable of life in Gehenna. Here the damned are spoken of as being totally unfit for eternal life. St. John the Evangelist bears witness in his Apocalypse of the eternal punishment of sinners beyond the grave and consequently of their eternal torment: "And the smoke of their torment ascendeth up for ever and ever: and they have no rest day nor night, who worship the beast and his image, and whosoever receiveth the mark of his name" (Revelation 14:11); "And the devil that deceived them was cast into the lake of fire and brimstone, where the beast and the false prophet are, and shall be tormented day and night for ever and ever" (20:10). Chrysostom takes these words as meaning the eternal torment of the sinners beyond the grave in the life to come. The Apostle Jude writes: "Even as Sodom and Gomorrha and the cities about them in like manner, giving themselves over to fornication and going after strange flesh, are set forth for an example, suffering the vengeance of eternal fire" (verse 7). The Apostle Paul also writes thus about eternal torment to the Thessalonians (II Thessalonians 1:7–10): "And to you who are troubled rest with us, when the Lord Jesus shall be revealed from heaven with his mighty angels, in flaming fire taking vengeance on them that know not God, and that obey not the gospel of our Lord Jesus Christ: Who shall be punished with everlasting destruction from the presence of the Lord, and from the glory of his power; when he shall come to be glorified in his saints, and to be admired in all them that believe." Concerning the eternalness of torments, the Prophet David also bears witness thus: "The Lord is known by the judgment which he executeth: the wicked is snared in the work of his own hands" (Psalms 9:17);

and the Prophet Isaiah writes: "The sinners in Zion are afraid; fearfulness hath surprised the hypocrites. Who among us shall dwell with the devouring fire? Who among us shall dwell with everlasting burnings?" (33:14). The Forerunner of the Lord, John the Baptist, witnesses thus concerning eternal punishment: "Whose fan is in his hand, and he will throughly purge his floor, and gather his wheat into the garner; but he will burn up the chaff with unquenchable fire" (Matthew 3:12). This means that in the Old Testament the truth of eternal bliss and torment was known. The immortal soul of the condemned sinner, passing beyond the grave, enters into an eternal, never ending state, which in the Holy Scriptures is called eternal death, the second death.

There were, and, perhaps even now, there are no small number of false sages, bandying sophistries according to the flesh, that supposedly there could not be eternal torment, but only temporary, and they present their false reasoning. Such are the disciples or followers of Origen who taught that demons and sinful souls in Gehenna will be tormented only till a certain time, after which they will again be returned to their sinless primal state. The Fifth Ecumenical Council condemned and rejected this false teaching as completely at odds with good sense, contrary to the truth, and contradicting the word of God, offending the mystery of the Redemption of the human race which took place only by the merits of the Son of God, our Lord Jesus Christ Who granted eternal life only to those who believe in Him. All those, however, who deny Him, will depart unto torment, not temporary, but as Jesus Christ Himself teaches, unto eternal torment. Thus, first of all their false teaching does not recognize as true the words of Jesus Christ Himself Who called torment eternal while they consider it temporary. Why, indeed, should the Saviour have come to earth? For what reason did He come to deliver sinners? He came only to deliver those who believe from eternal torment, prepared for the devil and unrepentant sinners. After this can one regard their arguments as true when their teaching on this subject is completely contrary to the teaching of Jesus Christ on the eternal character of punishment? Origenists find eternal torments not to be in agreement with the mercy of God, and in their error they do not notice that in denying the eternalness of torment, they make God out to be unjust, rewarding the worthy and the unworthy, both those capable and those incapable of bliss, rewarding all without exception, those who desire and those who do not desire bliss.

The words of God and experience in life bear clear witness that moral evil can turn to good only on earth, through penitence, and, at that, only active penitence which can no longer exist beyond the grave. It was said previously that earthly life is a preparation for the life beyond the grave, either a life of bliss in Paradise or one of torment in Gehenna. And so, the good or evil acquired by the soul while on earth, having become its nature, having entered into the flesh and blood, cannot be transformed beyond the grave from good to evil or evil into good. Both the kingdom of heaven and Gehenna are sought on earth, while beyond the grave we inherit what we have sought, desired here; in short, we inherit what we have lived for on earth, of our own will, and not by being forced. Paradise and Gehenna are obtained voluntarily. If the categories of souls beyond the grave can no longer change, then the evil person is unable to be a dweller in Paradise where love reigns—just as, on earth, corrupt individuals are not found in the society of moral people, not because the latter would not accept them but only because they are incapable of it. Just as a fish is not able to live in the air or a bird underwater, so the wicked person withdraws and is separated by a great chasm from the virtuous; and the Lord Jesus Christ Himself bore witness to the impossibility of passing from one moral state to the other in the parable of the Rich Man and Lazarus. And since life is a development of either good or evil, the life of sinners after death in Gehenna is an unceasing development of evil alone. For this very reason, it is impossible for demons to be turned into good angels or lost souls to become the souls of the righteous.

In His endless wisdom and grace, God made man according to His holy will, not demanding man's desire, wish, or agreement; and He made him for bliss. But, so that man would have bliss on earth and beyond the grave, it was needful on man's part to have an active desire to achieve blessedness, without which almighty grace alone will not save a man; "The kingdom of heaven suffereth violence, and the violent take it by force" (Matthew 11:12); therefore, can souls that do not seek the kingdom of God and His righteousness on earth ever find it beyond the grave? It is given only to those that seek and obtain it.

Consequently, both demons and lost souls committed to eternal fire will suffer everlastingly, not by the will of God but by their own choice to be in eternal torments together with evil spirits and evil souls rather than be eternally blessed with the good angels and with all the Saints. The blessed Augustine, defending the truth which the Lord Jesus Christ Himself expressed on the everlasting nature of bliss and torment, writes: "Eternal life beyond the grave is either bliss or torment. But if eternal bliss will have no end, then eternal torment will also have no end. With one and the same sense of the word, to say that eternal life will be unending, but eternal torment on the other hand will have an end—this is very foolish. And therefore, since the eternal life of the Saints will be endless, so, without doubt, eternal torment will also have no end."

From the words of Holy Scripture it is revealed that the death of the soul consists in not knowing its Creator, God, and therefore in drawing away from Him. Ignorance of God, and therefore the drawing away of the soul from God, naturally begins during life on earth. Knowledge and ignorance of God can be only on earth. Ignorance of God, distancing from God, the Source of life, constitutes eternal death for the soul. The content of eternal death is made up of: 1) ignorance of God, 2) lack of love for God, for holy spirits and souls, and hatred for everything holy, and 3) drawing away from God. Thus, the truth of eternal torment of sinners beyond the grave known to the Old Testament obtained the right of a dogma in the Christian Church. The Holy Fathers and Doctors of the Church left us their teaching on the everlastingness of the torments of sinners beyond the grave, and we believe what they have taught and preached to all the world: not the wisdom of the flesh, but truths of the Spirit Who chose them as His instruments for proclaiming to the world the lot of man on earth and beyond the grave. Thus, in the Athanasian Creed, there is this confession of faith: "And they that have done good shall go into life everlasting; and they that have done evil, into everlasting fire."

St. Clement of Rome: "Immortal are all souls, even those of the wicked for whom it would be better if they were not incorruptible, because, tortured by endless torment in the fire that never goes out and not dying, they will have no end to their anguish."

St. Polycarp: "Thou threatenest me with a fire that burns only for a time and is then extinguished, because thou knowest not of the fire of the judgment to come and of eternal torment which is prepared for the wicked."

Justin Martyr: "That he (the devil), with his army and the people that follow him, will be sent into the fire and be tormented there for ages without end, this Christ has proclaimed."

St. Irenæus: "To whom the Lord will say: Depart from Me ye accursed, into the eternal fire—these will be condemned forever. Eternal and without end will be the good things bestowed by God; therefore also, the deprivation of them will be eternal and without end, just as in the unlimited light those that have blinded themselves or been blinded by others will be forever deprived of the pleasantness of the light."

St. Cyril of Jerusalem: "If anyone is sinful, he will receive an eternal body that must suffer torment for sins, so as to burn eternally in fire and not be destroyed."

St. Basil the Great: "The Lord says definitely, 'These will go into eternal torment'; on the one hand, He sends some 'into the eternal fire, prepared for the devil and his angels,' while in another passage He names 'fiery Gehenna,' and adds: 'where their worm dieth not, and the fire is not put out'; and furthermore of old He foretold of some through the Prophet Isaiah that 'their worm shall not die, neither shall their fire be quenched' (Isaiah 66:24). Therefore, if with so many similar testimonies, in so many passages of divinely inspired Scripture, many yet seem to have forgotten all these pronouncements and sentences of the Lord and promise themselves an end to torment, so as to be bolder and freer in committing sin, then this is of course one of the devil's snares. For if there will ever be an end to eternal torment, then without doubt eternal life must have an end. But if we dare not think this of life, then what basis can there be to suppose an end to eternal torment? Both torment and life have one and the same word: eternal. It is said: 'These shall depart into eternal torment, but the righteous into life eternal.'"

St. John Chrysostom: "Let us assume thou shalt live even many years experiencing no change; but what is this in comparison with unending ages and with those severe and unbearable torments? Here both happiness and misery have an end, and a very rapid one at that; but there, both continue for undying ages, and their quality is so different from that of this place that one cannot tell it . . . If someone shall say, 'How can the soul put up with such a multitude of tortures, when it is at the same time to bear punishment for ages without end?'—then let such a one think of what occurs here, how often it happens to many to have a long and severe illness. Even if they died, this is not because the soul was completely exhausted, but because the body refused to serve; so that if it had not yielded, the soul would not have ceased to suffer. And so, when the soul receives an incorruptible body, then nothing will prevent torment from continuing for infinity . . . For this reason, let us not dispose ourselves now, as if the extreme severity of torments could exhaust our soul; for then, the body will no longer feel this exhaustion, but will be tormented eternally with the soul, and there will be no other end."

We find such thoughts in Tertullian, Theophilus of Antioch, Cyprian, Minucius Felix, Hippolytus, Athanasius, Gregory the Theologian, Hilary of Poitiers, Jerome, and others.

Sin—iniquity committed on earth—brings about a dual punishment: removal from the peaceable family, city, and comfort and exile to another place[135] where one must face various inconveniences, hardships, and unpleasantness amid a society that is not peaceable. In the same way, the punishment

---

[135]In the nineteenth century criminals were usually exiled from European Russia to settle in Siberia.

of the sinner beyond the grave is double: deprivation of the heavenly fatherland that should have been his own and of seeing the face of God—and incarceration in Gehenna, where there is weeping and gnashing of teeth, and the inextinguishable fire. Eternal death, or eternal punishment, which is the same thing, is twofold: 1) removal of the sinners forever from seeing the face of God, that is, their removal from God, removal from the kingdom of God, according to the Apostle's words: "Know ye not that the unrighteous shall not inherit the kingdom of God?" (I Corinthians 6:9). This is spiritual (inner) life. 2) But the Lord Jesus Christ defines the state of Gehenna not only as spiritual suffering alone but adds to it physical suffering as well: "Depart from Me ye accursed, into the everlasting fire" (Matthew 25:41). This is palpable, outward punishment.

Besides the spirit, man, after the resurrection of his body, will have two natures: the soul and the new, fine body. And since while on earth the spirit, soul, and body of man took part in his works, therefore, beyond the grave, according to the teaching of St. Paul, "each shall receive the things he hath done with his body, either good or evil"; punishment therefore must be for both the body and the soul: punishment, spiritual, inner torment, and outward torment, corresponding to the new, fine, ethereal body. This outward or palpable punishment consists of: 1) the very society in which the poor, rejected soul has to live forever, and 2) the elements which fully correspond to man's passion: eternal fire, never extinguished. The passion-filled state of sinners on earth corresponds to the state of sinners in Gehenna. There are people who admit only to inner torment—the gnawing of conscience—and who doubt the presence beyond the grave of a physical fire in Gehenna. If one were to admit doubts as to the presence of fire in Gehenna, then one would have also to allow the absence of warmth in man himself. What fire warms the blood so strongly in the human body? Whence does man have warmth, heat in the innards? The presence of fire, of warmth in the human body, has its basis, its cause which evoked this warmth. This fire is invisible to the eyes but visible in its action.

It is known that the harshest punishment people have sometimes used on earth for their criminals is burning, punishment by fire. It is a dogma that only God alone is a Spirit, while all else, His creation, is not a spirit, but spiritualized flesh, matter; and therefore angels, souls of men, and demons, in comparison to their Creator, are fine, ethereal beings. From all eternity it has been known to God what will be ahead with His moral, spiritual beings, how they will make use of their free will; and therefore from eternity there is prepared the kingdom of Heaven, or Paradise, and Gehenna, or eternal fire. Everywhere there is life, there is warmth; life and warmth are inseparable. Where there is no life, there is no natural warmth; warmth supports life. In Gehenna life goes on, consequently, there must also be warmth there. But warmth has its degrees; in one room the warmth is pleasant to man, but in another it reaches such a high degree as to burn or be unbearable for humans. Therefore, in the first room it is pleasant for humans to live, but in the other it is torment or impossible. At the same time, in neither room is there fire to be seen. The fire of Gehenna has its own characteristics that set it apart from earthly fire. The main one is that on earth fire destroys its victims, albeit not in every case; there have been cases when certain of the holy Martyrs given up to be burned, remained unharmed. The Old Testament bears witness to the three youths, Ananias, Azarias, and Misael, who were cast into the flaming furnace in which, nevertheless, they remained completely unhurt *(Lives of the Saints* for December 17). So exactly the fire of Gehenna does not destroy its victims; they remain eternally unconsumed. The fire of Gehenna with its peculiar, distinctive quality was prepared for a special purpose, the one mainly proper to it: for eternal punishment of the fallen angels, those fine, ethereal beings; consequently, it is different from earthly fire. Nevertheless, it has a direct external effect on moral beings. For the body which, no matter how ethereal it may be, is still a body—there must be a physical punishment: the fine, ethereal, but still palpable fire, that was prepared by God for the fallen spirits. Human souls while in the body on earth, by their activity against God which corresponded to that of the evil spirits, have made themselves associates of the evil spirits and inherit the same fate that was prepared for them from all eternity, that is, eternal, undying fire. This is the outward torment of Gehenna. The internal and external torment of sinners in Gehenna is the teaching of our Church. Thus, Jesus Christ, representing the condition of Gehenna beyond the grave in the first period in the parable of the Rich Man and Lazarus, says clearly that the unfortunate rich man was in flame: "And he [the rich man] cried and said, Father Abraham, have mercy on me, and send Lazarus, that he may dip the tip of his finger in water, and cool my tongue; for I am tormented in this flame" (Luke 16:24). If in the preliminary stages of torment the sinners already suffer so from the flame, then what will the effect of the fire be in the full torment of the second period of life beyond the grave, that is, after the universal judgment of Christ. As Jesus Christ represents the state of Paradise in the second period of blissful life in images, for example, in the image of a feast, so also here, in order to depict the second period of the life of sinners beyond the grave in Gehenna, He employs the prophetic imagery of Isaiah (Isaiah 66:24). The Prophet, describing the glorious kingdom of the Messiah when there will be a new heaven and a new earth, says that then the members of this kingdom will see the bodies of sinners on which the worm does not die and the fire does not go out. The enemies will be conquered; the people of God will triumph. All the imagery of the Saviour's words about the eternal torment of sinners beyond the grave is taken from the heaps of bodies of those killed in battle, according to prophetic vision. The worm, which thrives on dead bodies, will not die, because these bodies will last for all eternity, and the fire by which the remains of the dead were burned after a battle will not be extinguished, so many will the corpses be (Archimandrite Michael,[136] *Gospel Commen tary*, Mark 9:42). The Lord Jesus Christ, in order to teach us to shun the temptations that draw us toward sin, warns people thus of the lot of Gehenna beyond the grave: if, for example, thine eye, hand, or foot, or some limb tempt thee, then cast it away, as it is better to be without some limb in the kingdom of Heaven than to be with it, rather than in fiery Gehenna where the worm dieth not and the fire is not extinguished. Here what is to be understood is not the actual amputation of body parts, as practiced for example by the *Skoptsy*[137] and others like them who are accused by the Lord, but rather the cutting off of the will, the annihilation of sinful desires in oneself, the rejection of evil thoughts, the conquering of evil by good. For those who indeed carry out the desires of their ill will, there awaits fire beyond the grave. And these prophetic words of Isaiah: "the bodies of the dead, with the worm upon them and fire, with which they were burned," served the Lord Jesus Christ as a symbol of the lot of sinners beyond the grave where their eternally new bodies will fall prey to worms and fire. This is the outward torment of sinners in the second period of life beyond the grave (Archbishop Makary of Kharkov, *Theology*, Volume II, p. 657). The same teaching of the Lord on temptations was stated by the Evangelist Matthew (Matthew 5:29–30). Regardless of how long the first period of life beyond the grave might be, souls without bodies will not receive a full retribution which God has prepared for the devil and his cohorts, specifically they who do not believe in the Lord Jesus Christ sent by God for the salvation of mankind.

As the Lord Jesus Christ, preparing to give His soul, prayed for His enemies, so He demands perfect love of His followers, a love that does not even allow evil in thoughts; therefore speaking ill of one's neighbor, as a matter concerning the honor of another, is a lack of love and, consequently, a breach of the commandment of love; and those who break this commandment face fiery Gehenna beyond the grave. At the universal judgment, Jesus Christ will pronounce to the

[136]"Archimandrite" theoretically is the head of a monastery. In earlier passages in this book, "Archbishop" is used for the author of the same work referred to here.

[137]The Skoptsy were a sect in nineteenth-century Russia that practiced castration.

sinners standing on the left the following sentence, judging them to remain and suffer eternally in the fire: "Depart from Me, ye accursed, into the eternal flame, prepared for the devil and his angels." St. Paul bears witness to the outward torments of the sinners in Gehenna, when he says, "[The future Judge] in flaming fire [shall] take vengeance on them that know not God, and that obey not the gospel of our Lord Jesus Christ" (II Thessalonians 1:8).

Thus also did the Holy Fathers of the Church teach regarding external torments in Gehenna. St. Basil the Great says, "Then (that is, after the Judgment) one who has committed many bad deeds in life will be faced with fearsome and grim angels whose glance is fiery and breath is fiery from the cruelty of their will, and faces like unto night with dolefulness and misanthropy; then an impassable void, a deep darkness, fire without light, which in the darkness has a burning power but is deprived of any glow; then some sort of poisonous and carnivorous worm, voraciously devouring, never satisfied, and by its eating, causing unbearable pains; then the most cruel of all torments—eternal shame and eternal ignominy."

St. John Chrysostom teaches thus about the fire of Gehenna: "Think not, that the fire there is like that on earth: *this* fire burns whatever it catches on to and turns it into something else; but *that* fire—of Gehenna—whomever it once embraces it will burn forever and never stop, for which reason it is called inextinguishable. For even sinners are to be vested in immortality, not for honor but in order to be eternally the victim of the torments that are there." Chrysostom, so as to give at least some idea of eternal torment in the fire of Gehenna, suggests imagining oneself closed up in a bath-house heated above the normal temperature or lying in a fever. If in such a case the bath or fever causes discomfort, nevertheless, the torment has an end. If one were to make such a torment endless, what would be the plight of such a person? Now one can go on to that terrible, indescribable, endless fire of Gehenna. And so, the outward torment for sinners in Gehenna, according to the teaching of the Church, will consist of an undying worm and a fire that is never extinguished (Archbishop Makary of Kharkov, *Theology*, Volume II, p. 657), and finally of that society of evil spirits as well with whom they are judged to abide eternally and together in the fire prepared for fallen spirits. It is to this that sinful souls are sentenced. Thus the fire, the worm, the society: here is where the activity of the outward senses of the new, fine, ethereal body is to be. Nothing will bring joy to the sight, to the hearing, to the feelings, the taste, and the sense of smell. The objects that are subject to the senses are unbearably sad.

In Gehenna, every sense will suffer with particular grief. Thus, the eyes will suffer from the darkness and the smoke and if the fire of Gehenna sheds any light at all, then it will be for the greater fear and trembling of the condemned so they might see the frightful form of the demons whose very sight is more terrible than any torture, and see the tormented faces of the sinners with whom they angered the Lord during their lives by their sins. The ears will hear only the incessant sound of wailing, complaints, and curses; the sense of smell will suffer from the stench; the taste, from intense thirst and fearful hunger. For this reason these unfortunate captives—suffering in fire, tortured by terrible punishment—weep, moan, wail, despair, but do not find, and never will find either relief or consolation. Since the activity of the mind, the will, and heart depends on or is determined by the action of the senses, therefore the lost, rejected souls in Gehenna, having distanced themselves of their own will from God whilst on earth, will enter into the condition of evil spirits. The activity of the mind is one of not seeing or knowing God, the activity of the heart is one of hatred for God, and the activity of the will is blasphemy against God. The state of the lost is a state of embitterment against God and against everything divine, everything that is true, good, and beautiful.

Testimony to the eternal torment of sinners by fire in Gehenna we find in the Apocalypse: "The same shall drink of the wine of the wrath of God, which is poured out without mixture into the cup of his indignation; and he shall be tormented with fire and brimstone in the presence of the holy angels, and in the presence of the Lamb" (Revelation 14:10); "But the fearful, and unbelieving, and the abominable, and murderers, and whoremongers, and sorcerers, and idolaters, and all liars, shall have their part in the lake which burneth with fire and brimstone" (Revelation 21:8). Chrysostom writes that here the word "wine" refers to torment, deprived of all mercy or relief.

The Apostle Jude bears witness to the fire that is to be a punishment for sinners in the life beyond the grave: "Even as Sodom and Gomorrah, and the cities about them in like manner, giving themselves over to fornication, and going after strange flesh, are set forth for an example, suffering the vengeance of eternal fire" (Jude 1:7).

The Apostle Paul teaches that everyone will receive according to his works in the life beyond the grave: "For we must all appear before the judgment seat of Christ; that every one may receive the things done in his body, according to that which he hath done, whether it be good or bad" (II Corinthians 5:10). Hence it is understood that since the soul and body took part in activity on earth, therefore the soul and body both receive recompense in the life beyond the grave: an inner, spiritual recompense and an outward, palpable one, because the new body, with all its fineness and lightness, nevertheless remains material, and it needs a positive, palpable recompense.

According to Metropolitan Philaret of Moscow, fire, so often mentioned in the Holy Scriptures, acts quite apart from the torments of conscience; not to receive positive torments would signify only a criminal arbitrariness. The spiritual bodies of the condemned, of course, will not remain without a palpable punishment appropriate to them, since judgment will be passed on both soul and body. And the finer the spiritual bodies will be, the more painful will be the action of the fire, corresponding to their qualities. In this way, as much as they might remove the properties of crude matter from the state of the condemned, they would not weaken but only increase the excruciating effect of Gehenna fire, given that positive torments must exist *(Dogmatic Theology*, Volume II, pp. 513–514). The Teachers of the Church considered this fire an invisible one which consumes and nourishes its victim, itself being nourished by the victim's incorruptibility (p. 515). St. Basil the Great says that this fire is not bright, having in its darkness a burning power, but deprived of any glow.

St. John of Damascus teaches: "The fire to which sinners will be committed is not the same material one as ours on earth but such as is known only to God." In general, the ancient Doctors of the Church pictured the Gehenna fire as not being like the one that we know here; it will burn but neither burn anything up nor consume it; it will act not only on the bodies of sinners but also on their souls, and on the spirits themselves, the bodiless demons. It will be some sort of murky fire, without light, and mysterious. Some thought (the Blessed Augustine and Jerome) that this inextinguishable fire and undying worm could be taken in a figurative sense as symbols of the bitterest torments of Gehenna, that the worm chiefly expresses the inner gnawing of conscience, while the fire symbolizes terrible outward, hellish tortures (ibid., p. 658).

And so, the inner torments of sinners in Gehenna consist of the eternal clawing of incurable passions and the incessant reproaches of conscience for failing their duty to be the image and likeness of the Divinity. The action of passions and conscience in Holy Writ is called the unsleeping worm and inextinguishable fire. St. Theophylact[138] writes that the worm and the fire that tear at sinners in Gehenna is the conscience of the sinner. The action of the

---

[138]St. Theophylact, bishop of Nicomedia, an opponent of the iconoclasts, was banished to Caria where he died in 845 A.D. His memory is kept on March 8 (21). Another Theophylact, Archbishop of Ochrid in the eleventh century, was a noted theological writer and commentator on Scripture, but not considered a Saint.

conscience he likens to the action of eternal gnawing by a worm and the burning of fire.

Nevertheless, the view that the unsleeping worm signifies inward torment is only a private opinion and for the most part it belongs to the Western Church. The Orthodox Church sees the worm as a worm without seeking to explain what was said of it, simply, without an explanation of that which could never be satisfactorily understood at our present level. St. Basil the Great recognizes the worm of hell as existing in reality and not figuratively, not in reflection or abstraction. St. John Chrysostom also places the worm among the palpable torments of Gehenna: "From the grave and the worm," says he, "transfer thy thought to the worm unsleeping, to the fire that never goes out, to the gnashing of teeth, to the outer darkness, to sorrow, and oppression." Here, as also in Basil the Great, inner punishment is clearly separated from the outward punishments; among the latter, both Saints note the unsleeping worm as an outward and palpable punishment. Here is the inward and outward torment mentioned by St. Dimitri of Rostov: "There, that is, in Gehenna, there will be the inextinguishable fire, the bitter winter, the undying worm, the unbearable stench, the inexpressible anguish, the outer darkness, fearful hunger, un-slaked thirst, and oppression that cannot be told" (*Homily 2* on Palm Sunday). The words of Scripture on the delights of Paradise and on the torments of hell should be taken simply and directly, insists St. Tikhon of Zadonsk: "The misfortune that occurs in the world is, as it were, a shadow and an image of the future and eternal misfortune. It is hard for those who are regarded as among the villains and counted among the wicked and dishonest, but it will be far more grievous to be counted with the devil and his evil angels and to share their fate forever. It is hard to be under the power of some tormenter here and to suffer abuse, mockery, and all manner of coercion and offense from him; but it will be far worse to be with Satan, the enemy of God, and to suffer abuse, mockery, and cruelty from him forever. It is hard here to put up with beatings, sufferings, sickness, inflammation, fever, toothaches, and paralysis of the body; but it will be far worse to undergo the everlasting burn of hellfire, fierce and unbearable illness, the gnawing of teeth, and the unsleeping worm, and to suffer these in both soul and body. It is hard here to be incarcerated in prison, deprived of light, and not to feel any consolation; but far worse to be enclosed in the prison of hell, and never to see the light, and to be deprived of all consolation forever. It is hard here to put up with thirst and to desire, but not to have some coolness; but it will be worse eternally. In a word, any temporary suffering is hard, either for the soul or for the body, as everyone knows; but eternal suffering is incomparably

harder, both for its greatness and its continuance, as something endless which
the damned will suffer in soul and body. Temporary suffering is a shadow of
eternal suffering. The shadow is nothing by comparison with the reality; and
temporary suffering is nothing when compared to eternal. From temporary
suffering, therefore, know what eternal suffering is and take care not to fall
into the latter. Now, in the mind's eye, go down into hell so as not to go down
later in soul and body. How shalt thou bear the fire that sears, but destroys not;
the worm that gnaws, but does not consume; the gnashing of teeth, the outer
darkness, the hungry look of the demons, and the weeping, and the moaning,
and the wailing, and the other sufferings, how shalt thou bear these? Reflect
on these things, compare temporary suffering with eternal, and vanity will be
driven away, as by a whip, from they heart."

The main basis of inner torment in Gehenna is eternal expulsion from
God—the source of life and bliss—and consequently being deprived as well of
everything that comes of abiding and communion with God—deprivation of
all that is good; this is the basis of inward and outward torments in Gehenna.
The state of torment is a state opposite to that of bliss, just as the state of sickness is opposite to that of health. Torment is a sorrowful state in which all the
senses suffer, while bliss is a state that brings joy in all the senses. The former
state overflows with eternal sorrow, the latter with joy.

Regarding the torments of sinners in Gehenna, Archbishop Makary of
Kharkov in his *Dogmatic Theology* (Volume II, pp. 656–657) writes: "Then there
shall be fulfilled upon them, in all fullness, the words of the Apostle: Tribulation and anguish, upon every soul of man that doeth evil' (Romans 2:9). The
remembrance of a life that has passed which they have so thoughtlessly wasted
on base works; the incessant reproaches of conscience for all the iniquities ever
committed; late remorse for neglect of the God-given means for salvation; the
overbearing awareness that there is no more possibility to repent, correct oneself
and be saved—all this will claw at the unfortunate without ceasing."

With the ending of the kingdom of Grace and the arrival of the kingdom of
Glory, in the future life beyond the grave, the righteous anger of God will befall
the sinners, as David bears witness: "The face of the Lord is against them that
do evil, to cut off the remembrance of them from the earth" (Psalms 33:17),[139]
that is, the Lord, seeing their iniquity, will pronounce upon them the sentence
of eternal ruin. Solomon depicts the internal torments of sinners in Gehenna
thus: "And they, repenting and groaning for anguish of spirit, shall say within
themselves: . . . We have erred from the way of truth, and the light of righteous-

[139]This passage is numbered Psalms 34:16 in the King James Version.

ness hath not shined unto us, and the sun of righteousness rose not upon us. We wearied ourselves in the way of wickedness and destruction: yea, we have gone through deserts where there lay no way; but as for the way of the Lord, we have not known it. What hath pride profited us? Or what good hath riches with our vaunting brought us? All those things are passed away like a shadow, and as a post that hasted by . . . Even so, we, in like manner, as soon as we were born, began to draw to our end, and had no sign of virtue to show; but were consumed in our own wickedness" (Wisdom of Solomon 5:3,6–9,13).

"Those," writes St. Basil the Great, "who have done evil, will rise from the dead unto reproach and shame, so as to see in their own selves the abomination and stamp of the sins they have committed. And perhaps, more fearful than the darkness and eternal fire will be that shame with which the sinners will be immortalized, having constantly before their eyes the traces of sin committed in the flesh, like some indelible paint, always remaining in their souls' memory." St. Paul writes of the inner torments of sinners in Gehenna: "[They] shall be punished with everlasting destruction from the presence of the Lord, and from the glory of his power" (II Thessalonians 1:9).

According to the teaching of the Lord Jesus Christ Himself, Gehenna is the inheritance of unbelievers (Mark 16:16), the unbaptized: "He that believeth on the Son hath everlasting life: and he that believeth not the Son shall not see life; but the wrath of God abideth on him" (John 3:36). Just as from faith there proceed submission and obedience, so, on the contrary, from unbelief proceed obstinacy and disobedience. Obstinate unbelief is eternal ruin, and such an unbeliever will not see life eternal. The one path to salvation is faith in the Redeemer; therefore unbelievers depart into eternity as sinners, awaiting the anger of God, un-reconciled with God, and the wrath of God remains upon such sinners. Here on earth the sun shines on the righteous and the sinners, and the rain waters both, and grace itself often acts through the unworthy, since we, for example, are sanctified even by priests that are unworthy, not through their own worth, but only for Jesus' name's sake, Whose name all beings adore in heaven, on earth, and in the abyss, for the sake of this Almighty name, even those that are not true Christians are able to do that which is above nature. Nevertheless, these works do not justify them, and they, being crafty, not having that love which serves as the foundation of all virtue, even if, in the words of St. Paul, they were to speak with the tongues of angels, all the same they will go down to hell for their wicked heart: "And then will I profess unto them, I never knew you: depart from me, ye that work iniquity" (Matthew 7:23). In another place, the Lord Jesus Christ clearly taught that all those without mercy will be denizens of Gehenna as being alien to the love that was commanded unto them and therefore not commiserating, not having sympathy with the state of those in need of our spiritual and material help. Among the baptized, those shall inherit Gehenna who blaspheme the Holy Spirit: that is, embittered, unrepentant sinners. Unbelievers are condemned to Gehenna because they did not believe, and therefore were not baptized, and remained in the state of original sin—that is, in the state of condemnation for their own sin, since without active faith, the fruits of the redemptory sacrifice of the God-man are not acquired. As they did not recognize the Redeemer, they remained outside of redemption—unredeemed. In another passage the Lord says that after the resurrection and the joining of the bodies with their souls, those that have done evil will depart unto the resurrection of condemnation (John 5:29), that is, all those that have not justified themselves on earth by deeds and life that are according to faith will rise to be condemned to eternal death (torment). And the Evangelist Matthew writes that the workers of wickedness shall be cast into the fiery furnace where there will be weeping and the gnashing of teeth. "Those that work iniquity" means those that lead a life not as befits Christians, immorally—those whose moral state corresponds to that of the evil spirits. And so, all the wicked, that is, those who do not believe in Christ, and all the impious, that is, heretics, as well as those of the Orthodox Christians who have lived a life of sin or have fallen into some "sin which is unto death" and not healed themselves by repentance, inherit eternal torment together with the evil spirits. Desperate malice makes up the character of the evil spirits; their faces are like the villainous faces of malefactors and criminals among mankind. This character is stamped on the faces of the lost souls in Gehenna. These latter words of the Lord, "Depart into the fire, prepared for the devil" bear direct witness that the sinners in Gehenna will also be together and in the company of the evil spirits at that, because the fire was prepared for them and their cohorts, the lost and outcast souls. This is the common place for spirits and souls, where there is weeping, cursing, and the gnashing of teeth, where there is neither kinship nor friendship nor acquaintance, nor good will; where there is no communion. This is the company of the outcast souls with the fallen spirits of which the Lord Himself bore witness, just as He did of the community of the saved in the kingdom of Heaven: "Many shall come . . . and recline with Abraham, Isaac, and Jacob, in the kingdom of Heaven."

St. Paul defined the character of the second period of life beyond the grave in Paradise (I Corinthians 2:9) which will be so blissful that those who live on earth cannot even imagine its delight any more than they can picture the blessed life of our first ancestors in the garden of Eden; time has concealed both past and future bliss from the present. Not only can those who live on earth not imagine the future bliss of the second period, but even those that dwell in Paradise do not know their bliss that is to come. This definition can, without error, also be applied to the distinctive characteristic of the second period of the state of Gehenna which will be so fearful that not only those living on earth but even those that are already beyond the grave in Gehenna can imagine the full horror of the torments of the second period—which the eye of man has never seen anywhere nor has the ear heard and yet which exist—prepared exclusively for the devil, and then also for all the souls that follow his suggestions and lead an earthly life without faith in Christ and without repentance. Consequently, it is impossible to describe the state of Gehenna in the second period exactly, according to the chosen vessel of the Holy Spirit, St. Paul.

If all the evil on earth, all the misfortunes, sorrows, illnesses, failures, offenses, and the like are a barely perceptible shadow of the future ills to be suffered in the first period in Gehenna, then what must be the misfortune of the condemned in Gehenna in the second period, the like of which was nothing either on earth or in the punishment of sinners in the first period: a punishment, concerning whose unbearable nature we quote an account of a monk of the Holy Mountain.[140]

Just how inexpressibly torturous it is to be in Gehenna is shown by the example of one paralytic who, his spirit of patience failing him, with wailing begged the Lord to bring his life of suffering to an end. "Very well," said an angel that appeared to the sick man, "the Lord, as One Who is ineffably good, has agreed to the petition of thy prayer; He ends thy temporary life, only with the condition if, in place of one year of suffering on earth, sufferings by which every man, like gold in a fire, is cleansed, thou agreest to spend three hours in the place of eternal torment? Thy sins demand cleansing in the suffering of thine own flesh; thou wast to have spent another year in paralysis; because neither for thee nor for all the other faithful is there any path to heaven other than that of the Cross laid down by the sinless God-man. Thou art become tired of this path on earth, so make a test and discover what eternal torment in Gehenna is like, in the place whither sinners go. However, thou shalt try it only for a period of three hours, and afterwards, through the prayers of the holy Church, thou shalt be saved."

The sufferer was plunged in thought. A year of suffering on earth would be a frightfully long time! Better I should get through three hours of suffering in these endless torments, said he to himself, rather than a year on earth.

[140]That is, of Mt. Athos in Greece.

"I agree to Gehenna," said he at last to the angel.

The angel quietly took his pain-filled soul and, enclosing it in the uttermost regions of hell, departed from the sufferer with these words of consolation: "In three hours I will come for thee." The darkness that prevailed everywhere, the oppression, the sounds that were wafted to him of indescribable moaning of sinners, the sight of the spirits of malice with their hellish ugliness, all of this blended together for the poor sufferer into an unbearable fear and weariness. Everywhere he saw and heard only affliction and wailing, without the slightest bit of joy, there in the bottomless pit of hell; only the fiery eyes of demons glittered in the abyss of darkness, and their gigantic shadows were carried about before him, ready to crush him, devour, and burn him with their hellish breath. The poor sufferer began to tremble and cried out; but his cry and wailing were answered only by the echo that died out in the distance of the abyss and by the seething of the flame of Gehenna which swirled about like a tremulous prisoner. It seemed to him that whole ages of misery had already gone by, and from one moment to the next he waited for the light-bearing angel to appear to him, but there was no angel. Finally, the sufferer despaired of his return and, gnashing his teeth, began to moan, but no one paid any attention to his wailings. All the sinners that languished in the pit of Gehenna were occupied with themselves, only with their own torment, and the demons in hellish joy mocked at the tortures of the sinners. At last the gladsome light of angelic glory poured over the abyss. With the smile of Paradise, the angel approached this sufferer and asked: "Well, how goes it with thee, brother?"—"I never thought there could be a lie on the lips of an angel," the sufferer whispered in a barely audible voice, broken with tribulation.—"Why, what is it?" retorted the angel.—"How canst thou ask?" said the tormented one, "after promising to take me from here after three hours, but instead whole years, whole ages have gone by in my inexpressible agonies."—"But hold on now, what years, what ages?" replied the angel modestly and with a smile: "Only an hour has passed since I left, and thou hast yet two hours to serve here."—"But how can it be two hours?" asked the sufferer in fright. "Two hours? Has only one hour gone by? Oh! I cannot bear any more! I have no strength! If only it can be, if only it be the will of the Lord, I beg thee, take me from hence! Better to suffer years and ages on earth, even till the last day, even till the very Coming of Christ for judgment, only take me from here. Have pity on me!" with wailing cried the prisoner, stretching out his hands to the angel of light.—"God, as the Father of mercies and consolation, makes wondrous His grace on thee; but thou must know and remember, how cruel and unbearable are the torments of Gehenna" (The *Monk of the Holy Mountain*, Part I, Letter 15).

> The next, in place and punishment, are they
> Who prodigally threw their souls away:
> Fools, who, repining at their wretched state,
> And loathing anxious life, suborned their fate.
> With late repentance, now they would retrieve
> The bodies they forsook, and wish to live;
> Their pains and poverty desire to bear,
> To view the light of heaven, and breathe the vital air:
> But Fate forbids; the Stygian floods oppose,
> And, with nine circling streams, the captive souls enclose.
> (Virgil's *Aeneid*, Book 6)[141]

The above is a picture of the life beyond the grave of suicides in the religio-moral understanding of the Romans as set forth by Virgil. The religious and moral sense of the Greeks and Romans did not admit of this means of willfully ending one's life. Cicero also condemned suicides. And Plato taught that the sacred obligation of a Greek is to bury the dead conscientiously, becomingly, with honor, which served as a foreboding of their happy life beyond the grave; yet suicides were deprived of certain honors at burial, which was a source of shame for the deceased as well as a sign that joy did not await him in the other world. And so, the death of suicides was considered a disgrace on earth, among the living; and Virgil stated how, in their concept, suicides live beyond the grave.

2. Concerning the Prayer of Absolution at Funerals

Every more or less attentive Christian has seen and heard the intercession of the Church for his well-being on earth during his entire earthly life and her concern for the life beyond the grave of all her members. And here, in the last moment of the soul's presence by its body on earth, the soul hears a consoling prayer, absolving the Christian soul of sins, and with full faith and hope it goes to its eternal repose in that place where, through Jesus Christ, all are to live together eternally. Here is that last prayer that the soul hears, and with which it at once leaves the earth and all that dwell therein forever, remaining, however, in an indissoluble spiritual bond with the living.

---

[141]From the translation by John Dryden (1631–1700).

Prayer: Our Lord Jesus Christ, by His Divine grace, as also by the gift and power vouchsafed unto His holy Disciples and Apostles, that they should bind and loose the sins of men: (For He said unto them: Receive ye the Holy spirit: Whosesoever sins ye remit, they are remitted; and whosesoever sins ye retain, they are retained. And whatsoever ye shall bind and loose upon the earth shall be bound or loosed also in heaven.) By that same power, also, transmitted unto us from them, this my spiritual child is absolved, through me, unworthy though I be, from all things wherein, as mortal he (she) hath sinned against God; whether in word, or deed, or thought, and with all his (her) senses; whether voluntarily or involuntarily; whether wittingly, or through ignorance. If he (she) be under the ban or excommunication of a Bishop, or of a Priest; or hath incurred the curse of his (her) father or mother; or hath fallen under his (her) own curse; or hath been bound, as man, by any sins whatsoever, but hath repented him (her) thereof, with contrition of heart: he (she) is now absolved from all those faults and bonds. May all those things which proceed from the weakness of his (her) mortal nature be consigned to oblivion, and be remitted unto him (her): Through His loving-kindness; through the prayers of our most holy, and blessed, and glorious Lady, the Birthgiver of God and Ever-Virgin Mary; of the holy, glorious, and all-laudable Apostles, and of all the Saints. Amen.

The custom of putting this Prayer of Absolution into the hands of the dead began in Russia in the eleventh century, and it began with the following instance. Prince Simeon, desiring to receive absolution of his sins after death, as he had in life, asked the venerable St. Theodosius of the Monastery of the Caves in Kiev, "to bless his soul, as in life, so also after death, and entreated him to give this blessing in writing." Therefore the Saint decided to give him this document, under the condition of his adhering to the Orthodox faith, and wrote out for him the words of the priestly absolution. Preparing to die, Prince Simeon left in his will that this prayer of absolution be put in his hand; his desire was carried out. From that time, according to the witness of St. Simon, bishop of Vladimir, it became the custom to put this prayer into the hands of the dead after their funeral (from the *Kievan Patericon*, p. 16).

Reviews of the Original Russian Book "How Our Departed Ones Live, and How We Shall Live after Death" The Russian-Language Edition

I.

From the Educational Committee of the Holy Synod, 196, 1882:

The main subject of Monk Mitrofan's book is the teaching about life after death. The author explains this subject from various angles and in great detail; his whole book, which makes up 476 pages in medium-size print, is divided into four parts. In the first part, the author discusses death; in the second part, he speaks of the inward tie and mutual relations between the living and the dead; in the third part, the dogma or teaching of the Church on intercession by the living for the departed and the asking of pardon of sins for certain deceased sinners is expounded; and finally, in the fourth part, which is the most important and fundamental one, the author depicts the actual life beyond the grave, in a very vivid and pictorial way, as seen from all sides. Each part, besides its main theses, is subdivided into many separate points, connected with the main theme of one or another part. But the fourth part, being the largest, dealing with life beyond the grave, consists of four sections. Section I is about life beyond the grave in general; Section II is on the first period of life after death; Section III is on the Second Coming of Jesus Christ to earth, the resurrection of the dead, the Last Judgment, and the end of the world; and Section IV is on the second period of life beyond the grave. Each of these sections has its divisions and subdivisions with many individual points or questions.

The book by Monk Mitrofan, spoken of here, has already come out in a second edition; and this fact speaks quite clearly of the value of the book itself and of the benefit that it can bring both to readers of the educated class and to less educated readers. In fact, the subject taken up by the author in his book, [*How*

Our Departed Ones Live, and How We Shall Live After Death] is a profoundly religious subject, a highly edifying one, and most interesting for anyone who even now and then reflects on the mysteries of life and death. The author begins his composition precisely with thoughts about death and its relationship to eternal life; he speaks of the appearance of death on earth, of the reasons for death, and of its benefit; of the departure of the soul from the body, of the aerial toll booths through which the soul passes after its separation from the body, and of the significance of the third, ninth, fortieth days, and the anniversary of death for the soul. Then, in his book he unfolds that joyous truth for us that the soul after departing from the body and passing into the world beyond the grave, does not cease to have an inner tie and a mutual relationship with living persons. He shows the basis for such a bond, a union, and a spiritual communion between this world and the next, and answers the question, "What does this bond between the living and the dead consist of?" He then demonstrates that the link between this world and the next should have a visible expression and, so to speak, a physical one: such a communion exists between earth-dwellers and the Angels and Saints.

Further on the author sets forth the teaching of the Church on the intercession of the living for the deceased, on asking that the sins of certain sinners be forgiven. He points out the basis for the Church's teaching that some deceased sinners can be saved and speaks of prayer and alms as the best expression for the intercession for the dead. He shows what a special, great strength the prayers of the whole Church have for the departed and mentions the individual prayers of those who remain on earth: relatives, friends, acquaintances of the departed. Then he unfolds the truth that not all the prayers of the living are helpful to the departed, and that not all the departed are helped by the prayers of the living.

Finally, the author depicts the actual life beyond the grave, that is: How do our souls live beyond the grave? As they did while on earth or otherwise? What is life after death, and what sort of a life is it?

Having defined life after death, the author names the states of the soul beyond the grave and indicates its periods; age; personal, conscious and active life. He defines the first period in life after death, and speaks of the inward and outward life and activity of the soul and its faculties. He tells of the life of the soul in Paradise, the places where the Saints dwell, the life of bliss of the first period, the habitations of Paradise, the character of the saved and of the sexes, the number of the Saints; he tells of incomplete bliss, and so on.

Then he tells of the life and activity of souls in Hades and Gehenna, shows the beginnings of these states, of Hades and Gehenna on earth, and lists the various names of the places where undetermined and condemned souls are. He describes the degrees in the status of the undetermined; of Hades and others, and speaks of the dwellings of Hades and Gehenna, of the distinguishing characteristics of souls whose state is undetermined or condemned, and so on.

Further, the author writes of the Second Coming of Christ to earth, of the resurrection of the dead, of the final Judgment on moral beings, and of the end of the world. He points to the signs by which one can judge the time when these events are to be. He sets forth the basis for the resurrection of the dead and shows the teaching of the Old and New Testaments on the resurrection of the body, as well as the characteristics of risen bodies. Then he discusses the general judgment on Christians and non-Christians and the end of the world.

The author concludes his book with a reflection on the second period of life beyond the grave. Here he gives a description first of life in Paradise with the abodes of the Saints, the degrees of bliss of soul and body, and the character of eternal life in Paradise in the second period. He then shows the same points in his reflection on the second period in Gehenna, that is, he describes the dwellings of the lost and discusses the degrees of eternal torment and so on.

Having put together such a broad and detailed program of theses for his work on life beyond the grave—as can be seen from the table of contents at the beginning of the book—the author unfolds and explains each thesis succinctly, clearly, rather convincingly, and, for the most part, fully enough. He bases each of his explanations, for each separate point, first on his own view or thought, or, one might better say, the general view of humanity on the given matter; and then he confirms these general thoughts with the evidence of the Old and New Testaments, the teaching of the Fathers of the Church, and the universal tradition of the Orthodox Church. Often he cites passages from the liturgical books, from the *Prologue* and the Lives of the Saints, or refers to the words and teachings of glorified Saints: St. Dimitri of Rostov, St. Tikhon of Zadonsk, and others. He quotes excerpts from the works of St. Philaret, Metropolitan of Moscow, from the Orthodox dogmatic theology of Metropolitan Makary of Moscow, Archbishop Anthony of Kazan, from the writings of Archimandrite Theodore Bukharev, from the Gospel commentary of Bishop Michael, and others.

In this respect, Monk Mitrophan's book bears the mark of a truly Orthodox Christian faith and of the piety of old. Indeed, it stands out by the richness of its proofs and explanations taken from Scripture, the writings of the Fathers of the Church, the lives of the Saints, and other sources of Orthodox faith on one or another question. But, setting forth in his book the teaching of the Orthodox

Church on life beyond the grave, the author did not lose sight of the views of other non-Christian peoples of the ancient and modern world.

Thus, he cites the views and beliefs of pre-Christian peoples, various wild tribes, and the ancient classical peoples—Greeks and Romans—about death, life beyond the grave, Paradise, Hades, and so forth. He recounts the views of Homer on heaven and hell, as expressed in the *Iliad* and the *Odyssey*. He sets forth the teaching on heaven and hell as Dante expressed it in his time, according to the generally accepted views of the Middle Ages. He also refers in certain cases to Flammarion (his *History of Heaven*), to Zimmerman, and others.

Regarding the expectation by some peoples of the approaching end of the world, the author points out an interesting fact: such an expectation arose gradually and continuously, beginning in the first ages of Christianity, so that there was never a century without its predictions of the end of the world. He cites the names of various scholars, be they astrologers, mathematicians, or preachers, from various ages, each of whom in his own way determined the day and hour when the world was to end. The author, in this connection, did not omit modern-day rumors, such as spread in Europe and Russia, based on the predictions of the fourteenth century Leonardo Aretino who announced that the world would end on November 15, 1881.

Such varied information on the topic of the book bears witness to the author's knowledge of the history of his subject matter, that is, the doctrines on life after death, as well as to his broad reading and diligence. His book brings together not only everything found in the acts of the Orthodox Church, but also in the theoretical deductions of science, and in the sayings of general literature, all of which makes his book not only edifying for the average reader, but also of interest for those philosophically inclined or curious about scientific evidence on the subject.

Regarding the style of the book, one can say the following: on the one hand, the author obviously sought to present the contents in as simple, clear, and straightforward a manner as possible. To this end, he tried to avoid unclear expressions, scientific terminology, foreign terms, and artificial turns of speech, even in explaining abstract truths and scientific investigation. On the contrary, his language is direct, vivid, clear and, at the same time, fully appropriate to the height and dignity of the book's content. As a result, the book, *How our Departed Ones Live, and How We Shall Live After Death*, is not only easy and pleasant to read, but evokes the most important questions of religion and life, for example: on the existence of God, the personal existence of the spirit, immortality, the ultimate goal and purpose of mankind, and so on. Reflecting deeply on such questions, the reader is at the same time stimulated in his heart towards the highest, heavenly hopes and expectations. All of this constitutes the value of the book's presentation.

Monk Mitrophan's book on life after death can bring an undoubted benefit to any attentive reader.

Bearing in mind all that has been said above regarding the book, *How Our Departed Ones Live, and How We Shall Live After Death,* with its rich material and many-sided research about the author's chosen subject matter, so important in a religious context, the Committee has approved this book for the basic libraries of theological seminaries and schools.

II.

From the periodical "Tserkovno-Obschestvenny Vestnik," for October 6, 1881, Issue Number 107.

In the short period (no more than a year and a half) since its first publication, this book has already sold out, and a second edition was found necessary. Such a demand for a book bears witness more clearly than any review or any recommendation in words.

Indeed, this book is of major and undisputed value.

Its first value lies in the fullness of information it provides on the subject matter. In this regard, the attentive and diligent author has gathered together what is found not only in the positive statements of the Orthodox Church, but also in the theoretical deductions of science and in the sayings of general literature.

The second value of this book should be considered its generally accessible presentation: scientific terminology is replaced by commonly understood expressions, and instead of abstract turns of speech, a direct and unobstructed language is used that can be understood by anyone, even those of limited education.

The third value of the book can be felt in the very tone of its research. Reading through the book attentively, we experience, one might say, the way that it touches the highest spiritual and religious chords. First and foremost, the mental powers of the reader are touched and led to a clear recognition of the nature and personality of his own spirit: and, at the same time, to a certain "feeling after the Lord," as a prototype, "in Whom we live, and move, and have our being." (Acts 17:28) Such a self-examination brings forth in the depths of our soul a direct certainty of the existence of God, such as was expressed in 1781 so happily by the poet Derzhavin: "I am; therefore, Thou art (that is, my God)." With such a double sense of the origins of our spirit, is it possible to think of death as a cutting off or destruction of our existence? Of course not!

On the other hand, in this work are concentrated the religious hopes of faithful hearts who even during their life on earth "have tasted the heavenly gift" (Hebrews 6:4) and the holy joy of the world to come (Romans 14:17). Thus the attentive reader is given, through all of this, a more palpable precedent. Our bodily death, which came into the world through sin (Romans 5:12), is to be thought of now, after the redeeming death of Christ the Saviour, as nothing else than a passage or conveyance into a better and unending life and in no way as a ceasing to exist, as desired only by evil and godless persons.

The highest science, in the opinion of St. Basil the Great, is to be considered "the science of dying in good will." We might add to this that he who does not learn to live devoutly here cannot attain such a science. Only by attaining the secret of this life can we understand the secret of death.

—Archimandrite Joseph.

III.

From the "Pravitel'stvenny Vestnik" for December 30, 1884, Number 286.

The first edition of this book, which came out almost simultaneously in Russian and French, was met with approving reviews not only in this country, but abroad as well. It was also, after being examined by the Educational Committee of the Holy Synod, approved for all basic libraries and recommended for popular reading.

At the present time, this work is already in its third edition, corrected and expanded by the author. It is divided into four parts, joined into one well-constructed whole by the same religious thought. In the first part, the author considers death in relation to immortality: in the second part, he discusses the internal bond and mutual relationship between the living and the dead; the third part contains the teaching of the Church on intercession by the living for the departed and the asking of pardon for the sins of certain sinners: and, finally, the subject of the fourth part is life beyond the grave.

The last, and most extensive part, comprises the main theme of the work, and is subdivided into four sections: life after death in general, its first period, the end of the world and the resurrection of the dead, and the second period of the life to come.

As he develops his basic idea, Father Mitrophan bolsters it with the witness of the Scriptures, the teaching of the Holy Fathers, and of the Doctors of the Church. In his evaluations, he also refers to the works of our renowned hierarchs and spiritual writers quoting the words of Metropolitan Philaret, the dogmatic theology of Metropolitan Makary, the Gospel commentary of Bishop Michael, and others.

But in setting forth the teaching of the Orthodox Church on life after death, the author at the same time conveys an idea of what views on the subjects were held by non-Christian peoples both in ancient and modern times. Based on the poems of Homer and the famed epic of Dante, he tells of the views of Hades that existed in various ages. At the same time, quotes from Zimmermann, Flammarion, and other scholars show that the author is thoroughly acquainted with modern studies of his subject as well.

As a composition of this character, the book is not only of theological value, but of scientific value as well, and at the same time can be read by the general public, since the author made every effort to avoid terminology not understood by everyone. As to style, Father Mitrophan's book is written in a simple and easy language, which is not always the case in such works.

The French version of this book received the most cordial reviews in the "Journal de St.-Petersbourg" and the newspaper "Le Nord."

On the French-Language Edition

From the Newspaper "Journal de St.-Petersbourg," for March 17, 1884, Number 72.

How Our Departed Ones Live, and How We Shall Live After Death—Under this title a few days ago was published a translation of the excellent work of the monk Mitrophan of the Konevsky Monastery, which had appeared in Russian two years ago. As proof that any evaluation of ours would be superfluous, it is enough to say that the original went through two editions in a year and a half.

We, for our part, can say only that, after a splendid review by the Educational Committee of the Holy Synod, which recommended the book for the people and approved it for all basic religious school libraries, and after the recommendations of other authorities, we too would like to note, especially for our readers abroad, this rare occurrence. A learned theological work, the fruit of the study and reflection of one of the monastic members of the Orthodox Church, has come out in St. Petersburg in French.

The aim of this translation is to acquaint foreigners with Father Mitrophan's wonderful book, and therefore, for our part, we hasten to say a few words about it, in the certainty that theologians and clergy of the West, and, in general, all lovers of spiritual literature, regardless of denomination, will read it with equal interest. This collection of the beliefs of the Orthodox Church on the life to come is as complete as it is detailed. The reader cannot but gain from the attention he gives to this book. Alongside of the Church's dogmas on the life to come, the author sets forth the beliefs of pagan peoples, both ancient and modern. Alongside of information taken from the Scriptures and the Fathers of the Church, we find Homer's views from antiquity, those of Dante from the Middle Ages, and those of noted modern-day scholars as well.

Besides the Synodal Committee's splendid review of the Russian original, there was also a recommendation in the "Tserkovno-obschestvenny Vestnik" that noted the merits of Father Mitrophan's book, such as the abundant information, the readable style, and the spirit that permeates the work and makes it both interesting and edifying.

As concerns the French translation, which has now come out, the translator had no small task. Not able to attain the excellent style, he tried only to convey the author's thoughts faithfully, but he was rather successful in this.

We might also add that the French version is marked by very correct typesetting, no easy matter for a lengthy work in a foreign language.

In closing, we might give our view of the book's title, *How Our Departed Ones Live, and How We Shall Live After Death*. This we do not approve; it is too long and too hard and will not please a Frenchman. Instead, we would have used one of the sub-headings in the first part of the book: *Death in Relation to Immortality*, or even better, *Life Beyond the Grave*. This last title, in our opinion, is the most appropriate: short, clear, expressive, and broad enough to embrace the whole content.

From the Author. In the sorrowing heart of man, the word "death" has always touched upon a living chord. The author therefore considered it natural to set out the concept "life" as an antidote to the poison of "death." The misconception of "nonexistence" is replaced by a living awareness of being (Luke 7:14; 8:52,53; John 11:11–44). The sorrowing heart, overcome by grief, had whispered to the cold mind, "Where is he (she) now? What has become of him (her)? Is he (she) no more? What is he (she) doing?"

The heart, assured by the spirit of man that there is immortality, had not doubted that the departed live (as witnessed by the history of religion). Yet, not satisfied by this, the heart of mankind throughout all the stages of its religious and ethical development, has always asked the question: "But how do they live?" "Do our departed live beyond the grave as they did on earth or otherwise?"

The heart of man, darkened by the fall, replied: "They live not," or "They live as on earth"—thus, for example, in all of paganism. Even the Hebrews asked Jesus Christ about this (Matthew 22:30); to which the Lord and Knower of hearts gave an answer to the age-old question of the human heart: they live as angels.

A heart overcome by grief at the death of someone close is in need of healing. Distressed at the absence of an object of love, the heart, living by hope and faith, hears that the one wept for as gone, is alive, lives! It is enough, and the sad heart is relieved again!

A detailed reflection on the title chosen for my book, *How Our Departed Ones Live, and How We Shall Live After Death*, is to be found in the first part of the second volume, which contains the beliefs and teachings of pagans and so-called "natural religion."

V.

From the Belgian newspaper "Le Nord," for April 26, 1884, Number 17.

I cannot pass in silence over the interesting work of Father Mitrophan, monk of the Konevsky Monastery. It is, after all, a bibliographic rarity, as a book of religious content that was published almost simultaneously in Russian and French.

This book bears the title, *How Our Departed Ones Live, and How We Shall Live After Death*. The title is puzzling enough, and at first glance could be taken for a presentation of spiritism or of some other mysterious teaching. Yet it turns out to be nothing of the kind.

On the contrary, it may well be that up to now no such work as that of Father Mitrophan has yet been inspired by such living and profound faith.

I do not take it upon myself to labor through a critical analysis of the matter on which the author based his truly splendid work since it is beyond my theological knowledge. Instead, I must give credit that this book, much spoken of in our society, is worthy of special attention; and that the translation makes it possible for those foreigners who are curious about everything Russian, to acquaint themselves with the teachings of Orthodoxy—till now, a kind of *terra incognita*[1] for us.

In this respect, Father Mitrophan has done a great service by giving a mass of information on his subject in clear and fine language. Not stopping at a detailed study of the Scriptures, the author at the same time makes use of scientific data and information from general literature. Thus, for example, reflecting at the close of the book on the end of the world, the author found it necessary to include even the mythological sayings on this subject, and the writings of Dante were not hidden from Father Mitrophan.

This new work on eternal life, whose success has been so great as to call for a second edition after six months, has the value, so rarely met with in Russian theological writings, of being understood by a general audience. The elimination of scientific terminology, replaced by words understood by all, combined with a pleasant variety given by the anecdotes, make this book more and more wonderful.

[1]"An unknown land."

Acknowledgements

Valentina N. Obermaier (née Saiapina) arranged for the first edition of *How Our Departed Ones Live* to be published with the help and support of His Grace Kyrill Archbishop of San Francisco and Western America, Father David Moser, Ksenya Anagnostopulos (editing and proofreading), Galina Hanover, Fr John R. Shaw, and Father Stefan V. Pavlenko.

The first edition was published in honor of St John of Shanghai and San Francisco. It was dedicated to Mrs Obermaier's husband Ioann (Hans) Obermaier, a convert to the Orthodox Faith who knew English better than he did Russian as well as to Anna Z., Stephanie Z., Nikita A. Saiapin, Zechariah, Alexi, Anna, Tatiana, Martha, George and all Mrs Obermaier's departed relatives.

As the demand for *How Our Departed Ones Live* continues long after the last copies of the first edition were sold, Holy Trinity Publications wishes to thank Father Stefan V. Pavlenko for permission to reformat and publish this second edition. May this publication continue to offer edification and encouragement for those seeking the Divine gift of salvation.

HOW OUR DEPARTED ONES LIVE

The Experience of the Orthodox Church